RENEWALS 458-4574

D0803537

WITHDRAWN
UTSA LIBRARIES

The International Monetary System, the IMF, and the G-20

WITH...
UTSA LI...

COMMITTED TO
IMPROVING THE STATE
OF THE WORLD

The International Monetary System, the IMF, and the G-20

A Great Transformation in the Making?

RICHARD SAMANS, MARC UZAN, and **AUGUSTO LOPEZ-CLAROS**

Copyright © 2007 by the World Economic Forum

All rights reserved. No reproduction, copy or transmission of this
publication may be made without written permission.

No paragraph of this publication may be reproduced, copied or transmitted
save with written permission or in accordance with the provisions of the
Copyright, Designs and Patents Act 1988, or under the terms of any licence
permitting limited copying issued by the Copyright Licensing Agency, 90
Tottenham Court Road, London W1T 4LP.

Anyone committing an unauthorized act in relation to this publication
may be liable to criminal prosecution and civil claims for damages.

The authors have asserted their rights to be identified as the authors of this
work in accordance with the Copyright, Designs and Patents Act 1988.

First published 2007 by
PALGRAVE MACMILLAN
Houndmills, Basingstoke, Hampshire RG21 6XS and
175 Fifth Avenue, New York, N. Y. 10010
Companies and representatives throughout the world.

PALGRAVE MACMILLAN is the global academic imprint of the Palgrave
Macmillan division of St. Martin's Press, LLC and of Palgrave Macmillan Ltd.
Macmillan® is a registered trademark in the United States, United Kingdom
and other countries. Palgrave is a registered trademark in the European
Union and other countries.

ISBN-13: 978-0-230-52495-8
ISBN-10: 0-230-52495-8

This book is printed on paper suitable for recycling and made from fully
managed and sustained forest sources.

A catalogue record for this book is available from the British Library.

A catalog record for this book is available from the Library of Congress.

10   9   8   7   6   5   4   3   2   1
16 15 14 13 12 11 10 09 08 07

Printed and bound in Great Britain by Creative Print & Design (Wales),
Ebbw Vale

**Library
University of Texas
at San Antonio**

Acknowledgments

The International Monetary System, the IMF, and the G-20: A Great Transformation in the Making? was published by the World Economic Forum within the framework of the International Monetary Convention Project, in partnership with the Reinventing Bretton Woods Committee.

This volume constitutes the project's final report, which has been supported by the Forum's Strategic Partner, Credit Suisse. It consists of some of the most interesting papers prepared for the Roundtable events, which were generously supported by the seven host governments as well as SEB, Banca Intesa, Garanti Bank, Morgan Stanley, and Standard Bank.

Special thanks to all of the contributing authors of this publication as well as to Carina Larsfälten and Lauren Johnston for their invaluable project management and research assistance.

We also wish to thank AmadeaEditing, Hope Steele, and Ha Nguyen for their excellent editing and graphic design work.

Richard Samans
Managing Director, World Economic Forum

Marc Uzan
Executive Director, Reinventing Bretton Woods Committee

Augusto Lopez-Claros
Former Chief Economist, World Economic Forum

Contents

Foreword xi
    by Rodrigo de Rato y Figaredo

Introduction: The International Monetary Convention Project:
A Public-Private Exploration of the Future of the International
Monetary System xiii
    by Richard Samans, Marc Uzan, and Augusto Lopez-Claros

Part 1: Reconstitution of the International Monetary System

1.1 What Prospects for the International Monetary System? 3
    by Patrick Artus

1.2 What Should We Think About When Refounding
    the International Monetary System? 23
    by J. Bradford DeLong

1.3 Reforming Bretton Woods to Promote World
    Harmony and Stability 37
    by Li Ruogu

1.4 The US Current Account Deficit and the Future
    of the World Monetary System 43
    by Robert Skidelsky

1.5 Implications of Structural Changes for Management
    of the Global Economy 53
    by Edwin M. Truman

Part 2: New Players, New Responsibilities: Asia and Emerging Markets in the International Monetary System

2.1 The BRIC Dream: An Update 65
by Michael Buchanan

2.2 Institutions to Promote Financial Stability:
Reflections on East Asia and an Asian Monetary Fund 73
by Gordon de Brouwer

2.3 East Asian Economic Regionalism: Update 109
by Masahiro Kawai

2.4 The Role of ASEAN+3 in Regional Policy Surveillance
in East Asia 141
by Yung Chul Park

2.5 The Internationalization of Markets for Local
Currency Bonds 159
by Philip Turner

2.6 The Evolving Exchange Rate Regimes in East Asia 171
by Yu Yongding

Part 3: Global Imbalances and their Implications for the International Monetary System

3.1 Understanding Global Imbalances......................................187
by Richard N. Cooper

3.2 Remarks on Global Imbalances..203
by Dietrich Domanski

3.3 Global Imbalances: The New Economy, the Dark Matter, the Savvy Investor, and the Standard Analysis 223
by Barry Eichengreen

3.4 Ongoing Risks from the US Current Account Deficit 237
by Brad Setser

3.5 Domestic Investment and External Imbalances in East Asia.............257
by Jong-Wha Lee and Warwick J. McKibbin

Part 4: A New IMF in the Making?

4.1 Sixty Years After Bretton Woods:
Developing a Vision for the Future 295
by Jack Boorman

4.2 Assessing the Future of the IMF:
Its Role, Relevance, and Prospective Reform......................................307
by John Lipsky

4.3 Reforms of the International Monetary System 321
by John Williamson

4.4 The Future of the International Monetary Fund 331
by Nouriel Roubini and Brad Setser

4.5 Rethinking the IMF Business Model:
Proposals for Assessment and Reform of the
IMF's Medium-Term Strategy 343
by Angel Ubide

About the Authors 361

Foreword

RODRIGO DE RATO Y FIGAREDO, Managing Director, International Monetary Fund

ince March 2004, the International Monetary Convention Project has examined the salient challenges facing the international monetary system in the 21st century. The series of roundtable discussions co-hosted by the World Economic Forum, the Reinventing Bretton Woods Committee, and several G-20 countries marked the 60th anniversary of the 1944 Bretton Woods Conference that founded the International Monetary Fund and the World Bank. This initiative has allowed policymakers, academics, and private sector participants the opportunity for meaningful deliberation and exchange of ideas on issues critical to the future effectiveness of the international monetary system, including the reconstitution of the system, the new role of emerging market countries, global imbalances, and the future role of the IMF.

Through the publication of the conference papers in this anthology, *The International Monetary System, the IMF, and the G-20: A Great Transformation in the Making?* the momentum garnered by the roundtables will endure and promote further dialogue on the pressing challenges facing the international monetary system. The collection is rich in the depth of its coverage of each of the multifaceted issues facing the international monetary system, but also in the quality of the evaluation, analysis, and advice regarding each issue.

The first section, dealing with the reconstitution of the international monetary system, provides an excellent introduction to the anthology, cultivating the themes on global imbalances and IMF reform, which are discussed at greater length in subsequent sections. The second section, on the new role of emerging markets, assesses a number of issues relating to the international monetary system that are of particular importance to emerging market countries, but also ponders the new roles and responsibilities of emerging market countries. In the third section, on global imbalances, the papers provide a comprehensive overview of the debate regarding the various perspectives on the nature and eventual outcome of such imbalances. The final section on the future role of the IMF touches on many of the issues the IMF is presently addressing, including issues related to quota reform, surveillance of the global economy, and lending policy in the face of crises.

The IMF has been not only a focus of attention in the roundtable discussions, but also a participant in these discussions, with senior IMF officials participating on several occasions.

As the international institution charged with enhancing global economic stability and growth, the IMF has already recognized that it must adapt its policies to reflect the changes in the wider world, so that its members can continue to benefit from globalization. Indeed a number of the proposed reforms discussed at the roundtables have been moving forward. In 2005, the IMF approved a new medium-term strategy to help countries face the effects of globalization, and in the spring of 2006, it approved a new global surveillance tool. At the 2006 Annual Meetings in Singapore, the IMF took concrete steps toward implementing changes in its governance structure, recognizing the need for a rebalancing to reflect the rise of new economic powers, especially emerging market countries. As agreed in Singapore, the first step toward reform will see an increase in the quotas of the four most under-represented countries, while the second step will involve a broader reform of the quota process over the next two years. The quota reforms are but one part of the IMF's overall medium-term strategy of reform, which will reshape various aspects of the IMF's work and direction. The strategy also calls for deepening the IMF's surveillance efforts, updating tools, adapting its support of emerging market countries, and refocusing its role in helping low-income countries to achieve the Millennium Development Goals. Undoubtedly, the anthology will spur additional debate on these, and subsequent, reform proposals in the coming years.

Transforming the international monetary system will confer important benefits on all citizens working and interacting in it, and will help them respond to growing changes in financial markets. The question is whether the international community is prepared to work together to grasp the opportunities and meet the challenges that presently confront the system. The reforms currently underway in the IMF will play an important role in achieving this, but there is a long journey ahead of us, and, through initiatives like the International Monetary Convention Project, the likelihood of further success is strengthened.

The International Monetary Convention Project: A Public-Private Exploration of the Future of the International Monetary System

RICHARD SAMANS, Managing Director, World Economic Forum
MARC UZAN, Founder and Executive Director, Reinventing Bretton Woods Committee
AUGUSTO LOPEZ-CLAROS, Former Chief Economist, World Economic Forum

The ongoing international integration of product and capital markets is posing challenging questions about the adequacy of international governance arrangements and institutions, including those related to the international monetary system. In particular, a shift in the composition of global economic activity toward Asian and other emerging markets, a marked expansion of cross-border capital flows, and large, persistent economic imbalances are exposing weaknesses and structural inadequacies in an international financial architecture whose main features were constructed in the 1940s and 1970s.

To put things in perspective, it is necessary to go back to 1944, when 735 delegates from 44 countries locked themselves up for three long weeks in July at the Mount Washington Hotel in Bretton Woods, New Hampshire, to deal with the issue of how to patch up the international financial system. Efforts to contend with the effects of the depression via currency devaluations and trade barriers had not only been ineffective, but also had made matters worse in the inter-war period. International trade, in particular, had collapsed. The conference was dominated by J. M. Keynes, the head of the British delegation, who, at the outset wrote to a friend in London that the gathering was "the most monstrous monkey house assembled for many years" and that the only thing one could predict with some reliability about the likely outcome was that "acute alcohol poisoning would probably set in before the end."

Maybe this dour assessment reflected frustration with the fact that the US Treasury had vetoed some of his more ambitious initiatives for the conference. As Robert Mundell has noted, Keynes' original plan for Bretton Woods was to create a world currency. As recounted by John Cassidy in *The New Yorker*, much of the attention of delegates during the off hours was focused instead on Keynes' wife, Russian ballerina Lydia Lopokova, who was reported to have practised her dance steps everywhere and at all hours.

In the end, however, much was accomplished, and Keynes' own assessment had turned considerably more positive. "All of us here have the greatest sense of elation. All in all, quite extraordinary harmony has prevailed. As an experiment in international cooperation, the conference has been an outstanding success," he wrote to a friend back in London.

Five features of the Bretton Woods system

What exactly was agreed at Bretton Woods? Volumes have been written on the subject, but most would agree with Richard Cooper's five-point characterization of the need for:

1. Greater freedom for national economic policy to allow for national economic objectives—employment, price stability, economic growth—to prevent another 1930s-style depression;

2. Fixed exchange rates—desirable against the turbulence of the 1930s and the distortionary effects of competitive devaluations;

3. Convertibility of currencies for trade in goods and services, the result of dissatisfaction with extensive use of exchange controls and wartime restrictions. Governments would no longer interfere with private sector decisions on the allocation of foreign exchange, and so on;[1]

4. Medium-term lending to cover balance of payments deficits of a temporary nature, leading to the creation of the International Monetary Fund, which became the focus of this particular initiative;[2]

5. The possibility for countries to alter their exchange rates, in the event that deficits turned out not to be temporary.[3]

The system implied a bargain between the United States and the rest of the world, along the lines of: "We (the U.S.) will maintain domestic economic stability; you (the rest of the world) will fix your currencies to the US dollar and will accumulate reserves in dollars which will be gold-convertible." There seems to be consensus—and nothing that was said at the Rome conference, or thereafter, contradicted this—that this system implied enormous implicit gains for the U.S., which, with unlimited access to capital markets, could buy goods abroad without selling an equivalent value of its own goods, an arrangement akin to paying for such goods with checks that are not cashed. In his paper in this *Report*, Robert Skidelsky has noted that the accumulation of US dollar reserves in the European Union during the 1960s was part of this contract: protection against communism, financed by an "imperial tax."

Perhaps because the historical backdrop was so horrible, the system proved very successful, and led to close to 30 years of growth and stability, with trade expanding by leaps and bounds. It also saw the emergence of the EU as an attempt to build upon this global framework. However, as summarized by Cooper, the system had two major flaws, which did not become apparent until much later:

- Gold convertibility of the dollar would gradually become doubtful as the volume of dollar liabilities outpaced the growth of the US gold stock. To have otherwise halted the accumulation of foreign-held dollar reserves would have stifled growth of the world economy;

- The prospect of devaluation gave way to speculation. Capital controls were allowed under the Bretton Woods system, but with improved communications, and electronic money, capital transfers became much more difficult to control. Indeed, over time, the distinction between a current account transaction (for which the currencies were convertible) and a capital account transaction (for which they were not) became blurred. Most countries in the end gave up, making them at times vulnerable to swift changes in market sentiment and expectations. New terms, such as "bandwagon effects" and "self-ful-filling prophecies" found their way into the economics literature. Cooper refers to "expectations feeding on expectations," perhaps echoing Keynes' earlier sentiments that: "nothing is more certain than that the movement of capital funds must be regulated," for if this did not happen, money would "shift with the speed of the magic carpet and these movements would have the effect of disorganizing all steady business." In fact, Klas Eklund, chief economist of Skandinaviska Enskilda Banken (SEB), has observed that today only 3 percent of foreign exchange trading is linked to current account transactions, adding that FX markets suffer from herd behavior, instability, fickleness, unaffected by the fundamentals which used to guide them.

So, in 1973 the system eventually collapsed, with the dollar ceasing to be convertible into gold, and the major economies moving to a non-system of floating exchange rates characterized by:

- Considerable variability in exchange rates, including, by now, probably well over 100 episodes of runs on countries' currencies, and with short-run movements in real exchange rates fairly detached from what policymakers have come to recognize as "economic fundamentals."

- A greater degree of uncertainty for trade and investment. Indeed, the perception that unpredictable movements in real exchange rates can severely complicate macroeconomic management—against a background of increased international integration—was a key factor in pushing the EU to adopt the euro in early 1999.

- Manipulation of exchange rates for national gain—e.g., to fight high inflation through monetary tightening and an appreciated currency.

Since then, the world economy has continued to change dramatically. Manufacturing has begun to go the way of agriculture in many countries, real per capita incomes have increased markedly, and markets have become electronically interconnected, leading to a much greater degree of integration of financial and other services and a seven-fold increase in cross-border capital flows. Exchange rate movements are now potentially more disruptive of profits, production, and employment because of the greater possibilities for substitution of geographic location in all types of production. With the on-going globalization of manufacturing operations, the concept of "country of origin" is becoming fuzzier by the day, as is the meaning of "current account balance" and, hence, the willingness of countries to deal with imbalances when they emerge.

The Fund's Articles of Agreement have not kept pace with these changes. In the words of one noted observer: "the crisis prevention and resolution mechanisms embodied in the Fund's Articles and the Fund's practices had become dysfunctional."[4] This failure of the international monetary system to adapt adequately to contemporary conditions is more than a simple academic matter. It imposes significant real and opportunity costs as well as higher systemic financial risk:

- Real costs include the misallocation of resources stemming from a prolonged exchange rate misalignment, as well as the contraction of economic activity and major social dislocation caused by an unnecessarily severe currency crisis.

- Opportunity costs include the suppressed rate or skewed pattern of economic development which can accompany a government's decision to accumulate an unusually large amount of foreign exchange reserves as insurance against a currency crisis.

- Systemic risks include the increased uncertainty and volatility in financial markets accompanying investor perceptions that delayed adjustment to large, persistent economic imbalances may result in a hard economic landing in one or more systemically significant countries.

These increased costs and risks have been visible in a wide range of countries in recent decades, leading the governments in many emerging market economies and the international business community to take a greater interest in international monetary reform. Fortunately, the world's most influential international monetary authorities (the Group of 7) have begun to perceive both the need for reform and the value of broadening participation in their deliberations to include key emerging market countries and the private sector. In particular, they have begun to make greater use of the Group of 20 as a forum to explore ideas and build consensus.

Created in 1999 in the aftermath of the Asian financial crisis, the G-20 consists of the finance ministers and central bank governors of the 20 countries deemed to be of greatest significance for the international financial system. As documented by Edwin Truman, G-20 members collectively account for about 75 percent of global growth, 50 percent of the growth in world trade, and 70 percent of the growth in reserves since 1990. While the International Monetary Fund's board remains the formal locus of decision-making on immediate questions of Fund policy, the G-20 appears to be evolving into the most influential forum for exploration of longer-term issues and institutional reform, by virtue of the greater legitimacy conferred by its more representative character. By all accounts, it played an important role in preparing the ground for the important governance and surveillance reforms adopted by the IMF in 2006, suggesting that it is coming of age as a policy-making institution after a number of uneven, initial years in which it appeared at times to be in search of a clear purpose.

In 2004, this growing private sector interest in international monetary reform and a new willingness by G-7 policy-makers to engage in serious discussion with a wider set of interested parties prompted the World Economic Forum's Centre for Public-Private Partnership and the Reinventing Bretton Woods Committee to approach a number of G-20 governments about co-convening a series of public-private roundtables to examine how to improve the functioning of the system, in light of the emergence of a wider range of important national actors and the increased role of private capital flows. Known as the International Monetary Convention Project, this series of intensive, two-day discussions was inaugurated at the Ministry of Economy and Finance of Italy in July of 2004, on the 60th anniversary of the conclusion of the Bretton Woods conference. Over the succeeding two years, six additional sessions were held, in cooperation with the finance ministries and central banks of the Netherlands (during its presidency of the European Union), China, Turkey, France, Australia, and South Africa. Over 50 research and discussion papers were prepared for these sessions by participating governmental, private sector, and academic experts. All of the discussions were conducted on an off-the-record basis to encourage candid and expansive dialogue.

These roundtables effectively became an informal, rolling forum on the international monetary convention, a latter-day, multi-stakeholder exploration of many of the same fundamental questions and policy dilemmas that preoccupied Bretton Woods conference participants in 1944. In the process, they provided a stimulating laboratory for policy-makers, offering them a means for structured intellectual outreach to some of the world's leading private sector and academic experts. In two cases, sessions were held immediately before the first G-20 deputies' annual meeting, helping the incoming G-20 chairs (China and Australia) to explore potential agenda items for the year to come. And participants were invited to continue the discussion online in an electronic platform provided by the Centre for International Governance Innovation known as IGLOO.

This volume constitutes the project's final report, which has been supported by the Forum's Strategic Partner, Credit Suisse. It consists of some of the most interesting papers prepared for the roundtable events, which were generously supported by the seven host governments as well as SEB, Banca Intesa, Garanti Bank, Morgan Stanley, and Standard Bank. It seeks to convey to the reader the depth and range of ideas and arguments advanced across the two years of discussion.

A number of the concepts and themes presented in the roundtables were embraced by policymakers in the 2006 reforms adopted by the IMF on multilateral surveillance and governance. However, as the papers that follow illustrate, the need for further reform is significant and political momentum toward it probably inescapable. Part I explores the context by asking what fundamental forces are likely to shape the pattern and pace of reform in the years to come. Parts II and III examine more closely the nature and potential implications of two of these likely drivers of change: the growing economic weight of Asian and other emerging market countries, and the persistence of large global macroeconomic imbalances, respectively. Finally, Part IV presents a number of promising, specific proposals presented at the roundtables, aimed at improving the management of the international monetary system and strengthening the structure and governance of its principal institution, the International Monetary Fund.

What emerges from these observations and proposals, and from the reactions they provoked in the roundtables, is a reform agenda about which there is considerable, albeit far from universal, agreement. A critical mass of governments clearly wishes to create a stronger set of institutional arrangements and instruments to support international financial stability in a world characterized by increasingly large cross-border private capital flows, wider geographic distribution of economic activity, and deepened regional macroeconomic and international trade policy coordination.

But they represent only the beginning of the thought process about how to achieve this objective—a process that the G-20 is poised to play a central role in advancing. Indeed, we conclude this project with the impression that an important transformation of the international monetary system has just begun in which the G-20, by virtue of its relatively informal and highly representative nature, may well prove to be the crucible in which its primary features are forged.

Goldman Sachs economist Michael Buchanan states in his paper: "Every few decades, a seismic shift occurs in the world economy that has far-reaching implications across a wide range of markets. The rise of the US economy in the late 19th century, the post-war rebuilding of Japan and Western Europe and the rise of the East Asian production network have all been events of this kind. We have speculated that the rise of the four largest emerging economies, the so-called BRICs—Brazil, Russia, India, and China—could be the same kind of transforming event over the next few decades." And to this list, we might add from our perspective Mexico and South Korea, among others.

As a result, the big questions that policy makers are grappling with today, from the persistence of large global imbalances, to the huge accumulation of reserves in surplus countries, to the day-to-day functioning of the IMF, can no longer be viewed through the traditional prism of core and periphery (the G-7 vis-à-vis the rest of the world). In ways implicit and explicit, the G-7 has begun to accept that its influence will have to be shared, as evidenced by the medium-term strategic review initiated by the IMF's Managing Director, which has set in motion negotiations likely to yield significant additional shifts in the institution's distribution of quotas and votes within the next two years.

In short, a new geography of international finance is beginning to emerge. And just as the U.S. and Europe found it difficult at times to accommodate the rise of Japan as an economic power, so they are likely to be somewhat anxious about the emergence of China, India, Brazil, Korea, and other countries. Some of this concern is grounded in legitimate questions: will these new actors be up to the task of being both constructive and assertive? For example, will they be able to elaborate a vision of their own for the future of the IMF? Will they be prepared to act, as challenged by Truman in his paper, in response to the fact that their economic policies have spillover effects that can significantly affect the global economy? At root, are they prepared to shoulder part of the responsibility for leadership in managing the international financial system?

Judging from the roundtable discussions, conditions are ripe for creative leadership in three aspects of the international monetary system: strengthening the international adjustment process, improving crisis prevention and resolution instruments, and modernizing and rationalizing the governance of its principal institutions.

Adjustment process

In the roundtables in Italy, China, France, and Australia, global imbalances were a dominant theme. The United States current account deficit in 2005 was about US$800 billion, or close to 7 percent of GDP. It is now being financed mainly by fixed income flows, particularly purchases of government securities by central banks of surplus Asian and other countries, rather than the large net private equity flows of several years ago. Perhaps no other issue attracted greater attention and disagreement in this project than the sources, sustainability, and implications for global economic stability and progress of these imbalances (see, for example, the papers of Cooper, Eichengreen, Skidelsky, De Long, and Setser).

Nevertheless, there was widespread agreement on the utility of upgrading the IMF's surveillance capabilities and responsibilities. In 2006, the IMF's Executive Board approved a strengthened role for the institution in monitoring and facilitating the adjustment of large, persistent economic imbalances. The so-called multilateral surveillance process which was launched is intended to sharpen appreciation of the systemic implications of individual country policies, and facilitate a greater degree of peer pressure for governments to act in the global interest. Consultations have been taking place with Saudi Arabia, the United States, euro zone countries, Japan, and China, but it is too early to tell whether this initiative will be any more effective in spurring a coordinated response by both debtor and creditor countries than previous efforts.

The International Monetary and Financial Committee (IMFC) has called for an ongoing review, with the aim of updating the 1977 Decision on Surveillance over Exchange Rate Policies, in order to achieve a common understanding and consensus on responsibilities under Article IV and the foundations and objectives of surveillance, covering monetary, fiscal, financial, and exchange rate policies. This provides a welcome opportunity to reevaluate the exchange rate system and consider how the IMF could be reconfigured to help improve its performance. In his paper, John Williamson shows how the new multilateral surveillance process could be strengthened by giving the Fund authority to issue independent, public evaluations of the sustainability of national exchange rates, indicating at what parity countries would be presumed to be acting against the interests of global economic stability, if they intervened in the markets to block movement by their currency back toward its long-term equilibrium rate. Giving the Fund genuine independence to prepare and publish fundamental analyses of this sort could strengthen moral suasion and sharpen market information—two of the primary sources of its leverage in these matters—without prejudging whether sensitive aspects of

Article IV consultations concerning the policy dialogue with the government in question should be similarly made public.

In this spirit, the Fund may wish to reflect on the even more ambitious proposals of former IMF US Executive Director Sam Cross. He has suggested that the IMF shift its focus from prices (exchange rates) to quantities (payment imbalances). The underlying concept is that the IMF adjustment program should not be limited to members which had to rely on the Fund for financing, but that any nation that had a serious imbalance in its external payments should be obliged to work toward reduction or elimination of that imbalance, in a program taking due account of the broader interests of the international economy. Under his proposal, each IMF member with a large prospective payment imbalance, either deficit or surplus, would be required to present to the IMF an explanation of the factors leading to the imbalance, a program for reducing the imbalance toward an acceptable level over the medium term, and a description of how the imbalance would be financed in the interim.

The IMF would either bless or withhold approval of the program, with non-approval representing a kind of a moral censure or vote of no confidence regarding whether the government was fulfilling its responsibilities for international good behavior. In effect, there would be three rings of IMF surveillance:

- Member exchange rate policies with respect to the avoidance of manipulative practices;

- The implications of member imbalances for the international balance of payments adjustment process;

- The implications of member imbalances for world capital markets.

Efforts to strengthen the IMF's surveillance capabilities should not be limited to macroeconomic policies. The system would also benefit greatly from a serious examination of its market surveillance capabilities and functions. Given the expansion of private capital flows in recent decades and, in particular, the proliferation of derivative and off balance sheet instruments, there is an urgent need to improve official sector understanding of these new sources of systemic risk and fully integrate this insight into policy dialogue regarding exchange rate policy and macroeconomic adjustment. This is a topic ripe for future public-private dialogue and collaboration.

Crisis prevention and resolution

Almost ten years after the Asian financial crisis, the rules of the game for IMF lending have still not been clarified (see the papers by Jack Boorman and Angel Ubide). The IMFC stated recently that it supports the strengthening of IMF policies to better assist its emerging market members and "welcomes the recent discussion in the Executive Board on a new liquidity instrument for countries that are active in international capital markets, aimed at supporting these countries' own strong policies, and ensuring that substantial financing will be available if needed while safeguarding IMF resources. The Committee calls on the Executive Board to continue its work on the necessary design features of a new instrument, while paying due regard to the interaction with existing IMF facilities, and invites the Managing Director to present a concrete proposal by the time of its next meeting."[5]

The roundtable series spent considerable time examining several aspects of this question, including stronger regional arrangements (see de Brouwer and Kawai) and improved multilateral instruments such as Richard Portes' and Daniel Cohen's proposal to create an International Lender of First Resort and Angel Ubide's proposal to create an automatic and universally available insurance mechanism (see Ubide).

All of these potential reforms raise the question of resources. If in a world of extensive private capital flows the opportunity cost for economic and social progress represented by the enormous reserve accumulation of many developing countries is to be reduced, then the international monetary system will need to create a much more credible lender (or coordinated set of lenders) of last resort. To this end, most roundtable participants supported an expansion of the Fund's resources through a major quota increase, as well as an increase in country access limits. However, many were skeptical that the necessary political consensus could be assembled any time soon to endow the Fund with substantially increased resources. Perhaps the will to address the adequacy of the Fund's lending resources will be strengthened by the widespread perception, frequently articulated in the roundtables, that its business model—the way in which it finances its day-to-day operations—is even more deeply in need of repair. As fewer countries have chosen to avail themselves of Fund lending facilities and more of its outstanding credits from previous crises have been repaid, the ability of the IMF to fund its ongoing activities has been questioned, prompting management to appoint a Committee of Eminent Persons "to provide the Fund with an independent view of the available options for ensuring that it has a sustainable and durable income base with which to finance its running costs over the long term."[6] It is expected that the Committee will report to the Managing Director in the first quarter of 2007.

Finally, it should be noted that most expert roundtable participants approved of the recent addition of collective action clauses to emerging bond market issues, as well as efforts to create a voluntary code of conduct by parties to a debt restructuring process. Most were optimistic that these innovations would make a significant difference. Nevertheless, many thought that it was only a matter of time before the debate about a more formal sovereign debt restructuring mechanism, such as the IMF's unsuccessful initial proposal, resurfaced because of doubts about the ultimate ability of a purely voluntary process to deal with large and complex cases in which the holdings of key creditors are unable to be aggregated into a general settlement.

Governance

Probably no aspect of international monetary policy received more attention from governments during the life of this project than institutional governance (see the papers by Boorman, Lipsky, and Truman). In particular, the drive to make IMF's voting rights and quotas better reflect economic reality—a key focus of the 2006 Australian and 2005 Chinese G-20 presidencies—bore initial fruit in 2006. At the Singapore annual meeting, the Fund's membership agreed to a substantive realignment of IMF quotas to recognize the growing weight of emerging market economies in the world economy. The proposal to begin a fundamental reform of the IMF was approved by 90.6 percent of the votes of member countries. Supported by all the Fund's large shareholders, it will provide immediate additional voting power to China, Korea, Mexico, and Turkey. The initial ad hoc increases imply new quotas for the four countries and involve an aggregate increase in quotas of SDR 3.81 billion (about US$5.66 billion), or 1.8 percent of IMF's total current quotas of SDR 213.48 billion (about US$317.26 billion). In addition, the decision launched what is expected to be a two-year effort to redistribute votes more broadly, and in ways that will boost the voice of the poorest nations of Africa, as well as other countries accounting for a larger share of the world economy than their current IMF shares would suggest.

UK Chancellor of the Exchequer Gordon Brown has called these steps "the biggest reform to the governance of the International Monetary Fund for

60 years." And while the overwhelming majority of roundtable participants agreed that reforms to the IMF such as these are essential, there are at least two other aspects of international financial governance which also deserve priority attention. First, the time has come to clarify the responsibilities and quite possibly rationalize the array of institutions and country groupings concerned with the various aspects of international monetary policy. The Financial Stability Forum (FSF), Bank for International Settlements (BIS), IMFC, G-10, G-7, G-20, IMF Executive Board, and parts of the World Bank have a number of overlapping activities and areas of oversight. In particular, the relationship of the FSF to the G-20, that of the IMFC to the IMF's Executive Board, and that of the G-7 and G-10 to the G-20 would benefit from clarification. This, too, is an area ripe for further public-private dialogue and research.

Second, most roundtable participants took the view that the cause of international economic policy cooperation and coherence would be served by the creation of some sort of overarching coordinating process or mechanism. Despite the ambitions of its founders, the G-7/G-8 Summit process clearly does not serve this purpose. And project participants assigned a low probability to either the United Nations or the G-20 evolving into an alternative forum for presidents and prime ministers to provide coordinated direction of such principal international economic institutions as the IMF, the World Bank, the World Trade Organization, the International Labor Organization, and their corresponding groups of ministers.

Nevertheless, we believe that the G-20 has the potential to effect a substantial improvement in the coherence of international policy within its existing ministerial-level configuration. In addition to serving, as it has in its finest hours to date, as a caucus conducive for the deliberations of key countries about the agenda for international monetary reform, the G-20 could use its special convening authority—by virtue of its finance minister membership— to advance progress on a growing number of interdisciplinary challenges which have accompanied international economic integration. Progress on problems as diverse as domestic capital market development, unemployment, aid-for-trade, energy security, pandemics, climate change, and burden sharing, among others, all cry out for greater engagement by and coordination among ministers and international organizations with different portfolios. All inevitably implicate finance ministries by virtue of their relevance to national budgets or international financial institutions. The G-20 could contribute substantially to international economic policy management by serving as a locus of cross-ministerial consultations on selected, interdisciplinary economic problems, harnessing finance ministers' *primes inter pares* standing among economic policy ministers in most governments to catalyze such badly-needed coordination. The G-20 has already taken initial, tentative steps in this direction, most notably in the health meeting hosted by the Canadian government in 2005, and the energy security discussion held in conjunction with the recent Australian G-20 ministerial meetings. It should build upon these experiences by establishing a practice of incorporating at least one set of cross-ministerial workplans and consultations into its annual agenda.

In conclusion, we wish to thank the authors who submitted their research for this volume, the more than 200 experts, seven governments, and six financial services firms who contributed to the success of the project, and particularly our colleagues Carina Larsfälten, who managed it with diligence and initiative from start to finish, and Lauren Johnston. We believe that this innovative exercise in public-private partnership has demonstrated that effective reforms to improve the performance of the world economy and reduce the risk of regional and systemic financial crises are within conceptual reach. The growing complexity of the global economy and the financial mechanisms and institutions underpinning it highlight the central importance of continued dialogue on the reforms necessary to ensure the smooth functioning of the international monetary system. Only time will tell whether the political will to act will also be within reach before the next crisis.

NOTES

1 In his paper in this *Report*, John Lipsky expresses the view that this was the most important achievement of the Bretton Woods system.

2 Hence, the discussion below on the role of the IMF, the institution at the very centre of the Bretton Woods system.

3 For a thorough overview of the key relevant issues underlying the operation of the international monetary system, see Cooper, 1986.

4 John Lipsky, former Vice Chairman, JPMorgan.

5 IMF, 2006b, p. 3.

6 IMF, 2006b.

REFERENCES

Cooper, R. 1986. *The International Monetary System: Essays in World Economics.* Cambridge, MA: MIT Press.

International Monetary Fund. 2006a. Press Release No. 06/100. Washington, D.C.: IMF. 18 May.

———. 2006b.Communiqué. Washington, D.C.: International Monetary and Financial Committee, Board of Governors, IMF. 17 September.

PART 1

Reconstitution of the International Monetary System

CHAPTER 1.1

What Prospects for the International Monetary System?[1]

PATRICK ARTUS, Chief Economist, IXIS Corporate and Investment Bank

T he crucial question today regarding changes in the international
monetary system can be described as follows. The implementation of a
productive specialization, undoubtedly efficient, between some countries
(notably the United States), which specialize in goods and services not traded
internationally to a great extent, and others, such as China, which specialize in
industrial production—a very different specialization pattern from the one
economic theory suggests—implies that the former post a growing deficit
with the latter. In the near term, this deficit is easily financed, resulting in an
imbalance that is mutually advantageous for the United States and for China.

But how can one avoid this growing US external deficit from resulting, in
the medium term, in a crisis, if the countries posting surpluses and lending
to the others refuse to let their claims on debtor countries grow further, in
particular because of the induced currency risk?

Tradables or non tradables

We will see that the choice lies between the dollarization of creditor countries,
to prevent a crisis in the United States, and a change to exchange-rate flexibility
(between the dollar, the renminbi, etc.), in order to prevent serious drawbacks
stemming from the implementation of a single currency between countries
that present significant asymmetries, such as highly different growth rates.
We will also see that, even in the event of a crisis leading to a steep depreciation
in the dollar, the dollar is very unlikely to lose its dominant reserve currency
status and, as a consequence, will continue to suffer from the "reserve currency
curse."

We begin by pointing out that some countries have specialized in goods and services that are hardly or not at all tradable, while others have chosen industrial goods. To avoid ending up with a host of examples, we will draw most often upon the cases of the United States and China.

The type of international specialization that is being set up between the two groups of similar countries is quite different from the conventional pattern of specialization in international trade models, which presupposes that the emerging country specializes in not very sophisticated products requiring rather unskilled labor, and that of the advanced countries specializing in sophisticated goods requiring skilled labor. In fact, the United States has specialized in goods and services that are hardly or not traded internationally— e.g., services, construction, and retail—while China has specialized in factory products.

The structure of employment in the United States has shifted into sectors sheltered from competition: employment in construction has increased by 33 percent since 1996; employment in services by 18 percent; employment in manufacturing has decreased by 18 percent.

Since 1997, the stagnation in industrial production excluding electronics in the United States—i.e., production of all traditional industrial sectors: automobile, metallurgy, capital goods, chemicals, textiles, pharmaceuticals, food, toys, furniture, etc. —is impressive, and contrasts with the robust growth in industrial output in China, which has tripled since 1996.

What accounts for this significant divergence from the theoretical model of international specialization? Probably, the fact that the hypotheses of the model are not verified. For example, the level of education is high in many emerging countries. Others may not have full employment, and make use of internal migration to increase factory employment, as is the case in China; hence, the lack of convergence between costs of production factors or wages, relative to each level of schooling.

Among advanced countries, only Germany and Japan present a type of specialization in conformity with conventional theory, as shown by the fast increasing level of exports to emerging countries or the trade balance in capital goods and transport equipment (Table 1), in other words products in which advanced countries must normally specialize.

Table 1: Trade balance in capital goods and transport equipment (as percentage of GDP)

	2001	2002	2003	2004
United States	−1.25	−1.49	−1.56	−1.75
France	1.31	1.36	1.14	0.85
Germany	6.02	6.64	6.55	7.12
Italy	1.29	1.12	0.98	1.13
Spain	−1.83	−1.68	−1.78	−2.40
Japan	4.15	4.71	4.93	5.28

Source: OECD.

The argument often heard in the United States, to the effect that the shortfall in growth in the rest of the world is what generates its external deficit—that is, the external deficit is not a US domestic problem—is in direct contradiction of the facts.

As we have seen above, the stagnation in exports from the United States and in industrial production, excluding IT, clearly shows that there has been a noticeable deterioration in the situation and in the capacity to meet the demands of US industry.

Furthermore, for several years, global growth has been higher than growth in the United States, and this has not prevented the external deficit of the United States from growing further from less than 4 percent of GDP in 1999 to more than 6 percent in 2005.

Specialization between the United States and China

This type of specialization between the United States and China (or countries with the same characteristics) generates a growing trade deficit in the United States, which cannot be filled by the usual methods, but which does not give rise to a problem in terms of financing it in the near term.

Since the United States (and other advanced countries) specializes in non-traded goods and China (and other emerging countries) in traded products, it is natural that there appears a growing trade deficit in the United States with China and other emerging countries (Figure 1).

Figure 1: United States: Trade balance by region (US$ billion per year)

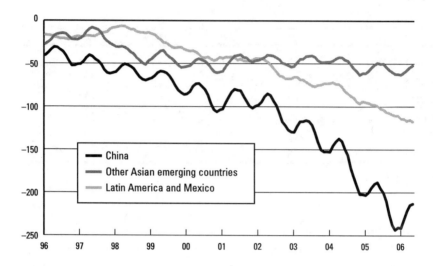

Sources: IMF, IXIS Corporate Investment Bank (CIB).

The external deficit cannot be corrected by the usual remedies, since it results from the gradual disappearance of US industry. Growth in domestic demand in the United States is met by imports and not by domestic production. From 1997 to 2005, domestic demand grew by 40 percent in real terms in the United States, imports by 81 percent, and industrial production (excluding IT) by only 8 percent. Furthermore, the export capacity of the United States is very low, and the gap between imports and exports has been widening steadily. Currently, US exports represent hardy more than the half of US imports.

A moderate depreciation of the dollar would not improve the US foreign trade significantly in volume terms, as its deterioration results from the contraction of industry, not a slight problem of cost-competitiveness. It might hurt the country's foreign trade in value terms, through the induced increase in import prices. Mild restriction of domestic demand in the United States would fail to rebalance foreign trade. Let us suppose that a country becomes a pure service economy, without any industrial production. It no longer exports and imports all its factory products. In consequence, its domestic demand would have to disappear to rebalance its foreign trade.

Figure 2: Official reserves (US$ billion)

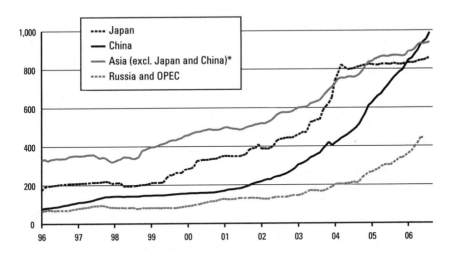

* Singapore, Korea, Taiwan (China), Malaysia, Hong Kong SAR, Indonesia, Philippines, Thailand.
Sources: IMF, IXIS CIB.

Note also that, even in the countries which produce exportable services (tourism, financial services, etc.), the surplus in services remains far too small to offset the deficit in goods ; the surplus amounts to 3 percent of GDP in Spain (tourism), for an overall trade deficit for goods of 8 percent of GDP; to 2 percent of GDP in the UK (financial services), for a trade deficit of 5 percent of GDP; to only half a percent of GDP in the US for a trade deficit of 6 percent of GDP.

The United States will therefore have an increasing trade deficit (US$900 billion at the annual rate in mid-2006), resulting from an efficient productive specialization with emerging countries (China). This will be impossible to correct using the usual (moderate) economic policies.

However, in the near term, the financing of this external deficit does not pose a problem, since China (and other countries posting surpluses with the United States) maintains its peg on the dollar and finances the external deficit of the United States by accumulating official reserves (Figure 2), a situation favorable for both groups of countries.

The United States can persist in its strategy of specialization in non-traded goods and services, without having to correct the external deficit and, therefore, without having to reduce domestic demand.

China can continue to let its growth be driven by exports, notably to the United States, and related investments, given that the average household income in China is still too low to enable its demands to be an engine of growth. In 2006, export growth in China was a high as 29 percent in real terms, with exports representing more than 40 percent of GDP, whereas world trade increased by only 8.5 percent.

Furthermore, it is impossible, in the near term, for the Chinese authorities to make the renminbi convertible for residents. Thus, it is difficult to imagine how the country could have an exchange-rate regime other than its peg to the dollar. The Chinese have substantial savings invested in banking deposits in renminbi, while domestic financial markets are hardly developed and illiquid, and thus unable to cope with domestic savings.

The Chinese hold more than US$3 trillion in the form of bank deposits, where the correlated market capitalization of the bound and equity markets amount to only US$1 trillion.

Under these conditions, making the renminbi convertible would run the risk of a dollarization of China, something the Chinese government certainly does not wish.

The present short-term equilibrium—growing external deficit of the United States financed by the accumulation of reserves by foreign central banks—is therefore quite robust.

The economic literature (see Aghion et al., 1999 and 2004, and Bacchetta and van Wincoop, 2000) clearly demonstrates that, at an intermediate stage of development, emerging countries suffer from credit constraints (rationing), and the liberalization of the capital account would result in a destabilization of the economy, resulting in massive capital outflows.

Furthermore, the accumulation of official reserves in Asia also plays the role of protection reserves (against an economic crisis, political strains, the end of capital inflows, and so forth). This point has already been well analyzed in Aizenmann et al. (2004) and Flood and Marion (2002).

The medium-term problem for China: Currency risk and excess liquidity

The issue we would like to tackle is as follows: it would be efficient for the global economy if the current equilibrium were to last. It enables the United States and China to specialize in the types of production in which they boast a comparative advantage—non-traded services in the United States and factory products in China—and this would be favorable for well-being.

It is obviously inefficient for the United States to manufacture clothing items or toys. But the perpetuation of this specialization implies, as seen above, that China, and other emerging countries, endlessly continue to accumulate claims in dollars on the United States. Such a development gives rise to two[2] critical problems:

First, a currency risk. If the dollar is not to become the currency of creditor countries, or if these countries are not to maintain a fixed exchange rate of their currency against the dollar, the accumulation of claims in dollars on the United States entails a currency risk for the holders of these claims, whose reference currency is, or will be, different from the dollar.

The increase in the holding of dollars in China or in other lender countries due to the accumulation of external debt by the United States (Figure 3) means that currency risk grows in the portfolios of lenders and leads to a fall in demand for dollars by these lenders.

If the fixed exchange rate between the currencies of these lenders against the dollar is maintained, a continuous rise in dollar interest rates will be needed for them to accept to increase their holding of dollar-denominated assets. Without such a rise in dollar interest rates, this holding of assets is limited, and, from a given point in time, there will no longer be any available financing of the external deficit of the United States. This point holds whether this financing is ensured by private or public (central banks) lenders. This point is important because an increase in the private financing of the external deficit of the United States might appear in China, for example, through acquisitions made by Chinese companies.

The literature offers a number of models which rationalize the idea described above. The growth in the external debt of the United States, at equilibrium, increases the (endogenously-determined) variability of the exchange rate. Such a development leads either to depreciation of the dollar, or an increasingly significant rise in interest rates in order to stabilize the dollar, since it decreased ex-antes the demand for dollars.

Figure 3: United States: External debt (US$ billion)

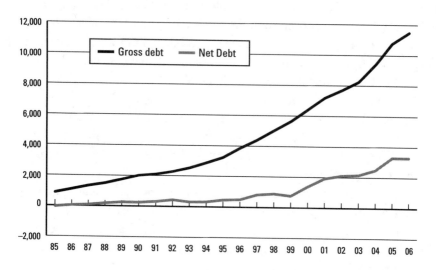

Sources: BEA, OECD, IXIS CIB.

The second problem is related to excess liquidity in China (and in other emerging countries). As long as the currency is pegged to dollar, monetary policy is far too expansionary, if, as in the case of China, growth is markedly stronger than in the United States. Several authors, including Goldstein and Lardy (2005), Roubini (2004), Roubini and Setser (2005), Eichengreen (2004) and Rajan and Subramanian (2004)) highlight the fact that the required massive growth in official reserves would mean that sterilization of the induced monetary creation would become impossible.

In countries where financial markets are not very developed, the accumulation of official reserves therefore leads to very rapid growth in the monetary base, and would gradually also result in very robust credit growth. Such a situation prevailed in China until quantitative credit control measures were taken in 2003, but again credit growth accelerated in the second half of 2005 (Figure 4).

Apart from this question of liquidity creation and sterilization—there would, in fact, not be any rapid growth in the monetary base if the recycling of capital in the United States were carried out by private lenders and not by central banks—the pegging of currencies, (e.g., the renminbi) to the dollar

Figure 4: China: Credit and monetary base (Y/Y as percent)

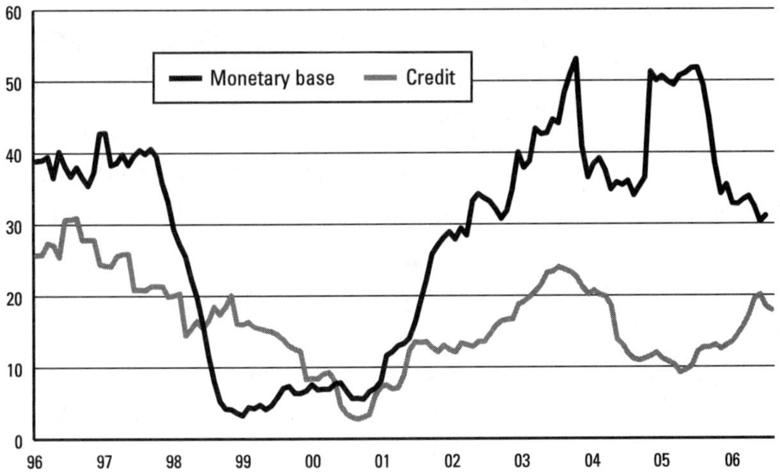

Sources: Economic Intelligence Unit (EIU), IXIS CIB.

means that interest rates (notably renminbi rates) have to be close to dollar interest rates. Such a constraint results in a far too expansionary monetary policy in China, given the growth gap between China and the United States. Interest rates in China are consequently ridiculously low as compared to nominal growth: a 10-year rate in China is, in the second half of 2006, just above 6 percent, while nominal GDP growth is, officially, above 13 percent, and in reality even higher—it is well-known that the official GDP growth date underestimates actual growth in China.

This dynamic is understandable, for if the exchange rate between the dollar and the renminbi is fixed in a credible manner, the external debt of the United States suffers from unstable dynamics and grows endlessly, but without any effect on the equilibrium. If investors think that the dollar will eventually depreciate against the renminbi, China's interest rate will decline, first because of the expectation of an appreciation in the renminbi and, second, due to the accumulation of external debt of the United States. If China changes to flexible exchange rates between the dollar and the renminbi, it will recover its freedom to set its interest rate as it chooses. In the context of quite strong international capital mobility, the change to flexible exchange rates is deemed preferable by China, if it prevents the appearance of bubbles in asset prices. These occurred, under fixed exchange rates, because of the excessively low level of interest rates in China.

Therefore, we can see two factors which would stop the accumulation of claims in dollars on the United States in the medium term, in those countries posting trade surpluses with the United States:

- currency risk, if these countries must eventually have a currency that fluctuates against the dollar;

- negative effects of a chronically too expansionary monetary policy, if these countries enjoy higher growth than the United States.

Note that the question of ascertaining whether the financing of the external deficit of the United States by emerging countries will continue indefinitely has given rise to a heated debate in the literature.

One side—e.g., Blanchard and Giavazzi-Sa (2005), Eichengreen (2004), and Obstfeld and Rogoff (2004)—argues that this financing will necessarily end, and that there will be a required correction in the external deficit of the United States. Such a development will lead to serious consequences: a slide in the dollar, which, as seen above, would be precipitous because of the deterioration in the situation of US industry, and the very high level of US imports in comparison with US exports.

The other side, including especially Dooley et al. (2002, 2004a, and 2004b), holds that the current equilibrium can persist for a variety of reasons:

- the mercantilist policies of Asian countries which base their growth on exports and, as a consequence, necessarily post external surpluses which they must recycle; (as explained earlier, we agree with this argument in the near term;)

- the superiority of the United States in carrying out financial intermediation, thus giving the rest of the world an alleged interest in lending its savings to the U.S., in the form of purchases of government securities for example, so that the U.S. can make these investments.

This second argument (re financial intermediation) is patently absurd. On the one hand, in order to finance its external deficit, the United States needs net capital inflows, and not inflows followed by equivalent outflows. On the other hand, for a long time, long-term capital has flown *into* the United States and not *out*. Since the end of the 1990s, there has been no sign that the United States has played the role of financial intermediary.

There is yet another argument pointing to an end, in the long term, of the policy of intervention in the currency markets: it leads to the risk of considerable inefficiencies in the allocation of savings, due to distortions a) in interest rates, b) between interest rates and growth rates, as seen above, and also c) between regulated interest rates (on deposits and government securities) and borrowing rates (see Higgins and Klitgaard, 2004).

Between a rock and a hard place

Crisis would result from the end of the financing of the US external deficit, and monetary unification between countries would present significant asymmetries. The foregoing arguments lead to a number of straightforward conclusions:

1. Because of the presence of currency risk, the only solution, if creditor countries of the United States are to continue to endlessly finance the external deficit of the United States, is to ensure that their currency remains perpetually fixed against the dollar, i.e., these countries (such as China) would have to set up a de facto currency area with the United States. For, within a currency area, trade surpluses or deficits of the various regions with one another are of no importance. They are automatically financed by private capital flows, for example in the interbank market. Such is clearly the situation in the euro zone, which posts an overall external surplus. For example, Spain's external deficit (more than 6 points of GDP) is automatically financed without posing a problem for Germany's external surplus, and without the need for any central bank interference. Once again, this does not give rise to problems, since both countries share the same currency.

2. Dollarization of the world—at least of emerging countries with large trade surpluses with the United States—would thus enable the move toward efficient specialization described above between the United States and such emerging countries as China to continue. Thus, the end of the financing of the US external deficit would not interrupt this process by causing excess currency risk.

But, if the United States, China, and other emerging countries were to set up a currency area, or a virtual currency area, with irrevocably fixed exchange rates, the problem already discussed above *would*, in fact, emerge: i.e., these countries do not form an optimal currency area. In particular, as we have seen, the growth gaps between China and the United States are so wide, that it is impossible to imagine that these countries could share the same interest rates.

This leads to a difficult choice: a) either give up the idea of a monetary unification between the United States and countries with a surplus with the United States (e.g., China), since a serious crisis would ensue. As we also saw above, it would lead to a marked slide in the dollar, a recession in the United States, as well as in those countries which have significant trade with the United States; or b) carry out this monetary unification, whereby China would definitively peg its currency in a credible manner against the dollar, i.e., have the dollar as its currency, in order to prevent a growing currency risk for lenders. However, the drawback would be that monetary policy would be ill-adapted in some countries because of structural asymmetries.

It may be noted that this problem does not arise solely between the United States and China, but also within the Euro zone. Let us look again at the example of Spain and Germany. The fact that both countries have the euro as their currency makes it possible for Spain, like the United States, to specialize in sheltered sectors—tourism, services, construction, etc.—from 1996 to 2006, employment in construction in Spain increased by more than 85 percent; employment in services and tourism by more than 45 percent)— and not experience problems in terms of financing the trade deficit implied by this type of specialization.

But, as is the case with the fixed exchange rates between the United States and China, euro interest rates are too high for Germany where growth is sluggish, and too low for Spain, where growth is robust: a 10-year rate in the Euro zone area is slightly under 4 percent, while nominal growth in Spain fluctuates at around 8 percent and in Germany around 3 percent.

What if monetary unification is not carried out?

If monetary unification is not carried out, the dollar will depreciate massively, but it will maintain its dominant reserve currency status.

Let us suppose that the asymmetry argument, i.e., the absence of an optimal currency area between the United States and China wins the day, that

China eventually stops financing the external deficit of the United States, and that the dollar therefore depreciates so significantly as to drive domestic savings in the United States upwards, and wipe out its external deficit.

Recent studies, such as those of Gourinchas and Rey (2005), Lane and Milesi-Ferretti (2001 and 2002) and Tille (2004), show that such a depreciation in the dollar would improve the current account balance of the United States through the increase in income drawn from the external assets of US foreign currencies, as their market value and return in dollars would rise after a depreciation in the greenback.

However, as interesting as this argument may be, it does not rule out a pronounced depreciation if the dollar if the US external deficit has to be reduced. On the one hand, a 10 percent depreciation in the dollar would increase income from the external assets of the United States by only 0.4 percent of GDP, and this is not a considerable figure. On the other hand, an expected depreciation in the dollar would result in the demand for an increase in the interest rates on the external debt of the United States, and would accordingly wipe out the effect of the increase in the return on its external assets.

Would the dollar lose its role as a reserve currency?

We would point out that the staggering depreciation in the dollar since 1971 (Figure 5) has not led to such a development.

The dollar is still, and by far, the dominant international currency in official reserves (Table 2) and in the invoicing of trade (Table 3).

In our opinion, regardless of the depreciation in the dollar stemming from the end of the financing of the US external deficit, the dollar would not lose its reserve currency status.

The economics literature explains the important role played as an international reserve currency by certain currencies by pointing to the size of the foreign-exchange market associated with these currencies. The concept is that transaction costs between two currencies decrease in line with the volume traded (see Krugman, 1980, Matsuyama et al., 1993, and Zhou, 1997).

As has been well documented for the dollar (Hau et al., 2003), this theory explains the role of certain currencies as vehicles currencies, i.e., as a third currency making trade between two other currencies possible via two transactions (Rey, 2001, Krugman (1984).

Figure 5: Exchange rate against the dollar

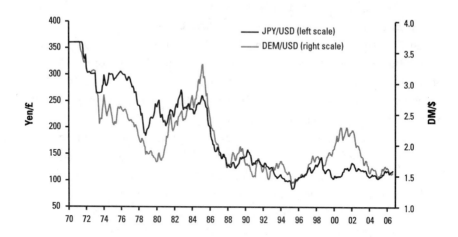

Source: Datastream, IXIS CIB.

The other approach indicated in the literature shows that if the exchange rate between two currencies becomes more volatile, the risk for market-makers increases, leading to a wider spread as well as lower liquidity, and does not allow them to become dominant international currencies. (See Black, 1991, Hartmann, 1998, Giovannini,1998, Devereux et al., 2004 and Bacchetta and van Wincoop, 2000 and 2002.)

Liquidity, which is necessary for the reserve currency, also results from the slope of supply curves (Hau and Rey, 2002) for the various currencies that affect variability, the level of transaction costs, and the transmission of information by the observation of market prices.

Lastly, it has been argued that the quest for a single currency is, above all, useful for sales of an industry in which products are not differentiated (McKinnon, 1979, Krugman, 1980, Goldberg and Tille, 2005).

The role of the dollar as the dominant reserve currency thus seems solid, with the observation that transaction costs in euros are higher than is the case for the D-mark (Hau et al., 2002a), and liquidity (stickiness of prices with respect to transactions) justifies the dollar's role as a vehicle currency (Lyons and Moore, 2005).

Table 2: Weight of different currencies in official reserves (percent)

As percent	1995	1996	1997	1998	1999	2000	2001	2002	2003	2004	2005	2006
ALL COUNTRIES												
US dollar	59.02	62.07	65.16	69.30	71.18	71.55	71.83	68.86	66.58	67.02	66.63	66.32
Yen	6.78	6.72	5.78	6.24	6.07	6.26	5.37	4.53	3.85	3.84	3.59	3.35
Sterling	2.12	2.69	2.58	2.66	2.81	2.79	2.69	2.75	2.56	2.36	3.65	3.96
Swiss franc	0.33	0.30	0.35	0.33	0.25	0.24	0.27	0.36	0.18	0.20	0.15	0.16
Euro	—	—	—	—	18.00	17.66	18.46	21.98	25.00	24.07	24.34	24.80

As percent	1995	1996	1997	1998	1999	2000	2001	2002	2003	2004	2005	2006
INDUSTRIALIZED COUNTRIES												
US dollar	52.34	57.37	59.09	67.65	72.60	73.82	73.07	70.45	69.63	73.04	73.68	73.81
Yen	6.67	5.69	5.87	6.89	6.50	5.15	5.93	3.48	3.96	3.50	3.31	3.48
Sterling	2.09	2.08	1.98	2.06	2.13	2.09	1.96	2.02	1.64	1.14	2.11	2.08
Swiss franc	0.14	0.10	0.15	0.15	0.08	0.21	0.32	0.51	0.23	0.19	0.13	0.20
Euro	—	—	—	—	16.98	15.69	17.12	16.04	22.55	19.74	19.14	19.25

As percent	1995	1996	1997	1998	1999	2000	2001	2002	2003	2004	2005	2006
DEVELOPING COUNTRIES												
US dollar	70.26	68.48	72.33	71.07	69.64	69.09	70.58	67.25	63.53	60.69	60.73	60.38
Yen	6.95	8.13	5.67	5.55	5.60	5.92	4.81	4.59	3.73	3.22	3.83	3.25
Sterling	2.15	3.51	3.29	3.31	3.53	3.55	3.43	3.49	2.73	4.40	4.95	5.45
Swiss franc	0.67	0.58	0.59	0.52	0.43	0.26	0.22	0.16	0.21	0.16	0.16	0.14
Euro	—	—	—	—	19.11	19.80	19.82	23.21	21.42	28.62	28.71	29.20

Sources: IMF (COFER).

Table 3: Weight of currencies in the invoicing of world trade (as percent)

Dollar	Euro	Other
52	25	23

Sources: ECB, CEP II, central banks.

What can be the effect of the accumulation of US external debt on the role of the various currencies as a reserve currency? First, there is both a network effect—as transaction costs in dollars decline when the size of the dollar market increases—as well as a currency risk effect. When the US external debt increases, it is the network effect which initially dominates: transaction costs in dollars fall, the dollar appreciates, variability in the dollar's exchange rate against the yen-yuan declines, and the weight of dollar-denominated assets increases in global wealth. Secondly, when there is a substantial US external debt, the currency risk effect dominates: there is a rise in the variability of the dollar's exchange rate, a depreciation of the dollar, and stabilization, but not decline, in the weight of dollar-denominated assets in global wealth. This shows that, even if the dollar depreciates, it remains the dominant reserve currency.

In our opinion, the size argument is significant. As we saw earlier, the external gross US debt exceeds US$12 trillion. What assets other than dollar-denominated could total such an astronomical figure? The asset markets in other currencies are far too small to make it conceivable to invest dollar-denominated assets held outside the United States in them. US$12 trillion represents about one quarter of the overall wealth held outside of the United States.

In addition to this "primary" size effect, there are the effects seen above: low transaction costs, and liquidity (price stickiness with respect to shocks). Even if the dollar were to depreciate drastically, keeping it as the reserve currency, the invoicing currency of trade would still be efficient.

This conclusion actually confirms the "reserve currency curse" theory. Let us look at the dynamics suggested above and how they correspond to the course of the dollar since the early 1970s. Despite crises, the dollar has kept its reserve currency status. This implies that demand for the dollar is strong and, relative to the economic situation of the United States (external deficit, fiscal deficit, etc.), the cost of capital is low in the U.S. This is a favorable factor, as it stimulates productive investment, as we saw during the 1990s in the United States.

But this low level of the cost of capital—despite the external debt and the fiscal deficits since 2001—also makes it possible to stimulate a type of debt that is not used to accumulate efficient capital. It mostly stimulates household debt, used to finance housing purchases (which drive prices or consumption upwards), as well as public debt, to finance tax cuts that boost consumption.

The net savings rate for households in the United States has declined from 6 percent in 1995 to below 1 percent in 2006.

Thus, in a country such as the United States, which issues a reserve currency, there is an accumulation of inefficient external debt, and possibly a currency crisis.

Conclusion

The critical choice is therefore between continuing the present move toward productive specialization between the United States (non-traded goods and services) and China (and other emerging countries in factory products) and the return to exchange-rate flexibility between the dollar and the renminbi (the won, etc.). If the financing of the US trade deficit is to continue indefinitely without the accumulation of excess currency risk, the current move toward specialization is efficient, but requires monetary unification between the United States and China (and the other emerging countries with trade surpluses).

The return to exchange-rate flexibility between the dollar and the renminbi (the won, etc.) would bring to an end this move toward international specialization, and trigger a severe depreciation in the dollar. On the other hand, it would make it possible to avoid having to form a currency area between countries which, because of the major asymmetries they present, clearly do not meet the prerequisites for an optimal currency area.

NOTES

1 This paper was originally prepared for the Roundtable "The Evolving Role of the Bretton Woods Institutions: Where do we stand?" Paris, 4–5 July 2005.

2 Note that Frankel (2005) offers a list of seven difficulties related to the maintenance of the peg to the dollar.

REFERENCES

Aghion P., P. Bacchetta, and A. Banarjee. 1999. "Financial Liberalization and Volatility in Emerging Market Economies." in P. R. Agénor, M. Miller, D Vines, and A. Weber, eds. *The Asian Financial Crises: Causes, Contagion and Consequences.* Cambridge: Cambridge University Press.167–90.

———. 2004. "Financial Development and the Instability of Open Economies." NBER Working Paper No.10246. January.

Aizenmann J., Y. Lee, and Y. Rhee. 2004. "International Reserves Management and Capital Mobility in a Volatile World: Policy Considerations and a Case Study of Korea." NBER Working Paper No.10534. June.

Bacchetta P. and E. van Wincoop. 2000. "Capital Flows to Emerging Markets: Liberalization, Overshooting, and Volatility." in S. Edwards, ed. *Capital Flows and the Emerging Economies—Theory, Evidence and Controversies*. Chicago: University of Chicago Press. 61–98.

———. 2002. "A Theory of the Currency Denomination of International Trade." NBER Working Paper No. 9039.

Black, S. 1991. "Transaction Costs and Vehicle Currencie." *Journal of International Money and Finance* 10:512–27.

Blanchard O., F. Giavazzi, and F. Sa. 2005. "The US Current Account and the Dollar." NBER Working Paper No.11137. February.

Devereux M., C. Engel, and P. E. Storegaard. 2004. "Endogenous Exchange Rate Pass-Through when Nominal Prices are set in Advance." *Journal of International Economics* 63(2):263–91.

Dooley M., D. Folkerts-Landau, and P. Garber. 2002. "An Essay on the Revised Bretton Woods System." NBER Working Paper No. 9971. September.

———. 2004a. "The Revised Bretton Woods System: the Effects of Periphery Intervention and Reserve Management on Interest Rate and Exchange Rates in Center Countries." NBER Working Paper No.10332. March.

———. 2004b. "The US Current Account Deficit and Economic Development: Collateral for a Total Return Swap." NBER Working Paper No.15727. August.

Eichengreen, B. 2004. "Global Imbalances and the Lessons of Bretton Woods." NBER Working Paper No.10497. May.

Flood R. and N. P. Marion. 2002. "Holding International Reserves in an Era of High Capital Mobility." In S. M. Collins and D. Rodrik eds. *Brookings Trade Forum 2001*. Washington, D.C.: Brookings Institution Press. 1–68.

Frankel, J. 2005. "On the Renminbi: the Choice between Adjustment Under a Fixed Exchange Rate and Adjustment Under a Flexible Rate." NBER Working Paper No.11274. April.

Giovannini, A. 1988. "Exchange Rates and Traded Goods Prices." *Journal of International Economics* 24: 45–68.

Goldberg, L. S. and C. Tille. 2005. "Vehicle Currency Use in International Trade." NBER Working Paper No.11127. February.

Goldstein M. and N. Lardy. 2005. "China's Role in the Reviewed Bretton Woods System: A Case of Mistaken Identity." Institute for International Economics, Working Paper No.WP 05-02. March.

Gourinchas P. and H. Rey. 2005. "International Financial Adjustment." NBER Working Paper No.11155. February.

Hartmann, P. 1998. "Currency Competition and Foreign Exchange Markets: the Dollar, the Yen, and the Euro." Cambridge: Cambridge University Press.

Hau, H., W. Killen, and M. Moore. 2002a. "The Euro as an International Currency: Explaining Puzzling First Evidence from the Foreign Exchange Markets." *Journal of International Money and Finance* 21:351–83.

———. 2002b. "Euro's Forex Role: How Has the Euro Changed the Foreign Exchange Market?" *Economic Policy*. April. 151–91.

Hau, H. and H. Rey. 2002. "Exchange Rates, Equity Prices, and Capital Flows." NBER Working Paper No. 9398. December.

Higgins M. and T. Klitgaard. 2004. "Reserve and Accumulation Implications for Global Capital Flows and Financial Markets." *Current Issues in Economics and Finance* 10(10). September/October. New York: Federal Reserve Bank of New York.

Krugman, P. 1980. "Vehicle Currency and the Structure of International Exchange." *Journal of Money, Credit and Banking* 12:513 –26.

———. 1984. "The International Role of the Dollar: Theory and Prospect." in J. Bilson and R. Marston, eds. *Exchange Rate Theory and Practice*. Chicago: University of Chicago Press. 261–78.

Lane P. and G. Milesi-Ferretti. 2001. "The External Wealth of Nations: Measures of Foreign Assets and Liabilities for Industrial and Developing Nations." *Journal of International Economics* 55. December. 263–94.

———. 2002. "External Wealth, the Trade Balance and the Real Exchange Rate." *European Economic Review*. June.

Lyons R. and M. Moore. 2005. "An Information Approach to International Currencies." NBER Working Paper No.11220. March.

Matsuyama K., N. Kiyotaki, and A. Matsui. 1993. "Toward a Theory of International Currency." *Review of Economic Studies* 60:283–320.

McKinnon, R. 1979. *Money in International Exchange: The Convertible Currency System*. Oxford: Oxford University Press.

Obstfeld, M. and K. Rogoff. 1996. "The Unsustainable US Current Account Position Revisited." NBER Working Paper No. 10869.

Rajan, R. and A. Subramanian. 2004. "Exchange Rate Flexibility: Is it in Asia's Interest?" *Financial Times*. 26 September.

Rey, H. 2001. "International Trade and Currency Exchange." *Review of Economic Studies* 68:443–64.

Roubini, N. 2004. "BW2: Are We Back to a New Stable Bretton Woods Regime of Global Fixed Exchange Rates?" Nouriel Roubini's Global Economics Blog. October 8.

Roubini, N. and B. Setser. 2005. "Will the Bretton Woods 2 Regime Unravel Soon? The Risk of a Hard Landing in 2005-2006." Symposium on the "Revived Bretton Woods System: A New Paradigm for Asian Development?" 4 February.

Tille, C. 2003. "Financial Integration and the Wealth Effect of Exchange Rate Fluctuations." New York: Federal Reserve Bank of New York. August. Mimeo.

Zhou, R. 1997. "Currency Exchange in a Random Search Model." *Review of Economic Studies* 64:289–310.

CHAPTER 1.2

What Should We Think About When Refounding the International Monetary System?

J. BRADFORD DELONG, University of California at Berkeley and National Bureau of Economic Research

Introduction

Sixty years ago, the Bretton Woods Conference saw the architects of the post–World War II international monetary system look back at the preceding 30 years and try to construct a system that would help to avoid the mistakes of the generation past. They were largely successful—that is, they avoided the mistakes of the previous generation, but they proceeded to make some of their. The classic Bretton Woods system which they created ran unevenly and imperfectly for nearly 30 years, but "uneven and imperfect" was good enough. The international monetary system that they established provided the underpinnings for the great Keynesian boom, dubbed by de Gaulle the "thirty glorious years," (1945–75), the fastest period of worldwide economic growth history had ever seen.

Now the world stands at another moment at which there is at least the potential for refurbishing the international monetary system. And once again, we are looking backwards, at the errors of the past generation. But I suggest that if there is any pattern to be seen in the evolution of the international monetary system, it is that reformers pay too much attention to the errors of the past and not enough attention to the challenges of the future. In this paper, I wish first to review how past episodes of reform have, to some extent, missed the boat, and then make some predictions about possible future errors, and how we might prevent them.

To telegraph my conclusions—or, rather, speculations—let us first look ahead. Forty years from now, somewhere on the globe, there will be a conference celebrating the 100th anniversary of the Bretton Woods Conference. What will the people there wish we had talked about here today? I think that it is a good bet that they will be discussing three sets of issues:

- Problems of *harmonization*—commercial and financial—created by *service-sector outsourcing*: over the next generation or two, the fiber-optic cable and the packet-switched network will make trade in services as integral a part of economic life as trade in goods has been over the past century; yet this process of expanded trade will only function smoothly if there are consistent expectations, operating procedures, rights, and dispute-settlement mechanisms across the globe.

- Problems of *political management*, also created by *service-sector outsourcing*: the expansion of trade in services will put enormous stress on distributions of income within countries; There will be more and more people in economic situations similar to those of the peasants (and landlords!) of Prussia at the end of the 19th century, when it became clear that the proletarians of Hamburg could buy American wheat more cheaply than Prussian rye.

- Problems of *economic autonomy*: ever greater interconnection means that the monetary affairs affecting a country's economy will take place less and less frequently within its borders; Mexico's economy over the past decade has not been greatly retarded by its failure to clean-up and recapitalize its banking system. Northern Mexico has functioned and grown by borrowing the US banking system.

Unfortunately, I have no answers to the big question that comes next: what reforms of the international monetary system *today* will put us in a good position to deal with these potential stresses on the world economy *tomorrow*?

A quick review of the history

At the end of the third quarter of the 19th century, the newly formed German Empire spent the war indemnity it exacted from France by shifting to the gold standard. The accession of the German Empire and United States to gold—the latter a decade and a half after the end of the American Civil War—

pushed the world economy past its tipping point: a "gold standard" that had not been worth joining when the gold block consisted principally of the United Kingdom became worth joining when the critical mass of the world's largest economic powers were on gold (Meissner, 2001).

The gold standard period from 1880–1914 saw the fastest worldwide economic growth and the greatest expansion of the international division of labor that the world had hitherto seen. Our estimates of world real GDP are little more than guesses, but our best current guess is that in the years around 1900, world real GDP was growing, albeit extraordinarily unevenly, at a pace of about 3 percent per year (Maddison, 2003).

We still know relatively little about the extent to which the gold standard was the cause or consequence of the tremendous pre–World War I expansion of trade.[1] That classical gold-standard period of growth, trade expansion, and world economic integration came to an end with the coming of the catastrophe of World War I.[2] In the aftermath of World War I, those who found themselves in charge of reforming the international monetary system that had been smashed to pieces by the war decided that the obvious thing to do was to try to rebuild the pre–World War I classic gold-standard system. For the experience of the pre–World War I gold-standard years had taught finance ministers and central bankers three important lessons:

- As long as a country's commitment to the gold standard is ironclad, financial crises will be rare and manageable: international financial speculators betting on the continuance of the gold standard will be a powerful stabilizing force.

- The security of asset values and the predictability of commodity prices flowing from the gold standard are powerful spurs to international trade, overseas investment, and economic growth.

- The gold standard with free trade and capital flows was a remarkably successful way of organizing the international monetary system in a period of extraordinary growth and change.

The reader should note that I am not claiming that these three lessons were a full, adequate, or best set of, lessons from the pre–World War I period. I am simply arguing that they were the lessons that the near-consensus *did* draw, and *did* seek to apply. Thus, after the end of World War I, in the more turbulent world economy that followed, central bankers and finance ministers tried to apply these lessons and to restore the classic gold standard. It was well known in advance that this would be difficult. John Maynard Keynes dedicated his 1924 *Tract on Monetary Reform* to the Governor and Court of the Bank of England, who, he wrote, faced much more severe challenges in the 1920s than those they had become used to facing in the years before the Great War. But it was widely believed that the task had to be accomplished. Continued prosperity and growth depended on a well-functioning international division of labor, and nearly all believed that this depended on price stability and confidence in the security of property produced by the gold standard.

The policy of returning to and maintaining the gold standard was seen, in the words of R.S. Sayers (1976), as "an employment policy." Keynes (1924) was more eloquent: "We leave Saving to the private investor.... We leave the responsibility for setting Production in motion to the business man.... [T]hese arrangements, being in accord with human nature, have great advantages. But they cannot work properly if money, which they assume as a stable measuring-rod, is undependable..."[3] Monetary theorists might propose new-fangled innovations such as targeting the value of a basket of commodities, but sensible people thought there was only one way to ensure that money would be stable: make it as good as gold.

It is going only a little too far to say that the result of the attempts to restore the pre–World War I gold standard was the Great Depression. The "golden fetters" with which interwar policy-makers bound themselves kept them from doing very much that was constructive once the Great Depression began to roll forward. The turbulent interwar period saw an unbelievable run of economic and monetary catastrophes, from German hyperinflation to the British General Strike, to the Great Depression itself. Against these problems the "golden fetters" had little power. Eichengreen (1996) believes that intelligent, creative policy-makers of the 1920s and 1930s would have been able to do a much better job in admittedly difficult circumstances, had they not been hindered by their long and thorough study of the lessons of the classic gold standard.

Toward the middle of the 20th century, as World War II came to an end, economists and analysts looked back at the interwar catastrophes, and reported to their finance minister and central banker masters that the interwar period taught three important lessons:

- Without an ironclad commitment to the gold standard, free international capital flows were seen to be destabilizing, the source of inflation, of financial crisis, and of depression.

- With the coming of universal suffrage, the political costs of the unemployment generated by strict adherence to the gold standard were too great; a functioning system had to have "give" and allow for periodic exchange-rate adjustments.

- A decentralized consortium of central banks, each responsible to their political masters was not enough; both more formal institutions and a strong commitment on the part of the largest economy to take on the role of hegemon were essential preconditions, if there was to be a chance for stability and prosperity.

The result was the Bretton Woods conference and the classic Bretton Woods system. With domestic autonomous control over monetary policy seen as a necessity, and with at least quasi-fixed exchange rates seen as highly desirable, it was international capital mobility that would be sacrificed on the altar of the international finance "trilemma" of Obstfeld and Taylor (2002). With the coming of mass suffrage, governments could no longer pretend that unemployment was unrelated to the government's economic policy, and so the idea of the fixed-but-adjustable-peg as a safety valve was adopted (Eichengreen, 1998).

Formal institutions were created, in the form of the IMF and the World Bank. And an attempt was made to deal with the fear that the United States would once again withdraw from world affairs by locating the IMF and the World Bank in Washington D.C. Today, most complaints about the Fund's and the Bank's location come from those who fear (correctly) that their location three blocks from the White House and four blocks from the US Treasury gives the current administration undue *influence* on Fund and Bank decisions: it is just too easy for the White House and the Treasury to "lobby" the Fund and the Bank. But half a century ago, there was a different calculus at work: it was believed that the current US administration had to be lobbied by internationalists. For this reason, locating institutions of international governance, such as the Fund, the Bank, and the United Nations *inside* the United States, rather than in Geneva, Basle, or London, seemed an easy way of strengthening the internationalist lobby.

The "Thirty Glorious Years" that followed World War II in North America and Western Europe saw the results of the efforts of central bankers and finance ministers to apply the lessons they drew from the interwar period. It is true that at the Bretton Woods conference and thereafter no one had the faintest idea how large and desperate Western Europe's post–WW II reconstruction needs would be. And it is certainly true that the Truman administration was slow to recognize how adverse Western Europe's post–WW II terms of trade and how poor and brutish immediate post–WW II standards of living would be, if trade had to be carried out at exchange rates where imports balanced exports. But although the Truman administration came late to the party, it brought lots of refreshments: the United Nations Relief and Rehabilitation Administration (UNRRA), loans, the Marshall Plan, Mutual Security Aid, and more (Milward, 1984).

There were always complaints. Charles de Gaulle and company complained about the "exorbitant privilege" the Bretton Woods system granted the United States, which produced international liquidity services at zero cost and sold them to the rest of the world at a handsome price year after year. American manufacturers pointed to undervalued European (and Japanese) exchange rates that allowed them to pursue policies of export-led growth and boost employment at the expense (so they said) of the American manufacturing sector. Restrictions on international capital flows did slow down processes of diversification, technology transfer, and international investment—but we do not know by how much or how important these would have been. The requirements for maintaining the system did put some constraints on domestic macroeconomic policies, but episodes in which countries ought to have wanted to escape from those constraints were few.

Until the end of the 1960s things went rather well. The results convinced them that they had discovered the key to the riddle of history—at least, to the riddle of international monetary history.

Then, of course, things fell apart. Western European and Japanese policymakers were unwilling to acquiesce in having what they saw as an uncomfortably high rate of expansion of their money stocks dictated to them by the United States, and the United States was unwilling to take serious steps to curb domestic inflation, if it was the price for maintaining the fixed-but-adjustable-peg system that was at the heart of classic Bretton Woods. "Go home and tighten money," Treasury Undersecretary Paul Volcker snapped at Federal Reserve Chair Arthur Burns after one too many lectures on the importance of maintaining classic Bretton Woods. And Burns retreated in silence (Gyohten and Volcker, 1992).

It is still not completely clear to me why the fixed-but-adjustable-peg exchange rates of the Bretton Woods System did not evolve into a crawling-peg based system in the 1970s. One factor was that economists and central bankers thought that they were signing on to more or less such a system by committing to floating rates. Dornbusch's (1976) insight that the real exchange rate was not a slowly changing ratio of relative national productivities but a rapidly changing asset price—the present value of expected future interest rate differentials—was still in the future. Another factor was US Treasury Secretary John Connelly and his master Richard Nixon. Paul Volcker described Connelly as a man with a strong bias toward "bold action" without caring much about the particular direction that bold action might take him (Gyohten and Volcker, 1992). Descriptions of Richard Nixon as economic steward are even less complimentary. It certainly seemed unwise to Western European and Japanese policy-makers to tie their economies to the mast of such an erratic and unstable hegemonic ship.

For whatever reasons, in the turbulent years of the 1970s and 1980s, those looking back on the first-generation post–World War II experience drew three important lessons from that experience:

- It was simply no longer possible to exercise a degree of control over capital movements that would make a fixed-peg-but-adjustable system viable, as long as different continents insisted on maintaining their policy autonomy; and there was no chance that the United States, Western Europe as a whole, or Japan would ever surrender their policy autonomy.

- Increasing communications and trade had made the world smaller, and the benefits from international capital mobility higher; thus, there was no longer reason to fear destabilizing speculation, except in cases where unsustainable government policies invited it.

- The world economy was subject to shocks of a magnitude which required sufficiently different macroeconomic responses on each continent that it made no sense to think in terms of an "optimum currency area."

Over the past three decades, as the international financial system has evolved, finance ministers and central bankers have tried to implement policies based on these lessons, which led to a system in which the major currencies floated against one another, with different governments on different continents pursuing their own macroeconomic policies for sensible—and senseless— reasons, and major-currency exchange rates fluctuating widely in response. Implementation of these principles led to a system of incipient blocs, as smaller economies sought to peg their currencies to that of their biggest trading partner (usually America) in order to diminish risk and promote trade. And the IMF took on a new role: it was no longer the referee that decided when a devaluation was in accord with Bretton-Woods principles. It became, rather, the janitor which tried to clean up the mess when governance failures or large adverse shocks to small economies produced balance-of-payments crises.

By now the pattern should be clear. Each generation the international monetary system is revamped to one degree or another. And each generation of economists and policymakers make a very careful study of the past generation, and try to build a system that will handle its crises and its mistakes.

Now I won't claim that these lessons, drawn after each and every historical period, were the right ones, either in the sense of being based on a true and faithful picture of the history they purported to analyze, or as providing good guides to policy in the subsequent period. This is clearly not the case. Moreover, it is humbling, for I am certainly not as smart, nor as wise as Keynes, Nurkse, Kindleberger, Friedman, and company. But I do claim that, every 30 years or so, people take a step back, try to draw new lessons about the international monetary system, and things change in response.

But one cannot look back at this history without noticing that each generation's lessons from the past are not necessarily the right ones for the future. Nothing was more disastrous than attempting to establish an ironclad commitment to the gold standard in the interwar period, for it was doomed to fail. And that failure dragged economies into the depths. The fear of capital mobility inherited from the interwar period reduced the growth of the international division of labor during the great post–World War II boom, a period of amazing economic stability and opportunity. The difficulties experienced in trying to manage a peg during the classic Bretton Woods system led central banks and finance ministries in directions that left them poorly prepared for the exchange rate-driven crises of the 1980s and 1990s, whether it was the Latin American debt crisis of the 1980s, or Mexico, or East Asia.

The current situation

It has now been 30 years since the end of the classic Bretton Woods system. What has been our experience over the past generation? What consensus has been arrived at from the lessons learned, and what are the institutions that are emerging? And are these the right lessons and institutions for the next 30 years?

Once again, we have a generation during which the flaws in current international monetary arrangements have been clear and apparent, and, once again, there are, I believe, widely accepted lessons that can be drawn since the end of classic Bretton Woods, the most important being the following:

- It remains the case that no component of the industrial core is willing to sacrifice its policy autonomy: for good or ill, the yen will float against the dollar, the dollar will float against the euro, etc.

- Free capital mobility in emerging-market economies is wonderful when properly regulated; but the chances, especially in emerging markets, that regulators will be properly prepared for the systemic risks created by whatever current financial innovation is going on are poor.

- Even a currency board and the certainty of disaster if governments follow unsustainable policies is not enough to allow one to confidently maintain a pegged exchange rate, as we saw in Argentina; for those wanting a fixed exchange rate, dollarization (or euroization) are the only possibilities.

- Even a world of largely floating rates is not hostile to rapid expansion in world trade, so very little is sacrificed if there is no policy coordination between Europe, the United States, and Japan.

The institutions that are being built in response appear to be twofold: first, there are attempts to construct large fixed-exchange rate areas via currency unification. The euro itself is a fascinating topic which cannot be dealt with here. However, it is important to note that it is only part of a broader movement which in Latin America goes under the name of "dollarization." Second, we now have an IMF which appears ready to somewhat more like a central bank, serving less as scolder-in-chief of countries that follow unsustainable macroeconomic policies than as lender-of-last-resort when currency or banking-sector mismatches within a nation generate large liquidity crises.

Much less has been done in the way of institution-building and institution-reforming than I, at least, expected to see six or seven years ago. The EMS 1992, Mexico 1994–95, East Asia, 1997–98, Brazil, Turkey, and Argentina were a very impressive run of crises, all of which seemed to me to call for a more institutionalized approach, rather than a continued series of one-off ad-hoc responses. I am strongly in favor of a much better-funded IMF, committed in times of crisis to following Bagehot's rule: lend freely on what would be good collateral, if asset prices and economies are in their normal configurations. And I do think these three most-recent conclusions are reasonably smart policy-oriented summaries of the lessons offered by the experience of the past generation.

Nevertheless, I cannot help but fear that our current focus on the difficulties of financial regulation and supervision, on the one hand, and on currency unions, on the other, is in all probability leading us to not talk about what we should be talking about, in other words, to neglect the intellectual and institutional investments that would do most to help the world economy in the next generation. That is the major lesson of the past. It seems only reasonable to apply this lesson to the future as we envision it now.

What should we be talking about?

What, then, are the big shocks that are likely to affect the international monetary system over the next generation, and what institutions and arrangements should we be building now to guard against them?

Outsourcing: The first and most obvious, a problem since the early 2000s, but one which has now practically vanished from view: *outsourcing*. In the late 19th century, the iron-hulled ocean-going steamship made international trade in staple agricultural and manufacturing products profitable, while the submarine telegraph cable made truly large-scale international investment possible for the first time in human history. A century ago, the technological underpinnings of the first era of the globalization came into being, and much

of the history of the classic gold standard should be read as an attempt to
construct institutions to take advantage of opportunities and ward off danger.

Now we have the fiber-optic cable, the packet-switched network, data
bandwidth and data storage capacity large enough to make international trade
in *white-collar services* as feasible as trade in commodities became a century
ago. There are many other items of startling economic news yet to come out
of the high-tech revolution. But this is the piece that has had the greatest
impact on the international economy.

A century ago, the institutions that developed to manage (and misman-
age) that era's tremendous expansion in international trade and investment
share were four: the gold standard (both to make sure payments could be
made and as a commitment to avoid inflation), the gunboat (to "secure"
property rights and market access), the creditors' committee (to clean up after
things went wrong), and either social democracy or protectionism, depending
on the country (to protect workers, or landlords and bosses from the consequences of expanded trade shares).

Right now, outsourcing, is dropping off the political radar screen and is
ceasing to be mentioned by politicians and media commentators. But it will
come back.

Consider: cross-country income gaps today are much greater than they
have been in the past. Thus the potential downward pressure on the wages of
workers in the richer countries is much greater today. Slow wage growth has
one set of political and social consequences. Large-scale income losses by
whole social classes has quite another, different set of political and social consequences. And there are no "anchors" to tie white-collar paper-shuffling production to durable long-run, unchanging "natural" factors of production
(ores, climate, soil quality, etc.), hence much more rapid change is possible. Of
course, the magnitude of the potential gains is greater as well. Consider India
today: if 10 million people are put to work at US$25,000 a year, providing
white-collar services to the industrial core, and India's standard of living will
have been boosted by at least a quarter.

This process of expanded international trade in services will come about
gradually, but it will come. And as it does, we will see not only a much greater
density of economic interconnections across continents, but a much greater
need for harmonization of work, commercial, and legal practices to settle the
disputes. These will inevitably arise as the world division of labor in services is
chopped more and more finely. Adding to this pressure will be the fact that

world finance is now sending its tendrils into regions in which the structures of title and obligations are very uncertain. The most important areas for international economic policy in the next few decades may well fall under the rubric of *harmonization*.

And as outsourcing comes to be a major force in the world economy, it is likely to put nearly unbearable long-run pressure on the internal income distributions of countries. The gains from trade will still be there. But the distribution of these gains and the losses to those in the wrong economic position will be sharper-edged than before. And the resulting political problems will be immense. We know the long-run political consequences of the fact, a century and more ago, that, as was noted earlier, steamships enabled the Minnesotans to sell their wheat to the proletarians of Hamburg more cheaply than the Prussians could sell their rye (Gerschenkron, 1962). We are likely to face even larger shocks in the next generation.

Unless people perceive that they are being pulled out of white-collar service-sector work by better opportunities in other sectors—and not being pushed out of white-collar service-sector work by unfair foreign competition—the political problems of maintaining support for expanded world trade over the next generation are likely to prove very difficult indeed.

Loss of control by central banks: second, there has long been speculation that central banks will lose control of their standard policy levers and tools, given the fact that, in the modern world, there are simply too many places to park money offshore, and too many financial instruments with too much liquidity for a monetary economic paradigm devised early in the last century—when currency and demand deposits were the only liquid assets—to be of much use. I have no fears for the Federal Reserve, or the ECB, or the Bank of Japan, or the Bank of England for generations to come. But fiber-optic cables, packet-switched networks, offshore electronic fund transfers, and alternative payment settlement mechanisms will have consequences for smaller central banks. The recent Argentinean crisis shows how much damage a government determined to wreck the structure of assets and settlements can do. But that may be one of the last such episodes.

Consider the course of the Mexican economy over the past decade: a sharp panic and crisis, followed by sustained growth at about 4.5 percent per year. But in the US Treasury in 1995, talking point #6 about the Mexican crisis was always, "Sustained recovery from the crisis requires a clean-up and recapitalization of the Mexican banking system." That clean-up and recapitalization did not happen, and the fact that it did not has hurt the Mexican economy, although not very much. Why not? Because in much of northern Mexico, commerce has borrowed from the US banking system.

Conclusion

Forty years from now, at what is sure to be a gathering to celebrate the 100th anniversary of the Bretton Woods Conference, what will people wish that we had talked about today? No doubt, the following:

- Problems of *harmonization*, commercial and financial, as the fiber-optic cable and the packet-switched network make trade in services as integral a part of economic life as trade in goods has been over the past century.

- Problems of *political management*, as the expansion of trade in services puts more and more people in an economic situation similar to that of the peasants and landlords of Prussia at the end of the 19th century.

- Problems of *economic autonomy*, as monetary affairs that affect a country's economy take place more and more outside its borders.

But we cannot yet answer the question which logically follows: what reforms of the international monetary system today will enable us to deal with potential stresses on the world economy tomorrow?

NOTES

1 Lopez-Cordova and Meissner (2003) present interesting evidence that without the gold standard, the world's "first globalization" of 1880–1914 would have been far less extensive.

2 Note that some see signs that it was running up against political limits which would have been likely to constrain the process and prevent further globalization, even if the general peace had held in the 1910s and 1920s; see O'Rourke and Williamson, 1999.

3 Preface to Keynes, 1924.

REFERENCES

Dornbusch, R. 1976. "Expectations and Exchange Rate Dynamics." *Journal of Political Economy* 84(6):1161–76. December.

Eichengreen, B. J. 1996. *Golden Fetters: The Gold Standard and the Great Depression.* Oxford: Oxford University Press.

———. 1998. *Globalizing Capital.* Princeton, NJ: Princeton University Press.

Gerschenkron, A. 1962. *Economic Backwardness in Historical Perspective: A Book of Essays.* Cambridge, MA: Belknap Press.

Gyohten, T. and P. Volcker. 1992. Changing Fortunes. New York: Random House.

Keynes, J. M. 1924. *A Tract on Monetary Reform.* London: Macmillan.

Lopez-Cordova, J. Ernesto, and C. Meissner 2003. "Exchange Rate Regimes and International Trade: Evidence from the Classical Gold Standard Era." *American Economic Review.* March.

Maddison, A. 2003. *The World Economy in Millennial Perspective.* Paris: OECD.

Meissner, C. 2001. "A New World Order: Explaining the Emergence of the Classical Gold Standard." Cambridge: NBER Working Paper 9233.

Milward, A. 1984. *The Reconstruction of Western Europe.* London: Methuen.

Obstfeld, M. and A. Taylor. 2002. "Globalization and Capital Markets." Cambridge: NBER Working Paper 8846.

O'Rourke, K. and J. Williamson. 1999. *Globalization and History: The Evolution of a Nineteenth-Century Atlantic Economy.* Cambridge: MIT Press.

Sayers, R. S. 1976. *The Bank of England: 1891–1944.* Cambridge: Cambridge University Press.

CHAPTER 1.3

Reforming Bretton Woods to Promote World Harmony and Stability

LI RUOGU, President, Export-Import Bank of China

The Bretton Woods institutions need further reform

The Bretton Woods institutions have been around for six decades. About 60 years ago, the international community began to design a post-war international monetary system to prevent a reoccurrence of the "beg-gar-my-neighbor" policy adopted by countries in the Great Depression. In 1944, representatives from 44 countries attended the United Nations Monetary and Financial Conference at Bretton Woods, in New Hampshire (USA), and adopted the Final Act as well as the Articles of Agreement of the International Monetary Fund and the Articles of Agreement of the World Bank Group. These provided for the establishment of a new international monetary system, which became known as the Bretton Woods system. The Bretton Woods institutions, i.e. the International Monetary Fund (IMF) and the International Bank for Reconstruction and Development (IBRD, also known as the World Bank) were founded in the following year.

Since then, the Bretton Woods institutions have performed important functions. However, with the earthshaking changes of the past 60 years in the international economic and financial situation, the functions of these institutions are very different from what they were at the time of their establishment. The purpose of the International Monetary Fund then was to promote international monetary cooperation, facilitate the expansion and balanced growth of international trade, promote exchange rate stability, and assist with the establishment of a multilateral system of payments, and provide temporary assistance to members experiencing balance of payments difficulties, the initial goal of the World Bank being to assist with the reconstruction of Europe in the aftermath of World War II. Today, the IMF's major objective is to promote international economic and financial stability, while the objectives of the World Bank are to eliminate poverty and narrow the gap between developed and less-developed countries. To put it another way, the functions of the Bretton Woods institutions currently are to promote the harmonious and steady development of the world.

Change in functions calls for corresponding reforms in the institutions. In fact, the Bretton Woods institutions have always valued reform, and have, through reform, contributed greatly to global economic development, and to the improvement of the international monetary system. However, faced with the challenges of a changed international economic situation, an entirely different global financial market, and the requirements of the building of a harmonious and stable world, the reforms that have been made in the Bretton Woods institutions are not sufficient, either in extent or scope. Therefore, reform of the Bretton Woods institutions should be intensified, so as to give full play to their roles in maintaining international economic stability and promoting the economic development of the world.

Three proposals for reform of the Bretton Woods institutions

1. Reform the IMF to promote a stable international monetary system

One obvious drawback of the current international monetary system is that the exchange rates are highly volatile. The major countries adopt floating exchange rates, either in the form of a single float or joint float, to suit their own interests, while most developing countries peg their currencies to a major one and float passively. The floating exchange rate regime has its own pros and cons, so it is hard to say whether it is good or bad. However, for the developing countries with relatively weak risk-management abilities, it is often the case that the pros are outweighed by the cons, as the latter sometimes even trigger monetary or financial crises. As the main agency charged with the task of safeguarding the stable international monetary system, the IMF is duty-bound to promote stable exchange rates.[1] Yet, regrettably, the IMF has not only failed to maintain the relative stability of exchange rates among the major currencies, but it has often suggested to developing countries that they adopt a floating exchange rate regime and liberalize their capital accounts. Given the damages of large exchange rate volatilities, the IMF should restore the concept of exchange rate stability, strengthen the monitoring of exchange rates of major countries and international capital flow, and advocate the establishment of a stable yet flexible exchange system.

Instability of international reserve currencies is another major deficiency of the current international monetary system. Ideally, a reserve currency should be issued by an institution independent of any national government, and maintain its value in relation to the demands of international trade and financial transactions. Apparently, the current international reserve currencies are nothing like that. Rather, they consist, largely, of foreign exchange reserves, and the policy-makers in the countries of these reserve currencies tend to make decisions in favor of their own economic interests, rather than the interests of international economic stability. These countries have reaped huge benefits by issuing reserve currencies, without assuming the corresponding responsibilities. Such asymmetry between risks and benefits in the international reserve currency-issuing mechanism has caused the exchange rates of major currencies to fluctuate sharply, something which is detrimental to international financial stability and global economic growth.

Since it is difficult for the currency issued by a sovereign nation to avoid such asymmetry, one feasible solution for establishing an ideal international reserve currency is to create a world currency and establish an international payments-adjustment mechanism based on institutional rules.

An alternative to a world currency would be Special Drawing Rights (SDR). As a currency unit created by the IMF, SDR has some of the basic characteristics of a world currency. But, it is still a long way away from functioning like a world currency. The IMF should, therefore, take effective measures to further promote the use of SDR, and optimize institutional mechanisms, so as to institute a world currency at an early date, thus laying the foundation for a more stable international monetary system.

2. Reform the World Bank to promote harmonious world development

Currently, the main task of the World Bank is to eliminate poverty and promote the harmonious development of the international community. In order to achieve this far- reaching, significant goal, the World Bank must make significant efforts in at least two areas. The first is to raise sufficient funds and use them effectively. To a certain extent, the development of low-income developing countries depends on international assistance. Although as early as the 1970s the UN set the target of official development aid at 0.7 percent of GNP for the developed countries, the majority of the developed countries have failed to fulfill this obligation over the past more than 30 years.[2] The World Bank, as an important channel of capital transfer to developing countries, has only limited amount of funds. In recent years, the World Bank has provided about US$18 to US$20 billion to the developing world annually.[3] For the 153 middle- and low-income economies around the world, this is utterly inadequate, if the World Bank is to be the catalyst for attracting private capital into developing economies.

This being the case, the World Bank should be innovative in its financing mechanism, in order to increase the amount of its funds and enable itself to provide more support to developing countries. In addition, the World Bank should not scatter its limited resources widely when providing loans. Rather, it should focus on a specific sector in a given region, to effectively solve one or two problems within a targeted period of time. For example, to improve transportation in Africa, the World Bank could put US$10 billion to use in Africa for improving the transportation infrastructure, building a network of railways, highways, airports, and ports. Once transportation had been improved, other problems would be easier to deal with. This would not only effectively solve the problem of fund shortages for development projects, but would demonstrate greater efficiency and encourage more private capital inflow.

The second point is that the development assistance institutions should function on the basis of a clear division of labor. In the last decades, the international community has established development financial institutions at the international, regional, and bilateral levels. However, the lack of efficient coordination and clear division of labor among them has resulted in either redundant or insufficient aid, and either overlapping or absent development responsibilities. This has seriously affected the efficient use of financial resources. Therefore, the development financial institutions should interact and communicate more effectively, in order to establish joint strategic objectives and scope of activity, respectively, so as to more reasonably allocate aid, and cover all development bases. As an international development agency, the World Bank should focus on infrastructure, the creation of a favorable environment, and enhancement of development capacities in developing countries.

3. Reform the operation and governance of the Bretton Woods institutions

The Bretton Woods institutions are an important pillar of the international economy. Their operational concept and governance structure are vital for the stability and development of the global economy. In their six decades of existence, the IMF and the World Bank already have members between them. As most of their decisions concern developing countries and have a vital impact on them, there should be extensive participation from the developing world in the Bretton Woods institutions.

However, the decision-making in these institutions has long been controlled by a small number of developed countries. Both the development programs designed by the IMF and the international development assistance programs of the World Bank are dominated by Western perspectives and operate in Western interests.

As a result, decisions made by the Bretton Woods institutions in Washington often do not correspond to actual situations in developing countries. Even those decisions guided by a well-meaning philosophy have often failed to produce the promised results in Africa, Asia, or Latin America. Therefore, it is understandable that the Bretton Woods institutions lack credibility in many developing countries. In order to change this situation and enable these institutions to play a positive role, we must rectify the current governance structure, to have a European at the head of the IMF and an American at the head of the World Bank. Those operational concepts which do not reflect reality in the developing countries should be abandoned, and the quota of developing countries and voting power should be increased. Individuals who are well-versed in and familiar with the problems of developing countries should be appointed as Managing Director of the IMF and President of the World Bank, respectively, and more qualified staff from the developing countries recruited.

Only through such significant reforms can the Bretton Woods institutions make decisions which correspond to the real needs of the developing country members. Only in this way will they increase their effectiveness, fairness, and credibility, and thus, promote growth in the developing countries, and ensure the stability of the world economy. Only when harmony and development become the norm, will it be possible to minimize warfare and terrorism in the world.

NOTES

1 For details, see Articles of Agreement of the International Monetary Fund.

2 According to data from the Development Assistant Committee (DAC) of the OECD, only five countries (Norway, Denmark, Luxemburg, the Netherlands, and Sweden) had reached the target by 2005. The average level of aid in GNP among DAC member states was 0.33 percent, far below the 0.7 percent target.

3 In fiscal year 2004, for example, the IBRD provided US$11 billion in loans to 87 projects in 33 countries, and the International Development Association (IDA) provided US$9 billion in loans to 158 projects in 62 countries. See the World Bank's *Annual Report* for details.

The US Current Account Deficit and the Future of the World Monetary System

ROBERT SKIDELSKY, Chairman, Centre for Global Studies and Professor of Political Economy, University of Warwick

Introduction

This paper seeks to challenge the conventional view that generalized floating is the desirable and inevitable goal of the international monetary system.

It argues that the breakdown of 20th century fixed exchange rate systems was due more to the privileged position of the United States in the system than to inherent weaknesses arising from domestic political pressures or financial liberalization. Specifically, the position of the dollar in the world economy has enabled the U.S. at various moments to print dollars without limit to finance its preferred pattern of spending. This has created unsustainable imbalances whose liquidation requires periodic changes of regime. The problem of adjustment is *not* solved by generalized floating, as the question of who adjusts to whom remains.

The paper challenges the view of Dooley et al. (2003) that the pegging of East Asian currencies to the dollar, like the earlier pegging of European currencies to the dollar, represents a deliberate policy of export-led growth by means of currency undervaluation and capital controls. It also argues against the view that, like the earlier European episode, this must be considered part of a progressive global evolution to floating systems. I contend that this distorts history and simplifies the motives of those who believe in fixed-exchange rates as a public good.

In the light of these considerations, the paper considers the issue of the sustainability of the current US account deficit. It concludes by stating that the deficit is sustainable in the very short run, but not in the medium-term when adjustment will occur through various ad hoc measures. However, the long-run liquidation of the unbalanced creditor and debtor positions requires a redefinition of the geopolitical role of the U.S. This will occur naturally as the incentives for other countries to accept this role—and the dollar seignorage which goes with it—are much reduced. The liquidation of unbalanced positions will in turn enable a system of stable currencies to re-emerge, with institutions which improve on those agreed at Bretton Woods.

It was to avoid a repetition of the currency wars of the 1930s that the Bretton Woods system of fixed exchange rates *adjustable by agreement* was set up in 1944. This still seems to be the best model for a globalizing economy.

Fixing and Floating

Economists are almost unanimous in preaching the virtues of floating, and its logical inevitability. Yet many, perhaps most, countries remain attached to some form of fixing. Is this a case of economists being out of touch with reality? Or is reality out of touch with economics?

The post-Bretton Woods world is far from being one of generalized floating. The countries of the world present a kaleidoscope of currency arrangements, ranging from "hard" fixers to "pure" floaters, with a large variety of intermediate arrangements. It is said that the floaters are gaining over the currency fixers and managers. There is wide academic acceptance of Stanley Fischer's argument[1] that soft pegs are unsustainable, that we are moving toward a bipolar world where most currencies float freely and a minority adopt hard pegs.

The evolution of the European monetary system from a "mini-Bretton Woods" in 1978 into a currency union seems a convincing example of the latter development. But how to explain the emergence of an a revived or "new" Bretton Woods, centered on the US-East Asian nexus? Dooley, Folkerts-Landau, and Garber[2] try to do this, contending that the East Asian countries are simply following in the footsteps of European countries, who, in the 1960s, undervalued their currencies relative to the dollar and controlled capital movements in order to grow. Now, having caught up, they have liberalized their capital accounts, requiring them to float. Thus, in their words, "the Bretton Woods system does not evolve, it just occasionally reloads a periphery."

There are at least three problems with this developmental perspective on monetary evolution. The first is that the incentives of the "fixers" are described solely in terms of their desire to maintain competitive exchange rates with the dollar, whereas fixed—and not undervalued—rates may be preferred for macroeconomic stability and to facilitate inter-regional trade expansion. Growing financial maturity did not lead the European countries to float against each other. Rather, it led them toward an extreme version of hard fixing. This brings out the point that the theory and advocacy of floating is a predominantly American phenomenon, the latest manifestation of a long-standing US monetary unilateralism.

Secondly, it assumes that the motives of the fixers have been predominantly economic, whereas in the 1960s they were at least partly geopolitical. The Western European countries accepted dollar seignorage in return for military protection against communism. This incentive is evidently lacking today, and the war against terrorism is a lame substitute. Acceptance by the EU countries of an upward float against the dollar is as much an assertion of political independence as it is an ineluctable consequence of financial liberalization.

Finally, the developmental perspective in concentrating on the incentives of the "periphery" to keep their currencies undervalued against the dollar ignores the incentives for the monetary hyper-power, the United States, to live beyond its means. Both in the 1960s and today, the U.S. took advantage of the world appetite for dollars to print as many as it wanted. That is, in both periods it placed the onus of adjustment to its self-chosen spending patterns on other countries. These could either revalue their currencies or accept dollars without limit. The latter was the chief mechanism by which *unbalanced* creditor and debtor positions arose and persisted in the post-war world, irrespective of whether exchange rates were fixed or floating. The alternative would have been for the United States to reduce its own consumption. It is just as accurate, then, to say that other countries' acquiesced in American overspending as that the U.S. acquiesced in their currency undervaluation.

The central monetary fact of the 20th century, it seems to me, was not the alternation of fixing and floating, but the failure to develop generally accepted rules of adjustment for either. Floating does not obviate the need for such rules: it is simply the most obvious consequence of not having them.

The unilateral US attitude to monetary adjustment has its parallel in the unilateralism of US foreign and security policy. At bottom it is the attitude that the United States is powerful enough to do whatever is in its own interest, and it is up to other countries to adjust to what it does. There is no hope of bringing the European and East Asians together into a single agreed system of monetary rules as long as the United States remains indifferent to the external value of the dollar, and indifferent to the consequences of its indifference. Even worse: in the long-run its unilateralism is destructive both of economic globalization and of any orderly system of international relations.

Is the US deficit sustainable?

The main contemporary example of America's monetary unilateralism is its indifference to its burgeoning current account deficit. Driven by a widening trade deficit, it stands at US$531 billion, or 4.9 percent of GDP, its highest ever as a share of the American economy.

The deficit has two sources: the government spends more than it raises in taxes, and the U.S. imports more goods and services than it exports; hence, the "twin deficits" (see Appendix). Currently the US government accepts no internal limits on the growth of either public or private spending. It is up to other countries to adjust their economies to the rate of US spending by allowing their currencies to appreciate against the dollar.

This attitude is based on the view that the US deficit is not the result of any profligacy by US consumers, but of the "undervaluation" of East Asian currencies against the dollar in order to secure an "unfair" trade advantage. This is a recipe for currency wars.

Traditional economics teaches that deficits of this magnitude are unsustainable, as foreigners will not go on financing them. Kenneth Rogoff, Chief Economist of the International Monetary Fund put it this way: "Suppose for a moment we were talking about a developing country that had a gaping [trade] deficit year after year as far as the eye can see, budget ink spinning from black into red, open-ended security costs, and an exchange rate that has been inflated by capital inflows. With all that I think it's fair to say we'd be pretty concerned."[3] To oversimplify, foreigners will withdraw their capital for fear of a default.

Catherine Mann wrote in 2000 that "Absent structural reforms in the United States and abroad, a large devaluation of the dollar, or significant changes in the business cycle, both the trade and the current account deficits will continue to widen until they become unsustainable, perhaps two or three years out."[4] Four years later, the deficit has widened and continues to be sustained.

In practice, the United States gets away with it for several reasons. The demand for a country's currency is not closely tied to its current account balance. This is particularly true of a currency which plays a key role in world trade and finance. The usefulness and reputation of a currency, that is, can survive the relative economic decline of the country which issues it, especially in the absence of viable alternatives. This was true of the pound sterling in the early 20th century[5] and is true of the dollar today.[6]

A different approach to the problem of the sustainability of the US deficit emphasizes the structural difference between the US economy and that of other countries. The US is essentially a productivity-growth economy, whereas others rely on export growth. The US therefore sucks in capital which forces up the value of the dollar. According to Dooley et al. (2003), "there have been complaints from US industry about the strong dollar, but overall the US has been happy to invest now, consume now, and let investors worry about its deteriorating international investment position."[7] This mechanism has been used to explain US success in financing its current account deficits in the boom years of the late 1990s. The role of the U.S. as consumer of last resort imparted an economic virtue to this unbalanced position. But European investors care about returns, and as the American economy started to stagnate, the inward flow from Europe shrivelled, and the dollar started to depreciate against the euro. This was a sign of the classic adjustment mechanism at work.

By contrast, this adjustment mechanism has been blocked on the Asian side. The widening US current account deficit is being financed by purchase of treasury bonds by the Central Banks of Japan, China, India, and other East Asian countries. The dollar's predominant weight in East Asian currency baskets has returned to its pre-1997–8 crisis levels. Most East Asian economies are becoming dollar creditors.[8]

The hypothesis is that their governments are accumulating dollar assets as a by-product of a strategy of export-led growth. East Asia is prepared to forgo better returns in order to keep its exchange rates down and export demand up, allowing the region's industries to compete on world markets and attract foreign investment. This explains the emergence of a "very asymmetric version of a fixed exchange rate system in which, for some time, periphery countries are willing to underwrite future deficits of the United States."[9] This is not the only explanation. McKinnon says: "The microeconomic rationale for stabilizing dollar exchange rates in East Asia stems from the need to limit foreign exchange risk in intra-regional trade and capital flows that are mainly invoiced in dollars [...] The macroeconomic rationale stems from the monetary need for a nominal anchor for domestic price levels—more against the threat of inflation before 1997, and now against threatened deflation in the new millennium."[10]

Most academic economists and US Treasury officials deplore the East Asian strategy of sterilizing dollar holdings rather than allowing their currencies to appreciate. The Americans forced through a G-7 statement in Florida calling for "more flexibility in exchange rates."[11] Martin Wolf thinks that East Asian reserve accumulations "will prove seriously destabilising... it would be better to let exchange rates move upward."[12]

Others emphasize the costs of the system. Lal, Perry, and Plant have argued that by accumulating foreign exchange reserves to keep the rupee competitive with the dollar, rather than investing the money, India sacrificed 2.7 percent annual growth in the 1990s, i.e., its growth would have been 2.7 percent per annum higher, had it let its currency float. Joshi and Sanyal have shown that this argument rests on a simple analytic mistake. (Lal and his colleagues assume non-absorption of all capital inflows and remittances, rather than just those represented by the reserve accumulation that actually took place.) In practice, India's growth rate was probably higher under exchange rate management than it would have been under floating. A clean float can enable a country to do without reserves. But the cost is an exchange rate which may be highly unstable or inappropriate. "Without the cushion of adequate reserves, the shelter of capital controls and the reassurance they provided to the authorities and the market, the exchange rate could have spun out of control and caused severe damage to companies and the private sector." [13] Exchange rate management kept the rupee "mildly undervalued" in real effective terms, which is good for GDP growth via growth of exports. Appreciation of the exchange rate would have discouraged export growth and made it more difficult to liberalise the capital account and imports and achieve productivity gains.

The debate over the sustainability of the US current account deficit has strong echoes of earlier debates about how the duty of adjustment should be shared between creditor and debtor countries. The orthodox view was that it was the duty of debtor countries to curtail their spending as a condition for the receipt of new loans. Keynes emphasized the duty of creditors to expand their spending so that debtors could earn the foreign exchange to repay their loans. This debate is not resolved by floating. How much appreciation or depreciation of one's currency is accepted by one's trading partner depends on some prior agreement between them about how the costs of adjustment should be shared, in other words, what the appropriate internal policies for both should be. Without such generally accepted rules of the game, floating can produce currency wars as readily as fixing can give rise to trade wars.

On the hypothesis that the US deficit is the counterpart to a rational export-led growth strategy by East and South Asian countries, it can be sustained until the limits of their growth are reached. But this hypothesis is flawed. Currency stability is desired for many reasons, of which maintaining competitive exchange rates with the dollar is only one. If we take the European precedent seriously, a group of East Asian countries (possibly together with India) will liquidate their creditor position with the United State over time by allowing their currencies to appreciate against the dollar, but will organize a regional zone of currency stability. With the elimination of unbalanced creditor and debtor positions in the major monetary centers, there is no inherent reason why a new and superior Bretton Woods system should not be constructed.

Conclusion

The competitive motive for accumulating dollar reserves blocks the global adjustment process, allowing the U.S. to continue to run large current account deficits. But it is not the only motive East Asian countries have for managing their exchange rates. The importance of stable currencies within the region will grow with the expansion of inter-regional trade. So a double process of liquidating creditor balances and regional monetary consolidation is probable.

In the very short-run the deficit is evidently sustainable. In the medium-term it will be shrunk through ad hoc measures. The strong recovery of the US economy may well restart private foreign investment, thus lessening the exposure of East Asian central banks. Unlike in the classic Bretton Woods system, there is an alternative store of value to the dollar (and the euro) and other currencies will follow. In due course, the U.S. will also bring its domestic deficit under control.

In the long run, the curing of monetary imbalance depends on restoring global political balance, a position which David Calleo has long argued in eloquent, if somewhat solitary, splendor. If the United States wants to run an empire, it has to be in position to tax the rest of world. Running up debt is a shadow tax, but payment is voluntary, and depends, at minimum, on acquiescence in US foreign policy, or to put it another way, in the perception that, via the deficit, the U.S. is providing public goods for the whole world. This is far from evident. Specifically, the geopolitical reason for accepting the seignorage of the dollar has become less important since the fall of Communism. Its puny substitute, the war against terrorism, is insufficient.

If the American empire is rejected, then other economic power centers have to assume responsibility for their own protection, the EU and Japan in particular. This means burden sharing, but others must help define how the burden is to be shared, and for what purposes.

If the imbalances caused by geopolitics are eliminated, then currencies will become more stable. That floating enjoys its present vogue is not because of theoretical arguments in favor of floating, but because US policy precludes the elimination of imbalances which are required to re-establish a global system of stable exchange rates.

It was to avoid a repetition of the currency wars of the 1930s that the Bretton Woods system of fixed exchange rates, *adjustable by agreement*, was set up in 1944. This still seems to be the best model for a globalizing world.

NOTES

1 Fischer, 2001.

2 Dooley et al., 2003, p. 6.

3 News item, *Wall Street Journal*, 10 April 2003.

4 Mann, 2000.

5 See Skidelsky et al., 1999.

6 For a good account of the contemporary role of the dollar as a unit of account, a medium of exchange, and a store of value, and the structural characteristics of the US economy which sustain this role, see Pollard, 2001.

7 Dooley et al., 2003, p. 6.

8 See McKinnon and Schnabl, 2004.

9 Dooley et al., 2003, p. 311.

10 McKinnon and Schnabl, 2004, op. cit. p. 4.

11 *Financial Times*, 8 February 2004.

12 Wolf, 2004.

13 Joshi and Sanyal, 2004.

REFERENCES

Dooley, M. P., D. Folkerts-Landau, and P. Garber. 2003. "An Essay on the Revived Bretton Woods System." Working Paper No 9971. National Bureau of Economic Research. September. Available at: http://www.nber.org/papers/w9971

Fischer, S. 2001. "Exchange Rate Regimes: Is the Bipolar View Correct?" *Journal of Economic Perspectives* 15:3–24.

Mann, C. 2000. "Is the U.S. Current Account Deficit Sustainable?" *Finance and Development Quarterly*. Washington, D.C.: International Monetary Fund.

Joshi, V. and S. Sanyal. 2004. "Foreign Inflows and Macroeconomic Policy in India." Barry Bosworth et al., eds. *India Policy Forum*. Vol. 1. New Delhi. Brookings Institution and the National Council of Applied Economic Research. May.

Lal, D., S. Bery, and D. Pant. 2003. "The Real Exchange Rate, fiscal deficits and capital flows: India, 1981–2000." *Economic and Political Weekly* XXXVIII (47):4965–76.

McKinnon, R. and G. Schnabl. 2004. "The Return to Soft Dollar Pegging in East Asia: Mitigating Conflicted Virtue." *International Finance*. July.

———. 2003. "A return to exchange rate stability in East Asia?" October. Available at: http://www.stanford.edu/~mckinnon/papers/Return.pdf

Pollard, P. 2001. "The Creation of the Euro and the Role of the Dollar in International Markets." The Federal Reserve Bank of St. Louis. September/October.

Rogoff, K. 2003. *Wall Street Journal*. 10 April.

Skidelsky, R., N. Lawson, J. Fleming, M. Desai, and P. Davidson. 1999. *Capital Regulation: For and Against*. London: Social Market Foundation.

United States House of Representatives. Available at: www.house.gov

United States Department of Commerce, Bureau of Economic Analysis. Available at: http://www.bea.gov/bea/international/bp_web/filter.cfm?anon=71&table_id=1

White House. Available at: http://www.whitehouse.gov/omb/budget/fy2005/hist.html

Wolf, M. 2004. "Asia: A New Economic Powerhouse." Asian Development Bank Annual Meeting. Jeju, Republic of Korea. 14 May.

Appendix: US current account and budget statistics

Year	GDP US$ billion	Balance on current account US$ million	Balance on current account % of GDP	Budget US$ million	Budget % of GDP
1980	2,725.4	2,317	0.1	−73,830	−2.7
1981	3,058.6	5,030	0.2	−78,968	−2.6
1982	3,225.5	−5,536	−0.2	−127,977	−4.0
1983	3,442.7	−38,691	−1.1	−207,802	−6.0
1984	3,846.7	−94,344	−2.5	−185,367	−4.8
1985	4,148.9	−118,155	−2.8	−212,308	−5.1
1986	4,406.7	−147,177	−3.3	−221,215	−5.0
1987	4,654.4	−160,655	−3.5	−149,728	−3.2
1988	5,011.9	−121,153	−2.4	−155,152	−3.1
1989	5,401.7	−99,486	−1.8	−152,456	−2.8
1990	5,737.0	−78,968	−1.4	−221,195	−3.9
1991	5,934.2	3,747	0.1	−269,328	−4.5
1992	6,240.6	−47,991	−0.8	−290,376	−4.7
1993	6,578.4	−81,987	−1.2	−255,087	−3.9
1994	6,964.2	−118,032	−1.7	−203,250	−2.9
1995	7,325.1	−109,478	−1.5	−163,972	−2.2
1996	7,697.4	−120,207	−1.6	−107,473	−1.4
1997	8,186.6	−135,979	−1.7	−21,958	−0.3
1998	8,626.3	−209,557	−2.4	69,213	0.8
1999	9,127.0	−296,822	−3.3	125,563	1.4
2000	9,708.4	−413,443	−4.3	236,445	2.4
2001	10,040.7	−385,701	−3.8	127,424	1.3
2002	10,373.4	−473,944	−4.6	−157,797	−1.5
2003	10,828.3	−530,668	−4.9	−375,295	−3.5

Sources: US Department of Commerce, Bureau of Economic Analysis; White House.

CHAPTER 1.5

Implications of Structural Changes for Management of the Global Economy[1]

EDWIN M. TRUMAN, Senior Fellow, Peterson Institute for International Economics

Introduction

Rapid economic expansion in a number of large emerging-market economies (LEMs) is changing the shape of the world economy.[2] This is now conventional wisdom. However, the implications of these developments for the performance and management of the global economic and financial system are controversial. On the one hand, some observers predict a tectonic shift of economic power. On the other, it is argued that the United States will remain the single global superpower and will continue to dominate the global economy and financial system, alongside the other traditional industrial countries, as far into the future as reliable predictions can be made. To be fair, Goldman Sachs (2006), the principal perpetrator of the BRIC (Brazil, Russia, India, and China) view of the world, takes an intermediate position: the world is changing; some of those changes will occur faster than others, and it is desirable to recognize and to adjust to these emerging realities.

My view is that the group of systemically important countries (SICs) has expanded and will continue to expand. The SICs are those countries whose economic performance and economic policies affect the performance of the global economy and the stability of the global financial system. They are the countries whose active and passive policies, including policy errors or omissions, generate substantial spillovers not only on their immediate neighbors but also well beyond their borders. They are not price-takers in the global economic and financial system. Importantly, they should not be free-riders in that system. They should be held responsible for the performance of the system as a whole, and if they are to be held responsible, they should have appropriate representation in the forums of governance for the system.

Which are the systemically important countries?

The group includes more than just the G-7 countries.[3] It includes more than just the G-7 countries and the BRICs.[4] As a first approximation, the SICs are the G-20 countries represented at the 2006 Roundtable on Global Savings and Investments Patterns and the subsequent meeting of G-20 deputies in Adelaide.[5] Appendix Tables 1, 2 and 3 summarize the relative positions of the G-20 members, their growth rates, and the expansion of their trade and reserves. The tables illustrate both the varied performance among G-20 countries over the past 5 to 15 years and the overwhelming importance of this group of countries to global growth?accounting for about 75 percent of the world total, more than 50 percent of growth in trade, and about 70 percent of growth in reserves. The tables demonstrate, as well, the increasing relative contributions of the non-industrial members of the G-20—the principal LEMs—to global economic and financial activity.

A more complete list of SICs today might include as many as 30 countries, depending on the issue. Moreover, the concepts of country and sovereignty today have become blurred, in large part by the forces of globalization, and also through political integration, in particular in Europe. Thus, Belgium and the Netherlands may not be as systemically important as they were in 1970, but the European Union of which they are members has more influence on the global economy and financial system than was the case 35 years ago. Switzerland is not a member of the European Union, and it has arguably less influence on the global economy than 35 years ago, but it still has an important influence on the global financial system, illustrating the basic point that not all countries are equally systemically important on every issue.

What are the implications of an expanding list of SICs for the management of the global economy? First, those countries have responsibilities for the performance and management of the global economy and financial system. Second, they should have appropriate representation in the forums of governance for the system. Global economic growth and financial stability cannot be perpetuated successfully without the active involvement of the SICs in both dimensions; they are two sides of the same coin. Too often, in my view, this issue is framed in terms of raw economic power, and the lessons are applied solely in terms of enhanced representation for the newer SICs, the LEMs, leaving aside the dimension of responsibility. For this reason, I will address first responsibility and second appropriate representation.

Responsibilities of the SICs

Each systemically important country has a special responsibility for global economic prosperity and financial stability. This does not mean that policymakers in these countries should be expected to act solely in the international interest, to the detriment of the performance of their own economies. What it means is that they should seek to internalize the fact that their policy actions and inactions can affect the performance of the global economy, and, in turn, affect the performance of their own economies. The task of global economic policy cooperation is not only about coordinated policy actions.

In international economic cooperation, it is more important for policymakers to endeavor to reach a shared diagnosis of potential problems, preferably based on a common analytical framework (Truman, 2004). If they are able to do so, their individual policy decisions are more likely to mesh smoothly. Moreover, on those occasions when coordination actions are agreed on, it is more likely that those actions will produce their intended result, if the various relevant policy-makers proceed on the basis of a shared framework. Sound diagnosis based on an agreed framework helps to minimize misunderstandings and maximize the consistency of policy actions. Following are two examples.

Consider the central issue of today (and the past several years): the resolution of global economic imbalances. Neither the diagnosis of the nature of the problem of global economic imbalances, nor the evaluation of their seriousness is agreed. Partly as a consequence, there is no consensus on the appropriate resolution. As I have described elsewhere (Truman, 2005), few countries have the incentive to move forward. Some stress the lack of US saving, others the lack of investment, still others excess saving in the rest of the world. Some say the US economy is growing too rapidly and sucking in imports at an unsustainable rate, while others point to the slow growth in some parts of the world, in particular, Europe and, until recently, Japan. (It is difficult in the fourth year of above-trend global growth to point to a serious deficiency in overall growth in the world.) Some emphasize that exchange rates should move, in particular in Asia, and others express concerns about an associated risk to financial stability. Because of this lack of a shared diagnosis, agreement as to which countries should take what actions, and in what sequence, has been elusive.

To a degree, this lack of consensus reflects institutional failures. The staff and management of the International Monetary Fund (IMF) have provided clear analyses, but the Fund has fallen short on applying imagination and leadership to encourage changes in underlying policies. The G-7 has held internal discussions and released communiqués calling for "vigorous action," but actual actions have been limited. Moreover, the G-7—or a G-7 augmented on a limited ad hoc basis by the BRICs plus sometimes South Africa, and occasionally Mexico—is the wrong institutional setting to address these issues. The G-20 is the place to address these issues collectively, but as an outsider, I have the impression that the G-7 has not encouraged this role for the G-20, and that the other members of the G-20 are perfectly content to engage in perfunctory discussions.

Global imbalances must be addressed in a multi-pronged manner: boost US savings, slow the growth of US domestic demand relative to domestic production, reverse that pattern in most of the rest of the world, and facilitate overall adjustment, via substantial changes in bilateral and effective exchange rates. For those countries with the largest surpluses—in particular those with substantial net capital inflows on top of their current account surpluses—the exchange rate adjustments will have to be larger, not only against the dollar but also on average against all currencies, what economists call an "effective" basis.

The SICs should shoulder their responsibilities and take these actions in their own interests and in the interests of global economic and financial stability. The IMF should spell out in specific detail not only the direction but also the size of the desirable policy actions, and should support specific adjustments in exchange rates, for example, by developing a set of reference exchange rates as an analytical tool. In *A Strategy for IMF Reform* (Truman 2006b), I call on the IMF to do a better job of policing the policies of the SICs, and those countries should pay more attention to the policeman, particularly if it becomes more active in the area of exchange rates.

Consider another important issue: the growth of international reserves. It is reasonable to ask whether the doubling of official foreign exchange reserves over the past four years—in particular, the more than 100 percent increase in non-Japan Asia and by Japan—has contributed to global economic prosperity and financial stability. That is a difficult case to make. Some argue that the increases in foreign exchange reserves are defensive in nature, but it is reasonable to ask whether this is the right type of defense or whether more fundamental policy reforms would not be more effective. Even if it were agreed that countries should build up their foreign exchange reserves, one could ask whether they should also, or preferably, seek to reduce their short-term external financial obligations.[6] Maybe there is a better way to augment countries' international reserves, for example, through allocations of special drawing rights that have less potential to distort the global adjustment process.

In addition, with regard to global financial stability, the diversification of official foreign exchange reserves is relevant. I have argued (Truman 2005, Truman and Wong 2006) that this issue is exaggerated in terms of the potential for financial disruption and the extent of actual reserve diversification. However, I have also argued that the financial market volatility associated with rumors and reports of such diversification by countries that are large holders of foreign exchange reserves should be addressed by the adoption of an International Reserve Diversification Standard. The standard would build on the transparency about official reserve holdings provided by the reserve template of the IMF's Special Data Dissemination Standard and the voluntary disclosure, as an element of that template, by 23 countries to date of the currency composition of their reserves. Increasing the number of countries adhering to that voluntary element would increase transparency and public accountability. Participants would also commit to a gradual adjustment of the currency composition of their reserve holdings.

The SICs should address these important issues associated with official reserve holdings in their own interests and in the interests of global economic and financial stability. Given that the members of the G-20 hold 64 percent of all foreign exchange reserves—25 percent by the industrial countries and 39 percent by the non-industrial countries—and given that they account for 72.6 percent of the increase in foreign exchange reserves from 2000 to 2005, the G-20 is an appropriate forum to discuss these issues, with a view to taking cooperative action in the form of adherence to an International Reserve Diversification Standard.

Representation of the SICs

The second topic, the appropriate representation of the SICs in the forums of governance of the global economic and financial system, has many dimensions. I will discuss two: first, the issue of representation on the IMF executive board (chairs) and voting shares in the Fund (shares); and second, the issue of a steering committee for the global economy.

The issues of chairs and shares are linked components of the governance of the IMF, as well as in its Bretton Woods twin, the World Bank. I argued in Truman (2006b), and in more detail in Truman (2006a), that rearranging chairs and shares is the most urgent and important issue in a desirable overall package of IMF reform. Without reform in this area, the Fund could, indeed, "slip into obscurity," quoting the warning recently delivered by the Governor of the Bank of England Mervyn King (2006). However, in this regard, I respectfully disagree with King on two fronts: first, the risk that the Fund will slip into obscurity derives not from what it does or does not do in carrying out its mission to support global economic and financial stability or how it is organized to carry out that mission; the risk derives from its perceived lack of legitimacy and lack of relevance to the real problems of the global economy and financial system. Unless the Fund promptly addresses concerns about its legitimacy and relevance, the majority of its members among the SICs will lose their remaining interest in the institution. It will have reached a tipping point into a downward spiral. Second, King's argument—that the members of the Fund, with their currently distorted voices and votes, should first address the larger questions he raises about the need for and the role of the IMF before addressing issues of chairs and shares—fails to recognize the extent of the IMF's governance crisis. I applaud the G-20 for its role in helping to promote a down payment on this important issue at the IMF/World Bank annual meetings in Singapore in September 2006. I hope that, with the down payment on the table, a substantial and comprehensive package of reforms can be implemented quickly.

With respect to representation on the IMF Executive Board, I argued that the members of the European Union, in both their individual and collective interest, should initiate steps toward a single seat, starting at the time of the election of Executive Directors in the fall of 2006. They failed to take my advice. Whenever it does occur, this first step would involve consolidating the members of the European Union into seven seats in EU-majority constituencies, compared with the current 10. This potentially would free up three positions as executive directors and three as alternate executive directors, adding new voices. Two year later, the seven seats should be consolidated into five, allowing for two new constituencies on the 24-member board, and generating perhaps one more for emerging Asia and another for Africa. Once the European Union completes its consolidation, members could discuss whether the four additional seats should be reallocated, or whether the size of the

Executive Board should be reduced to the 20 seats provided for in the Articles of Agreement.

With respect to voting shares, I think it is desirable to simplify the quota formula in the interests of transparency. I would favor the use of two variables, GDP on a purchasing- power-parity (PPP) basis and the variability of current receipts and overall capital inflows. However, it is desirable to appreciate that quota decisions involve political not technical negotiations, and the quota formula can only guide those negotiations not drive them. The place to conduct those negotiations is in the G-20, because its members make up 65 percent of existing quotas and about 70 percent of quotas based on my preferred, revised formula.[7] Moreover, most of the large absolute adjustments in quota shares involve the G-20 countries.[8]

It may be desirable to start with a limited number of ad hoc adjustments in quotas, but I believe that fundamental reform can only be achieved in the context of a substantial increase in the total of all IMF quotas, known as the size of the Fund, based on the objective of achieving parity in the voting shares of the United States and the European Union at about 18 percent. Thus, the issues of chairs and shares are joined, and it is essential to address them promptly in order to correct the imbalance in the governance of the IMF that has developed over the past 20 years or so.

On the matter of a steering committee for the global economy, C. Fred Bergsten (2006), among others, has written eloquently on the need for institutional change. He advocates replacing the G-7 with an F-16 where the F-16 would be the G-20 at the level of finance ministers and central bank governors with EU representation at parity with the United States—two seats.

This is another contentious topic. First there is the question of whether the global economy needs a steering committee. The proponents of democracy argue in the negative, but there are no pure democracies in the world, only representative democracies. The proponents of a more central role for the IMF in guiding the global economy argue for use of an IMF organ—the International Monetary and Financial Committee (IMFC), or for the creation of a Council in the IMF. However, in the past the IMFC has failed to deliver on anything more than narrow IMF issues. Steering the global economy involves areas—for example, energy—where the IMF has some expertise, but limited competence. As discussed in Truman (2006b, Chapter 4), some argue for a new group, possibly under the auspices of the United Nations. Some argue that the G-7 should be expanded, but expanding the G-7 will tend to perpetuate the old order and G-7 dominance, including excessive European influence in that group. Moreover, a slightly enlarged or reconfigured group of 10 or 12 only by chance is likely to be sufficiently representative with respect to substance as well as geography.

My view is that there is a perfectly serviceable group already, the G-20. Bergsten (2006) discusses its many advantages in terms of balance and getting the right countries to the table on most important global issues, including for example governance of the IMF. One objection is that the group is too large. On the other hand, a group of this size allows for a shifting emphasis in its agenda as the needs of the global economy shift. Moreover, it is always useful to have some members with less of an immediate stake in outcomes, which are able to play the role of facilitators of compromise.

The final issue is whether the G-20 should gradually assume a broader role, progressively taking over from the G-7, or whether a big bang would not be preferable. The truth is that the G-7 will only let go gradually, as was the case when the G-5 group at the level of finance ministers and central bank governors morphed into the G-7. Thus, it would be difficult to implement a big bang. The transformation process for the G-20 can be accelerated by a combination of three developments. First, the chosen few countries—the BRICs-plus—should henceforth decline invitations to breakfast, lunch, or dinner meetings with the G-7. Second, those countries, along with the other non-G-7 members of the G-20, should insist upon more substantive discussions on the problems of global economic growth and financial stability in the G-20, and take the initiative to put those topics on the agenda. Third, the non-G-7 members of the G-20 must approach meetings, including preparatory meetings of the G-20, with a willingness themselves to contribute to concrete progress on substantive issues. In this way, those countries will demonstrate increased responsibility commensurate with their appropriately increased representation.

NOTES

1 © Peterson Institute for International Economics. Taken from paper delivered at the Roundtable on Global Savings and Investments Patterns and the Changing Structure of the World Economy, by the World Economic Forum and the Reinventing Bretton Woods Committee, Adelaide, Australia, 18–19 March 2006.

2 See Boyer and Truman (2005) for an analysis of US policy toward the LEMs.

3 The G-7 countries are Canada, France, Germany, Italy, Japan, the United Kingdom, and the United States.

4 The Goldman Sachs BRIC group includes Brazil, Russia, India, and China. It is emphasized in many of the Goldman Sachs presentations that these four countries are representative of a larger group of emerging-market economies.

5 The members of the G-20 are the G-7 countries, Australia, and 11 emerging market countries (Argentina, Brazil, China, India, Indonesia, Korea, Mexico, Russia, Turkey, Saudi Arabia, and South Africa). The 20th country is the one holding the EU presidency, if it is not France, Germany, Italy, or the UK.

6 Dani Rodrik (2006) answers this question in the positive. He has a point even if does not agree with his associated endorsement of controls on short-term capital inflows.

7 In the context of consolidated EU representation in the G-20 and US-EU, voting parity in the IMF at 18 percent the G-20 total would be the same. See next paragraph.

8 Large absolute changes in quotas are relevant because it is those changes that can be politically disruptive at the same time that they are politically necessary to recognize changes in relative economic and financial weight.

REFERENCES

Bergsten, C. Fred. 2006. "A New Steering Committee for the New Economy? Chapter 9 in E. M. Truman, ed. *Reforming the IMF for the 21st Century.* IIE Special Report 19. Washington, D.C.: Institute for International Economics (IIE).

Boyer, Jan and Edwin M. Truman. 2005. "The United States and the Large Emerging-Market Economies: Competitors or Partners?" C. Fred Bergsten and IIE, eds. *The United States and the World Economy: Foreign Economic Policy for the Next Decade.* Washington, D.C.: IIE.

Goldman Sachs Global Economics Group. 2006. *The World and the BRICs Dream.* New York: Goldman Sachs.

International Monetary Fund (IMF). 2006a. World Economic Outlook Database. Washington, D.C.: IMF. April. Available at: http://www.imf.org/external/pubs/ft/weo/2006/01/data/index.htm

———. 2006b. *International Financial Statistics.* Washington, D.C.: IMF.

King, Mervyn. 2006. "Reform of the International Monetary Fund." Speech delivered at the Indian Council for Research on International Economic Relations. New Delhi, India. 20 February.

Rodrik, Dani. 2006. "The Social Cost of Foreign Exchange Reserves." Paper presented at the American Economic Association meetings. Boston, MA. 6–8 January.

Truman, Edwin M. 2004. "A Critical Review of Coordination Efforts in the Past." H. Siebert, ed. *Macroeconomic Policies in the World Economy*. Heidelberg: Springer.

———. 2005. "Postponing Global Adjustment: An Analysis of the Pending Adjustment of Global Imbalances." IIE Working Paper 05-06. Washington, D.C.: IIE.

———. 2006a. "Rearranging IMF Chairs and Shares: The Sine Qua Non of IMF Reform." Chapter 9 in Edwin M. Truman, ed. *Reforming the IMF for the 21st Century*. IIE Special Report 19. Washington, D.C.: IIE.

———. 2006b. *A Strategy for IMF Reform*. Policy Analyses in International Economics 77. Washington, D.C.: IIE.

Truman, Edwin M., and Anna Wong. 2006. "The Case for an International Reserve Diversification Standard." International Economics Working Paper no 06-2. Washington, D.C.: IIE. World Bank. YEAR. *World Development Indicators*. Washington, D.C.: World Bank.

World Bank. 2006. *World Development Indicators*. Washington, D.C.: World Bank.

World Trade Organization. 2005. Online database. Available at: http://www.wto.org/english/res_e/statis_e/statis_e.htm

PART 2

**New Players, New Responsibilities:
Asia and Emerging Markets in the
International Monetary System**

CHAPTER 2.1

The BRIC Dream: An Update

MICHAEL BUCHANAN, Co-Head of Global Macro and Markets Research,
Goldman Sachs

E very few decades, a seismic shift occurs in the world economy that has far-reaching implications across a wide range of markets. The rise of the US economy in the late 19th century, the post-war rebuilding of Japan and Western Europe and the rise of the East Asian production network have all been events of this kind. We have speculated that the rise of the four largest emerging economies, the so-called BRICs—Brazil, Russia, India, and China— could be the same kind of transforming event over the next few decades.

In 2003, Goldman Sachs Economics published a report, entitled *Dreaming with BRICs—the Path to 2050*, which looked at how the world might change between now and 2050 if the BRIC economies continued to grow strongly. The punch-line of that report was simple: the importance of the BRICs—as a source of new demand and as a share of global spending— could increase sharply over the next few decades. As a result, the world might look very different than it does today, and sooner than most people expected.

The original model

The model relies on a simple formulation of the overall level of GDP in terms of a) labor, b) the capital stock, and c) the level of "technical progress" or Total Factor Productivity (TFP). We assume that GDP is a simple (Cobb-Douglas) function of these three ingredients, a production function which seems to best represent long-term trends in the share of national income that go to labor and capital.

We then describe the process by which each of the different components change over time. The components are: labor (L) and capital stock and total factor productivity (K). For L, we simply use the projections of the working age population (15–60) from the US Census Bureau. For K, we take the initial capital stock, assume an investment rate (investment as a percent of GDP) and a depreciation rate to calculate the growth in the capital stock. For TFP, we assume that technology changes as part of a process of catch-up with the most developed countries. The speed of convergence is assumed to depend on income per capita, on the assumption that, as the developing economies get closer to the income levels of the more developed economies, their TFP growth rate slows.

The results are startling:

- If things go right, in less than 40 years, the BRIC economies together could be larger than the G-6 in US dollar terms.

- By 2025 they could account for over half the size of the G-6.

- In 2050, of the current G-6, only the US and Japan may be among the six largest economies in US dollar terms, and the list of the world's ten largest economies may look quite different.

- The largest economies in the world (by GDP) may no longer be the richest (by income per capita), making strategic choices for firms more complex.

About two-thirds of the increase in US dollar GDP from the BRICs should come from higher real growth, with the balance through currency appreciation. The BRICs' real exchange rates could appreciate by up to 300 percent over the next 50 years (an average of 2.5 percent a year).

The shift in GDP relative to the G-6 takes place steadily over the period, but is most dramatic in the first 30 years. Growth for the BRICs is likely to slow significantly toward the end of the period, with only India seeing growth rates significantly above 3 percent by 2050 (due to its much more favorable demographics). Individuals in the BRICs are still likely to be poorer on average than individuals in the G-6 economies, with the exception of Russia. China's per capita income could be roughly what the developed economies are now, about US$30,000 per capita.

As early as 2009, the annual increase in US dollar spending from the BRICs could be greater than that from the G-6, and more than twice as much in dollar terms as it is now. By 2025 the annual increase in US dollar spending from the BRICs could be twice that of the G-6, and four times higher by 2050.

Growth environment scores

In order to rank the ability of countries to meet their growth potential more formally and to monitor growth conditions over time, we have developed a Growth Environment Score (GES) that aims to summarize the overall environment in an economy, emphasizing the dimensions that are important to economic growth. Relying on the large body of research on the determinants of economic growth, we have constructed our GES using 13 subindexes, which can be divided into five basic areas:

- Macroeconomic stability: Inflation; government deficit; external debt
- Macroeconomic conditions: Investment rates; openness of the economy
- Technological capabilities: Penetration of PCs; telephones; Internet
- Human capital: Education; life expectancy
- Political conditions: Political stability; rule of law; corruption

The basic notion is that strong growth is best achieved with a stable and open economy, healthy investment, high rates of technology adoption, a healthy and well-educated workforce, and a secure and rule-based political environment. We rank a country's performance on each measure on a 0–10 scale and create an overall score, the GES, which also ranges from a possible minimum of 0 (poor conditions) to a possible maximum of 10 (perfect conditions). The GES is consistent across countries and over time, can be easily updated and tracked on an ongoing basis, and is based on hard evidence.

Encouragingly, the BRICs themselves are all in the top half of the rankings for developing countries and above the developing country mean. China ranks the highest (16th), followed by Russia (44th), while Brazil and India are further behind (58th and 60th, respectively), out of a total of 133 developing countries. This validates our decision, in our BRICs projections, to use a lower convergence speed in the initial period projections for Brazil and India. Importantly, China clearly tops the list of the large-population developing economies (BRICs plus N-11), and by a sizeable margin.

The GES sub-components highlight the strengths and weaknesses of each of the BRICs, and indicate where there is room for improvement:

- Brazil scores relatively well on measures of political stability, life expectancy, and technology adoption, but quite poorly on investment, education levels, openness to trade, and government deficit.

- Russia also scores well in terms of education, fiscal position, external debt position, openness to trade, technology adoption, and life[1] expectancy, but it does less well on measures of political measures stability and corruption, investment rates and inflation.

- India scores relatively well in terms of rule of law, external debt and inflation, but quite poorly in terms of levels of secondary education, technology adoption, fiscal position, and openness.

- China ranks well above the mean on macro stability, investment, openness to trade, and human capital. Its rankings on technology adoption are more mixed (PC usage is still quite low) and corruption measures are also a little worse than the mean.

Update: "RIC"s look good, but Brazil is at a crossroads

Do we still believe these results are indicative of the long-term trends in the global economy? In a word, yes. Since our original work, all of the BRICs economies have grown faster than predicted by our model.[2]

China has thus far defied talk of a crash landing, and while the economy has slowed (both on official data and on our proprietary indicators), it is still likely to grow by more than 10 percent in 2006 and more than 9 percent in 2007.

- This is far above the long-term average growth rate our model predicted for China (4.7 percent), and also well above the forecast for this decade (before the demographics really start to bite into growth).

- We do have concerns, however, about the unbalanced nature of the economy. China's growth is still far too dependent on a booming external sector.

- With policy-makers trying to cool investment at home, China's growth story is at risk from a combination of rising trade tensions abroad and weaker global demand that could threaten exports. A revaluation of the Chinese yuan would help to re-balance the economy away from an overheated trade sector to domestic-driven growth.

- The banking sector remains a risk, with NPLs falling, primarily because of loan growth and a carve-out of bad debts, rather than a more deep-seated reform of banking p, However, progress is now being made and this should not derail the long-term BRIC story.

India is also doing better than our model implied, but this year may slip fractionally below the average implied growth rate for this decade.

- It grew in excess of 8 percent last year, well above the long-term model prediction of 5.8 percent and above the forecast for this decade of 6.1 percent.

- Longer term, while growth in the G-6, Brazil, Russia, and China is expected to slow significantly over the next 50 years, India's growth rate remains above 5 percent throughout the period.

- With the only population, out of the four BRIC countries that continues to grow throughout the next 50 years, India has the potential to raise its US dollar income per capita in 2050 to 35 times current levels. Still, its income per capita will be significantly lower than any of the countries we look at.

Russia, benefiting from high oil prices—which we expect to be a lasting phenomenon given the long-term lack of investment in infrastructure in the oil sector—has far exceeded the model projections:

- It grew at over 6 percent last year against a long-term model projection of 3.2 percent and an average projection of 4.7 percent for this decade.

- We expect growth to slow just a touch in 2007, due to a drop in energy sector investment, and failure of other sectors to fill the void, but household demand growth remains very strong, thanks to loosening fiscal policy, leading to a surge in imports. In the longer term there is still a need to further diversify away from energy.

- The overall macro stance remains prudent, helping to ensure sustainability. The budget is likely to remain in surplus to the tune of more than 7 percent of GDP this year, and reserves and the stabilization fund continue to grow strongly.

- The legacy of Yukos affair is diminishing, but, given the continued unresolved legitimacy of privatized property, has emboldened state bodies, intimidated the private sector, and worsened the climate for foreign investment.

- The 2008 presidential succession is uncertain, particularly in light of the Orange Revolution in Ukraine. The Putin regime is likely to survive, but the hand-over to a new president could be accompanied by more pressure on oligarchs. In the long term, Russia must find a political system that is representative, but which leaves the country effectively governable.

Brazil is the country for which our model was least optimistic, but the projections are in the greatest danger of proving *too* rosy.

- Broadly speaking, the outlook for the Brazilian economy for the next Lula administration remains favorable in our view, buoyed by the persistence of strong global growth and liquidity, and if underpinned by sound demand management policies, growth could increase to about 3.4 percent this year, and 3.5 percent next year.

- Such conditions are so extraordinary that it would not be an exaggeration to say that the Lula administration could use one of the most favorable macroeconomic conditions in the last 40 years to push hard for deep structural reforms intended to bolster real GDP growth in Brazil.

- Unfortunately, we believe that the government is not taking full advantage of these extraordinary conditions to lay the foundations of a stronger economy.

- On the contrary, over the last six months or so, political developments have not been encouraging, and suggest that politicians may undermine the pillars of stabilization, rather than use global prosperity to boost potential GDP growth.

Conclusion

That BRIC performance has been even better than the model we predicted is hardly surprising, as we had been deliberately conservative at each stage of the process. However, this only serves to highlight the fact that our projections were far from an extrapolation of the recent past.

The key assumption underlying our projections is that the BRICs maintain policies and develop institutions that are supportive of growth. Each of the BRICs faces significant challenges in keeping development on track. This means that there is a good chance that our projections will not be met, either through bad policy or bad luck. But if the BRICs come anywhere close to meeting the projections we set out in 2003, and if they continue to be a useful guide to the long-term changes afoot in the global economy, the implications for the pattern of growth and economic activity could be very large.

NOTES

1 The effects of the one-child policy mean that China is not just aging at a relatively early stage of development, but it is aging more rapidly than today's G-6.

2 Note: the model results differ from our short-term forecasts for growth in each of the BRICs.

REFERENCES

Goldman Sachs Economics. 2003. *Dreaming with BRICs—the Path to 2050*. Global Economics Paper No. 99. Available at: http://www2.goldmansachs.com/insight/research/reports/99.pdf.

Institutions to Promote Financial Stability: Reflections on East Asia and an Asian Monetary Fund[1]

GORDON DE BROUWER, General Manager, G-20 and APEC Secretariat, Department of the Treasury, Australia, and Professor, Crawford School of Economics and Government, Australian National University

Introduction

A regional financial architecture has started to emerge in East Asia. Although still in its early stages, it has many dimensions, spanning improved policy dialogue and surveillance, the development and integration of financial markets and systems, financial cooperation to prevent or manage balance of payments crises, and possible cooperative exchange rate arrangements.[2] One aspect of regional financial arrangements that comes up in discussion from time to time is a regional fund or, more specifically, an Asian Monetary Fund (AMF).[3]

There is widespread recognition in policy and academic circles that the way in which institutions are designed and structured determines their incentives and whether they can in fact achieve their aims. This paper looks at some issues about the design of a possible AMF. It does not presume that such a regional institution will be set up, nor does it argue the merits or disadvantages of such an institution. Ultimately, judgment on an Asian Monetary Fund will be a pragmatic decision based on a specific proposal, made with an open mind.

Rather, the paper seeks to help contribute to the preliminary debate by canvassing some of the key principles that are useful in thinking about the substantive responsibilities of a regional fund and its organizational features. It is by no means an exhaustive commentary on the issue. It aims to look at practical ways to ensure that a regional institution, if it is set up, is designed to maximize the likelihood of its success.

To provide some context, there have been several important developments in regional financial cooperation in East Asia since mid 1997 and these are outlined below. East Asia now has the financial resources to fund a regional entity. And it is now trialling forms of financial cooperation. An AMF, if it occurs, will emerge out of this experience.

The paper then outlines some recent developments in the global financial architecture. The point of this discussion is that East Asia has a fundamental interest in the global architecture. However, its interests are not adequately represented in global forums and institutions. It is incumbent on the region to exercise its ownership in global forums and institutions, since it is, after all, a major shareholder of the IMF. But the region is dissatisfied with its partici- pation rights, and recent proposals (examined in the paper) which seek to limit East Asia's role in global forums even further may produce a counter- productive backlash in the region. This raises the risk that a more inward- looking regional architecture will develop. The paper argues that the G-20 is still the best bet for general debate on international financial issues.

I then explore the economics and political science literature for some general ideas about the importance of institutions and what makes for a "good" institution. The ideas that recur in the literature are the importance of incentives and path-dependence. A good institution is one which has clear aims and responsibilities, can achieve its aims under pressure, and embodies the preferences of its owners. The paper explores some general implications for the building of institutions in East Asia.

Following this, I look at some specific design issues for a possible Asian Monetary Fund, and argue that the primary aim of a regional fund would be to enhance regional stability. I then explain how possible responsibilities of a regional fund—particularly surveillance and financial support in a balance of payments crisis—can be made consistent with that aim, especially when there is a global institution that has the same objective. I also look at a couple of different organizational forms that a regional institution could assume, and explore which of these is most consistent with the characteristics of a good institution.

I conclude by summarizing the key arguments and end with the observa- tion that the evolution of the regional architecture is not pre-determined. I point out how East Asia, in particular, engages with the rest of the world, and show how US and European engagement with East Asia will affect the outcome.

Background

The debate in East Asia on a regional financial architecture has not been occurring in isolation. There are two ways to put the regional debate in context. The first is what the region has done so far in terms of regional financial cooperation since the start of the crisis in July 1997, indicating that regional financial cooperation has some steam behind it. The second is that the nature of, and progress in, the broader international debate on financial architecture may affect the way in which East Asia approaches regional financial cooperation. The less inclusive the global debate is of East Asia and the region's needs, the stronger is the East Asian constituency for regional institutions and solutions.

Recent developments in regional financial cooperation in East Asia

The debate about a regional monetary fund in East Asia is not new. And the region now has some experience in thinking about, and dealing with, regional financial cooperation. To put the thinking about a possible regional fund in context, there have been four specific developments regarding regional financial cooperation in East Asia.

The first is the region's initial experience with providing crisis funding, notably the meeting of the Friends of Thailand in Tokyo in August 1997. Following in-principle agreement on supplementary financing among Executives' Meeting of East Asia-Pacific Central Banks (EMEAP) in Shanghai on 25 July, officials from the larger regional economies (Japan, China, South Korea, Hong Kong SAR, Australia, Indonesia, Malaysia, and Singapore) committed formally at the Tokyo meeting to provide substantial financial support for Thailand to supplement IMF funding.[4]

This meeting was the first time the region had agreed to, and actually did, provide substantial funds to an East Asian country in financial crisis.[5]

Besides the IMF, the World Bank and the ADB, only countries from the region provided direct financial support to Thailand. The United States declined to participate, in part because the Administration was prevented by the D'Amato Amendment from accessing the Exchange Stabilization Fund. The psychological impact of the Friends of Thailand was considerable: at the same time as it revealed the difficulty in garnering supplementary support from outside the region, it showed that the region itself was able to come together quickly and resolutely provide support for one of its own. In subsequent international financing packages, the region committed US$14 billion to Indonesia (out of a total US$35.1 billion) and US$11.1 billion to South Korea (out of a total US$58.4 billion).

The second development in regional financial integration was the proposal by Japan in late 1997 for an Asian Monetary Fund. Japan's Ministry of Finance started work on a proposal for an Asian Monetary Fund in late August 1997. The AMF was to raise US$100 billion to support adjustment in the crisis-affected economies, with Japan providing half of the funds. Its members were to be the Friends of Thailand group (Hamanaka, 2003).

The proposal was opposed because of concerns that a regional fund would apply weaker conditionality in its crisis funding, thereby weakening the authority and leverage of the IMF in advancing macroeconomic and structural reform in the crisis-affected economies. There was also concern that the AMF would be tantamount to a bailout, rather than reform, of some Japanese banks, with funds being directed to distressed sectors (via their banks) in the crisis-affected economies.

The AMF proposal failed because of the opposition of key countries, notably the United States and China.[6] It is significant, nevertheless, because it put the creation of a regional institution for financial cooperation in East Asia on the policy agenda.

The third development was the Chiang Mai Initiative (CMI) of ASEAN+3.[7] Under the CMI, ASEAN+3 governments in May 2000 agreed to set up a system of bilateral swaps to lend foreign exchange reserves between particular countries in the event of a financial crisis. There are now 16 bilateral swaps in place with an aggregate value of US$79 billion (as of September 2006),[8] more than double the amount available only a few years ago. The CMI is widely viewed as a useful step in formalizing regional financial cooperation.[9] But it is also seen as a first step. There are a number of aspects about the CMI that regional commentators talk about changing, but about which there is no consensus as yet among ASEAN+3 countries.

One is the dependence on IMF conditionality for triggering the facility. Under current arrangements, only 20 percent of the facility is available without IMF conditionality either in place or about to be put in place, and it is only available for a maximum of six months (compared to two years for the component attached to IMF conditionality).[10]

Another area of possible change of the CMI would be increasing the amounts available to individual countries under the CMI swap arrangements.

The most that a member country can access under regional arrangements ranges from around US$3 billion (Singapore) to US$22 billion (Korea). This is still below the speculative positions that were established in individual regional foreign exchange markets in 1997 and 1998 and well below the amounts of the original financing packages.[11]

The final area of possible change would be to multilateralize the CMI system of bilateral swaps. ASEAN+3 finance ministers have indicated their intention to multilateralize the arrangement. The simplest way to multilateralize a bilateral network is to coordinate activation of the swaps, either on an informal pragmatic basis, or under a specific memorandum of understanding between parties to the CMI to consult with other parties when a country seeks to use the swap facility.

Other, more complex approaches to multilateralizing the CMI could be taken. For example, the funds available under the CMI could be available under regional arrangements-to-borrow, akin to the New Arrangements to Borrow (NAB) of the IMF.[12] Or they could be an actual pool of foreign exchange reserves. This would mean that countries in crisis could probably access more funds from the region than is currently possible. But it also means that limits may have to be set on access to these funds, with effective mechanisms to minimize and deal with associated risks.[13] The CMI could also be multilateralized by setting up a regional monetary fund.

The final aspect of regional financial arrangements is the accumulation of foreign exchange reserves in East Asia, especially of US dollar assets. The region now has foreign exchange reserves in excess of US$3 trillion, up from US$715 billion at the end of 1996.

While many economies in the region have increased their holdings of foreign exchange, the most spectacular in the past few years are China and Japan, with US$954 billion and US$872 billion at the end of July 2006 (Figure 1). This is significant. With this sort of reserve in hand, it is hard to see how the region would be exposed to a play of events similar to that which occurred from mid 1997 to late 1998.[14]

Reserves of this order naturally lead to the question of how they might be used. Such reserves can not only costly to carry but they also have an

Figure 1: Foreign exchange reserves of selected Asian economies

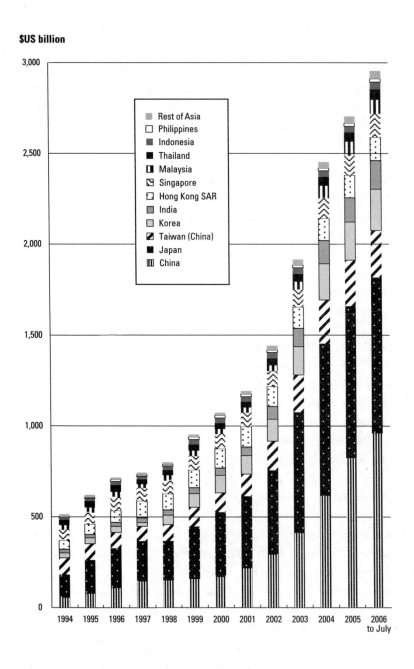

$US billion

Legend:
- Rest of Asia
- Philippines
- Indonesia
- Thailand
- Malaysia
- Singapore
- Hong Kong SAR
- India
- Korea
- Taiwan (China)
- Japan
- China

Source: IMF, International Financial Statistics.

opportunity cost which is high for some developing economies. Some countries, therefore, may want to use them for domestic purposes, as China did in January 2004 by allocating US$45 billion of its reserves to fund bank recapitalization.

But the main holders of these reserves, while probably not wanting to build up reserves further, may keep them on the official balance sheet.[15] As such, some portion of them might be used in some form of financial cooperation. If the region did decide to multilateralize the CMI arrangement, for example, in the form of an Asian Arrangements to Borrow or central reserve fund, some of these reserves could be hypothecated to that purpose. Amounts that are talked about in the region range as high as US$100–200 billion, substantially more than the aggregate value of the bilateral swaps. In this case, Japan is talked about as the most likely candidate to increase the amount of funds in such an arrangement.

Certainly, the region now has the resources to deal with regional financial crises alone if it so wants. At the end of 2003, the IMF's total resources were US$326 billion, but its one-year forward commitment capacity was a more modest US$81 billion. Supplementary funding of around US$50 billion is available through the General Arrangements to Borrow and the New Arrangements to Borrow.[16] The catalytic role of external funding for a country in crisis can now be provided by either the IMF or East Asian financial resources. But, at this stage, in the absence of a credible regional surveillance and enforcement mechanism, IMF involvement would probably have the most powerful catalytic role in establishing policy credibility for a country in crisis.

The international debate

The East Asian debate about regional financial cooperation also needs to be seen in the context of the international debate about global financial arrangements. The global debate has a long history and is clearly ongoing. It focuses on issues of substance about financial cooperation. It includes the following:

- the pre-conditions for avoiding financial crises

- the amounts, terms and conditions for providing financing in a crisis that are compatible with the desired incentives for borrowers, lenders and financial markets in general

- the coordination mechanisms between the official sector and the private sector in dealing with and resolving crises

- technical assistance

And the global debate has increasingly focused on the operation and governance of the forums and institutions by which financial cooperation is effected, especially the International Monetary Fund and policy dialogue forums, such as the Financial Stability Forum, G-7, and G-20.[17]

The global debate is one in which East Asia has a direct interest and is active. The region participates in a variety of ways.[18] Japan is the only East Asian country that is part of the G-3, G-7, G-8 and G-10, and it reports developments back to countries in the region on an informal basis. Japan, Australia, Hong Kong SAR, and Singapore are part of the Financial Stability Forum.[19] Japan, China, Indonesia, Australia, and South Korea are part of the G-20. Japan, China, Australia and Thailand are also members of the International Monetary and Financial Committee (IMFC) of the IMF.[20] There have also been non-G-7 discussions on the global financial architecture in the region, notably those led by South Korea.[21]

But many in the region are dissatisfied with the debate. In the first instance, most of East Asia is under-represented in the decision-making of the IMF while Europe is over-represented.[22] This is an ongoing sore point in the region and has become the talisman of the region's discontent. Eichengreen (2003b) regards the need for rebalancing regional representation as one of the basic issues for reforming the governance of the Fund. It is an increasingly widespread view.[23]

And dissatisfaction runs deeper. There is concern that the credibility of the Fund is undermined by its pliability in meeting the short-term strategic objectives of its major shareholder. There is concern that the concentration of the IMF's lending to Argentina, Brazil and Turkey increases the Fund's—and hence its shareholders'—exposure to risk and creates moral hazard. While these are (now) systemically important countries, they are not as strategically important to East Asia as they are to the United States or Europe.

East Asia has a direct interest in the ways that weaknesses in the Fund's governance can be resolved.

There are different views on how to do this. Eichengreen (2003b), for example, argues that the IMFC is the natural place to reform the IMF—even if the IMFC itself needs reform.

He argues that alternative forums, especially the G-20, are not ideal because they lack broad support from Europe, especially from the smaller European countries who are members of the G-10 but not the G-20.[24] Yet it is hard to see how these countries could be happy with changes to quotas and representation on the IMF Executive Board and IMFC. From East Asia's perspective, there must be better grounds for rejecting the G-20 than simply because it is opposed by some small, otherwise over-represented European countries.

Henry et al. (2003) argue that groupings based on the G-7 or G-10 are not balanced globally and, hence, lack credibility. The IMFC is certainly a key and essential forum for debate and decision. But it has the foot print of the G-10 and hence lacks geographic balance.[25] Henry et al. argue that the G-20 is the better and more credible forum in which to take up these issues, and advance, among other things, reform of the IMF.

Kenen et al. perceive a shift toward informal groupings rather than formal institutions as the way to discuss and resolve international financial policy issues.[26] They argue for a consolidation of groupings, explicitly recommending closing down the G-10.[27] They advocate reform of the IMF, upgrading the role of the Executive Board, rationalizing EU representation, and revisiting the allocation of quotas which determine voting rights.[28] And they recommend that the G-20 call for the formation of a new Council for International Financial and Economic Cooperation (CIFEC) to set the global agenda. The CIFEC would be limited to 15 country members.[29]

The idea of a CIFEC is new and has not yet been fully debated. East Asia is likely to be suspicious of this proposal, for three reasons. It was made by North Americans and Europeans without Asian involvement and consultation.[30] It is unclear who the 15 members are that the authors have in mind. The concern in this case would be that it would wind back further the gains in East Asian representation made in the G-20. And it is the creation of yet another forum when there is already a plethora of them—although there would be no net increase in their number, since the G-10 would be disbanded. The Council, by its name and function, would be a paramount forum. All in all, from East Asia's perspective, the CIFEC might be seen as a proposal made by those outside the region without consultation with them, for a new and powerful forum which would likely reduce East Asian participation and voice in international economic and financial policymaking.

It is worth noting here that the G-20 itself was a compromise which weakened a key gain in East Asian international participation and voice. The G-20 was set up by the G-7 after the experience with the G-22, also known as the Willard Group.[31] The G-22 was an initiative of President Clinton at the APEC meeting at Vancouver in November 1997. The success of its three working groups on international financial crises, strengthening financial systems, and transparency and accountability in the aftermath of the financial crisis showed the value of fresh, practical, and less institutionally based dialogue and cooperation.[32] But its provenance and the inclusion of so many East Asian countries made it unacceptable to the Europeans.

The G-20 carries the same membership as the G-22, adding Saudi Arabia and Turkey, but dropping Hong Kong SAR, Malaysia, Singapore, Thailand, and Poland. Given the region's experience with the metamorphosis of the G-22 into the G-20, East Asia is naturally wary of further changes that would weaken its participation in international economic policy dialogue. The view from East Asia may be that the effort should be in making the G-20 work rather than setting up another forum.

This context is important in understanding the pressures for further change in regional financial cooperation in East Asia. The more the region is dissatisfied with global arrangements and feels that it is marginalized in, or excluded from, international policy debates, the more likely it is to focus on regional solutions. This is a process which has the dangerous potential to spiral and feed back on itself. There is a need for better engagement of North America and Europe with Asia on these issues, and vice versa.

The onus is also on East Asia to make the case for change. By using the voice it does have in a range of forums and behind the scenes, East Asia can strengthen its case for wider representation in global forums. This entails, among other things, the region forming its own views on the global financial architecture and projecting them in key forums. This is a work in progress. East Asia's authority would be enhanced by showing that it is not just seeking to advance its own interests but wants to secure outcomes which improve global well-being.

The design of institutions

Before proceeding to look at some specific issues about the design of a possible Asian Monetary Fund, it might be useful to highlight some of the key, if rather ethereal, insights from the political science and economic literature on the design of institutions. There are two elements that are worth noting here. The first is the importance of institutions and getting their design right. The second is the set of characteristics that make for a "good" institution.

The importance of institutions

There is widespread recognition that institutions are important. Goodin, for example, argues that the basic value of institutions is that they provide stability and reliability, by enabling a nested system of rules to govern current and future behavior.[33] In this respect, they can provide more certainty about the future, and hence improve predictability and reduce risk. And because transactions are not costless, institutions matter.

North makes the powerful assertion that institutions "are the underlying determinant of the long-run performance of economies."[34] The recent work of Hall and Jones (1999), Caballero and Hammour (2000) and Acemoglu et al. (2004), among others, are attempts to support this claim. These authors argue that economic institutions embody a set of incentives in the economy, and that these incentives constitute the "underlying determinants of economic performance."[35] Incentives and institutions can also vary considerably over time.

Institutions lock in, and set a future path for, sets of relationships, forms of action, and responses to events.[36] Because of this path-dependence, the incentives and behaviors embodied in institutions are carried forward, as the decisions of today affect what happens in the future. Moreover, the creation of a new institution induces its own responses, a new set of constraints, and persistent informal and formal rules that will govern and influence future behavior.[37]

In this context, "institutions" are defined broadly as "the rules of the game in a society or, more formally, ... the humanly devised constraints that shape human interaction."[38] North's definition of institutions includes bricks-and-mortar institutions, as well as the broader systems of networks and interactions between people and groups in the economy.

Three implications of this type of analysis for setting up a new institution such as an Asian Monetary Fund make it clear that the task is not to be taken lightly.

In the first place, it is essential to get the incentives and the structure of the institution right. If poorly designed, then an institution can not only *cause* damage but, because it creates its own set of interests in its preservation, also make it difficult to undo or correct. There are learning costs in setting up a new institution which must be managed and which should enter the cost-benefit analysis of setting the institution up in the first place. And, looked at from a broader perspective, to the extent that the current focus on regionalism is, at least in part, transitory—part of a cycle or long oscillating wave between globalism and regionalism—it is important to ensure that setting up a regional institution does not lock East Asia into a set of regional solutions without ready recourse to global solutions at some later stage.[39]

Second, given that institutions are devised from the self-interest, circumstances, and particular "transactions costs" existing at the time,[40] there is no presumption that an institution created for the needs of East Asia at a given point in time will necessarily have the attributes of some other similar institution elsewhere. In other words, what suits the region should be informed by insight from elsewhere, but it does not necessarily have to mimic what is done elsewhere. The mind should be full, but the paper blank.

Finally, practical policy-makers should focus on the substance and effectiveness of institutional arrangements and not just the form that they may take. There is an array of different types of institutions, ranging from informal networks to bricks and mortar. Formal institutions might not be the most effective type of institution for the issues at hand. Flexible relatively informal arrangements may in fact deliver better results than formal rigid ones. East Asian policy-makers might end up deciding that a bricks-and-mortar type AMF is the right way to go, but they need not feel compelled to think that that route is the only, or indeed the best, one, in order to indicate their support for regional financial cooperation and community building.

What defines a "good" institution?

Given that they are important, what makes for a good institution? There are four aspects that emerge from the literature, with varying degrees of specificity.

The first is that the responsibilities of the institution have to be well defined, and it must have a clear sense of its mission (Wilson, 1989; Tirole, 2002). This is not as anodyne as it sounds. The staff and management of an institution must have a practical understanding of its function, and an institution's oversight body must have some terms of reference to judge performance. Governance is harder when an institution has multiple and competing objectives.

The second is that the institution must be resistant to pressure, i.e. be able to meet its stated purpose under internal and external pressure. A crisis-management institution has to be able to operate under the pressures of a crisis. The pressures may come from politicians and the political process. This implies that some independence from the political process is necessary, at least in terms of the analysis of, and advice about, economic and financial vulnerabilities in the region.

The pressures may come from the particular national interests of large countries within the region, especially if the region comprises a few very large countries, as does East Asia. This means that decision-making may have to be shared across countries. The region as a whole will be reluctant to choose institutional forms or practices which allow one large country to dominate a regional institution in the same way as the United States is perceived to dominate the IMF.[41] And pressures may arise from outside the region. In East Asia's case, this is principally the United States. This means that effective communication channels have to exist across regions, not just within them.

The third element of a good institution is that it embodies the preferences of its members/owners. It is hard to identify common preferences for a region as heterogeneous as East Asia, and the assessment that follows is subjective and tentative. But, given that caveat, three strong preferences can be identified: a simple and streamlined process with minimal bureaucracy; retention of political control over decision-making to ensure that, while guided by technical advice, decisions are under political control; promotion of harmony and community-building in the region, i.e. balancing the interests of large and small countries in the region and of north and south East Asia.

In terms of crisis management, its experience with the 1997–98 crises means the region wants to be able to make decisions quickly in a crisis. Below, I will look at ways to accommodate these preferences in the responsibilities and organizational design of a regional fund.

And it is not enough that an institution satisfies the short-term needs of its owners. It must also meet the basic preferences of its shareholders in the long-run. A relevant example of the importance of time-consistency is the IMF's recent experience with lending to Argentina. The provision of funds by the IMF prevented an immediate crisis, but it came at the expense of moral hazard for Argentina and a concentrated country-exposure by the Fund, both of which potentially undermine international financial cooperation and stability.

The final element of a good institution is a set of micro conditions relating to flexibility. Goodin (1996) argues that well-designed institutions must be flexible enough to change as the circumstances change, i.e. to deal with complex agendas and motives. And they must be flexible in dealing with new situations, experimenting, and trying new ways to get things done. Openness to the rest of the world can help promote flexibility.

At times a trade-off may exist between some of these conditions for a good institution. For example, there may be occasions when the various intense pressures that emerge during a crisis challenge the regional institution to remain fully consistent with the preferences of its owners. How the conflict between goals is achieved may depend on the organizational design of the institution. For example, an independent advisory body within the organization may be a practical mechanism to help decision-makers resist some of these pressures.

The design of a possible AMF

The design of a regional institution covers two basic areas. They are the responsibilities of the institution and its organizational structure.

Possible responsibilities of an AMF

The pivotal rationale for a regional entity is to ensure stability. The guiding principle for selecting the responsibilities of an AMF, therefore, is that the institution should promote regional financial and economic stability in a practical fashion. It can do this

- by seeking to reduce the risk of crises occurring
- by providing funding to prevent or minimize a crisis

The second of these methods may be linked to the first. For example, increasing the pool of financial funds available to deal with a crisis may be a way to reduce the likelihood of the crisis if it is a credible demonstration of the fundamental strength of the economy concerned.[42]

But if it is not credible, it may simply serve to increase the size of the bets, and, instead of reducing the risk of a crisis, it may even exacerbate it.[43]

In thinking about the scope of activities that are compatible with the aim of promoting regional stability by a regional institution, it is natural to consider them in comparison with what the IMF does as a global institution responsible for global stability. The IMF has four main functions: surveillance of the global economy and the economies of its members; provision of technical assistance to its members; serving as an international forum for consultation and collaboration on international monetary problems; lending to its members (Fischer, 2003).

At least in some respects, the responsibilities of a regional institution cannot mimic those of a global institution. A regional body, for example, cannot carry out global surveillance or facilitate global collaboration itself. And there are some forms of cooperation that can probably only be done at the global level. Private-sector involvement (PSI), for example, requires global coordination to be effective. East Asian governments have no jurisdiction over the activities of US or European banks and other financial institutions outside East Asia.

But even if the regional cannot mimic the global, a properly designed regional institution might echo some of the functions of the global institution.

The literature looks at the responsibilities of a *regional* body in terms of surveillance, collaboration and crisis funding at a *regional* level.[44] Some of the literature discusses the possible role of a regional fund as coordinator and manager of regional cooperative exchange rate arrangements. I will now consider these in turn.

Surveillance

Effective surveillance is uniformly regarded as one of the lynchpins of financial stability. It is an essential part of reducing the risk of crisis, and a prerequisite for the provision of crisis funds. There can be no financial cooperation without it. Effective surveillance requires not just the sharing of information about key economic and financial developments, but also frank and open discussion, albeit behind closed doors, of policy responses to the economic and financial issues in play.[45]

There is a large body of opinion that East Asia has too little effective regional surveillance and collaboration.[46] This is multidimensional, given that much of East Asia consists of developing economies with diverse income levels and faces basic problems of adequate data and information collection and exchange. There has been considerable work in recent years on improving data systems, through the work of the IMF, ADB, and other agencies.

Commentators also talk about a lack of frank and critical dialogue on policy issues in the region. There is some reticence to cause offence or criticize others, especially potential providers of funds, and to be open about domestic problems. The ASEAN principle of non-interference in the internal affairs of other countries can lurk in the background when discussion turns to sensitive issues. Nevertheless, the region is aware of the need to develop frank and open exchange and is working to improve it.

There is considerable scope for learning by doing, as policy-makers in East Asia experiment with different ways of talking about issues. These include the use of independent or academic trigger speakers, secretariat staff, independent chairs, and peer review.[47] Some of these may work better than others. For example, outsiders can play a useful catalytic role in discussion, at least early on, by providing analytical insight and raising sensitive issues. Given the economic imbalance between countries in East Asia, it is hard to see how peer review can produce effective surveillance. How, for example, can the region's small transition economies address the economic issues facing the region's big industrial economies? And how willing are the large countries of the region to be assessed by the smaller countries?

The case for enhanced regional economic policy dialogue in East Asia is powerful. East Asia is a rapidly growing, increasingly inter-connected economic region, with markets, institutions and regulatory systems of varying strength. Substantive and frank policy dialogue not only helps policymakers understand better their mutual dependence, but is a tool to articulate practical policy responses to the issues they face. It can provide ideas and help create a constituency for a particular policy or reform. Dialogue can also be a way to soothe bilateral tensions or sort out thinking on how developments elsewhere affect countries in the region and the region as a whole. Regional dialogue can be a forum to flesh out regional approaches and coalitions for wider global reform.

The aim in the region is to achieve something like the level of debate of Working Party 3 (WP-3), a policy dialogue forum of the 10 largest industrial countries, held under the auspices of the OECD (Ito and Narita, 2004). The history of WP-3 is instructive. It was set up in the early 1960s as a forum for the larger OECD countries to discuss monetary and balance of payments problems. In the early 1960s, for example, it was the forum in which the Europeans talked about the US balance of payments deficit and the United States talked about the underdevelopment of European capital markets.[48]

From the start, WP-3 was also a forum in which the largest industrialized countries discussed international financing arrangements, including terms and conditions for access to IMF funds and establishing the General Arrangements to Borrow (GAB). To quote Solomon, WP-3 "and the deputies of the Group of Ten would play an important role in the decisions whether or not to lend to the Fund and how to apportion any loan among participants. In deciding whether or not to lend to the Fund they would, in most cases, also be determining whether the Fund would be in a position to lend to any country in need of financing."[49] Not surprisingly, "[s]ome other members of the Fund found this arrangement less than pleasing."[50]

There are three points from this. Surveillance and policy dialogue in the WP-3 was, and is, substantive and frank. From the start, industrial-country surveillance was tied to industrial-country crisis lending arrangements. And from the start, industrial country surveillance was outside the IMF—even if it also involved the IMF Chief Economist as chair of the meeting. Indeed, at the IMF Executive Board discussion on this matter, the Dutch Director described the [GAB] agreement as a "compromise between the ideology of the Fund as a global monetary institution and a newer ideology which sought solutions through closer cooperation between the main industrial countries."[51]

Financing

It is appropriate, at this point, to turn to thinking about possible principles for determining financial arrangements in a regional fund. As discussed earlier, East Asia already has a regional mechanism for financial cooperation, the CMI. The issues that arise with respect to review of the CMI are attachment to IMF conditionality, the sufficiency of the amounts available to individual countries, and whether the bilateral arrangements should be multilateralized in some form. They also appear in the debate about a possible AMF.

The need for regional financing is well-accepted. The IMF's financial resources have always been limited and the need for "outer perimeter defences" has been recognized for over 40 years since the creation of the GAB in 1961.[52] As expressed in the above quote by the Dutch Director of the IMF on the GAB, it has long been recognized by the major powers that cooperation outside the IMF can be consistent with the IMF. This has resonance in East Asia. In the 1997–98 financial crisis, especially for Thailand, countries in the region were a, if not *the*, major source of funds. While supplementary funding is available through the GAB and NAB, triggering them depends on the agreement of regional outsiders and can take time.

And the general basis on which financing is provided is also well-accepted. Funding is provided to support adjustment for countries experiencing short-term balance of payments difficulties. This has always been the basis for IMF funding. In their monograph advocating an Asian Monetary Fund, Bergsten and Park (2002) carefully use the same language in relation to a regional fund. This is intentional, and highlights the fact that the purpose of a regional institution is managing the external dimensions of financial crises, and not general lending or transfering funds between countries or supporting domestic financial institutions—although that still remains open at the bilateral level.

The debate is not on the need for supplementary funding for balance of payments difficulties, but rather the arrangements under which it is provided. This paper does not focus on technical issues such as limits to access, triggers for funding, rules for disbursement, reporting arrangements and transparency, and the role of countries outside ASEAN+3 in an East Asian fund. These are clearly important but might be thought of as details to be worked out if there is agreement to set up a regional fund.[53] Rather, the focus is on the basic prerequisites for a well-functioning regional fund. In this respect there are three core issues to examine: surveillance and conditionality, enforcement mechanisms, and the relationship between a regional entity and the IMF.

The need for surveillance has already been discussed. But the institutional framework in which it is delivered has not. Objective and high-quality economic analysis is needed if a lending agency is to reduce the likelihood of instability. The difficulty, as Eichengreen argues, is to ensure that "staff... have the independence and insulation from internal pressures to call a spade a spade."[54] One way to resist the many pressures to compromise assessments and advice would be to locate the surveillance function in an economic office independent of those who make the decision to lend. I will return to the organizational aspect of this later. It is also essential to have high quality analysis. This means it is necessary to staff the economic office with highly qualified and experienced economists from the region and beyond.

Regional financing arrangements require appropriate terms and conditions. This is met in the CMI by a detailed contract, signed by both parties to the bilateral swap agreement, and setting out the mechanics for using the facility and the requirement for IMF conditionality (either actual or expected in good faith). The region might decide to continue relying on IMF conditionality if it set up a regional fund. In this case, setting up a regional fund would simply be a device to formalize "Friends of Thailand"-type financial cooperation. Indeed, Bergsten and Park do not seem to envisage independent conditionality, arguing that "a regional financial arrangement could rely on the IMF for designing and enforcing policy conditionality to be imposed on borrowing countries."[55]

The region might decide to substantially ease or remove the attachment to IMF conditionality. This would then require it to set out its own economic and structural conditions for the putative borrower to access the region's funds. As is widely appreciated in East Asia, failing to do so could create substantial moral hazard. This would require careful analysis beforehand of what conditionality is necessary in dealing with a crisis. Is it restricted to monetary and fiscal policy settings? Or does it also extend to particular financial and structural policies and, if so, which ones?

The prospect of independent conditionality in a regional fund invariably leads to the raising of issues such as crisis-management arbitrage (the "race to the bottom" to "lowest common denominator conditionality"), the loss of reputation and credibility of a new institution, and the risk of inconsistent monitoring (Tirole, 2002). These are serious issues. But they are also ones of which East Asian policymakers are aware. Creditor countries in East Asia have no desire to waste public resources.[56] It really is not possible to say *ex ante* that conditionality set by a regional body would be weaker than that provided by the IMF, or that a regional body would be less credible than the IMF. It depends on perceptions about the quality of economic analysis, policy debate, and incentives in the region.[57] Again, the credibility of a regional fund depends on the strength of its surveillance and independence of its assessment and advice. This is why a primary focus in financial cooperation in East Asia in recent years has been on improving policy dialogue.

There is an associated issue of the enforcement of terms and conditions. It is one thing to have appropriate terms and conditions set out in lending documents. It is another to enforce them in a crisis under intense internal and external political and commercial pressure. Again, this is not just a potential problem for a regional fund. It is also a problem for the IMF, as recent experience shows. This is complicated further by the need to retain flexibility in selecting and enforcing conditionality as the economic and political situation progresses, again, as the evolution of Letters of Intent in IMF-managed crises shows. The attraction for creditor countries of the CMI arrangements as they currently stand is that they effectively delegate enforcement to the IMF. This way, the IMF suffers the opprobrium and lender countries do not directly expose their bilateral relationship with borrower countries to the pressures unleashed by enforcing the terms and conditions on lending.

There are mechanisms that strengthen incentives on lenders to enforce conditions on borrowing. One is to use the head of the regional body or institution as the interface with the borrowing country. In this case, appointing an influential, powerful, respected, and impartial person as leader is essential. The regional institution could subject itself to scrutiny through, for example, the publication of the independent analysis of its economic office, the creation of an independent office of review, or the use of the IMF or its Independent Evaluation Office as an agent for performance assessment.[58] Public scrutiny, through independent media and financial markets, can also exert a powerful discipline for ensuring that lending conditions are being met. Ultimately, if countries are not willing to enforce conditionality, then an AMF would likely increase the risk and severity of crises in the region.

The final issue on regional financial cooperation is the relationship of a putative regional body with other international financial institutions. The significant other is the IMF.[59] If an AMF is purely an associated financing agency of the IMF, then the question of space between institutions does not arise. If an AMF has substantial independent financing capacity, then the crucial issue is avoiding gaps in the management of financial crises.

Parkinson et al. (2004) explain this risk in more detail. The gist is that if a regional entity starts as the lead manager of a financial crisis in the region, there has to be an effective mechanism to pass management of the crisis to the global crisis manager if the crisis becomes unmanageable at the regional level, say, because it extends to many other countries in the region or spreads beyond the region. This means that a regional institution, even if it is independent, must be compatible with, complementary to, and underpin global mechanisms.

Even if a regional fund is independent of the IMF, there have to be effective and strong links between the two institutions. These links must be formalized, for example, by requiring regular meetings to discuss recent developments and issues, extensive staff exchange and interaction, and perhaps even involving each institution in discussions on possible lending. The WP-3 has always been closely connected to the IMF even if it is independent of it. However, the links must also be informal, with close and respectful working relationships. It is important in this case to avoid the damaging aspects of competition that emerge at times between other regional and global institutions, such as the development banks. One way to secure mutual respect is for the regional institution to develop and show particular expertise in the analysis of East Asian economies and systems, and for the IMF to listen to the insights about East Asia from the regional entity.

Exchange rate management

The third set of functions that are discussed in East Asia as a possible responsibility of an AMF is reserves and exchange rate management (Bergsten and Park, 2002). If the region were to decide to pursue a cooperative exchange rate arrangement, such as targeting a synthetic Asian currency unit or basket peg, then it would need a process to organize and coordinate exchange rate management. This paper does not canvas the arguments for and against coordinated exchange rate arrangements in East Asia.[60] At this stage, there is little support for intermediate cooperative exchange rate arrangements, although there is a broader ambition for currency and monetary union in East Asia, at least in parts of it, in the long run.

The implications of the debate on regional exchange rate arrangements for a possible AMF are twofold. Ultimately, ongoing deep cooperative exchange rate arrangements require some institutional backing, especially if they are an interim step to currency union. While the BIS could perform some of these functions, it is not owned by the region. And while the ADB would like to perform this function, doing so would appear to exceed its charter. An AMF might be the right institution, if the region were to pursue cooperative exchange rate arrangements.

The second is to ensure clarity in the functions of a regional institution. The function of exchange rate coordination (and implicitly reserves management) is distinct from the function of crisis prevention and management, although, of course, the selection of exchange rate regimes can matter for susceptibility to a financial crisis. This distinction would have to be embedded in the design and structure of the institution. If the region went this route, funds for dealing with financial crises would have to be separate from funds to support exchange rate parities.

There should also be some independence of the sets of countries which would participate in each of these two activities of the regional fund.

Participating in the financial cooperation function of an AMF should not necessarily imply participation in the exchange rate coordination function.

Possible organizational structure of an AMF

The other basic design feature of a putative regional fund is its organizational structure. The rather long and complex question posed here is: given a) the current state of communications and travel technology, b) our experience with the behavior of institutions and the importance of governance, and c) the general preferences of the region for bureaucratic simplicity and political control, what sort of organizational and governance structure would best deliver an effective institution for regional stability?

There are three guiding principles in thinking about organizational structure. The organization should be:

- able to make decisions sufficiently quickly; crises evolve quickly, so it is important to have a structure which enables decision-makers to confer and act quickly;

- directly representative of regional interests; the various national interests within the region should be reflected in the assessment and decision-making of the institution in a balanced manner;

- simple and streamlined; the decision-making process should be as simple as possible, and not be overburdened by excessive and costly bureaucracy.

What do these principles mean in practice for the design of a possible AMF? One way to assess this is to look at existing institutional models. There are two models that stand out. The first is the (Harry Dexter White) IMF model of an institution with a large independent bureaucracy which provides independent expert analysis of the issues, makes recommendations and decisions overseen by an on-site body representing the owners of the institution.

The second is the Bank for International Settlements (BIS)-type model or quasi Keynes-IMF model of an institution which provides independent expert analysis of the issues and secretariat support, but leaves actual decision-making to a group of senior officials from the core national institutions concerned, (in the BIS case, central banks). In the case of a regional fund, the decision-making body would be a meeting of finance deputies from the member countries, advised by a regional fund secretariat.

This is a quasi-Keynesian model, because while Keynes wanted decisions of the IMF to be made by national officials, he wanted those decisions to be based on technical rather than political grounds. As argued below, this is probably not feasible. Keynes argued that the governing body of the IMF should be "made up of high national officials (Treasury ministers or their deputies), who would travel to headquarters periodically to take key decisions, rather than a standing executive board that would meet in continuous session."[61]

The choice of model can be informed by the principles outlined above (which in turn embed the preferences of policy-makers in the region). The arguments probably stack up in favor of a BIS-type model. There are three steps to reaching this assessment.

The decision to provide lending in a crisis is one that must be made at the political level because, at its core, it involves national judgments about international economic and strategic relationships and possible fiscal commitments.[62] High-quality technical advice is necessary to inform the decision, but the decision is not ultimately just a technocratic one. This means that national governments in the region should retain control of the decision-making process.

National governments can make these decisions directly. They need not make them indirectly by passing responsibility to officials in an institution or to a board that is specially constituted to make decisions for them.

This eliminates the possibility of decisions being made by management with which the majority of governments, in fact, do not agree.[63]

National governments can make these decisions directly through meetings of deputies for finance ministers. Senior officials from the region can easily meet in person or by using tele/video-conference facilities. Regional proximity and the high quality of contemporary transport and telecommunications technology mean that officials can meet to decide issues among themselves without proxies. This is different from the situation that existed 60 years ago when the Bretton Woods institutions were established.

In making their decisions, the governing body of an AMF would also need specialized advice. While finance ministers and their ministry and central bank officials will have considered views on these matters, it is also important to have a vehicle which can develop expertise in surveillance and crisis analysis, as well as bring national views together and provide independent critical analysis. To this end, an independent management, with an economic office to provide analysis and a forum for debate and decision-making is essential, even if it does not have voting power itself. Having an independent advisory body might also provide decision-makers with a mechanism to shelter them, at least to some extent, from the pressures to compromise decision-making in the heat of a crisis.

In the final analysis, regional preferences would seem to dictate that a regional fund in East Asia should keep bureaucracy to a minimum. It should have a decision-making process which is as simple as possible, and which makes finance ministers (in the person of their deputies) the core decision-makers. But if the decision-making body comprises officials from the national level, the advice given to it should be regionally focused and as independent as possible. One way to guarantee the necessary distance between the provision of expert analysis and surveillance and the application of that advice is to ensure that the management of a regional fund and its office of economic analysis are independent.

There are two additional issues of importance to East Asia. One is voice. Given the region's concerns with the dominance in the IMF of its biggest shareholder, it is likely that the region will, in turn, be sensitive to dominance of a regional fund by the large countries of East Asia. There are a number of ways to deal with this. One would be to allow all East Asian countries which are members of the regional fund to participate in decision-making. Countries would not be required to participate, but would always have the option to do so.[64] Another way would be to expand membership of the regional fund to countries in the wider East Asian region or even beyond it. Each country could also be given one vote. The alternative of voting on the basis of country size or financial contribution would mean that the institution would be dominated by Japan and perhaps China.

The other issue is that setting up a formal regional fund requires bricks and mortar. This means choosing a location. This is a vexing question in East Asia, even now, as the region considers the merits of setting up a secretariat for ASEAN+3. In their discussion of an ASEAN+3 secretariat, de Brouwer and Ito set out three guiding principles for the selection of a location.[65] These might also be applied to thinking about a site for a possible AMF. The first principle is that it not be seen to be "owned" by a big country (the "Brussels solution"). They argue that this effectively rules out China, Indonesia, and

Japan. The second is that it must balance the broad regional interests of East Asia (particularly of the North and South) and not exacerbate intra-regional rivalry, especially in Southeast Asia. The third is that it must be situated in a relatively well developed economy which can provide infrastructure and stability to the region. No location is perfect but, on these grounds (and, as they say, at the risk of alienating everyone else), they argue that Seoul or Bangkok would appear to be the strongest candidates. Whatever the case, meetings need not be restricted to the location of the bricks-and-mortar institution, but could be held in all member countries at some stage.

Conclusion

A regional financial architecture has begun to emerge in East Asia. It has many dimensions, spanning improved policy dialogue and surveillance, the development and integration of financial markets and systems, financial cooperation, and cooperative exchange rate arrangements. One aspect of regional financial arrangements that comes up in discussion from time to time is a regional fund or an Asian Monetary Fund (AMF).

The aim of such an institution, if it were to be set up, would be to enhance regional financial stability. In this paper I have focused on the practical means of structuring the responsibilities of such an institution and on how it should be organized, in order to ensure that its incentives are consistent with its aims and responsibilities. I do not presume that an AMF will be set up. And I do not argue the merits or otherwise of an AMF. Ultimately, judgment on an AMF rests on the specific proposals made by policy-makers.

There is much greater awareness now, in both official and academic circles, of the importance of getting the design of institutions right. If new institutions are to be set up, it is important that they end up doing what they were intended to do. As the literature on institutional design points out, there is a risk that any new institution may, under unforeseen pressures and circumstances, not deliver on its promise. To reduce this risk, careful thought must be given to devising mechanisms and structures which are consistent with the aims and incentives of the institution and shareholders' preferences. This applies to a possible AMF, as indeed it does for any institution.

Likely responsibilities of a regional institution such as an AMF would cover economic policy dialogue, surveillance, and external financial support in a balance of payments crisis. It may also include managing cooperative exchange rate arrangements for some members. A necessary precondition for effective crisis management is substantive and frank policy dialogue and surveillance; in this respect, the region should aim for policy interaction of the quality of Working Party 3 of the OECD.

The region is a major shareholder in the IMF and that institution remains essential to regional and global stability. If East Asia were to set up a regional fund, it would have to ensure that the objectives and operation of its two institutions were consistent, and I have made practical suggestions how to do this. As owners of both Funds, regional policymakers might choose either to apply IMF conditionality in the regional fund, or to manage localized balance-of-payments crises and apply conditionality independently. In the latter case, they would have to ensure that regional mechanisms to identify and enforce conditionality were in place. Whatever the case, smooth crisis management would require close coordination and consultation between the two institutions.

A regional institution could be organized in a number of different ways. It could be an independent bureaucracy with a resident governing board. Or it could be a secretariat which provides expert advice on an independent basis, with the final judgment being made by finance ministry deputies acting under direction from their ministers. The latter model is more likely to fit with the preferences of regional policymakers for quick decision-making, minimal bureaucracy, and political control. But securing credibility and making these decisions enforceable would require that finance deputies be advised by an independent and highly reputable body within the institution. The reputation of a regional institution depends not only on getting the substance of its responsibilities and organizational structure right, but also on the perceived quality, expertise, and independence of its staff and management.

I have argued in this paper that the route taken by East Asia—and perhaps Asia more generally—in developing a regional financial architecture depends on how it is engaged with, and involved in, the debate about the global financial architecture. East Asia participates in a range of international policy forums and is itself a major shareholder in the IMF. It is incumbent on the region to actively exercise its ownership responsibilities in these forums and institutions. But it is also necessary for other regions, especially North America and Europe, to engage constructively with East Asia as a partner in debates about reform. And it is also necessary for the IMF to engage more directly with the region. The more exclusive other regions are, the less likely

East Asia will be to see itself as a stakeholder in the global architecture and the more insular will be the route that it may be inclined to take.

NOTES

1 This paper is based on the presentation made to the Conference, "Sixty Years After Bretton Woods: Developing a Vision for the Future," held in Rome, 22-23 July 2004, and organized by the Reinventing Bretton Woods Committee, the World Economic Forum, and the Ministry of Economy and Finance of Italy. The author is grateful for comments from Roger Brake, Guy Debelle, Stephen Grenville, David Gruen, Randy Henning, Adam McKissack, Janine Murphy, and Martin Parkinson, and for research assistance from Scott Mitchell and Jenny Chang. The views expressed in this paper are those of the author and should not be represented as the views of the Australian Treasury, the Australian Government, or the Australian National University.

2 See, for example, Asian Development Bank (2004a, and 2004b), de Brouwer and Wang (2004), and de Brouwer and Kawai (2004).

3 For want of a better term, a possible regional fund is called an Asian Monetary Fund in this paper. De Brouwer and Ito (2003) call it, alternatively, an Asian Financial Stabilisation Fund. In the 1944 discussions for what became known as the International Monetary Fund, the institution was initially called the International Stabilization Fund by the Americans (Skidelsky 2000, p. 325).

4 The funds committed to Thailand by economies in the region were provided to the Bank of Thailand through baht-US dollar denominated swaps by participating EMEAP central banks. EMEAP central banks include the monetary authorities of Australia, China, Indonesia, Hong Kong SAR, Malaysia, Japan, New Zealand, the Philippines, Singapore, South Korea, and Thailand. The Philippines attended the meeting (and so was part of the "Friends of Thailand" group) but was not in a position to commit funds. Japan committed US$4 billion, Australia, China, Hong Kong SAR, Malaysia, and Singapore each committed US$1 billion, and Brunei, Indonesia and South Korea each committed US$0.5 billion, for a total of US$10.5 billion from the region. The IMF provided US$4 billion, the World Bank US$1.5 billion, and the Asian Development Bank (ADB) US$1.2 billion. The total package was US$17.1 billion. A summary of international financing packages for Mexico, Thailand, Indonesia and South Korea is provided on page 6 of the website of the Reserve Bank of Australia, available at: http://www.rba.gov.au/ PublicationsAndResearch/Bulletin/bu_may98/bu_0598_2.pdf.

5 The Association of South East Asian Nations (ASEAN) swap arrangement, established in August 1977, predates the East Asian financial crisis. Under this arrangement, the five original ASEAN members agreed to provide up to US$40 million to other members. It has been used four times but was not used in the 1997-98 crisis.

6 It was also opposed by the European Union, Hong Kong SAR, Australia, Canada, and New Zealand. Hamanaka (2003) argues that China's opposition might be explained less by "strategic competition" with Japan than by then President Jiang Zemin's forthcoming visit to the United States and China's negotiations with the United States about China's entry into the WTO and its quota with the IMF.

7 ASEAN+3 includes China, Japan, and South Korea.

8 See the web page, http://www.mof.go.jp/english/if/CMI_060504.pdf (4 May 2006), on the Japanese Ministry of Finance website (accessed 22 September 2006). This amount does not include bilateral swaps under the New Miyazawa Initiative (which includes a US$5 billion swap from Japan to Korea). The amount includes the ASEAN Swap Agreement (US$2 billion). The figure in the text takes account of the recent doubling of the China-Indonesia swap to US$4 billion.

9 See, for example, Henning (2002), Rajan and Siregar (2004), and Wang (2004). The ADB also provides information on the CMI: see http://aric.adb.org/default1.asp?handler=infocus&switch=73.

10 Initially, only 10 percent of the facility could be accessed without Fund conditionality but this share was raised by ASEAN+3 finance ministers on the margins of the 2006 ADB annual meetings in Hyderabad, India.

11 For estimates of some speculative positions in the East Asian financial crisis in 1998, see de Brouwer (2001). The overall notional packages, as mentioned above, were US$17 billion for Thailand, US$36 billion for Indonesia, and US$58 billion for South Korea.

12 Wang (2004) proposes an "Asian Arrangements to Borrow."

13 See Wang (2004), and Rajan and Siregar (2004).

14 This is *not* to say that the region is immune from a financial crisis. To the extent that structural weaknesses exist, the region would still be exposed to the risk of a crisis. The enforcement of limits on non-resident access to the domestic foreign exchange swap markets and limited offshore markets in the domestic currency contain speculation by non-residents. But the possibility of speculation by residents and capital flight still remain; see de Brouwer (2001).

15 There is an ongoing debate about the sustainability of East Asia's accumulation of foreign exchange reserves. Dooley, Folkerts-Landau and Garber (2003) argue that the process can go indefinitely. Eichengreen (2004) and Park and Yoon (2004) provide persuasive rejoinders.

16 See Reserve Bank of Australia (2004).

17 See, for example, De Gregorio et al. (2000), the May 2003 American Economic Review Papers and Proceedings discussion on the IMF, Eichengreen (2003a and 2003b), Henry et al. (2003), Vines and Gilbert (2004), and Kenen et al. (2004).

18 See http://www.imf.org/external/np/exr/facts/groups.htm#G20 for a list of forums and their members. Because I am referring to East Asia and not Asia as a whole, I am including Australia but not India. India is a member of the G-20 and the IMFC.

19 Japan is represented by the Ministry of Finance, Bank of Japan and Financial Services Agency, Australia by the Reserve Bank of Australia, Hong Kong SAR by the Hong Kong Monetary Authority, and Singapore by the Monetary Authority of Singapore.

20 For two years from November 2004, South Korea will replace Australia on the IMFC because South Korea will lead the shared IMF constituency for that period.

21 See, for example, SaKong and Wang (2000) and Kim and Yang (2001).

22 See de Brouwer (2004a), p. 261. Based on GDP, Europe is over-represented by about 6 percent in IMF quotas, while the United States and Japan are under-represented by 12 and 9 percent. The Dutch, Saudi, and Belgian constituencies are the most over-represented in terms of IMF quotas.

23 The editorial in the Financial Times of 3-4 July 2004, marking the 60 year anniversary of the Bretton Woods conference, argues that "financial 'quotas' and voting power must be revised to give nations such as the emerging Asians clout in the fund that reflects their economic size." (p. 6).

24 These are Belgium, the Netherlands, Sweden, and Switzerland.

25 For example, it has nine European country members, compared to five from Asia (and four from East Asia), five from the Americas, three from Africa , and two from the Middle East.

26 See Kenen et al. (2004), p. 43. The examples they use are the G-20, FSF, and Basel 2 processes.

27 Ibid., pages 94 and 98.

28 Ibid., page 99.

29 Ibid., pages 105-6.

30 The authors are eminent North Americans and Europeans and the text contains little reference to the issues or literature from East Asia. Contrast this, for example, to the geographic balance in the monograph on IMF reform by De Gregorio et al. (2000).

31 Its members were the G-7, as well as Argentina, Australia, Brazil, China, Hong Kong SAR, India, Indonesia, Malaysia, Mexico, Poland, Russia, Singapore, South Africa, South Korea, and Thailand.

32 The three working group reports are available on the websites of the IMF, World Bank, BIS and OECD.

33 Goodin (1996), p. 23.

34 North (1990), p. 107.

35 Ibid, p. 135. See also Brennan (1996).

36 George Soros calls this "reflexivity."

37 North (1990), p. 83.

38 Ibid, p. 3.

39 Kenen et al.. (2004) present an interesting commentary on the waves of policy dialogue and cooperation in the post-war period.

40 See North (1990), p. 48.

41 While the region has some frustration with US veto power in the IMF, the United States is not the only shareholder with veto power. Coalitions in excess of 15 percent of voting rights have formed at times in the IMF and have exercised veto. It is also open to European and East Asian constituencies forming coalitions to do likewise.

42 See, for example, Corsetti et al. (2000) for a model which associates higher reserves with better economic fundamentals.

43 The speculative short positions of the macro hedge funds in the Asian financial crisis, for example, were larger, prompting the greater willingness of the authorities to defend what the macro hedge funds judged to be an indefensible exchange rate. The short positions on the baht in 1997, for example, were larger than those on other regional currencies (apart from the yen) in either 1997 or 1998 (de Brouwer, 2001). These select hedge funds faced no constraint in borrowing from banks and other financial institutions, giving them greater freedom to increase their short positions as they wanted. In some instances, increasing the amount of funds to defend a particular financial price may just have raised the stakes in the speculative game and not have prevented the crisis. The counter-factual is unknowable.

44 The discussion here does not take up the issue of technical assistance. Technical assistance already exists at the bilateral, regional and global level.

45 This is true for regional and global surveillance. The IMF biennial reviews of surveillance and reports of the IMF Independent Evaluation Office are an indication of how seriously this is taken.

46 See, for example, Bergston and Park (2002), Wang and Yoon (2002), Grenville (2004), Kuroda and Kawai (2004), de Brouwer and Wang (2004).

47 Suggestions are made, for example, by Wang and Yoon (2002), Balls (2003), and de Brouwer and Wang (2004).

48 Solomon, 1982, p. 42.

49 Ibid., p. 43.

50 Ibid., p. 44. To continue the quote: "[T]he Australian Director spoke of a 'very exclusive club' and the Indian Director feared that the Fund Board might find itself obliged to concur in decisions taken elsewhere."

51 Ibid.

52 Solomon (1982, pp. 42-3) attributes this term to Robert V. Roosa, US Under-Secretary of the Treasury for Monetary Affairs in the late 1950s.

53 And some of these issues are still ongoing ones for the IMF. See the discussion in Eichengreen (2003a and 2003b).

54 Eichengreen, 2003b, p. 29. See also Balls (2003) for a discussion of these issues with respect to the IMF.

55 Bergsten and Park, 2002, p. 17.

56 Japan, for example, declined informal requests from Thailand and South Korea for bilateral funding to supplement their foreign exchange reserves in 1997 (de Brouwer, 2004a).

57 See de Brouwer (2004a, p. 272-7) for a more detailed exposition.

58 The creation of an independent office of review is unappealing, since it would be both expensive and create more bureaucracy than the region probably wants.

59 See Henning (2002), pp. 68-74, 77-84, and 93-5 for a discussion on East Asian regional financial cooperation and the IMF.

60 There are now many papers on this subject. See, for example, the references in Bergsten and Park (2002), de Brouwer (2002), and de Brouwer and Kawai (2004).

61 Eichengreen (2003), p. 5. In order to minimize the likelihood of the Fund being captured by its local host, Keynes also proposed that the institution not be based in Washington, D.C. See also Skidelsky (2000), pp. 345-6 and 465-7.

62 Fischer (2003) makes a similar argument.

63 This is somewhat controversial. Reflecting on his experience as First Deputy Managing Director, Fischer (2003) argues that management of the Fund cannot make decisions without the support of the Executive Board. This may be right in general, but it is not so in all cases. The Executive Board is sometimes brought late into the decision-making process, after senior management has already announced to the press that agreement on a package to a particular country has

been reached or is imminent. A case in point was the 1998 package for Russia, when the Executive Board felt it had no choice but to support management, even though a number of Board members had serious reservations about the package.

64 This is different from the proposal of Kim et al. (2000), to the effect that the decision-making body comprise officials from China, Japan, South Korea, and three other member countries on a rotating basis. Their proposal is unlikely to give sufficient voice to the mid-sized and smaller countries of the region.

65 De Brouwer and Ito (2003), p. 8.

REFERENCES

Acemoglu, D., S. Johnson and J. Robinson. 2004. "Institutions as the Fundamental Cause of Long-Run Growth." NBER Working Paper No. 10481.

Asian Development Bank. 2004a. *Monetary and Financial Integration in East Asia, Volume 1*. Hampshire and New York: Palgrave Macmillan.

———. 2004b. *Monetary and Financial Integration in East Asia, Volume 2*. Hampshire and New York: Palgrave Macmillan.

Balls, E. 2003. "Preventing Financial Crises: The Case for Independent IMF Surveillance." Remarks made at the Institute for International Economics, Washington, D.C., 6 March. Available at: http://www.iie.com/publications/papers/balls0303.htm

Bergsten, C.F. and Y.C. Park. 2002. "Towards Creating a Regional Monetary Arrangement in East Asia." ADB Institute Research Paper No. 50. December.

Brennan, G. 1996. "Selection and the Currency of Reward." Chapter 10 in Robert E. Goodin, ed. *The Theory of Institutional Design*. Cambridge: Cambridge University Press. 256–75.

Caballero, R. J. and M. L. Hammour. 2000. "Institutions, Restructuring, and Macroeconomic Performance." NBER Working Papers No. 7720.

Corsetti, G., A. Dasgupta, S. Morris, and H. S. Shin. 2000. "Does One Soros Make A Difference? The Role of a Large Trader in Currency Crises." Cowles Foundation Discussion Paper No. 1273. New Haven, CT: Yale University.

de Brouwer, G. J. 2001. *Hedge Funds in Emerging Markets*. Cambridge: Cambridge University Press.

———. ed. 2002. *Financial Markets and Policies in East Asia*, London: Routledge.

———. 2004a. "East Asia and the IMF." David Vines and Christopher L. Gilbert, eds. *The IMF and Its Critics: Reform of the Global Financial Architecture*. Cambridge: Cambridge University Press. 254–87.

————. 2004b. "IMF and ADB Perspectives on Regional Surveillance in East Asia." G. de Brouwer and Y. Wang, eds. *Financial Governance in East Asia: Policy Dialogue, Surveillance and Cooperation.* London: RoutledgeCurzon. 38–49.

de Brouwer, G. J and T. Ito. 2003. "Financial, Monetary and Economic Cooperation in East Asia: Where We Are, Where We Want to Be, and How To Get There From Here. Paper presented at the PECC Finance Forum Meeting at Hua Hin Thailand, 8–9 July. Available at: http://apseg.anu.edu.au/staff/gdebrouwer.php

de Brouwer, G. J and Y. Wang. 2004. "Policy Dialogue, Surveillance and Financial Cooperation." Chapter 1 in G. de Brouwer and Y. Wang, eds. *Financial Governance in East Asia: Policy Dialogue, Surveillance, and Financial Cooperation.* London: RoutledgeCurzon. 1–15.

de Brouwer, G. J. and M. Kawai, eds. 2004. *Exchange Rate Regimes in East Asia.* London: RoutledgeCurzon.

De Gregorio, J., B. Eichengreen, T. Ito, and C. Wyplosz. 2000. *An Independent and Accountable IMF.* London: CEPR.

Dooley, M., D. Folkerts-Landau, and P. Garber. 2003. "An Essay on the Revived Bretton Woods System." NBER Working Paper No. 9971.

Eichengreen, B. 2003a. "Strengthening the International Financial Architecture." Dilip K. Das, ed. *An International Finance Reader.* London: Routledge. 65–86.

————. 2003b. "Governing the IMF." Paper prepared for the conference on Governing the Global Economy. Washington University, St Louis. November 2003. University of California, Berkeley. Mimeo.

————. 2004. "Global Imbalances and the Lesson of Bretton Woods." NBER Working Paper No. 10497.

Fischer, S. 2003. "The Future of the IMF and World Bank: Panel Discussion." *American Economic Review Papers and Proceedings* 93(2):45–46. May.

Goodin, R.E. ed. 1996. *The Theory of Institutional Design.* Cambridge: Cambridge University Press.

————. 1996. "Institutions and Their Design." Chapter 1 in R. E. Goodin, ed. *The Theory of Institutional Design.* Cambridge: Cambridge University Press. 1–53.

Grenville, S.A. 2004. "Policy Dialogue in East Asia: Principles for Success." Chapter 2 in G. de Brouwer and Y. Wang, eds. *Financial Governance in East Asia: Policy Dialogue, Surveillance, and Financial Cooperation.* London: RoutledgeCurzon. 16–37.

Hall, R. E. and C. I. Jones. 1999. "Why Do Some Countries Produce So Much More Output Per Worker Than Others?" *Quarterly Journal of Economics* 114:83–116.

Hamanaka, S. 2003. "Future Prospects for an Asian Monetary Fund: Lessons from Japan's Unsuccessful AMF Proposal in 1997." Mimeo.

Henning, C. R. 2002. "East Asian Financial Cooperation After Chiang Mai." *Policy Analyses in International Economics*, No. 68. Washington, D.C.: Institute for International Economics. September.

Henry, K., A. McKissack, M. Parkinson, A. Peterson, and K. Taylor. 2003. "Australia and the International Financial Architecture(60 years on." *Sir Leslie Melville Lecture*, 16 July 2003. Treasury Roundup, Spring, (accessed 8 July 2004. Available at: http://www.treasury.gov.au/documents/710/PDF/Australia_IFA.pdf

Independent Evaluation Office. 2003a. *Annual Report 2003*. Independent Evaluation Office of the International Monetary Fund. Washington, D.C.: IMF.

———. 2003b. *The IMF and Recent Capital Account Crises: Indonesia, Korea, Brazil.* Independent Evaluation Office of the International Monetary Fund. Washington, D.C.: IMF.

Institute of Southeast Asian Studies (ISEAS). 2003. *Concept Paper on the ASEAN Economic Community.* Singapore: ISEAS. 26 February. Mimeo.

International Monetary Fund. International Financial Statistics.

Ito, T. and K. Narita. 2004. "A Stocktake of Institutions for Financial Cooperation." Chapter 6 in G. J. de Brouwer and Y. Wang, eds. *Financial Governance in East Asia.* London: RoutledgeCurzon.

Kenen, P. B., J. R. Shafer, N. L. Wicks, and C. Wyplosz. 2004. "International Economic and Financial Cooperatron: New Issues, New Actors, New Responses." Centre for Economic Policy Research. April. Mimeo.

Kim, T. J, J. W. Ryou, and Y. Wang. 2000. "Regional Arrangements to Borrow: A Scheme for Preventing Future Asian Liquidity Crises." *Policy Analysis* 00–01. Korea Institute for International Economic Policy.

Kim, T. J. and D. Y. Yang, eds. 2001. *New International Financial Architecture and Korean Perspectives.* Seoul: Korea Institute for International Economic Policy.

Kuroda, H. and M. Kawai. 2004. "Strengthening Regional Financial Cooperation in East Asia." Chapter 7 in G. de Brouwer and Y. Wang, eds. *Financial Governance in East Asia: Policy Dialogue, Surveillance, and Financial Cooperation.* London: RoutledgeCurzon. 136–66.

March, J. G. and J. P. Olsen. 1984. "The New Institutionalism: Organizational Factors in Political Life." *American Political Science Review* 78:734–49.

North, D. 1990. *Institutions, Institutional Change, and Economic Performance.* New York: Cambridge University Press.

Park, Y. C. and D. R. Yoon. 2004. "The Transpacific Imbalance: What Can Be Done About It?" Paper presented at the Third PECC Finance Forum Conference. Santiago, Chile. 20–21 June.

Parkinson, M., P. Garton, and I. Dickson. 2004. "The Role of Regional Financial Arrangements in the International Financial Architecture." Chapter 12 in G. de Brouwer and Y. Wang, eds. *Financial Governance in East Asia: Policy Dialogue, Surveillance, and Financial Cooperation*. London: RoutledgeCurzon. 263–86.

Rajan, R. S. and R. Siregar. 2004. "Private Capital Flows in East Asia: Boom, Bust and Beyond." Chapter 4 in G. de Brouwer, ed. *Financial Markets and Policies in East Asia*. London: Routledge. 47–81.

Reserve Bank of Australia. 2004. "Recent Developments in IMF Financing Activities." Reserve Bank of Australia Bulletin. June. 1–8.

Rutherford, M. 2001. "Institutional Economics: Then and Now." *Journal of Economic Perspectives* 15(3):173–94. Summer.

SaKong, I. and Y. Wang, eds. 2000. *Reforming the International Financial Architecture: Emerging Market Perspectives*. Seoul: Institute for Global Economics and Korea Institute for International Economic Policy.

Skidelsky, R. 2000. *John Maynard Keynes, Volume 3. Fighting for Britain 1937–1946*. London: Macmillan.

Solomon, R. 1982. *The International Monetary System 1945–1981*. New York: Harper Row.

Tirole, J. 2002. *Financial Crises, Liquidity, and the International Monetary System*. Princeton: Princeton University Press.

Vines, D. and C. Gilbert. 2004. *The IMF and Its Critics: Reform of the Global Financial Architecture*. Centre for Economic Policy Research. Cambridge: Cambridge University Press.

Wang, Y. and D. R. Yoon. 2002. "Searching for a Better Regional Surveillance Mechanism in East Asia." Korea Institute for International Economic Policy Discussion Paper No. 02–01.

Wang, Y. 2004. "Instruments and Techniques for Financial Cooperation." Chapter 9 in G. de Brouwer and Y. Wang, eds. *Financial Governance in East Asia: Policy Dialogue, Surveillance, and Financial Cooperation*. London: RoutledgeCurzon.

Wilson, J. Q. 1989. *Bureaucracy: What Government Agencies Do and Why They Do It*. New York: Basic Books.

CHAPTER 2.3

East Asian Economic Regionalism: Update[1]

MASAHIRO KAWAI, Special Advisor to the President, and Head, Office of Regional Economic Integration, Asian Development Bank

Introduction

O ver the last two decades, the East Asian economies have liberalized sub-stantially foreign trade and direct investment (FDI) regimes within the frameworks of GATT/WTO and Asia-Pacific Economic Cooperation (APEC). The resulting expansion of trade and FDI has become the engine of economic growth and development in East Asia. Since the early 1990s, many emerging East Asian economies have also liberalized their financial systems and capital accounts. The consequent financial openness has contributed to rapid economic growth by attracting both long-term and short-term capital and, together with trade and FDI openness, deepened market-driven economic interdependence in East Asia. But it added financial vulnerabilities, culminating in the form of a financial crisis in 1997–98.

Following the crisis, the East Asian economies embarked on various ini-tiatives for economic regionalism in the areas of trade and investment, and money and finance. The crisis prompted the regional economies to realize the importance of economic cooperation among themselves and to make efforts to institutionalize the region's deepening economic interdependence. For example, Japan and Singapore implemented an economic partnership agree-ment (EPA); ASEAN-China and ASEAN-Korea each implemented a free trade agreement (FTA) on trade in goods, and many official discussions and negotiations for bilateral and sub-regional FTAs, such as Japan-Korea EPA, Japan-ASEAN EPA and India-ASEAN, are currently underway. In the financial area, the ASEAN+3 members, comprising ASEAN, China, Japan, and Korea, have begun to undertake initiatives for regional economic surveillance, currency swap arrangements (the Chiang Mai Initiative), and Asian bond market development.

In this paper, I first discuss the logic of recent economic regionalism in East Asia, and emphasize the importance of increasing economic interdependence among the regional economies and the lack of regional institutions and mechanisms that respond to such interdependence. It emphasizes the surprising extent to which the regional economies are integrated through trade, FDI, and finance and are interdependent in macroeconomic cycles.

Next, I discuss past and present economic cooperation initiatives in East Asia and analyze the issues and challenges for closer economic regionalism— or greater institutionalization of regional economic integration in East Asia— that can potentially lead to the creation of an East Asian economic community. I argue that deeper economic integration in trade, investment and finance and further institutionalization of such integration are mutually reinforcing. Trust building and political leadership are essential to transforming the current drive for economic regionalism into a much higher level of integration.

The logic of economic regionalism in East Asia

Deepening of economic interdependence

The fundamental rationale behind the emergence of recent economic regionalism is the deepening of regional economic interdependence in East Asia. Economic regionalism, through various types of policy coordination, can resolve the "collective action" problem by internalizing externalities and spillover effects that arise from interdependence.

The East Asian region has long enjoyed market-driven integration through trade and FDI, while embracing a multilateral liberalization framework under the GATT/WTO and, more recently, open regionalism through APEC. The region has avoided discriminatory trade practices. FDI flows to the East Asian economies, driven initially by Japanese multinational corporations after the Plaza Accord in the mid-1980s, have generated intra-industry trade within the region and have contributed to deeper economic integration. More recently, newly industrializing economies (NIEs) and some middle-income ASEAN countries have become active as investors, particularly in China, whose rise as a large trading nation has also strengthened trade (particularly intra-industry) linkages among the East Asian economies.

Trade integration. The degree of regional economic integration through trade in East Asia has been rising fast over the last 25 years. Table 1a summarizes changes in the share of intra-regional trade for various groupings in the world over the period 1980 to 2005. The table demonstrates that intra-regional trade as a share of East Asia's total trade has risen from 22 percent in 1980 to 45 percent in 2005 (excluding Japan) or from 35 percent to 55 percent over the same period (including Japan). Now almost 55 percent of East Asia's trade is with itself. Thus the intra-regional trade share in East Asia is still lower than that in the European Union-15 (60 percent), but exceeds that of the North American Free Trade Area (NAFTA) (45 percent) in 2005.

Table 1b summarizes changes in the intra-regional trade intensity indexes for the same groupings over the same period.[2] The table demonstrates that within East Asia, whether including Japan or not, the trade intensity index, at around 2.2, is higher than that for EU-15 (1.7), though it is lower than that for NAFTA (2.6) in 2005. This observation confirms that the degree of regional economic integration through trade in East Asia is quite high and comparable to levels seen in NAFTA or the EU. It must be emphasized that intra-East Asia trade has expanded rapidly, but not at the expense of extra-regional trade. This suggests that East Asia continues to maintain export competitiveness vis-à-vis countries outside the region.

FDI integration. Multinational firms from the major industrialized countries (the United States, Japan and the European Union) have traditionally been the main investors in emerging East Asia. In recent years, firms from the Asian NIEs, Singapore, Taiwan (China), Korea and Hong Kong SAR, have been active as foreign direct investors in ASEAN and China.[3] Furthermore, some middle-income ASEAN countries, such as Malaysia and Thailand, have started to invest in low-income ASEAN countries and China. Table 2 indicates that several emerging East Asian economies have accumulated sizable FDI assets abroad.

The traditional business activities of multinational corporations, together with the recent rise in emerging East Asian investment, have contributed to the integration of the East Asian economies through FDI and FDI-driven trade. Essentially, global and regional firms have established regional production networks and supply chains, through fragmentation of their production processes into different sub-processes, located in different countries for comparative advantage, such as relative factor proportions and technological capabilities. This strategy has stimulated vertical intra-industry trade in parts, components, semi-finished, and finished products across East Asia.[4] An important implication is that large inflows of FDI to emerging East Asia have

Table 1: Intra-regional trade shares and indexes

a. Intra-regional trade share[a] (%)

Regions	1980	1985	1990	1995	2000	2001	2002	2003	2004	2005
East Asia-15 including Japan[c]	34.6	37.1	43.0	51.7	51.9	51.5	53.4	54.5	55.1	54.5
Emerging East Asia-14[c]	22.1	27.5	32.8	39.0	40.4	40.7	43.0	43.7	44.1	44.7
NIEs-4	6.4	6.5	11.9	15.5	15.5	14.9	15.5	15.0	14.4	13.5
ASEAN-10[c]	17.9	20.3	18.8	23.9	24.5	23.9	24.3	23.8	23.8	24.0
NAFTA	33.8	38.7	37.9	43.1	48.8	49.1	48.4	47.3	46.4	45.0
MERCOSUR	11.1	7.2	10.9	19.2	20.3	17.9	13.6	14.7	15.2	15.0
EU-15	60.7	59.8	66.2	64.2	62.3	62.2	62.5	63.0	62.2	60.1
EU-25	61.3	59.8	67.0	67.4	66.8	67.2	67.8	68.6	68.0	66.2

b. Intra-regional trade intensity indexes[b]

Regions	1980	1985	1990	1995	2000	2001	2002	2003	2004	2005
East Asia-15 including Japan[c]	2.5	2.3	2.2	2.1	2.2	2.3	2.3	2.3	2.3	2.2
Emerging East Asia-14[c]	3.2	3.3	2.7	2.3	2.3	2.4	2.4	2.4	2.4	2.3
NIEs-4	1.9	1.5	1.5	1.5	1.6	1.7	1.7	1.7	1.6	1.5
ASEAN-10[c]	4.8	5.7	4.4	3.7	4.0	4.2	4.3	4.3	4.4	4.2
NAFTA	2.1	2.0	2.1	2.4	2.2	2.3	2.4	2.6	2.7	2.6
MERCOSUR	6.6	4.9	9.7	13.3	14.8	13.0	11.7	12.7	12.0	11.2
EU-15	1.5	1.6	1.5	1.7	1.7	1.7	1.7	1.7	1.7	1.7
EU-25	1.5	1.6	1.5	1.7	1.8	1.7	1.7	1.7	1.7	1.7

Notes:
a. The intra-regional trade share is defined as: $Xii/\{(Xi. + X.i)/2\}$ where Xii represents exports of region i to region i, $Xi.$ represents total exports of region i to the world, and $X.i$ represents total exports of the world to region i.
b. The trade intensity index is defined as: $[Xii/\{(Xi. + X.i)/2\}]/[\{(Xi. + X.i)/2\}/X.]$ where $X.$ represents total world exports.
c. East Asia-15 includes Emerging East Asia-14 and Japan. Emerging East Asia-14 includes four Asian NIEs [Hong Kong SAR, Korea, Singapore, and Taiwan (China)], nine ASEAN members (Brunei, Cambodia, Indonesia, Lao People's Democratic Republic, Malaysia, Myanmar, Philippines, Thailand, and Vietnam), and China. ASEAN-10 includes Singapore.
d. Computation is based on exporting economies' export data, except for Taiwan (China) in 1980 where importers' import data are used when necessary.

Source: Computed from IMF, Direction of Trade Statistics; CEIC database.

Table 2: Inward and outward FDI stock as a percentage of GDP, 1980–2005

Economy		1980	1985	1990	1995	2000	2001	2002	2003	2004	2005
Japan	Inward	0.3	0.3	0.3	0.6	1.1	1.2	2.0	2.1	2.1	2.2
	Outward	1.8	3.2	6.6	4.5	5.8	7.2	7.6	7.8	7.9	8.5
Korea	Inward	2.1	2.3	2.1	1.9	8.1	9.6	9.2	9.0	8.1	8.0
	Outward	0.2	0.5	0.9	2.1	5.8	6.8	6.5	6.5	5.8	4.6
China, PR of	Inward	0.4	2.0	5.4	14.4	17.9	17.5	17.1	16.2	14.9	14.3/
	Outward	—	0.3	1.2	2.5	2.6	3.0	2.9	2.6	2.4	2.1
Hong Kong	Inward	73.2	75.2	59.4	50.1	275.4	257.5	208.2	239.2	277.6	299.9
SAR	Outward	0.5	6.6	15.7	55.6	234.9	216.5	191.6	213.0	246.5	264.7
Taiwan	Inward	5.8	4.7	6.1	5.9	5.7	13.5	10.0	13.0	12.8	12.1
(China)	Outward	31.4	21.4	19.0	16.1	21.5	25.2	27.3	29.3	29.9	28.1
Singapore	Inward	52.9	73.6	82.6	78.2	123.1	143.1	157.3	160.2	150.2	158.6
	Outward	31.7	24.8	21.2	41.8	62.1	85.1	98.6	100.1	94.5	94.1
Brunei	Inward	0.4	0.8	1.1	12.4	89.8	106.0	127.0	161.0	135.9	145.2
	Outward	—	—	—	6.3	10.3	11.0	11.3	10.4	8.7	8.7
Malaysia	Inward	21.1	23.7	23.4	32.3	58.6	38.6	38.9	40.4	39.3	36.5
	Outward	0.8	4.4	6.1	12.4	23.6	9.5	10.7	11.4	11.7	34.0
Thailand	Inward	3.0	5.1	9.7	10.5	24.4	28.9	30.1	33.3	29.7	33.5
	Outward	0.0	0.0	0.5	1.4	1.8	2.3	2.0	2.1	2.1	2.3
Philippines	Inward	3.9	8.5	7.4	8.2	16.9	14.5	15.3	15.2	14.9	14.4
	Outward	0.5	0.6	0.3	1.6	2.1	1.0	1.0	1.5	1.9	2.1
Indonesia	Inward	6.5	6.7	7.7	10.2	16.5	10.8	4.1	5.0	4.4	7.7
	Outward	0.0	0.1	0.1	2.9	4.6	***	***	***	—	5.0
Vietnam	Inward	32.9	24.8	25.5	34.5	65.7	69.9	73.7	71.8	66.3	61.2
	Outward	—	—	—	—	—	—	—	—	—	—
Cambodia	Inward	1.8	1.6	2.2	10.8	46.9	50.7	50.9	49.9	47.2	45.6
	Outward	—	—	—	4.2	5.7	6.2	6.2	6.2	5.8	4.8
Lao, PDR	Inward	0.3	0.0	1.5	11.9	32.1	33.1	33.1	30.6	26.6	24.5
	Outward	—	—	—	0.4	1.6	1.6	1.5	1.4	1.2	1.0
Myanmar	Inward	0.0	0.0	1.6	5.3	9.3	8.1	7.6	7.8	7.9	43.6
	Outward	—	—	—	—	—	—	—	—	—	—

Notes:
a. — indicates that data are not available or not separately reported.
b. *** indicates negative accumulation of flows.

Sources: UNCTAD, online database from 1980 to 2003; UNCTAD, 2005 (Annex table B.3) for 2004; UNCTAD, 2006 (Annex table B.3) for 2005.

stimulated the region's engagement with trade, in a way that reflects the individual economies' stages of industrial development. More recently China and Vietnam have begun to actively participate in such production networks.

Financial and macroeconomic interdependence. Market-driven financial integration has also been underway as a result of the increased deregulation of the financial system, opening of financial services to foreign institutions, and liberalization of the capital account in several East Asian economies. Commercial banks have extended cross-border loans to banks and corporations throughout the region, and these have contributed to a closely connected banking sector within East Asia. The opening of securities markets, particularly equity markets, has attracted foreign portfolio capital inflows. Active commercial bank loans and portfolio flows have linked the economies in the region financially, creating positive correlations of asset price movements within the region. At least part of the contagion of currency crises in the region in 1997 was a reflection of such financial linkages.

Macroeconomic interdependence within the region has recently become stronger, as evidenced by a simultaneous contraction of economic activity throughout East Asia in 1998 and a simultaneous expansion in 1999–2000. Though the regional economies may have been affected by some common global factors such as US economic cycles and information technology (IT) stock price movements, many of the recent, synchronized economic activities in the region can be attributed to strong macroeconomic interdependence.

In view of the rising trade and FDI integration in East Asia, there is a growing need for setting up more formal institutional mechanisms for trade and investment liberalization and facilitation, for harmonization of rules, standards and procedures, and for dispute settlements. Deepening macroeconomic and financial interdependence also suggests a need for concerted efforts to internalize externalities and spillover effects, because the macroeconomic and financial developments and policies of one country can easily affect performance and developments in another. Joint action among East Asian economies to internalize spillovers would be easier because they are small in number, characterized by low transactions cost for collective action, and tend to face similar shocks and similar policy challenges.

Response to economic regionalism in Europe and North America

The initiatives for economic regionalism represent the efforts of East Asian economies toward greater institutionalization of *de facto* economic integration

—particularly through trade and FDI. They have made these efforts essentially for three reasons:

- As a defensive response to the emergence of regional trade arrangements (RTAs) elsewhere—particularly in Europe and the Americas—and due to their dissatisfaction with slow progress on trade/investment liberalization at the global and trans-regional levels;

- Out of willingness to enhance productivity and international competitiveness through exploitation of economies of scale and dynamic efficiency;

- In order to promote deeper integration and institution-building at the regional level.

Economic regionalism elsewhere—including the formation of an economic and monetary union in Europe, expansion of the EU to the east as well, as the success of NAFTA and its move to the Free Trade Area of the Americas (FTAA) in North, Central, and South America—has motivated the East Asian economies to pursue regional trade arrangements. Governments in East Asia fear that unless they strengthen their own regional trade arrangements, they will be disadvantaged in global competition and multilateral negotiations. They have increasingly realized the importance of uniting in order to strengthen bargaining power vis-à-vis the European Union, the United States and other groupings. The slow progress on the WTO-Doha liberalization process and the perceived ineffectiveness of the APEC process have stoked these fears.

Policy-makers in East Asia are increasingly of the view that they must create a larger market within their own region so that economies of scale and dynamic efficiency can be exploited. They believe East Asia's RTAs can help raise both productivity and international competitiveness, by encouraging trade and investment liberalization and associated structural reforms at the national level and creating an expanded market at the regional level. In addition, these RTAs can facilitate trade and investment, promote harmonization of rule-making, standard-setting and procedures, and provide dispute resolution mechanisms, particularly in the areas of services, labor mobility, investment, competition policy, intellectual property rights, contingency protection, and rules of origin—areas in which it is difficult to make substantial progress in a multilateral framework (OECD, 2003). This effort is basically one of institution-building for further deepening of trade and investment integration.

Response to the financial crisis

There are several significant driving forces behind the recent move to closer economic regionalism in the money/finance area:

- Hard lessons learnt from the Asian financial crisis of 1997–98, and the need to establish regional self-help mechanisms for effective prevention, management and resolution of regional financial crises;

- Dissatisfaction with the existing global financial arrangement governed by the IMF;

- Need for regional financial stability as a basis for global financial stability as well as the region's willingness to increase the Asian voice in, and for, global financial management.

The Asian financial crisis taught the countries of the region that there is a clear need for effective prevention, management, and resolution of financial crises, and for the control of contagion. The global initiative for the new international financial architecture intended to strengthen the international financial system has been unsatisfactory and disappointing. National efforts to strengthen individual economic fundamentals, to reduce the likelihood of home-grown crises, and to increase domestic resilience to crises and contagion —particularly through the Reports on the Observance of Standards and Codes (ROSC)—take time to bear fruit. More importantly, the East Asian economies have been dissatisfied with the way the IMF handled the crisis, particularly in Thailand and Indonesia. Hence, the general sentiment in East Asia has been that the regional economies must establish their own, self-help mechanisms through systematic macroeconomic and financial cooperation for prevention and management of possible crises in the future. Such cooperation should include information exchange, policy dialogue, a regional liquidity support arrangement, and joint policymaking in certain critical areas, such as exchange rate policy coordination.

There have been some proactive responses to the crisis. Since regional financial stability is one basis for global financial stability, effective regional financial cooperation is an obvious benefit, not only for the region, but for the global community. In this sense, East Asian regional financial cooperation can be made consistent with, and even strengthen, the IMF's global role. At the same time, given the perceived imbalance and unfairness in the current distribution of IMF quotas—unrealistically skewed to the disadvantage of East Asia—regional policy-makers have a sincere desire to make their voice heard in global financial management. Indeed, they believe they can play a greater role by joining forces.

Initiatives for economic regionalism

Early attempts

EAEG/EAEC proposal. Following the unsatisfactory progress of the Uruguay Round Ministerial meeting in December 1990, Malaysian Prime Minister Mohamad Mahathir proposed the formation of a regional trade grouping, comprised of major ASEAN countries, Japan, China, Korea, and Hong Kong SAR. This group of economies was called the "East Asian Economic Group (EAEG)." His objective was to establish a regional trade arrangement for the group, in response to the emergence of preferential regional trade arrangements elsewhere, including in North America, and to exercise a global impact on trade issues, such as the Cairns Group. In October 1991, ASEAN Economic Ministers considered Mahathir's proposal useful, and renamed the grouping "East Asian Economic Caucus" (EAEC).

The United States objected to the EAEG/EAEC proposal on the grounds that it could divide the Asia-Pacific, by excluding the United States, and reduce the effectiveness of the trade/investment liberalization process within APEC. Japan hesitated to support the proposal not only out of consideration for the US opposition—not wishing to exacerbate existing trade conflicts with the United States and jeopardize their bilateral relationship—but also because of the strategic priority it placed on the emerging APEC process. China also took a cautious approach. Interest in the EAEG/EAEC proposal waned eventually, in the absence of support from key countries in Northeast Asia.[5] But when the leaders of Japan, China, and Korea were invited to the informal ASEAN Leaders' meeting in December 1997, in the midst of the Asian financial crisis, the de facto ASEAN+3 process began, and was formally launched in April 1999.[6] Thus, the EAEG/EAEC proposal may be seen as a precursor to the ASEAN+3 process, since membership of the latter overlaps that of the former.

Asian Monetary Fund (AMF) proposal. Following the success of the August 1997 meeting in Tokyo to agree on a much-needed financial support package for crisis-affected Thailand, Japan, with support from South Korea and the ASEAN countries that participated in the Thai package, proposed in September to establish an Asian Monetary Fund (AMF), to supplement IMF resources for crisis prevention, management, and resolution. The aim was to pool foreign exchange reserves held by East Asian authorities, both to deter currency speculation, and to contain a currency crisis in a member economy. It was said that as much as US$100 billion would be mobilized. The United States and the IMF opposed this proposition, on the grounds of moral hazard and duplication. They argued that an East Asian country hit by a currency crisis would bypass the tough conditionality of the IMF and receive easy money from the AMF, thereby creating the potential for moral hazard; they reasoned that an AMF would be redundant in the presence of an effective global crisis manager, the IMF. Without China's support, the idea was eventually shelved.

New Miyazawa Initiative. Another highly successful example was the so-called "New Miyazawa Initiative," which actually contributed to the resolution of the Asian financial crisis. In October 1998, Japan pledged US$30 billion to support the economic recovery of the crisis-affected countries. Half of the pledged amount was dedicated to short-term financial needs during the process of implementing economic restructuring and reform, while the rest was earmarked for medium- and long-term reforms. Part of short-term financial support was dedicated to currency swap arrangements with Korea (US$5 billion) and Malaysia (US$2.5 billion). Long-term support was extended to assist the crisis-affected countries in restructuring corporate debt, reforming financial sectors, strengthening social safety nets, generating employment, and addressing the credit crunch. A commitment to provide substantial financial resources helped stabilize the regional markets and economies, thereby facilitating the recovery process. It is important to mention that the short-term financial support provided to Korea and Malaysia became a model for bilateral currency swap arrangements under the Chiang Mai Initiative.

Trade and investment initiatives

Moves for bilateral and sub-regional FTAs. Recently, many governments in East Asia have promoted bilateral and sub-regional trade arrangements. Notably, Japan implemented a bilateral EPA with Singapore in 2002. In response to the Japan-Singapore EPA negotiation, China and ASEAN began official negotiations to complete an FTA by 2010 with advanced ASEAN members, and by 2015 with less advanced members. They subsequently implemented "early harvest" measures in January 2004, and an FTA on goods in July 2005.[7] Japan and ASEAN then began negotiations in November 2005 on an EPA, with a view to achieving free trade by 2012, while at the same time pursuing parallel bilateral EPA negotiations with key ASEAN members, including Malaysia, Philippines, Thailand, Indonesia, Brunei, and Vietnam. Korea also started a similar negotiation with ASEAN, rapidly reached an agreement to complete trade liberalization by 2009, and implemented an FTA on goods in July 2006. India, Australia, and New Zealand have also become active in their negotiations with ASEAN and Northeast Asian economies. In this sense, there have been domino and bandwagon effects among Japan, China, and Korea in their drive for regional FTAs and EPAs with ASEAN. Proposals have been made for a larger FTA among China, Japan, and Korea, or among ASEAN+3 countries, or even among ASEAN+3, India, Australia, and New Zealand.[8]

Features of recent initiatives. One of the interesting features of the East Asian drive toward regional and bilateral trade arrangements is that these economies have also concluded, or have been negotiating, FTAs and EPAs with countries or groups outside of East Asia. For example, Japan has implemented an EPA with Mexico and is negotiating one with Chile and the Gulf Cooperation Council (GCC). Korea has put into effect its FTA with Chile, and is negotiating FTAs with Canada, Mexico, the United States, and India. China implemented an FTA with Chile and is negotiating with Australia, New Zealand, South African Customs Union (SACU), and the GCC. Singapore has implemented FTAs with Australia, New Zealand, India, the European Free Trade Area (EFTA), the United States, and other countries, and is currently negotiating with Mexico, Canada, and a handful of other non-East Asian countries. Thailand has implemented FTAs with India, Australia, and New Zealand and is negotiating with the United States, EFTA and others. ASEAN as a group has begun negotiations with India and Closer Economic Relations (CER) (Australia and New Zealand) and is also considering negotiations with the European Union. These attempts suggest that the economies in the region wish to maintain open trading relations with other parts of the world, rather than become inward-looking. These East Asian economies are focusing on stronger ties with India and CER and then Europe and North America.[9]

East Asia's move to regional trade arrangements symbolizes a change in its long-standing policy of pursuing trade liberalization only in a global or trans-regional framework, based on the WTO and APEC—apart from ASEAN which has formed the ASEAN Free Trade Area (AFTA) and is heading toward the ASEAN Economic Community. The region has decided to shift its trade policy to a three-track approach, based on global (WTO-based) and trans-regional (APEC-based), regional (within ASEAN+3 or the East Asia Summit Group), and bilateral liberalization. For East Asian economies, regional and bilateral liberalization is an attempt to achieve deeper integration with their trading partners on a formal basis, going beyond reductions in border restrictions on trade in goods—i.e., pursuing investment liberalization, promoting greater competition in the domestic market, and harmonizing rules, standards and procedures.

Three pillars of financial regionalism

The East Asian economies have also embarked on initiatives for regional financial cooperation. Such initiatives are founded on three major pillars:

- Establishment of regional economic surveillance, particularly through the ASEAN+3 Economic Review and Policy Dialogue process;

- Creation of a regional liquidity support facility through the Chiang Mai Initiative;

- Development of Asian bond markets through the Asian Bond Markets Initiative (ABMI) and the Asian Bond Fund (ABF) project.

Regional economic surveillance. Establishing processes for regional economic surveillance and policy dialogue is an obvious first step for meaningful financial cooperation. Economic surveillance involves not only analyses of macroeconomic and financial conditions and policies of member economies but also identification of vulnerable aspects of the economies and their financial markets as well as appropriate policy responses. This process requires frank and candid exchanges of views and policy dialogue among other member economies, and will hopefully induce good policies through peer pressure.

There are several mechanisms for regional policy dialogue for information sharing and economic monitoring. In May 2000, ASEAN+3 finance ministers agreed to introduce an ASEAN+3 Economic Review and Policy Dialogue (ERPD) process, which turned out to be the most important policy dialogue mechanism of all.[10] The purpose of this process is to facilitate policy dialogue, coordination, and collaboration on the financial, monetary and fiscal issues of common interest. Its primary focus is on global and regional economic monitoring, individual country monitoring, macroeconomic risk assessment and management, and banking and financial system conditions. Steps have been taken for cooperation in monitoring short-tem capital flows and developing a regional early-warning framework to assess regional financial vulnerabilities, with a view to preventing future financial crises. Many ASEAN+3 members have set up National Surveillance Units for economic and financial monitoring and are developing their own early warning systems. However, there is no independent, professional organization which prepares comprehensive analyses or assessments or identifies issues for discussion.[11]

Liquidity support facility. The hallmark liquidity support facility in East Asia is the Chiang Mai Initiative (CMI), which was designed to reduce the risk of liquidity crises or manage regional currency attacks, contagion, and crises once they occur. The Asian financial crisis highlighted the importance of establishing an effective financing facility, so that the economies in the region can prevent currency crises or respond effectively to crises when they occur in an increasingly globalized world. The finance ministers of ASEAN+3 who met in Chiang Mai in May 2000 agreed to establish a regional network of swap arrangements for its members, thus launching the CMI. It consists of two elements: expansion of the existing ASEAN Swap Arrangement (ASA), in both amounts and membership, and the creation of a new network of bilateral swap arrangements (BSAs) among ASEAN+3 members.[12] By May 2006, sixteen BSAs had been concluded in line with the main principles, amounting to a total of US$75 billion—excluding the commitment made for Malaysia under the New Miyazawa Initiative. This marked the conclusion of all conceivable BSAs at the time.

One of the important features of CMI BSA is that members requesting liquidity support can immediately obtain short-term financial assistance for the first 20 percent of the facility. The remaining 80 percent is provided to the requesting member under an IMF program. Linking CMI liquidity support to an IMF program—and hence its conditionality—is designed to address the concern that balance of payments difficulties may be due to fundamental problems, rather than a mere panic and herd behavior by investors, and that the potential moral hazard problem could be non-negligible in the absence of tough IMF conditionality. The general view is that, due to the region's limited capacity to produce and enforce effective adjustment policies, the CMI members will have to rely on the IMF, at least for the time being.[13]

Asian bond market development. Initiatives have been taken to develop Asian bond markets in view of the need to channel a vast pool of savings to long-term investment for growth and development within the region. This effort reflects the recognition that the financial system in East Asia has been too dependent on bank financing domestically and on short-term, external foreign-currency financing, and, hence, needs to be strengthened through the development of national and regional capital, in particular of bond markets. Development of well-functioning, local-currency denominated bond markets is expected to reduce incentives for banks and corporations to rely on bank financing and/or short-term external borrowing. It is expected to mitigate the "double mismatch" problem (currency and maturity mismatches) of international capital markets—i.e., borrowing short term in foreign currency and lending long term in domestic currency—and to make the national financial markets more balanced, with sound banking sectors and more developed capital markets.

The EMEAP process introduced the Asian Bond Fund (ABF) project. Its idea was to help expand the bond market through demand-side stimulus from purchases by central banks of sovereign and quasi-sovereign bonds using foreign exchange reserves. The initial ABF-1 was launched in June 2003, and focused on purchases of US dollar-denominated bonds. Given that local currency-denominated bonds needed recognition and promotion—in order to address the "double mismatch" issue—EMEAP launched ABF-2 in December 2004, which involved purchases of sovereign and quasi-sovereign local-currency-denominated bonds. ABF-2 consists of two components, a Pan-Asian Bond Index Fund (PAIF) and a Fund of Bond Funds (FoBF). PAIF is a single bond fund index investing in local currency bonds, issued in eight EMEAP emerging economies.[14] FoBF has a two-tiered structure with a parent fund investing in eight sub-funds, each of which invests in local currency sovereign and quasi-sovereign bonds issued in their respective markets. PAIF and the eight sub-funds are passively managed by private fund managers against a Pan-Asian bond index and predetermined benchmark indexes in local markets. ABF-2 is designed to facilitate investment by public and private sector entities.

The ASEAN+3 finance ministers adopted the Asian Bond Market Initiative (ABMI) in August 2003 to develop local currency-denominated bonds through supply-side stimulus. The initiative intends to create a better balance between banking sectors and capital markets in East Asia's financial system and encourage direct channeling of regional savings to regional investment, by establishing a solid market infrastructure for local-currency bond issuance and trading. Originally, six voluntary working groups on the ABMI were formed, later revised to four. The present working groups focus on the creation of multi-currency bonds, establishment of a regional credit guarantee mechanism, exploration of an Asian settlement system, and strengthening Asian credit rating agencies, and raising comparability of their ratings across countries.

East Asian economic community

One recent, significant development is the November 2004 agreement by East Asian Leaders in Vientiane to form an "East Asian Community" and hold an East Asian Summit for this purpose. The first East Asia Summit (EAS) meeting was held in Kuala Lumpur in December 2005, with the participation of ten ASEAN members, as well as China, Japan, Korea, India, Australia, and New Zealand. The idea of creating an "East Asian Community" was proposed by the East Asia Vision Group (2001).[15] Its principal aims, relating to trade and investment integration and regional financial cooperation, can be summarized as:

- Establishment of the East Asian Free Trade Area (EAFTA) and liberalization of trade well ahead of the APEC Bogor Goal;

- Expansion of the Framework Agreement on an ASEAN Investment Area to all of East Asia;

- Promotion of development and technological cooperation among regional countries, to provide assistance to less developed countries;

- Realization of a knowledge-based economy and establishment of a future-oriented economic structure;

- Establishment of a self-help regional facility for financial cooperation;

- Adoption of a better exchange rate coordination mechanism, consistent with both financial stability and economic development;

- Strengthening of the regional monitoring and surveillance process within East Asia to supplement IMF global surveillance and Article IV consultation measures.

The Group thus envisioned the progressive integration of the East Asian economies, ultimately leading to an "East Asian economic community." Once a region-wide FTA is formed and institutions for international financial management and exchange rate coordination are established, the basic foundation for an East Asian economic community will have been prepared. The ASEAN+3 government officials responded to the Vision Group's recommendations by submitting their report to the ASEAN+3 Summit meeting in 2002). They accepted most of the recommendations and laid out some concrete, practical short-run measures—to be implemented by 2007—as well as some medium- and long-term goals.

Future economic cooperation in East Asia, leading to an East Asian economic community, is likely to evolve around the multiple agreements under ASEAN, ASEAN+1, ASEAN+3 and East Asia Summit (EAS) processes.[16] It is important to point out that the "ASEAN Economic Community," to be created by 2015, is the center of East Asian economic cooperation. It is now understood that the core of East Asian cooperation lies in ASEAN as the "driving force," with ASEAN+3 as the "main vehicle" for the realization of an eventual East Asian economic community, with the EAS contributing to the overall evolving regional architecture.

Challenges for closer economic regionalism in East Asia

Strategy for closer economic regionalism

Creation of an East Asia-wide FTA. If an East Asian economic community is to be created, the region must become a single market. A starting point for this would be the formation of the "ASEAN Economic Community, the creation of a single East Asia-wide FTA, which should evolve into an East Asian customs union and/or a common market. Creating a single East Asia-wide FTA, however, is no easy task, given the proliferation of FTA and EPAs in the region, each with its own provisions, rules of origin, external tariffs, and exclusion lists. One challenge is how to avoid the so-called Asian "noodle bowl" effect, by ensuring consistency and transparency across these different trade arrangements. Convergence toward identical rules and common tariff rates, standards and procedures is highly desirable.

CMI multilateralization and surveillance. A second area is financial regionalism. The ASEAN+3 countries have strengthened the CMI since May 2005: the total amount covered by the CMI has been expanded, linkage to IMF programs reduced, collective decision-making introduced for CMI activation, and the need for a strong linkage between CMI and economic surveillance recognized. In the medium term, the CMI could be centralized and multilateralized so that the swaps can be activated promptly and effectively in the event of a crisis.[17] The linkage to IMF programs could be further reduced or even eliminated, as the quality of regional economic surveillance improves. The central issue here is how to improve the quality and effectiveness of surveillance within ASEAN+3, along the line of the G-7 and OECD processes. One way to strengthen regional surveillance would be to set up a competent Secretariat, whose primary role would be to assist the ASEAN+3 surveillance process by providing high-quality and in-depth economic reviews and assessments, timely identification of emerging issues and vulnerabilities affecting the region, and effective policy advice. This secretariat must have adequate professional staff to monitor regional capital flows and financial and exchange market developments, update early warning indicators, and analyze regional and country economic conditions.

Exchange rate policy coordination. A third area is exchange rate policy. A variety of exchange rate regimes exist in East Asia, but no concrete steps have been taken so far to coordinate exchange rate policy. Given the rising degree of economic interdependence among the East Asian economies through trade, investment, and financial flows, it is increasingly important to maintain intra-regional exchange rate stability, which requires closer policy coordination among the financial and monetary authorities in the region, since one country's exchange rate adjustment can have serious, competitive implications for neighboring economies. Essentially, intra-regional exchange rate stability is a public good for regional growth and economic stability. Another reason for regional policy coordination is the fact that crisis contagion and economic spillovers tend to be concentrated within a region.

Although no consensus yet exists, even within ASEAN+3, on a regional exchange rate arrangement, I offer here a possible scenario for the development of such an arrangement. East Asia's exchange rate policy coordination could evolve in three stages (see Table 3):[18]

1. Loose policy coordination—information coordination, initial institutional coordination, and resource coordination;

2. Tight policy coordination—macroeconomic and exchange rate policy coordination for intra-regional exchange rate stabilization;

3. Complete policy coordination—economic and monetary union with a single currency.

Table 3: Requirements for policy coordination in East Asia

Stages of policy coordination	Exchange rate policy	Institutions	Trade-Investment
Current state	Uncoordinated exchange rate arrangements	CMI; Regional economic surveillance; Asian bond market initiative	Uncoordinated FTAs, investment agreements
Loose coordination	ACU as monitoring index; a currency basket system	Independent secretariat for CMI and surveillance; regional infrastructure for bond markets	East Asian Free Trade Agreement (EA FTA)
Tight coordination	"Asian Snake" or "Asian ERM"	Asian Monetary Fund; regional regulatory authority	Asian customs union
Complete coordination	Asian monetary union	Asian central bank	Asian common market

At the initial stage of loose policy coordination, East Asian policy-makers can strengthen information, institutional and resource coordination. They are already in the early phase of this stage, including the strengthening of ongoing financial cooperation initiatives, with ERPD, CMI, ABMI, and ABF under the aegis of the ASEAN+3 finance ministers and EMEAP central bank governors. Authorities have already begun to study ways to further strengthen the reserve pooling arrangement, going beyond the current CMI toward multilateralization, together with enhanced regional economic surveillance. They have made significant progress in developing local currency-denominated bond markets through ABMI and ABF.

At this stage, the regional authorities should strengthen institutional coordination through various measures. First, they should create a regional common unit of account, the Asian Currency Unit (ACU) as a basket of regional currencies, including the 13 currencies for ASEAN+3.[19] Second, they should adopt policies that stabilize exchange rates against a common basket of both regional and external currencies (the US dollar, the euro, and the ACU) to ensure relative stability of both their effective exchange rates and intraregional exchange rates. A well-balanced currency basket would provide a better buffer to an economy due to yen/dollar and yen/euro rate volatility.[20] Initially, the degree of exchange rate stabilization can be left to an economy's specific conditions and preferences, but adoption of a common currency basket would be useful.[21] By using an ACU index and divergence indicators,[22] the regional surveillance process can focus more intensively on exchange rate issues, such as the impact of a possible exit of the Chinese renminbi from a de facto US dollar peg, and the policies needed to facilitate adjustments of global payments imbalances.

Before moving to the next stage, regional policy-makers could consider strengthening resource coordination. This involves expanding the CMI into a centralized, multilateral administration, with substantially larger stocks of resources than are presently available. This expanded reserve pooling arrangement would be increasingly independent of IMF programs and, hence, require alternative conditionality to be developed for currency crises. With a centrally administered CMI with its own secretariat, the ASEAN+3 countries will have effectively established an Asian Monetary Fund (AMF). The region would then be in a position to address the earlier concern that an AMF would lend too generously and with too little conditionality, and create a moral hazard both for governments at the receiving end and for investors with stakes in the countries in question.[23] It is therefore essential to improve economic surveillance, acquire capacity to formulate appropriate adjustment policy in the event of a liquidity crisis and, to the extent necessary, enforce effective private sector involvement.

Tight policy coordination could take one of two paths: one would be to initiate intraregional exchange-rate policy coordination along the line of European monetary integration. As East Asian economies become more integrated, achieve greater economic and structural convergence, and are better positioned to commit to meaningful policy coordination, a common framework for intraregional exchange rate stabilization can be developed. This could be done by establishing an Asian "Snake" or an Asian "Exchange Rate Mechanism." After a period of gathering experience and building confidence, all participating economies—Japan together with emerging East Asia—could shift from stabilization of their exchange rates against a common basket of external and East Asian currencies (comprising the US dollar, euro, and ACU) to a formal exchange rate stabilization, perhaps against a common basket of East Asian currencies alone—that is, the ACU. Such an exchange rate stabilization scheme requires: a) well-defined rules for currency market interventions and monetary policy coordination, so as to establish a credible monetary anchor within East Asia; b) a fully elaborated short-term liquidity support arrangement capable of allowing central banks' frequent interventions in foreign exchange markets; and c) fiscal policy rules designed to lend credibility to the exchange-rate stabilization scheme.

Another alternative is the "parallel currency approach" advocated by Eichengreen (2006), where the ACU is allowed to freely circulate as legal tender alongside component national currencies.[24] As the ACU is used increasingly by the market as a unit of account, store of value, and medium of exchange in East Asia, the role of national currencies may diminish, and there will be greater willingness to shift the role of national currencies over to the ACU. This market-led evolution will naturally create conditions for monetary unification. This option emphasizes the role of market forces, rather than political commitment, in dictating transition to a monetary union, the goal of the third stage.

Whichever option is taken, a practical approach in this stage is to adopt a multi-track, multi-speed approach where economies ready for tighter policy coordination start the process, while others prepare to join later. A group of economies largely fulfilling optimum currency area (OCA) conditions in East Asia—such as Japan, Korea, China, Hong Kong SAR, and Macau SAR, Singapore, Malaysia, and Brunei Darussalam—and with sufficient political commitment, may wish to initiate sub-regional currency stabilization schemes. This group could intensify monetary and exchange rate policy coordination and welcome others when they are ready.

In the last stage, complete policy coordination, the region would establish economic and monetary union with a common currency, like the euro regime. A common currency arrangement, however, cannot be expected in the very near future, because of the absence of political will, political and economic convergence, and deeper complementary institutions.[25] Such an arrangement would require member economies' readiness to accept strong coordination of monetary policy—and closer coordination of other economic policies—long before its implementation.

Overcoming impediments to closer economic regionalism

There are several possible impediments to deepening economic integration and advancing economic regionalism in East Asia:

- East Asia's global orientation in trade, FDI, money and finance, and its openness to North America and Europe;

- Concern about possible conflict with global economic systems governed by the WTO and the IMF;

- Fear of protectionism, discrimination, trade diversion, and proliferation of financial crises;

- Diversity in economic, financial, and social developments within East Asia, such as differences in per capita incomes, industrial and financial structures, and domestic institutional and human capacities;

- Lack of political consensus for closer economic regionalism.

Skeptics argue that East Asia is more closely integrated with the United States and Europe than with the economies in its own region, with more to gain from further integration with the global market than with the regional one. Hence, according to this view, forming an East Asia-wide FTA, excluding the United States and Europe, is not wise, as they are still important markets for the region's final products. The belief is that the expansion of intra-regional trade in East Asia, supported by FDI, has been made possible by open markets in the United States and Europe which absorb East Asian finished products. In the money and finance area, the region's global orientation should provide greater risk sharing for smooth consumption. The region's economies are also still highly dependent on the US dollar for exchange rate stabilization, trade invoicing, external asset holding, foreign exchange reserve holding, and external liabilities.

One corollary of this view holds that global frameworks of trade and investment liberalization and of cross-border financial management are more important for East Asia than regional ones. This implies that trade and investment liberalization within the WTO, or at least within APEC, would be more desirable than through regional FTAs. This argument tends to be supported by those who are wary of East Asian trade regionalism because it might undermine the WTO principle of maintaining a liberal, non-discriminatory, and multilateral trading system.[26] It also implies that cross-border financial management under the umbrella of the IMF, rather than a regional framework, would be more beneficial to East Asia.

The East Asian economies are, indeed, diverse and varied in their economic systems and stages of financial and social developments—such as per capita income levels, industrial and financial structures, trade openness and patterns, scope and extent of exchange and capital controls, institutional and human capacities, and health and other social conditions.[27] Such heterogeneity implies that low-income countries—where market infrastructure is insufficiently developed—will be slow in trade, investment and financial liberalization and market opening and, hence, will integrate only with difficulty with the rest of fast-paced East Asia. Moreover, given such economic diversity, economies in the region have different policy objectives and priorities and desire to maintain national sovereignty over economic policies. In order for the economies to take joint action at the regional level, there must be substantial economic convergence.

Finally, it is argued that there is no political consensus for economic integration within East Asia, due to differences in political systems, unresolved historical issues, and the lack of mutual trust. No single economic power plays a dominant role in East Asia similar to that of the United States in the Americas, nor does any bipolar relationship exist along the lines of the Franco-German alliance in Europe. Japan has been mired in economic stagnation over the last decade, and China, while recently emerging as an economic power, has yet to achieve transition to a market economy and, more fundamentally, political transition.

Assessment of the impediments. Some of these impediments are real, but they are not insurmountable. There is no doubt that global frameworks for trade and investment liberalization (WTO) and cross-border financial management (IMF) remain important. Yet there is room for regional frameworks to play complementary roles. In the trade and investment area, the United

States is no longer the most dominant economic partner for many East Asian economies, and the regional markets for final products are expanding fast. Large inward FDI flows in the region now originate from within the region. In addition, East Asia is in no way inward-looking, as evidenced by the fact that many of them are negotiating on FTAs with countries outside of the region, and are at the same time focusing on domestic structural reforms, higher productivity, and economic growth, thus minimizing trade diversion effects. The East Asian approach is to regard the WTO and principles as the basic infrastructure for international trade rules, and to achieve greater liberalization beyond the commitments of the WTO and APEC, what some are calling the "WTO-plus" or "APEC-plus" approach.

In the money and finance area, regional policy-makers have found it absolutely necessary to manage financial globalization through various measures, including the strengthening of a regional financial architecture. They have also found the cost of excessive reliance on the US dollar very high, and so have embarked on measures to increase the use of regional currencies, such as the Asian bond market. These regional efforts are not a substitute for, but a complement to, global and national efforts for crisis prevention, management, and resolution.

While diversity and heterogeneity are not the ultimate impediments to economic regionalism, the lack of political will could be. One clear observation is that, despite heterogeneity and differences in economic and social systems among the countries in the region, they have increasingly come to realize that the economic logic for strengthening regional frameworks for trade and investment integration and international financial management is overriding. They have found that the benefits of economic integration and its institutionalization outweigh the costs of not doing so. It is extremely important to raise the economic basis of poor members within East Asia and to encourage them to grow. For the time being, a realistic approach would be multi-track: countries ready for deeper integration and closer cooperation may negotiate on FTAs and financial arrangements, while those countries not ready are advised to pursue structural, institutional and governance reforms, assisted by Japan, Korea, advanced ASEAN members, and multilateral development banks, to enable them to gain from further liberalization and integration. As these low-income countries catch up with their more advanced peers, they can start participating in closer economic regionalism.

Trust building and leadership

On the issue of political consensus, it is important to point out that the region's governments have initiated efforts to form an "East Asian Community," whose important component is an East Asian economic community. Though a unified, deeply integrated ASEAN—through the formation of the "ASEAN Economic Community"—remains the core driver in East Asian integration,[28] Japan and China are also important players and they must form a solid bipolar alliance and joint leadership. For this purpose, they must resolve the issues impeding deeper economic integration between them and re-establish mutual trust.[29] Without this, the region cannot make substantial progress on economic regionalism that may eventually lead to an East Asian economic community. To some extent, healthy rivalry between the two major powers is desirable as long as it enhances market-driven competition and does not impede mutual trust and sense of community in East Asia. The two countries can jointly work hard on key issues by taking bold and forward-looking political gestures

- to resolve their historical issues permanently, so that the two countries can rebuild mutual trust for greater economic integration;

- to cooperate as bipolar partners to nurture emerging economic regionalism in East Asia, particularly on trade, investment, and financial issues, so that an East Asia-wide FTA, a zone of stable Asian currencies, and eventually an East Asian economic community can be created;

- to strengthen various types of economic policy dialogue including, for example, investment rules, protection of intellectual property rights, macroeconomic policy management, food and energy security, etc.

It is important to realize that China is now adopting a multilateral approach to regional economic cooperation. The payoff for such a policy appears high for China, because its economic growth depends on the political stability, peace, and security of the region. China's FTA initiative with ASEAN is one important sign of willingness to deepen economic and political relationships with its Southeast Asian neighbors. Its active engagement with the CMI and ABMI is another sign.

China faces two major challenges: first, it must complete its economic transition from a planned system to one which is market-driven. In particular, further liberalization of trade, investment, and capital accounts is crucial for China's gradual integration with the regional and global economy. Second, China must make an orderly political transition to ensure stability for her own people as well as the rest of East Asia and the world.

The absence of a solid, region-wide security arrangement should not be viewed as a serious obstacle to regional economic cooperation, or to the creation of a region-wide FTA and eventually an East Asian economic community. This absence may be partly attributed to the difference in political systems, the lack of common culture, religion, value, shared history, and mutual trust across East Asia. However, a convergence toward similar political systems will inevitably occur, as China and other socialist countries continue to pursue market-based structural reforms, achieve further economic development, integrate with the global and regional economies, and produce a large middle class within their societies. It is just such a middle-class which will encourage movement toward a more open, rule-based society.

Conclusion

This paper has demonstrated that the East Asian economies have achieved strong economic interdependence, particularly through domestic structural reforms, external liberalization and market-driven integration with the global and regional economies. Expansion of foreign trade, direct investment, and financial flows has created a naturally integrated economic zone in East Asia. Reflecting rising economic interdependence and in response to the trauma caused by the financial crisis of 1997–98, East Asia has embarked on various initiatives for economic regionalism, including several bilateral FTAs, negotiations for regional FTAs, regional surveillance mechanisms, a regional liquidity support system (CMI), and Asian bond market development. These constitute de facto economic integration and interdependence in East Asia, complementing the global frameworks of the WTO and the IMF.

I have outlined the major challenges for the region: first, the need for negotiations for a region-wide FTA, as a basis for further integration and interdependence, coherence of rules, standards and procedures across countries in the region, and consistency with the WTO framework. The middle-income member states of ASEAN must reform their economies to cope with greater international competition, particularly vis-à-vis China, while its low-income members must pursue institutional and governance reforms to enable them to benefit from trade and FDI openness. These efforts will accelerate the pace of creating an "ASEAN Economic Community."

Second, the regional economies must make greater efforts to strengthen the liquidity provision mechanism (CMI), regional economic surveillance, and Asian bond market initiatives, all of which are crucial for enhancing the CMI through enlargement, multilateralization of the currency swap arrangements, and reduction of its IMF linkages. Once the region strengthens its capacity to formulate appropriate adjustment policy in the event of liquidity crises and enforce effective private sector involvement, East Asia will have effectively established an Asian Monetary Fund that can contribute to regional financial stability without creating fears of moral hazard.

Third, is the need for coordination of exchange rate policy, including the joint monitoring of regional exchange rates based on an Asian Currency Unit, and adoption of a currency basket arrangement based on the US dollar, the euro, and the ACU. Greater economic and political policy coordination will eventually lead to greater integration and commitment to establish the formal institutions capable of supporting intra-regional exchange rate stability.

Finally, the region will have to take steps to overcome the impediments to closer economic regionalism, by integrating low-income ASEAN members with the regional and global markets, nurturing mutual trust by resolving thorny historical issues, and developing a long-term vision for an East Asian economic community which can be shared by all in the region.

NOTES

1 Based on the paper, "East Asian Economic Regionalism: Progress and Challenges," presented to the "International Economic Cooperation for a Balanced World Economy" held in Chongqing, 12–13 March, 2005. See original version in *Journal of Asian Economics* 16:1:29–55). The author is grateful to participants at the Chongqing conference and Michael Plummer for their constructive comments and views on the earlier version. The findings, interpretations, and conclusions expressed in the paper are those of the author alone and do not represent the views of the Asian Development Bank (ADB), its executive directors, or the countries they represent.

2 The advantage of using trade intensity indexes over trade shares is that the former control for a region's relative size in world trade and, hence, present a better measure of closeness of the economies within a region. However, a small regional group tends to have a high trade intensity index.

3 However, the large volume of Hong Kong SAR's FDI flows to China may contain "round tripping" from China, which aims to take China's tax and other favorable advantages given to "foreign" direct investment.

4 See Kawai (1997 and 2005a), Kawai and Urata (1998, 2004), Athukorala (2003), Fukao et al. (2003) and Urata (2004) and Kawai (2004).

5 Nonetheless, this proposal was not completely forgotten. When the Asia-Europe Meeting (ASEM) was created in 1996, the Asian participants were essentially EAEG/EAEC economies.

6 Stubbs (2002) takes the view that the ASEAN+3 will rise as a major regional and international player. See Kawai (2002a) and Kuroda and Kawai (2002).

7 "Early harvest" refers to provisions of the Framework Agreement on China-ASEAN Comprehensive Economic Cooperation, intended (before the full completion of the FTA), to reduce tariffs in priority sectors of interest, and implement other trade and investment measures of immediate benefit to ASEAN and to China.

8 However, no timeframe has been set for such negotiations for a larger FTA. Japan is indeed cautious about such an arrangement with China at this point. Its official view is that before negotiating on an FTA or EPA, it believes that China must clearly show its compliance with all the commitments made in WTO accession negotiations.

9 In this sense it is not surprising to see closer ties merging among ASEAN+3, India and CER as a new framework called the "East Asia Summit" group.

10 Its first surveillance meeting was held in April 2002. Other major mechanisms include the ASEAN Surveillance Process, EMEAP (Executives Meeting of East Asia-Pacific Central Banks), and trans-regional forums such as APEC and ASEM.

11 The ASEAN Secretariat provides some logistic support to the ASEAN-ERPD process, and the Asian Development Bank provides papers for discussion at the meeting of finance ministers, finance, and central bank deputies. The IMF used to play the role of a secretariat for the Manila Framework Group (MFG).

12 The ASA, established in August 1977 by the members of the original ASEAN-5, with a total facility of US$100 million, was augmented to a total of US$200 million in 1978. Under the CMI, ASA membership was extended to include all ASEAN members, and its facility was further augmented to US$1 billion. It was agreed in April 2005 to further augment ASA to US$2 billion.

13 On the other hand, some ASEAN+3 members, such as Malaysia, believe that the CMI should not be linked to IMF programs.

14 These eight economies include: China, Hong Kong SAR, Indonesia, Korea, Malaysia, Philippines, Singapore, and Thailand.

15 The East Asia Vision Group recommended: a) economic cooperation, b) financial cooperation, c) political and security cooperation, d) environmental cooperation, e) social and cultural cooperation, and f) institutional cooperation.

16 ASEAN+1 processes include ASEAN-China, ASEAN-Japan, ASEAN-Korea, ASEAN-India and ASEAN-CER mainly in the form of free trade agreements (FTAs) and comprehensive economic partnership agreements (EPAs).

17 Rajan and Siregan (2004) propose to establish a centralized reserve pooling system.

18 See Montiel (2004) and Kawai (2006). Although there may be other scenarios, the one proposed here is general enough to capture the substance of necessary elements of any other scenario.

19 Just like the European Currency Unit (ECU) under the EMS (1979–98), the weights of the regional currencies would reflect the relative importance of the countries in the region. The ACU could be used to denominate economic transactions (current and capital accounts) and asset stocks (foreign exchange reserves and cross-border bonds) and measure the degree of each currency's exchange rate deviation from the regional average provided by the ACU exchange rate.

20 In the post-crisis period, Korea and Thailand appear to be shifting to a de facto currency basket system, on the model of Singapore. See Kawai (2002b). However, McKinnon (2000 and 2001) takes the view that the East Asian economies have resurrected the US dollar standard system. See also Kawai (2004 and 2006).

21 This approach is consistent with what Goldstein (2002) calls "managed floating plus." A "managed float" is a system with occasional intervention to limit excessive short-term fluctuations in exchange rates without being accompanied by a publicly announced exchange rate target; the "plus" is inflation targeting and aggressive measures to reduce currency mismatches. Williamson (2001, 2005) has suggested the adoption of a G-3 currency basket as an exchange rate reference in the context of "managed floating plus." Even when a currency basket system is desirable for the region as a whole, it may not be easy for any single economy to move unilaterally away from the current US dollar-centered exchange rate arrangement to a new one in which the relative weight of the dollar is smaller than that of the yen and euro. When neighboring countries stabilize their exchange rates primarily against the US dollar, there may not be much incentive for any one country to unilaterally alter its exchange rate policy. This demonstrates a potential "collective action" problem associated with a move to a currency basket arrangement (Ogawa and Ito 2002). Overcoming this problem requires a concerted move among the economies concerned.

22 ACU index movements and divergences of component currencies from the basket can provide meaningful information, particularly once China moves to a more flexible exchange rate regime.

23 Nonetheless, Rapkin (2001) takes a pessimistic view of an AMF.

24 Eichengreen (2006) considers the "parallel currency approach." According to his findings, Europe should have developed the "parallel currency approach" but did not, and adopted the ERM instead.

25 See Wyploz (2004) for the importance of institutional integration for a currency union.

26 Lloyd (2002) argues that bilateralism and FTAs are more likely to lead to, and not impede, multilateralism, while Brown, Deardorff and Stern (2003) continue to believe in the superiority of multilateralism.

27 Ravenhill (2001) argues that diversity of membership and conflicts of power and interest sharply limit potential for cooperation in East Asia, while Terada (2003) provides a constructive and relatively optimistic account of the regional grouping.

28 Ba (2003) argues that while important differences remain, the relationship between China and ASEAN has improved markedly over the past decade.

29 Rozman (2002) argues that China continues to see Japan as both partner and rival, struggling to balance the two.

REFERENCES

Athukorala, Prema-chandra. 2003. "Product Fragmentation and Trade Patterns in East Asia." Working Paper No. 2003/21. Division of Economics, Research School of Pacific and Asian Studies, Australian National University.

Ba, Alice D. 2003. "China and ASEAN: Renavigating Relations for a 21st-Century Asia." *Asian Survey* 43(4):622–47. July/August,

Eichengreen, Barry. 2006. "The Parallel Currency Approach to Asian Monetary Integration." Manila: Asian Development Bank. Mimeo.

Fukao, Kyoji, Hikari Ishido, and Keiko Ito. 2003. "Vertical Intra-industry Trade and Foreign Direct Investment in East Asia." *Journal of the Japanese and International Economies* 17(4):468–506.

Goldstein, Morris. 2002. "Managed Floating Plus." *Policy Analyses in International Economics* 66. March. Institute for International Economics, Washington, D.C.

Kawai, Masahiro. 1997. "Japan's Trade and Investment in East Asia." David Robertson, ed., *East Asian Trade after the Uruguay Round*. Cambridge: Cambridge University Press. 209–26.

———. 2002a. "Global, Regional and National Approaches to the International Financial Architecture: Lessons from the East Asian Crisis." *International Economy* 7:65–108.

———. 2002b. "Exchange Rate Arrangements in East Asia: Lessons from the 1997–98 Currency Crisis." *Monetary and Economic Studies, Special Edition* 20:167–204. December.

———. 2004. "The Case for a Tri-polar Currency Basket System for Emerging East Asia." Gordon de Brouwer and Masahiro Kawai, eds., *Exchange Rate Regimes in East Asia.* London and New York: Routledge Curzon. 360–84.

———. 2006. "Toward a Regional Exchange-rate Regime in East Asia." Revised paper presented to the Bellagio Conference on New Monetary and Exchange-rate Arrangements for East Asia. 23–26 May.

Kawai, Masahiro and Shujiro Urata. 2004. "Trade and Foreign Direct Investment in East Asia." Gordon de Brouwer and Masahiro Kawai, eds., *Economic Linkages and Implications for Exchange Rate Regimes in East Asia.* London and New York: Routledge Curzon. 15–102.

Kuroda, Haruhiko and Masahiro Kawai. 2002. "Strengthening Regional Financial Cooperation in East Asia." *Pacific Economic Papers* 51. October. Australian National University.

Lloyd, Peter. 2002. "New Bilateralism in the Asia Pacific." *World Economy* 25(9):1279–96.

McKinnon, Ronald I. 2000. "The East Asian Dollar Standard: Life after Death?" *Economic Notes* 29:31–82. February.

———. 2001. "After the Crisis, the East Asian Dollar Standard Resurrected." Paper presented to the international conference Monetary Outlook on East Asia in an Integrating World Economy, 5–6 September. Bangkok: Chulalongkorn University.

Ogawa, Eiji and Takatoshi Ito. 2002. "On the Desirability of a Regional Basket Currency Arrangement." *Journal of the Japanese and International Economies* 16:317–34.

Organisation for Economic Co-operation and Development (OECD). 2003. *Regionalism and Multilateral Trading System.* Paris: OECD Secretary General.

Rapkin, David P. 2001. "The United States, Japan, and the Power to Block: the APEC and AMF Cases." *Pacific Review* 14(3):373–410.

Ravenhill, John. 2001. *Asia Pacific Economic Cooperation: The Construction of Pacific Rim Regionalism.* Cambridge: Cambridge University Press.

Rozman, Gilbert. 2002. "China's Changing Images of Japan, 1989–2001: The Struggle to Balance Partnership and Rivalry." *International Relations of the Asia-Pacific* 2(1):95–130.

Stubbs, Richard. 2002. "ASEAN + Three: Emerging East Asian Regionalism?" *Asian Survey* 42(3):440–55.

Terada, Takashi. 2003. "Constructing an 'East Asian Concept' and Growing Regional Identity: From EAEC to ASEAN+3." *Pacific Review* 16(2):251–77.

UNCTAD. Online database.

———. 2005. *World Investment Report 2005.*

———. 2005. *World Investment Report 2006.*

Urata, Shujiro. 2001. "Emergence of an FDI-Trade Nexus and Economic Growth in East Asia." Joseph Stiglitz and Shahid Yusuf, eds. *Rethinking the East Asian Miracle.* New York: Oxford University Press. 407–59.

Williamson, John. 2001. "The Case for a Basket, Band and Crawl (BBC) Regime for East Asia." David Gruen and John Simon, eds. *Future Directions for Monetary Policies in East Asia.* Sydney: Reserve Bank of Australia. 96–111.

———. 2005. "A Currency Basket for East Asia, Not Just China." *Policy Briefs in International Economics*, No. PB05-1. Washington, D.C.: Institute for International Economics. August.

Wyplosz, Charles. 2004. "Regional Exchange Rate Arrangements: Lessons from Europe for East Asia." Asian Development Bank, ed., *Monetary and Financial Integration in East Asia: The Way Ahead*, Vol. 2. Houndmills and New York: Palgrave MacMillan. 241–84.

CHAPTER 2.4

The Role of ASEAN+3 in Regional Policy Surveillance in East Asia

YUNG CHUL PARK, Director of Center for International Commerce and Finance, Graduate School of International Studies, Seoul National University

Global surveillance of the IMF

One of the core responsibilities of the IMF is to maintain a dialogue with its member countries concerning the national and international repercussions of their economic and financial policies. This process of monitoring and consultation is normally referred to as surveillance. At its inception, the IMF had a mandate, under its Articles of Agreement, to exercise firm surveillance over exchange rates and current account convertibility, in order to oversee the international monetary system and ensure its effective operation.[1] Until the Bretton Woods fixed exchange rate regime collapsed in the early 1970s, IMF members were obliged to declare par values, and to consult regarding their adjustment These obligations were fundamentally oriented toward stabilizing and sustaining international trade rather than international capital flows (Eichengreen, 2001). However, the growing cross-border repercussions of national economic policies, caused by unprecedented, large capital flows led to the Second Amendment of the IMF Articles of Agreement, empowering the IMF to conduct "firm surveillance" of its members' macroeconomic policies. A series of emerging market crises in the 1990s further underscored the necessity to expand the scope of surveillance for the purpose of coping with the intensified global integration of financial markets.

The scope of Fund surveillance has been so widened over time that it can no longer be seen as one unified concept. According to Crow et al. (1999), as currently practised, surveillance reflects a number of overlapping but conceptually distinct purposes, identified as follows:

Policy advice: The Fund offers advice and proposals and serves as a sounding board for policy dilemmas facing member countries.

Policy coordination and cooperation: The Fund facilitates policy consultation among groups of countries, by providing input such as reliable data, forecasts and analysis, and the machinery through which policy coordination can take place.

Information gathering and dissemination: The Fund maintains databases for use in policy formulation, and disseminates information beneficial for both private market participants and the general public.

Technical assistance and aid: In many developing countries, where expertise in macroeconomic policy-making is scarce, surveillance is tantamount to providing technical assistance.

Identification of vulnerabilities: This is an extension of the information and policy advice role that is particularly relevant when a country's policies are likely to be unsustainable. In this context, early warnings and policy advice given by the Fund to vulnerable countries play a role in formulating prompt corrective policy measures.

Delivering the message: The Fund provides countries with policy prescriptions on numerous topics, from the advantages of moving toward a system of indirect instruments of monetary control, to the need to liberalize labor markets. In so doing, the Fund makes it possible for the prevailing consensus of the economics profession to be shared with governments and policy-makers.

Traditionally, there have been two levels of surveillance practiced by the Fund: bilateral and multilateral. Bilateral surveillance refers to the Article IV consultations undertaken by the Fund with individual member countries; multilateral surveillance refers to the systemic analysis and forecasting of the world economy, published in the *World Economic Outlook* and *International Capital Markets Report*. In addition, the IMF and the World Bank have adopted a program of Reports on the Observance of Standards and Codes (ROSCs) which serve to stimulate member countries to adopt and improve adherence to internationally recognized standards and codes of good practice.

Bilateral surveillance

Bilateral surveillance is conducted through Article IV consultation. The IMF holds consultations, normally every year, with each of its members. These consultations focus on the following aspects of each member's economic policies: exchange rate, fiscal, and monetary policies; balance of payments and external debt developments; the influence of its policies on the country's external accounts; the international and regional implications of those policies; and the identification of potential vulnerabilities. These consultations are not limited to macroeconomic policies, but touch on all policies which significantly affect the macroeconomic performance of a country. Depending upon circumstances, these may include labor and environmental policies and the economic aspects of governance. With the intensified global integration of financial markets, the IMF is taking into account more explicitly capital account and financial sector issues (IMF, 2001).

Multilateral surveillance

Multilateral surveillance is geared more toward analysis of recent world developments, projection of future development, identification of the risks of international economic instability, and the proposal of ensuing policy recommendations. The primary vehicle for the Fund's multilateral surveillance is the biennial publication World Economic Outlook, which provides a comprehensive set of economic forecasts for the world economy. It usually covers the broad areas of the world economic situation, global economic prospects, and related policy issues, especially policy stances in industrial countries.

Regional surveillance

Regular discussions are also held with regional economic institutions, such as the Economic and Monetary Union (EMU) in Europe. The Fund has been active in providing input to other regional mechanisms for policy consultations. It has been designated as the technical secretariat to the Manila Framework Group. The Fund has also been invited to present economic briefings for the meetings of ASEAN+3 Finance Minister. Similarly, the Fund has provided input to the Asia-Pacific Economic Cooperation forum. Although the Fund's main contribution has been the preparation of background papers, these focus not so much on regional issues as on the results of bilateral and multilateral consultations. The Fund conducts regular discussions with regional entities of a number of currency unions, such as the West African Economic and Monetary Union, the Central African Economic and Monetary Community, and the Eastern Caribbean Currency Board.

As noted in External Evaluation of IMF Surveillance prepared by Crow et al.(1999), European monetary unification poses not only special challenges for Fund surveillance, but also new opportunities. For euro area countries, only monetary policy has been centralized, although trade policy has already been centralized for all members of the EU. Budgetary and structural policies continue to be a national responsibility, though the Pact for Stability and Growth subjects such policies to intensive monitoring by the Commission and by the Council of Finance Ministers (ECOFIN). Monitoring of the aggregate performance of the euro area is not yet well developed, apart from the European Central Bank (ECB), which is charged with reviewing its monetary stance on the basis of aggregate indicators. This asymmetry in the policy framework implies that it will initially be complex to focus Fund surveillance of the euro area on the aggregate performance. However, Fund surveillance may gradually be facilitated by an evolution in the policy framework, which is already under way. The *External Evaluation of IMF Surveillance Report* concludes that Fund surveillance is more likely to have an impact at the euro area level than at the level of individual countries. Consequently, Article IV missions to participants in the euro area should become less frequent, more focused, and leaner, with the resources devoted to Fund surveillance considerably reduced, as it should be possible for Fund surveillance to rely largely on the work of the European Commission.

Transparency and observance of standards

In the wake of the Mexican crisis in 1994–95, and the turmoil in the financial markets of East Asia in 1997, data issues have received increasing prominence in the IMF's work. In aiming to strengthen IMF surveillance, the Executive Board has emphasized the need for provision of timely, reliable, and comprehensive economic and financial data by members. The Fund encourages member countries to introduce greater policy transparency, for instance, by providing detailed data on external reserves, related liabilities, and short-term external debt. This is currently done through the IMF's data standard initiatives: the Special Data Dissemination Standard (SDDS) and the General Data Dissemination System (GDDS). The international community has also called upon the IMF and other standard-setting agencies to develop standards or codes of good practice, covering a number of economic and financial areas. The IMF and the World Bank have jointly adopted a program of Reports on the Observance of Standards and Codes (ROSCs).[2]

Development of a regional surveillance system in East Asia

Policy dialogue, along with a regular information exchange and surveillance process, is essential, if a regional financial architecture could serve as a defensive mechanism for crisis prevention. The collected information will help detect and identify the characteristics of a looming crisis at an early stage, so that proper and timely remedial action can be taken. A joint exercise, based on a region-wide early warning system will facilitate closer examination of financial vulnerabilities in the region. In addition, the regional policy dialogue process will contribute to ensuring effective implementation of individual or collective policy targets through peer pressure or rule-based enforcement mechanisms.

Economic and financial sector monitoring will keep a close watch over: (a) macroeconomic trends and policy changes, (b) financial market developments including cross-border capital flows, and (c) institutional and legal changes. This rather broad coverage of economic monitoring will serve the functions of supporting an effective management of the Network of Bilateral Swap Agreements (NBSA) promoting orderly economic integration in the region, and facilitating policy consultation and deepening financial cooperation among its members.

An independent monitoring and surveillance unit as an effective institution is required to develop a surveillance mechanism to enforce (a) implementation of common standards agreed upon by the members, (b) policy changes and reforms required of the swap-drawing countries from the Chiang Mai Initiative (CMI) (including policy conditionality attached to the swap borrowing), and (c) economic policy coordination or consultation agreed upon by the members. A proposal for the institutional structure and functions of a monitoring and surveillance unit is discussed in this paper.

As part of the institutional structure of the CMI, a regional policy dialogue mechanism is being discussed under the ASEAN+3 framework. This chapter explores the possibility that this mechanism could be used to support the operation of the CMI. Different institutional settings will require different mechanisms for effective monitoring and surveillance. As the scope of financial cooperation increases and economic integration deepens, different mechanisms and institutions for monitoring and surveillance will evolve, along with other pillars of regional financial arrangements, such as liquidity assistance and exchange rate policy coordination.

The rationale for regional policy dialogue and surveillance

One of the major implications of the growing interdependence in the world economy, being brought about by financial integration, is that financial instability in any given country is not likely to be isolated. As the East Asian and other experiences of crises have shown, financial shocks affecting a particular country can be transmitted to other countries through various channels of contagion (Claessens et al. 2000). Thus, cooperative efforts at both regional and global levels are needed to counter the negative spillovers or externalities of contagion. The surveillance activities of the IMF are just such an example of providing global public goods. By the common-sense logic that two heads are better than one, regional initiatives could complement the IMF surveillance process. The wisdom of having a second opinion on important matters clearly argues in favor of the case for regional monitoring and surveillance.[3]

At the initial stage of the CMI development, the focus of monitoring and surveillance activity has been placed on broadening and intensifying policy dialogues among the participating countries, which, together with the ASEAN regular monitoring and surveillance process, can lay the groundwork for an efficient system. Monitoring and surveillance form the bedrock upon which coherent regional policy-making rests. A regional monitoring and surveillance process would provide prompt and relevant information exchange for assessing the situation of countries in trouble and the potential contagious effects of a crisis on neighboring countries.

Another focus of the present surveillance process is stabilizing and strengthening East Asian financial systems, which, in general, suffer from inadequate economic and legal infrastructure. This results in inefficient allocation of high savings, inordinately large short-term debt markets, and the general absence of arm's length transactions. The regional policy dialogue process should, therefore, pay particular attention to the root problems of East Asia's weak financial systems. Besides strengthening prudential supervision, risk management, and corporate governance, the financial authorities in the region must also actively promote long-term capital markets. This is a case for financial cooperation to deepen and enhance regional financial markets.[4]

Like private bank loans, official financial assistance needs economic surveillance to ensure that assistance is provided and effectively used. Like the international financial institutions, such as the IMF and World Bank, the CMI requires surveillance for its lending to member countries. Economic surveillance is not merely an observation of economic indicators, but also an assessment of macroeconomic, financial, and structural policies of member countries. Only when the creditworthiness of borrowers is warranted on the basis of economic surveillance, will a group of lenders be able to make loans. At the same time, regular surveillance would enable quick disbursements in times of crises. If an assessment process for financial assistance begins only after a request from a borrower is made, then disbursement will be prolonged until a final decision is forthcoming.

As a supporting instrument and mechanism for regional financial arrangements, regional monitoring and surveillance will vary, depending upon given policy objectives, and the stage of regional financial and monetary integration. When the region has a more integrated institutional form, more comprehensive and binding policy coordination will be required. Therefore, the spectrum of the modality of monitoring and surveillance can be wide, ranging from simple information exchange and informal consultation forums to a supranational entity like the EMU. If common policy objectives were more broadly spelled out, an informal exchange of views and non-binding policy recommendations would be sufficient. If more specific policy objectives were pursued, such as the convergence criteria in EMU, tighter coordination and penalties on violations would be required. Thus, the exact form of monitoring and surveillance is a function of the degree of integration.

At the most elementary stage of zero institutional integration, governments simply take the policies of other governments as given, and do not attempt to exert influence. The existence of policy spillovers means that it would still be useful for governments to exchange information and consult each other, without formal pressure. When regional cooperation moves to the level of mutual liquidity provision, then moral hazard creates a strong case for monitoring and surveillance, and a clear need for specific enforcement mechanisms. An appropriate reference point for such regional activities would be IMF consultation and conditionality. Finally, when the regional grouping agrees on deepening regional integration through exchange rate coordination, monetary policy coordination then becomes as crucial as mutual economic surveillance.

The appropriate reference point in the progression from independence to integration is, of course, the movement of Europe from the Common Market to the European Union. Between independence and integration lies coordination, that is, joint identification of problems, and the pursuit of mutually beneficial policy objectives. Various forms, such as informal consultation, peer pressure, and rule-based penalties may be used for encouraging and enforcing certain common policies (UN ESCAP 2000).

The ASEAN+3 policy dialogue process

The necessity for and the structure of the surveillance mechanisms depend on the objectives of the group of countries engaged in policy dialogue. Both intensive and extensive cooperation cannot be carried out in a vacuum, unless the expected benefits are great enough to induce the support of all participating countries. A policy dialogue bereft of concrete action agendas and visible outcomes results only in empty rhetoric. For this reason, an effective surveillance mechanism presupposes well-defined objectives and ensures sufficient benefits for cooperation.

The surveillance mechanism in East Asia envisages the following objectives:

- sustaining stability of financial markets
- promoting economic integration in East Asia

At present, the ASEAN+3 group feels that it is critical to enhance the policy dialogue process among the participating countries as part of the CMI. Better monitoring and surveillance could help in identifying emerging issues and potential problems, and thus enable countries to take prompt corrective action at the national level, or jointly at the regional level, if necessary. As often observed in the IMF surveillance process, the symptoms of the crises and economic vulnerabilities have not been effectively delineated. Regional initiatives could complement the IMF surveillance process, since the economies in the region have become much more interdependent through trade and financial channels over the last decade. Precisely because spillover effects in the region are insidious, there is a pressing need to engage in regional monitoring and surveillance.

Although regional surveillance initiatives provide a potentially meaningful and substantive value-added contribution to existing multilateral and other mechanisms, East Asian countries do not yet have specified common policy objectives. Crisis prevention or financial stability is rather broad and ambiguous as a policy objective for surveillance. A more sophisticated mechanism of surveillance will result from the intensification of monetary and financial cooperation. As the scope of the ASEAN+3 financial cooperation framework is broadened, and other initiatives such as exchange rate coordination emerge, the objectives of a concomitant surveillance mechanism will be more clearly spelled out. In this regard, policy dialogue through peer review will be a good starting point, but it will not operate in a vacuum. The next main issue, then, is to identify the appropriate modalities, and to design the necessary instruments, techniques, and institutions for an effective system of monitoring and surveillance.

The ASEAN+3 group recognizes the importance of establishing an effective system of policy dialogue to complement the CMI operations. An enhanced regional policy dialogue process could promote sound macroeconomic policies and prevent any moral hazard problems that might arise in operating the CMI.[5] Despite this recognition, the ASEAN+3 countries have been cautious, and as a result, slow in creating a formal mechanism of surveillance. Since the inception of the CMI, informal economic reviews and policy dialogues have taken place at the ASEAN+3 Finance and Central Bank Deputies' Meeting (AFDM+3) and ASEAN+3 Finance Ministers' Meeting (AFMM+3). In order to enhance the existing process of economic reviews and policy dialogues, this group of countries decided to establish a Study Group at their meeting in Honolulu on 9 May 2001. The task of the Study Group is to examine ways of enhancing the effectiveness of ASEAN+3 economic reviews and policy dialogues to complement the Bilateral Swap Agreements (BSA) under the CMI. It was agreed that Japan and Malaysia would co-chair the Study Group and that its membership, which is voluntary, would consist of finance and central bank officials from the ASEAN+3 countries.

The first meeting of the ASEAN+3 Study Group was held in Kuala Lumpur on 22 November 2001. The main purpose was to discuss a joint paper prepared by Bank Negara Malaysia and the Ministry of Finance of Japan, entitled "Possible Modalities to Enhance the Effectiveness of Economic Reviews and Policy Dialogues among the ASEAN+3 Countries." The paper recommended an action agenda to be implemented in two phases. Phase 1 was to enhance the existing process of economic reviews and policy dialogues among the member countries, while phase 2 would see the emergence of a new strengthened policy dialogue mechanism. At this meeting, they agreed to this two-phase approach for enhancing a regional surveillance mechanism.

During phase one, the ASEAN+3 countries were to move one step forward in formalizing the current process. More specifically, they agreed to hold an informal meeting of the AFDM+3 to focus on economic reviews and policy dialogues in September or October, back to back with the IMF/World Bank annual meeting. This meeting was to be informal, in the sense that participation would be voluntary. However, it was essential that all of the countries involved in the network of the bilateral swap arrangements (namely the CMI countries) assume the responsibility of participating in the informal meeting, and that they circulate brief reports on their respective recent economic development. A common template or format for the report was to be developed to ensure the comparability of the reports submitted by countries at the meetings. This format would then serve as a guide, and each country would be given some flexibility in preparing the report. In addition, the report could include issues of concern to the participating countries, such as economic and policy assessments made by the IMF, World Bank, and the ADB.

The second meeting of the ASEAN+3 Study Group was held in Myanmar on 2 April 2002. There was more intensive discussion of the possible specific modalities for phase 2 proposed by Malaysia. Under phase two, it was proposed that a group or an institution be designated to undertake high quality and in-depth reviews and assessments. The following were proposed in order to determine the participants in this new discussion group:

- to develop an ASEAN secretariat

- to use existing institutions, such as regional multilateral institutions, think-tanks, or universities

- to form a working group.

Whichever option was chosen, however, the proposal made it clear that the group or institution was not to be a substitute for the Fund surveillance process, and would certainly not be another bureaucracy. Instead, the assessment by a working group or an institution could be used in negotiations for those countries requesting financial assistance from the IMF, or under IMF programs, by providing information and possible policy recommendations different from those prescribed by the IMF. The ASEAN+3 countries would also use these assessments, but they were only to be used for peer review at the AFDM+3 and not for public use.

For the next two years, ASEAN+3 policy-makers shelved the two-phase plan for creating a surveillance system for the CMI. At the annual meeting of the ADB in April 2004, the finance ministers of ASEAN+3 revived the surveillance issue and agreed to undertake it, as part of an overall assessment and further consolidation of the CMI. A working group, chaired by China, was created to conduct the review. The working group was expected to deliberate and produce a report on the five major issues related to a further development of the CMI. The amount of liquidity any country could draw from the CMI was small, and at this stage of development, there was no guarantee that the Bilateral Swap Agreements (BSA) would be activated, as some of the swap-providing countries could exercise their right to opt out. In order to remove this uncertainty, the CMI members sought to institutionalize joint activation of the BSAs to ensure the timely availability of liquidity from the system.

Multiple contractual parties

Under the current arrangement of the CMI, any country wishing to obtain short-term liquidity must discuss the activation with all swap-providing countries separately. If a large number of the members refuse to provide swaps and the various swap providers demand different terms and conditions, then the CMI may cease to be an efficient liquidity support system. Such time-consuming discussion of the swap activation with multiple contractual parties may deprive the swap-requesting country of the ability to mount an effective and prompt defense against a speculative attack. In order to avoid this bias inherent in the system, it has been proposed to create a secretariat or committee to determine joint activation of all swap contracts from countries requesting them, so that disbursements can be made in an efficient and timely manner.

Increasing the drawing limit

A second issue requiring resolution is how to mobilize support within ASEAN+3 for an increase in the automatic drawing limit. As noted earlier, the swap-requesting country can draw up to ten percent of the contract amount without subjecting itself to the IMF conditionality on policy adjustments. Some members of the CMI argue that the limit should be raised to 20 or 30 percent. However, the CMI members realize that multilateralization, together with an increase in the drawing limit would not be possible unless a more effective surveillance system is established. As pointed out earlier, creating a surveillance mechanism for the CMI has been a controversial issue, and it is uncertain whether the working group will be able to develop a system acceptable to all members.

Structure and location of CMI secretariat

Assuming that CMI members agree to its creation, and if members agree on multilateralization and on the creation of a regional surveillance unit, then their agreement would amount to establishing an institution similar to a regional monetary fund. The ASEAN+3 members may feel that it is premature to set up such an institution, but they do need an institution that can manage and set terms and conditions of bilateral swap transactions and perform secretariat functions for the meetings of AFMM+3, AFDM+3, and other formal and informal meetings for policy dialogues and coordination among the members. There have been several proposals for organizing an ASEAN+3 secretariat, but none has been seriously considered, because the member countries have been divided on its structure and location.

Enlargement of CMI membership

Several non-member Asian countries have expressed their interest in joining the CMI. At present, the consensus view is that until some of the operational issues of the CMI are settled, enlargement should be postponed for the time being. Only the possible inclusion of some of the less developed ASEAN members in the CMI will be discussed at the working group.

Monetary integration

Finally, in recent years, foreign exchange policy issues have dominated policy debates and dialogues within ASEAN+3. With the growing need to stabilize bilateral exchange rates among the ASEAN+3 states, proposals have been made to strengthen the CMI network so that it could serve as an institutional base for monetary integration in East Asia in the future. Although a formal discussion of monetary integration has been put on hold, this issue may come up again at future meetings of the AFMM+3.

Enforcement mechanisms: Does peer pressure work?

Under a loose and informal policy dialogue framework, formal enforcement mechanisms to impose sanctions and fines on countries that do not comply with agreed-upon policy guidelines and recommendations may not be needed. In keeping with the ASEAN policy of non-interference, the regional surveillance process in East Asia should be built on the basis of consensus and informality (Manzano, 2001).[6] At this stage of development of the CMI, the participating countries are not prepared to negotiate regional agreements that include provisions for sanctions and fines for countries that do not adjust their domestic policies as in conformity with common policy objectives. This unwillingness would then make it difficult for a regional surveillance process to impose politically unpopular policies on the member countries and, hence, may pose a serious moral hazard problem.[7]

Realizing this difficulty in creating a regional monitoring and surveillance unit as part of the CMI, the ASEAN+3 have chosen to rely on the IMF to impose and enforce policy conditionalities on those countries drawing from the BSAs. However, in the long run, the participating countries are planning to wean themselves from their reliance on the IMF. If the CMI develops into a regional financial arrangement, independent of the IMF, the architect(s) of the CMI will have to decide whether the arrangement could be supported by a surveillance mechanism based on peer review and pressure, instead of formal policy conditionalities and sanctions. In our view, economic policy dialogues and peer monitoring may not provide an institutional framework that can minimize the moral hazard problem. In this regard, it is important to distinguish conceptually two different types of moral hazard in connection with regional financial arrangements and related surveillance processes.

One is related to liquidity assistance, while the other is related to collective actions required for common policy objectives. Peer pressure or review may not be effective in rectifying the former, and should be supplemented by the surveillance and its conditionalities attached to the liquidity provision. If the CMI develops into a financial arrangement more or less independent from the IMF, then the regional financial arrangement should be designed to discipline the borrowers to adhere to sound macroeconomic and financial policies, by imposing conditionalities and pre-qualification. Otherwise, the Asian financial arrangement will go bankrupt.

The second type of moral hazard is not necessarily related to liquidity assistance. When common policy objectives are set, joint policy coordination is required to achieve a desirable outcome. Peer pressure is likely to work best when observable policy parameters exist and policy impact on neighboring countries is neutral. However, conceptually, three types of surveillance processes can be considered in the case of policy coordination.

First, a simple peer review process, without a specific enforcement mechanism, may be found among various policy dialogue groups. For example, the current ASEAN+3 policy dialogue process, the Manila Framework Group (MFG), and Group of Seven (G7) carry out economic reviews of the countries involved without an enforcement mechanism. Informal peer pressure is the only tactic used to encourage members to voluntarily implement policy recommendations.

Second, some groups may require strict obligations for membership. For instance, the Organization for Economic Cooperation and Development (OECD) is often referred to as a club of advanced countries, satisfying a list of high qualifications for current and capital account liberalization, labor relations, environment standards, and many other economic policies. The OECD conducts annual reviews of its members and goes through a transparent process of drafting and approving reports. Annual country reports include policy recommendations or warnings, to encourage member countries to correct unsatisfactory policies and practices. However, those policy recommendations are not necessarily compulsory.

Third, the surveillance process may require strict policy conditionalities, sanctions, and fines for countries which do not satisfy the obligations. IMF lending in support of adjustment programs is conditional on the country undertaking certain agreed policy measures. Under the Economic and Monetary Union (EMU) in Europe, peer pressure is a means to achieve the objective of economic policy coordination among members. However, budgetary policy surveillance according to the Stability and Growth Pact contains the possibility of pecuniary sanctions, beyond other coordination procedures based on peer pressure.

Under what conditions would peer pressure be likely to work? In the absence of an incentive-compatible mechanism, countries may have less incentive to achieve collective objectives. Without an institutional setup, mere peer pressure or a peer review process cannot provide an effective incentive to commit member countries to perform the collective activities required to achieve common policy objectives. To ensure that peer pressure is effective as a motivational device, a set of policy objectives should be clearly defined.

To prevent free-rider problems, effective monitoring is also essential to identify which parties do not comply with particular policy efforts. However, policy efforts are not always observable, so that moral hazard prevails in this kind of uncertainty.

Kandel and Lazear (1992) note the usefulness of classifying peer pressure as either internal or external. Internal pressure exists when a country or individual experiences a disadvantage (disutility) from hurting others, even if others cannot identify the offender. External pressure exists when the disadvantage depends specifically on identification by others. Internal pressure is like guilt, whereas external pressure is more like shame. In the context of surveillance, the important issue is observability. A country feels shame when others can observe its actions. Without observability, only guilt can be an effective form of pressure. The surveillance and monitoring process should exert peer pressure to motivate member countries to perform the required activities. Key observable policy parameters (expected policy efforts) should be developed in order to give a clear message to the offenders. Otherwise, some offenders may feel guilty, but not make the maximum effort required for common policy objectives.

Team spirit and partnership should be based on mutual trust and a sense of responsibility. Those psychological components may be more important than institutional settings or rule-based norms. However, both internal and external pressure will fail if there is neither self-imposed guilt nor a feeling of shame. Thus, a group of participants should design a credible punishment mechanism. That punishment should not be random, but should be deliberately designed, specifying under what conditions penalties or sanctions will be imposed. As long as the enforcement mechanism works as a credible threat, the common policy objectives can be achieved through maximum collective effort.

The surveillance and policy coordination may have a double-decker structure in policy formation and implementation. Under EMU, only specific common policies such as monetary and exchange rate policies are binding at the level of the Community, while economic policies, such as budgetary and structural policies remain under the national sovereignty of member countries. In the European Community, the framework of broad economic policy guidelines (BEPGs) provides a basis for policy coordination. This structured surveillance process has contributed to assessing the consistency of each member country's economic policies. At their current stage of development, the ASEAN+3 countries do not seem well prepared for establishing a policy coordination mechanism in the surveillance process. In the case of European integration, a more effective and structured surveillance process started only when the European countries sought monetary integration in the 1990s. Thus, it will take more time for the ASEAN+3 countries to agree to establish more comprehensive and structured surveillance systems.

NOTES

1 The origin and legal basis of the surveillance function stem from Article IV, section 3(b) of the Articles of Agreement, which states that "the Fund shall exercise firm surveillance over the exchange rate policies of members and shall adopt specific principles for the guidance of all members with respect to those policies. Each member shall provide the Fund with information necessary for such surveillance, and, when requested by the Fund, shall consult with it on the member's exchange rate policies.

2 ROSCs summarize the extent to which countries observe certain internationally recognized standards on a voluntary basis. The IMF has recognized 11 areas and associated standards as useful for the operational work of the Fund and the World Bank. These include data dissemination, monetary and financial policy transparency, fiscal transparency, banking supervision, securities, insurance, payment systems, corporate governance, accounting, auditing, and insolvency and creditor rights. Reports are used to help sharpen policy discussions with national authorities by rating agencies in their assessments and in the private sector for risk assessment.

3 Wang and Woo, 2004, p. 429.

4 Eichengreen (2003) advocates the establishment of an Asian Financial Institute to promote financial cooperation as the appropriate regional response to the 1997–98 Asian crisis. One of the tasks which should be undertaken by the ASEAN+3 policy dialogue group is to strengthen its technical expertise in financial sector regulation and financial market development.

5 Although the CMI does not need to design its own conditionality at this point, it is important for it to establish its own surveillance mechanism. Under the CMI framework, 10 percent of the swap arrangements can be disbursed without IMF involvement. But because this 10 percent of swap can be disbursed only with the consent of swap-providing countries, these should formulate their own assessment of the swap-requesting country. At present, the current practices under the ASEAN+3 process cannot effectively capture emerging problems.

6 In contrast to Europe, East Asia lacks both the tradition of integrationist thinking and the web of interlocking agreements which encourage monetary and financial cooperation. Eichengreen and Bayoumi (1999) stress that East Asia does not meet the necessary intellectual preconditions for regional integration. For this reason, they conclude that it is unrealistic to speak of pooling national sovereignties.

7 The IMF will play the role of an insurance firm, with its own monitoring and surveillance programs. However, the presence of a regional fund as a cooperative partnership fund will complicate the welfare consequences, depending on whether the regional fund is in a better position to monitor the effort than the IMF. If the regional fund cannot effectively harness its monitoring capabilities, to reduce the moral hazard problem, countries may become less cautious. The IMF will tend to provide less insurance. The regional fund may crowd out the more effective insurance provided by the IMF, thus becoming completely dysfunctional. In this regard, peer monitoring is essential for controlling the moral hazards involved in the partnership, and may even improve social welfare by enhancing countries' risk sharing.

REFERENCES

Bank Negara Malaysia and the Ministry of Finance of Japan. 2001. "Possible Modalities to Enhance the Effectiveness of Economic Reviews and Policy Dialogues among the ASEAN+3 Countries." Paper prepared for ASEAN+3 Study Group. Kuala Lumpur. 22 November.

Claessens, S., R. Dornbusch, and Y. C. Park. 2000. "Contagion: How It Spreads and How It Can Be Stopped." *World Bank Economic Review*. September.

Crow, J., R. Arriazu, and N. Thygesen. 2000. "External Evaluation of Surveillance Report." *External Evaluation of IMF Surveillance Report*. 1999. Washington, D.C.: IMF, Available at: http://www.imf.org/external/pubs/ft/exev/surv/index/htm

Eichengreen, B. 2002. "Capital Account Liberalization: What Do the Cross-Country Studies Tell Us?" *World Bank Economic Review*. March.

———. 2003. "What to Do with the Chiang Mai Initiative." *Asian Economic Papers* 2(1):1–49. January.

Eichengreen, B. and T. Bayoumi. 1999. "Is Asia an Optimum Currency Area? Can It Become One? S. Collignon, J. Pisani-Ferry, and Y. C. Park, eds., *Exchange Rate Policies in Emerging Asian Countries*. London: Routledge.

International Monetary Fund. 1999. *External Evaluation of IMF Surveillance Report*. Washington, D.C.: 14 September.

———. 2001. "IMF Surveillance: A Factsheet." Available at: http://www.imf.org/external/np/exr/facts/surv.htm

Kandel, E. and E. P. Lazear. 1992. "Peer Pressure and Partnerships." *Journal of Political Economy* 100(4):801–17. August.

Manzano, G. 2001. "Is There Any Value-added in the ASEASN Surveillance Process?" *ASEAN Economic Bulletin* 18:94–102.

United Nations Economic and Social Commission for Asia and the Pacific. (ESCAP). 2000. Available at: http://www.unescap.org

Wang, Y. and W. Woo. 2004. "A Timely Information Exchange Mechanism, An Effective Surveillance System, and an Improved Financial Architecture for East Asia." *Monetary and Financial Integration in East Asia: The Way Ahead* 2: 425–58. ADB.

The Internationalization of Markets for Local Currency Bonds

PHILIP TURNER, Head of Secretariat Group, Bank for International Settlements[1]

Introduction

The efficient allocation of resources, effective macroeconomic policies, and financial stability in large emerging market countries all depend on the existence of liquid bond markets in the local currency. The period between the mid-1990s and the present has indeed been one of phenomenal growth in emerging economies' bond markets. In the mid-1990s, the outstanding stock was about US$1 trillion. It is now close to US$4 trillion (Table 1). This rapid pace of issuance was fuelled by Latin American borrowers scaling back international bond issuance, by heavy public sector borrowing in the wake of the Asian crisis and, most recently, by substantial issuance to finance massive foreign exchange reserves accumulation.

In addition, major reforms have taken place, and several countries have established programmes to nurture local bond markets. But the results in many markets have been rather disappointing. Despite a huge increase in issuance, market liquidity has not developed as much as had been hoped.

Why such limited success? I have argued elsewhere[2] that developing bond markets raises issues and policy dilemmas that range across the whole spectrum of policies, fiscal, monetary, and financial. In many cases, these dilemmas are resolved in ways that, in effect, undermine bond market development. Quite often bond markets are stifled by the unintended consequences of seemingly unrelated government policies. The three main points can be briefly stated. First, government bond markets should be as liquid as possible. The market, not government, must price the bonds. The authorities in each country must constantly ask market participants about constraints they perceive on bond trading. Taxation, settlement practices, custodial arrangements, fragmented

Table 1: Domestic debt securities outstanding[1] (in US$ billion)

	1994	1995	1996	1997	1998	1999	2000	2001	2002	2003	2004	2005
Latin America[2]	274	316	394	466	522	449	493	544	441	567	686	913
Argentina	30	26	29	34	40	43	47	37	32	46	51	72
Brazil	173	231	297	344	391	294	298	312	212	300	372	523
Mexico	40	23	26	38	44	63	93	137	140	153	184	227
China[3]	42	63	83	111	160	208	259	307	391	48	672	907
India[3]	64	71	81	75	86	102	114	130	156	23	249	279
Korea	185	227	239	130	240	265	269	293	381	446	569	656
Other Asia[4]	199	229	284	254	305	374	387	409	457	518	578	607
Central Europe[5]	39	47	52	50	65	68	71	90	130	164	213	206
Russia	3	17	43	65	8	9	8	5	8	12	21	25
Turkey	16	21	27	30	38	43	55	85	92	140	170	185
South Africa	101	102	82	83	71	71	59	40	53	80	107	107
TOTAL[6]	923	1,093	1,285	1,264	1,495	1,589	1,715	1,903	2,109	2,610	3,265	3,885

Notes:
1. As of 8 August 2006.
2. Latin America includes Argentina, Brazil, Mexico, Chile, Colombia, and Peru. For the first time, the data for Argentina include domestically targeted issues in foreign currency, and domestically targeted repackaged issues.
3. For the first time, the data for China include issues by the central bank. The central government sector data of China included at end-2005 relate to end-2004.
4. Other Asia includes Malaysia, Taiwan (China), Hong Kong SAR, Singapore, the Philippines, Thailand, and Indonesia.
5. Central Europe is the total of the Czech Republic, Hungary, and Poland.
6. The total is the sum of the countries and areas shown.

Source: BIS.

issuance, trading rules on particular institutions, and many other factors require regular and careful review. It is hard for outside observers to generalize about such impediments, but market insiders will usually know, all too well, what is wrong. Secondly, the investor and issuance base must be as wide as possible. Finally, the banking system has to adapt to a new world where bond markets lay the foundations for a very different approach to the pricing, the management and the trading of credit risk.

The question addressed in this paper is what can be done to encourage foreign investment in emerging markets through local bond markets. Given what has happened in just a decade—which has confounded those who were pessimistic about the possibilities of local bond markets—it is tempting to reply "nothing special need be done" because local currency bond markets are already very large, and because the reforms needed to make bond markets liquid are often necessary anyway.

Nevertheless, the implicit question of this symposium, whether enough is being done by emerging market borrowers to take advantage of innovations in the financial industry, is a good one. The four questions posed in this paper are the headings to what follows.

What are the advantages of using international markets?

International markets are attractive because they have a stable and predictable infrastructure, clear legal arrangements, and efficient tax arrangements. The liquidity of such markets is high, and this facilitates the hedging of positions. Indeed, constant technical progress makes these markets ever more complete and so, prima facie, attractive to borrowers.

One key, recent structural development in global financial markets, which has implications for emerging markets, is the growing importance of credit derivatives markets. One aspect is the development of markets for so-called synthetic instruments, in which credit default swaps (CDS) are used to transfer and restructure credit risk. This is also the case for emerging market debt, where a visible development has been the growing liquidity in the market for CDS, based on emerging market sovereign debt, denominated in US dollars and euro. A related recent development is the creation of indices based on sovereign debt CDS contracts. These indices are still in their infancy, but, in time, should boost liquidity, and could potentially provide an alternative market benchmark for emerging market sovereign debt denominated in foreign currencies.[3]

The great bulk of international bonds are in fact issued in just two currencies: 43 percent in US dollars and 41 percent in euros.[4] These currency percentages are much more concentrated than, say, the US or euro area share of world GDP. This is presumably because investors value the liquidity of these markets and the ease with which credit risks can be hedged.

Spreading over additional currencies would almost certainly dilute liquidity. In addition, issuance in international markets could divert liquidity from local markets. At present, there are no signs that a market for credit derivatives based on local currency bonds is being created, although it may not be long before creative investment banks offer OTC products. Therefore, the development of credit derivatives based on foreign currency emerging market debt may well increase the relative attractiveness of foreign currency-denominated debt. All this suggests that issuance of local currency debt in international markets is likely to remain rather limited.

What is true is that weak domestic infrastructures or even impediments to non-resident investment in domestic markets may mean that, as Tovar (2005) concludes, issuing local currency bonds in international markets may be a second best solution—at least until domestic markets can be made to work well.

Are domestic bonds issued in local markets attractive to foreigners?

There is increasing evidence that foreign investors' appetite for domestic bonds is growing. Data on bond trading from the Emerging Market Trading Association show that foreign trading in local paper has risen sharply. Particularly notable is that trading in paper of two countries which have had recent crises (Brazil and Turkey) has risen sharply. In addition, a recent survey by the IMF finds that the share of foreign creditors in domestically issued debt has risen from under 6 percent in 2000 to over 12 percent by 2005.[5]

To understand the attractions of local currency bonds issued by emerging market entities for foreign investors, it is useful to consider three dimensions of returns on investment in local currency bonds: the mean return; the variance of returns; and the covariance of such returns with other assets in a global portfolio. The following paragraphs examine these three aspects,[6] using statistics on the performance of local currency bonds over the period January 2002 to February 2006. These are summarized in Table 2 (prepared by Srichander Ramaswamy). It should of course be remembered that this was an exceptionally good period for emerging markets, so the results discussed below should be viewed critically.

Average annual return of an unhedged portfolio

The average annual return of an unhedged portfolio modelled on JPMorgan Chase's Government Bond Index of emerging market bonds was 18.75 percent in dollar terms. Hedging the exchange rate risk, however, would have produced the much lower average return: only 6.10 percent. This is still higher than a global government bond benchmark of developed countries (GBI–G in Table 2).

Table 2: Risk-return characteristics and diversification benefits of emerging market government bonds (January 2002 to February 2006)

Description	Annual return (%)	Annual volatility (%)	Sharpe ratio[1]	Excess return vs. GBI-G[2] (%)	Correlation vs. GBI-G
GBI-EM, unhedged	18.75	9.35	1.79	14.80	0.264
GBI-EM, hedged into $	6.10	3.30	1.23	2.15	0.598
GBI-EM Broad, unhedged	16.80	6.80	2.17	12.60	0.271
GBI-EM Broad, hedged into $	6.97	2.86	1.72	2.77	0.509

Notes: GBI-EM = JPMorgan Chase's Government Bond Index–Emerging Markets. GBI–EM Broad = (GBI–EM) + bonds issued in China, India, and Russia.

1. Ratio of the excess return of the index to the risk-free return in US dollars and the index volatility.

2. Excess return vs. a duration-neutral global government bond benchmark of developed countries.

Sources: JPMorgan Chase; BIS calculations.

The size of this hedged/unhedged difference shows that exchange rate movements have played a crucial role. In particular, the uncovered interest rate parity condition has been violated—that is, the rate of nominal depreciation of EM currencies proved to be less than the initial interest rate differential vis à vis US dollar rates. This is partly because of the risk premium earned from holding a more volatile currency. But it seems mainly to reflect the fact that fundamentals in several emerging market countries have improved much more during the past two to three years than markets had expected in 2002. Hence, a large proportion of the high returns from investing in local currency bonds over the past four years is unlikely to be replicated.

Variance of the returns

A second important dimension is the variance of the returns. Calculations show that the Sharpe ratio—the mean return divided by the variance—of portfolios of emerging market bonds has, in recent years, been well above that for classic dollar, euro, and yen government benchmarks.[7] One fund manager recently noted that the mean return on its emerging market local currency debt portfolio (with a large Asian weight) was only a little lower, but the variance much lower, than on its flagship dollar-denominated fund.[8] The conclusion the fund manager drew was that emerging market local currency debt provided foreign investors with a lower risk alternative to comparable dollar debt.

Covariance

A third aspect is the covariance between a portfolio of local currency bonds and that of the global portfolio. The lower the covariance, the greater would be the diversification offered by such bonds. Several studies confirm that the covariance of a portfolio of emerging market local currency bonds with traditional portfolios of government bonds from developed countries is rather low.[9] Hence local currency bonds from emerging markets should enhance diversification possibilities for international investors.

Confronted with evidence of average returns and correlations calculated over periods of comparative calm, a wise investor will nevertheless ask, "But what happens in periods of stress, when markets fall?" In such periods, correlations between different markets tend to rise, sometimes dramatically. The absence of a major crisis in international capital markets during the past few years makes it impossible to assess this argument in a definitive way. It is not difficult to find episodes that call into question the diversification benefits of EM bonds. During the widespread market downturn in spring 2001, for instance, emerging market local currency bonds did fall more sharply than other assets. And during the sell-off in US Treasuries that began in mid-2003, Asian local bond markets did not perform well. An examination of several recent down-turns at the BIS, however, found no *general* evidence of an increase in correlations during times of market stress that was large enough to jeopardize the diversification benefits of local currency emerging market bonds. Even the dramatic resurgence of turbulence in global financial markets during May 2006 does not appear to have decisively contradicted this reassuring conclusion.

There is, in short, little doubt that local currency bonds can offer valuable diversification benefits to foreign investors. This means that those countries that develop "better" local bond markets (better infrastructure, no tax impediments, etc.) will be more successful in attracting foreign money, without having to risk the dangerous currency exposures that can come from dollar debt in international markets.

There is, however, a potential danger if only a few countries that develop deep markets, while other similarly placed countries do not: proxy hedging strategies may be used by traders to offset positions in thin markets that are difficult to liquidate quickly. For instance, Australian and Hong Kong paper were apparently used in this way when the Asian crisis broke in 1997. There have been signs in recent months, for instance, that speculative pressure on the Chinese currency has been diverted to other Asian markets, which are convertible and have deep financial markets. If such proxy hedging effects are large, there could be a case for cooperation among countries in developing their debt markets.

Some innovations to exploit

How far emerging market borrowers could make greater use of recent financial innovations to deepen markets is worthy of careful exploration. An obvious theoretical possibility is to structure bonds in ways that share risks with creditors. For instance, bonds with coupons related to commodity prices could help protect commodity exporters. GNP-indexed bonds are another possibility. This symposium reviews some recent suggestions. An important constraint, however, is that the issuance of different types of bond inevitably fragments liquidity.

Another idea would be the greater use of securitization. In developed countries, banks have become adept at bundling bank loans into packages to be sold in the market. This can work best for home mortgages and consumer credits, two areas of recent strong growth in several developing Asian economies. The reason is that decisions about the pricing of such loans tend to depend not on any special knowledge or relationship, but rather on "objective" criteria (such as income, valuation of the collateralized asset, and so on). As this process develops, new debt instruments come on to the market. A recent BIS study on the Danish mortgage market underlined how such bond markets could develop, even in a small market.[10] Wolfgang Fritsch (2004) has argued that the German Pfandbrief model (covered bonds, supported by mortgages) seems well suited for a bank-centered financial system.[11] The Pfandbrief represents the biggest segment of the German bond market. The twin lines of defense—the special supervisory procedures that apply to specialist issuing banks, and strict rules about the administration of collateral and other factors—made these instruments simple and transparent. Many central European countries have adopted such instruments.

Which international initiatives foster local currency bond markets?

The clear benefits from the development of local currency bond markets have led many to propose various international initiatives to foster such markets.

One of the most famous is by Eichengreen, Hausmann, and Panizza (2003). They propose that an emerging-market (EM) index be created, composed of an inflation-indexed basket of the currencies of roughly the 20 or so largest emerging economies, with the weights in the basket corresponding to each country's GDP (at purchasing power parity). The World Bank and other multilateral institutions would issue debt denominated in this index. G-10 sovereigns would also be asked to issue debt in the EM index, and would swap their currency exposure with countries whose currencies were included in the EM index.

The main drawback of this proposal is simply the absence of markets for many of the components of this index, which would make pricing difficult. Not all major emerging market currencies are fully convertible; comparatively few have tradable price-index-linked debt. Where markets exist, they are often illiquid, which inhibits trading and makes hedging strategies harder. Finally, governments in emerging markets are often reluctant to pay the high coupons required for local currency bonds. These issues are explored more fully in Chapter 8 of Goldstein and Turner (2004).

An alternative approach would be for IFIs to be ready to issue in non-dollar currencies, once liquidity in local bond markets has passed a certain threshold. In this way, liquidity could be further enhanced. The Asian Development Bank (ADB) recently floated a 10-year rupee bond, in order to offer private sector borrowers Indian rupee loans for projects in need of long-term currency financing. It is of particular interest that the ADB said that they would consider issuing similar bonds "in those developing member countries where the bond markets are sufficiently developed." This is, of course, quite different from indiscriminate IFI issuance in any emerging market currency.

Another important development is the Asian Bond Fund initiative of the Executives' Meeting of East Asia–Pacific Central Banks (EMEAP), in particular ABF2, which will invest in local currency-denominated Asian bonds.[12] At one simple level, this initiative could make sense in facilitating the investment of the reserves of Asian central banks in *Asian* financial assets, rather than in US Treasuries. But the project has much greater ambitions. Noting that the aim would be to promote the development of index bond funds in the regional markets, the EMEAP press statement puts emphasis on "[enhancing] the domestic as well as regional bond infrastructure." The statement further underlines that ABF2 is being "designed in such a way that it will facilitate investment by other public and private sector investors." The idea is to create a Pan-Asian Bond Index Fund (PAIF), which would accept investment from non-central-bank investors who want to have a well-diversified exposure to bond markets in Asia. A key complementary part of this project will be efforts to "improve the market structure by identifying and minimising the legal, regulatory and tax hurdles in [bond] markets." This is clearly crucial: see the exploratory work of Ismail Dalla and others at the ADB, on the areas where some form of harmonization might be needed.[13] Häusler (2003) also argues that very different institutional arrangements serve to unnecessarily segment local securities markets. This puts off potential foreign investors, and makes it more difficult for them to pool and hedge investment risks.

Conclusion

The markets for EM local currency bonds have developed very rapidly in recent years. The pace of this development has, doubtless, been stimulated by some special factors which are unlikely to persist. Bond prices have risen almost everywhere over the past two to three years, giving investors significant capital gains. And several emerging market currencies have appreciated in real terms. At some point, these favorable elements will reverse, and it remains to be seen how investors will react.

Nevertheless, the longer-term prospects of these markets do seem to be good. For borrowers, there are the attractions of borrowing in their own currency and, for foreign investors, the benefits of increased diversification. There is clear room for the greater development of corporate bond and asset-backed markets. Many market participants believe that the expansion of local currency debt markets has much further to go. More needs to be done to improve the working of local bond markets: the EMEAP and ADB initiatives should help in this direction.

Notwithstanding this positive assessment of a development, which has made financial systems in emerging markets much safer than they were a decade ago, there are two possible concerns:

1. The first is the lack of comprehensive data on the nature of domestic debt (e.g., short-term vs. long-term, exchange-rate-linked capital guarantees, etc.), which makes it difficult to assess the borrower's exposures to various risks. The ADB[14] and the IADB have both prepared comprehensive databases for their regions. Nevertheless, there is at present no comprehensive and consistent

international database on domestic debt securities similar to that for international debt securities. This must be corrected.

2. The second is that several years of heavy forex intervention have altered balance sheet positions in several emerging markets in a major way. Indeed, much of the rise in gross bond issuance in many emerging economies reflects the financing of a substantial rise in foreign exchange reserves.[15] Of course, increased foreign currency assets matched by local currency liabilities do not add immediately to the burden of net debt. But it does have significant implications for the balance sheet position of the country, and thus for risk exposures: if the local currency were to appreciate by a large amount, the net asset position of the country would worsen.

NOTES

1 This paper reflects my own views, and not necessarily those of the BIS. It draws on work by Jacob Gyntelberg, Thomas Jans, Srichander Ramaswamy, Marco Sorge, and Agustin Villar. Thanks are due to Bill White for helpful comments.

2 See Turner (2003) and Goldstein and Turner (2004). BIS (2002) provides a comprehensive review of these issues.

3 At present there are two broad emerging market CDS-based indices: one is CDX.EM diversified index, the other iTraxx Asia (Korea, Malaysia, China, Thailand, Philippines, and corporates from these countries).

4 Another 12 percent in sterling or in yen. The Swiss franc, Canadian dollar, and Australian dollar have only 1 percent each. These averages are for 1999 to 2004.

5 See IMF (2006), pp. 99–108.

6 A caveat is that return distributions are typically both skewed and have "fat tails" which cannot be simply identified by the mean and variance of returns.

7 Sharpe ratios for portfolios of developed country bonds and equities are generally below 0.5, as compared with Sharpe ratios above 1, as shown in Table 2.

8 The five-year annualized returns were (with the annualized standard deviation of monthly returns over three years in parentheses): local currency debt portfolio 23.9 percent (7.76 percent); dollar-denominated debt fund 25.4 percent (12.64 percent). This difference may have been partly due to a lower duration of the local currency portfolio and a somewhat better average credit quality. [Source: Booth (2003)].

9 See, for instance, Byun and Oswald (2006) and Giacomelli and Pianetti (2005).

10 See Frankel et al. (2004).

11 See the summary of the discussion in Bank of Canada (2004).

12 See the EMEAP press release of 15 April 2004.

13 Dalla, 2003.

14 See, for example, the Asian Bonds Monitor reports of the ADB (2006), available at: www.asianbondsonline.adb.org

15 See Mohanty and Turner (2005) for a fuller discussion of this.

REFERENCES

Asian Development Bank (ADB). 2006. "Growth in emerging East Asian local currency bond markets up 14 % in 2005." 24 March. *Asian Bond Monitor.* Available at: www.asianbondsonline.adb.org

Bank of Canada. 2004. "Summary of the discussion at the G20 Workshop on Developing Strong Domestic Financial Markets." *Quarterly Bulletin.* November. Available at: www.bankofcanada.ca/en/review/autumn04/stefan.html

Bank for International Settlements (BIS). 2002. "The development of bond markets in emerging economies." *BIS Papers* 11. June. Available at: www.bis.org/publ/bppdf/bispap11.htm

Booth, J. 2003. "Emerging market debt comes of age." *The Banker.* September.

Byun, J. and W. Oswald. 2006. "Emerging markets external debt as an asset class." JPMorgan Emerging Markets Research. 26 April.

Dalla, I. 2003. "Harmonisation of bond market rules and regulations in selected APEC economies." Manila: Asian Development Bank.

Emerging Market Trading Association. 2006. *Debt Trading Volume: Supplementary Analysis.* Available at: www.emta.org

Executives' Meeting of East Asia–Pacific Central Banks (EMEAP). 2004. Press release. 15 April.

Eichengreen, B., R. Hausmann, and U. Panizza. 2003. "The mystery of original sin." University of California (Berkeley), Harvard University, and Inter-American Development Bank.

Frankel, A., J. Gyntelberg, K. Kjeldsen, and M. Persson. 2004. "The Danish Mortgage Market." *BIS Quarterly Review.* March.

Fritsch, Wolfgang. 2004. Presentation at G20 Workshop. Bank of Canada.

Giacomelli, D. and F. Pianetti. 2005. "Expanding the Efficient Frontier." JPMorgan Emerging Markets Research. 6 April.

Goldstein, M. and P. Turner. 2004. "Controlling currency mismatches in emerging economies." Washington, D.C.: Institute for International Economics.

Häusler, G. 2003. "Trends in developing country capital markets around the world." Robert E. Litan, Michael Pomerleono, and V Sundararajan, eds. *The Future of Domestic Capital Markets in Developing Countries*. Washington, D.C.: Brookings Institution.

Hausmann, R. 2004. "Does currency denomination of debt hold key to taking away volatility?" *IMF Survey*. 15 March 2004.

International Monetary Fund (IMF). 2006. "Structural changes in emerging sovereign debt and implications for financial stability." *IMF Global Financial Stability Report*. Washington, D.C.: IMF. April.

McCauley, R. N. 2003. "Unifying government bond markets in East Asia." *BIS Quarterly Review*. December.

————. 2004. "Diversifying with Asian local currency bonds." *BIS Quarterly Review*. September.

Mohanty, M. S. and P. Turner. 2005. "Intervention: what are the domestic consequences?" in *Foreign exchange market intervention in emerging markets: motives, techniques and implications*. BIS Papers No 24. May. Available at: www.bis.org/publ/bppdf/bispap24.htm

Tovar, C. 2005. "International government debt denominated in local currency: recent developments in Latin America." *BIS Quarterly Review*. December. Available at: www.bis.org/publ/qtrpdf/r_qt0512.htm

Turner, P. 2003. "Developing bond markets: what are the policy issues?" Robert E. Litan, Michael Pomerleono, and V Sundararajan, eds. *The Future of Domestic Capital Markets in Developing Countries*. Washington, D.C.: Brookings Institution.

CHAPTER 2.6

The Evolving Exchange Rate Regimes in East Asia[1]

YU YONGDING, Director and Senior Fellow, Institute of World Economics and Politics, and Professor of World Economics, Postgraduate School of the Chinese Academy of Social Sciences

F or decades before the Asian financial crisis, East Asian currencies were pegged to the US dollar. In effect, their mutual link to the dollar was the collective nominal anchor for their domestic price levels. McKinnon (2000) coined the name "East Asian dollar standard (EADS)" for the exchange rate arrangement in East Asia.

Implications of the US dollar peg

After the Asian financial crisis, the pre-crisis peg to the US dollar was judged to be a failure. The experience of Asian countries indicates that a fixed exchange rate regime tends to invite speculative attacks, which lead to greater currency instability than a free floating exchange rate regime. There appear, currently, to be mainly two schools of thought on the future of exchange rate arrangements in East Asia. One school of thought argues for restoring the peg to the US dollar, the other for more flexible exchange rate regimes.

For the school in favor of the peg to the US dollar, nominal certainty and stability—whether implicit or explicit—is more important than real certainty and stability. East Asian countries, like other developing economies, are in a state of "fear of floating" (Reinhart, 2000). They fear appreciation, because it is unfavorable to capital inflows and exports; they fear depreciation, because it increases the liabilities expressed in domestic currencies of their enterprises. In a fragile financial system, depreciation leads to capital flight, speculative attacks, and the eventual collapse of the financial system. With regard to regional exchange rate arrangements, this school argues for a common monetary standard among trading partners in the region. According to McKinnon, such a common monetary standard, although not as good as a common currency which provides an independent anchor and full long-run exchange rate certainty, is still preferable to unrestricted exchange rate flexibility. The common monetary standard recommended by McKinnon is the US dollar.

For the school favoring a flexible exchange rate regime, the certainty and stability of the US dollar implies the uncertainty and instability of other major currencies. Kwan (2000) pointed out that with the yen fluctuating widely against the dollar, the traditional policy of pegging to the dollar has led to macroeconomic instability in Asian's developing countries. According to Kwan, since the Plaza Accord in 1985, there has been a clear tendency for economic growth in Asia to accelerate when the yen appreciates, and to decelerate when the yen depreciates. The weakening yen led to a marked deterioration in Asia's export performance and current account balances in 1996, paving the way for the currency crisis. Furthermore, for an individual country, nominal stability more often than not means real instability. For example, according to Deutsche Bank (March, 2005), though China's nominal exchange rate vis-à-vis the US dollar remained unchanged in 2004, in terms of the real effective exchange rate, the renminbi appreciated, due to rising domestic inflation for most of the year. Under a fixed exchange rate, adjustment is often made by means of changes in inflation.

The situation prior to the Asian financial crisis

For more than 15 years prior to the Asian financial crisis, China's exchange rate policy was based on the so-called real targeting approach (Zhang, 2000). During this period, the renminbi exchange rate underwent all sorts of changes: big bang, mini-devaluation, and so on. Determination of the exchange rate by the government was aimed at preserving export competitiveness. After the unification of the two exchange rates—official exchange rate and swap exchange rate in 1994—a managed floating regime was adopted. In the years leading up to the Asian financial crisis, the exchange rate of the renminbi vis-à-vis the US dollar appreciated 1 to 2 percent each year. The appreciation of the nominal exchange rate before the Asian financial crisis along with appreciation of the real exchange rate in 2004 shows that the

Chinese economy is not that vulnerable to appreciation. Does this explain why China has been so steadfast in refusing revaluation since 2003?

Measures taken during the Asian financial crisis

During the Asian financial crisis, in order to fence off a parallel crisis, the Chinese government adopted a no-devaluation policy. The arguments which convinced the government to shift to the dollar peg are summarized as follows (see Yu, 2001).

1. China needs financial stability more than anything else. With a very vulnerable financial system, devaluation and devaluation expectations would trigger financial panic, and lead to a financial crisis in China.

2. The devaluation of the renminbi would probably lead to the collapse of Hong Kong's peg to the US dollar, and a financial crisis in Hong Kong SAR.

3. Devaluing the renminbi could lead to competitive devaluation in Asia, which would worsen the Asian crisis and have a boomerang effect on China itself.

4. The substitution effects of the devaluation of the Japanese yen and other Asian currency on China's exports were much less obvious than the income effects of global recession on China's exports.

5. The foreign content of Chinese exports during the Asian crisis was as high as 57 percent; the competitive edge achieved by devaluation would immediately be offset, to a large extent, by price increases in foreign inputs of export goods.

6. Through the use of other policy measures, China is able to stimulate its exports effectively without resorting to devaluation.

7. Capital controls still in place were used to help reduce the pressure on the renminbi exchange rate by stopping or reducing capital flight.

8. The renminbi was not grossly over-valued. The pressure to devalue was created by the contagion effect, rather than by fundamental weaknesses in China's economy.

9. Maintenance of the current value of the renminbi would have the effect of forcing China's export enterprises to make extra efforts to raise productivity, so as to improve their competitiveness.

As a result of the adoption of the de facto peg to the US dollar, the real targeting approach, which had been fundamental to China's exchange rate policy since the early 1980s, was abandoned.

China's conversion to the US dollar peg contributed greatly to the recovery of the East Asian economy. As pointed out by McKinnon (2000b), if China were to let the yuan begin depreciating, no sustainable equilibrium for the East Asian economy would exist. In other words, if China had maintained the real targeting approach, a competitive devaluation in East Asia would be unavoidable, with the result that the crisis would have been much worse.

During the Asian financial crisis, it was acutely painful for China to have to peg to the US dollar. Everyone at the time was convinced that as soon as the devaluation pressure was reduced, China should delink the renminbi from the US dollar and return to a managed floating regime. However, only a few years after the Asia financial crisis, and before China could make headway in building market infrastructures that would make its economy resilient to exchange rate fluctuations, pressure to revaluate was building, suddenly and unexpectedly. While the renminbi was under pressure of appreciation, there was reluctance to delink, due to fear of a negative impact on the trade accounts. It was reasoned that a large appreciation would create too great a shock, whereas if appreciation were small, it would strengthen appreciation. The expectation of appreciation will, in turn, invite more capital inflows, and, hence, greater appreciation pressure. Furthermore, excessive capital inflows— to say nothing of speculative capital inflows—would create asset bubbles and weaken China's already fragile financial system.

Fear of the deflationary impact of appreciation was also a factor. However, this often-cited factor was no longer mentioned after 2004, when inflation became a major concern. Now (2006), the single most important concern for Chinese decision-makers is the possible negative impact of reval-uation on China's exports, and hence on unemployment. Unfortunately, no one has presented convincing evidence to show, , how much China's net exports would drop, and how many jobs would be lost if the renminbi were to appreciate by 15 percent. Faced with increasing unemployment, the hesitation of the Chinese authorities is understandable. However, on the other hand, China has no intention to ride with a US dollar that has been depreciating steadily since May 2002. It is very clear that any short-term gain will be offset by the rising trade protectionism of China's disgruntled trade partners, who are worse off, or who fail to be better off in the process.

Although China refuses to give a timetable, it has committed itself to a more flexible exchange rate regime and to allowing market forces to determine the exchange rate of renminbi at a reasonable equilibrium level. Delinking the renminbi from the US dollar is only a matter of time. Having eliminated the possibility of maintaining the dollar peg in the medium and long term, China is left with the following choices in reforming the exchange rate regime: managed floating, free floating, or participation in a regional common currency.

A managed floating regime

Among different forms of the managed floating exchange rate regime, China may choose a single currency, for example, the US dollar, as a reference point in determining the central rate, and then allow the rate to fluctuate within a specified range. This approach is basically a return to the exchange rate regime which China had adopted prior to the crisis.

It is also conceivable that China may also choose to peg to a basket of currencies. If this strategy is chosen, there would still be several options. It appears that most Chinese economists would prefer the exchange rate regime of three main elements, known as "basket, band, and crawling" (BBC). This exchange rate regime might reduce the variation of the home currency against those of its main trading partners, when the parity of foreign currencies against one another varies.

However, the net result for China of such a switch from a US dollar peg to one of a peg to a basket of currencies is still an unanswered question. The renminbi must have an anchor to maintain economic stability. The US dollar served well as such an anchor. Furthermore, because of the high complementarity between Chinese and Japanese goods, the negative impact of a devaluation of the Japanese yen on China's exports to Japan may not be as great as some people fear. This argument reinforces the opinion (Yongding, 2000) that, the weight of the US dollar in China's currency basket should be high, implying that the creation of a basket which includes the yen may matter less than people expect. More importantly, if major international currencies are variable without any clear direction, pegging to a basket of currencies will definitely make the renminbi more stable than the peg to the US dollar alone. However, if the dollar's long-term trend is in the direction of devaluation, China would be worse off by switching away from the US dollar peg.

Another important question, given the different exchange rate arrangements in the region, concerns the equilibrium, if any, which will result from the exchange rate game. BBC does not exclude government intervention, and BBC, per se, does not take away the incentive for competitive devaluation.

Free-floating regime

Owing to its fragile financial system and other factors, a full free-floating currency regime is out of the question for China in the foreseeable future. However, the majority of Chinese economists seem to regard a full free-floating regime as the ultimate goal of reform of China's exchange rate regime. For these economists, a regional common currency is not a goal China should pursue, as they have yet to be convinced of the virtue of an East Asian common currency. For most Chinese economists, BBC is the most attractive model, because, quite aside from its intrinsic virtue, it can serve as a path leading to either free floating or a common currency.

Asian common currency

What about a common currency in East Asia? It is argued in the literature that eliminating national currencies and moving to a common currency can be expected to bring gains in economic efficiency. These gains in efficiency have two different origins: one is the elimination of transaction costs associated with the exchange of national monies; the other is the elimination of risk of uncertain future movement of exchange rates. The elimination of transaction costs also has an indirect gain: consumers are able to see prices in the same currency unit and therefore to make better price comparisons. This in turn should increase competition and benefit all consumers. More importantly, the introduction of a common currency would stimulate financial integration. This in turn may set in motion dynamic integration in other areas. For example, financial market integration is likely to promote further harmonization of legislation. A decline in real exchange rate uncertainty, due to the introduction of a common currency would reduce adjustment costs. As a result, the price system would become a better guide for making wise economic decisions.

Reduced uncertainty in the exchange rate would lead to reduction of the real interest rate. Risk-averse investors will demand a lower interest premium, which in turn will promote economic growth.[2] All in all, a common currency, a monetary union, or a move toward monetary integration will promote trade–at least among members–and economic growth. The conclusion seems to be borne out by the empirical evidence.

Having accepted the virtue of a common currency, the next question is whether it is feasible for East Asia to create one. The feasibility of a common currency is based on the existence of an optimum currency area (OCA). It is assumed that asymmetrical shocks in an optimum currency area would be transmitted rapidly from one member country to another, and affect all members. As a result, idiosyncratic national policies, for example, changing exchange rates vis-à-vis those of other member countries, become unnecessary. For example, according to Mundell (1961), if a negative asymmetric demand shock hits one of the members of an optimum currency area, labor will move from this country to other members. With high labor mobility, labor migration between members will equalize wages as well as labor supply and demand in all members. As a result, a common monetary or fiscal policy can be used to stimulate the economies of all members. Hence migration is a channel through which adjustment to asymmetric shocks can take place, and flexible exchange rates between the members would no longer be necessary to restore fundamental balance.

The traditional literature suggests a set of criteria for creation of an OCA. Among the criteria are factor mobility (Mundell, 1961) trade integration (Mckinnon, 1963), regional production patterns (Kenen, 1969), policy preference, high correlation of shocks among members, and so on. Generally speaking, countries with strong trade and financial ties are identified as optimal candidates for optimum currency area.

According to this outline, many studies have found that East Asia fits the criteria for an OCA quite well, and that East Asian countries could form a monetary union, without incurring too many opportunity costs by losing monetary independence and policy autonomy.[3]

First, in terms of trade integration, East Asian countries have comfortably met the criteria for an OCA, especially when compared to the European countries at the time of the initiation of European Monetary Union. The intensity of intra-regional trade among East Asian countries is high and rising steadily. As we know, the intra-regional trade intensity index for East Asia is

2.2, while that for the EU and NAFTA are 1.7 and 2.1, respectively (Kuroda, 2004). Trade *among* these countries has already surpassed their trade with all trading blocks outside the region. This is especially true of the three key northern East Asian countries: China, Japan, and Korea.

Second, in terms of production patterns in the region, the international production network in the region has intensified East Asian countries' economic integration significantly during the past decade. Before the 1990s, the regional division of labor in the East Asian countries was roughly characterized by the so-called "flying geese formation." The development gaps between economies in the region—reflecting widely varying stages of the product cycle in their respective industries at any given point in time—give rise to the possibilities for forming a close regional of trade and investment network, based on the vertical division of labor in the region. Following the collapse of the flying geese formation in the last decade, a new pattern of regional division of labor seems to have taken shape, characterized by the establishment of a regional production network, resulting from the global strategy of multinationals. Owing to trade liberalization and technological progress, especially the IT revolution, corporate organization has changed greatly, with many activities outsourced to enterprises in other countries. Parts and components are produced and traded across borders before final products are completed. Processing trade is flourishing. In contrast to the traditional pattern of vertical inter-industrial division of labor, the new pattern of labor division is not only intra-industrial but also intra-product. As a result of closer trade and investment linkages, based on a newly emerged international production network, the correlation of cyclical economic change and rapid transmission of external shocks has increased significantly. The contagion effect during the Asian financial crisis is a case in point. It seems that East Asian countries have already laid a solid foundation for embarking on the process of monetary and financial integration.

If the economic arguments for the creation of an East Asian common currency are not sufficient, an even more convincing rationale for a common currency may be found in political economy. The most important characteristic of the current international monetary system is the domination of the US dollar. Milton Friedman once predicted that under flexible exchange rates, countries would not need reserves. He was wrong. Countries need more reserves today than ever before. And the principal reserve they use is the dollar. As a result, the United States is able to extract seignorage from other countries. According to Mundell (1997), the total amount of US currency in banks outside United States approaches US$400 billion. It is principally this currency that is being used as the international currency of the world. It has been estimated that only 10 to 15 percent of the US$400 billion in circulation is actually held in the United States. With the US dollar as the single most important international reserve currency, the U.S. is able to pay its huge current account deficits and accumulate more than US$1.5 trillion in foreign debt. On the other hand, the rest of the world has to rely on the mercy of Fed's self-discipline. As a result of the Asian financial crisis, East Asian economies, as a whole, now hold more than US$2 trillion in reserves, mainly in the form of Treasury bills and other dollar-denominated assets, earning very low return. In effect, East Asians are footing the bill for spendthrift American households. East Asian countries are now watching helplessly, as the value of their foreign exchange reserves is eroded, as a result of the depreciation of the US dollar. As pointed out by Mundell (1997), the United States is the last country to agree to international monetary reform which would eliminate this free lunch. As a superpower, the United States is unwilling to discuss international monetary reform, because it sees such reform as a threat to its own hegemony. The dollar liabilities of the United States have been rising alarmingly, and East Asia should not tolerate this situation forever. The formation of an Asian common currency, side by side with the euro, will help to end domination by the US dollar and impose discipline on the American administration.

The other equally important, if not more important, reason why East Asian countries must work together to create a common currency is purely political. To preserve peace, we need economic integration. To make integration irreversible, we need a common currency in the region. The formation of the European Economic Community was a political decision. The creation of the euro is the logical result of that decision. The literature indicates that the main costs of a common currency area are the loss of monetary policy independence, and giving up the possibility of changing exchange rates when it is necessary to achieve fundamental economic balance.

However, the costs of a common currency boil down to one thing: surrender of a degree of state sovereignty. Compared with this issue, the question of whether all East Asian countries (or ASEAN 10+3 specifically) fit the criteria for an OCA is not that important. If the countries concerned have the political will, and the physical and institutional capacity, an OCA area can be created. Better-developed financial markets, deeper trade, factor market integration, and liberalized capital markets are not only preconditions for monetary integration, but also represent the results of efforts to promote integration in the region. As Frankel and Rose point out: "Trade patterns and income correlations are endogenous…A country could fail the OCA criterion for membership today, and yet, if it goes ahead and joins anyway, as the result of joining, it could pass the OCA criterion in the future."[4] Unfortunately, in the current political atmosphere in East Asia, when one country is regarded as a threat to another, undermining mutual trust and good-will, would any country be prepared to take action, to say nothing of taking the lead, in this direction? The prospects for substantial progress in the creation of a common currency seem very dim, indeed.

The way forward

However, setting aside unpleasant and frustrating questions of international politics for the time being, if a common currency were to be accepted as the ultimate goal, how should the East Asian economies proceed? Kuroda (2004) presented a road map for achieving this goal. According to Kuroda, the first step toward a single currency in East Asia is already in place in the form of the Chiang Mai Initiative (CMI), which envisaged the establishment of a network of bilateral swap arrangements (BSAs), to avoid and resolve future currency crises like that in East Asia in 1997–98.

The second step is the Asian Bond Markets Initiative, aimed at promoting the development of functioning, integrated capital markets for tackling the problems of over-banking and maturity and currency mismatches in East Asia.

For Kuroda, free trade agreements (FTAs) represent the third step toward a common currency.

The fourth step refers to intra-regional exchange rate stability. According to Kuroda, a possible exchange rate arrangement could be a "basket regime," under which regional currencies are managed using as a reference a common basket of major currencies including the US dollar, the euro, and the yen. Finally, convergence criteria will be applied and a single currency would be introduced in the region.

I am sympathetic with many of Mr. Kuroda's views. Efforts should be sustained in order to consolidate the gains in regional monetary cooperation, for example, the CMI. However, because there does not yet exist a political atmosphere conducive to further progress in monetary integration—which necessarily implies surrender of a degree of state sovereignty for which they are not ready—the focus of the efforts should shift to the construction of the economic fundamentals of economic and monetary integration. Perhaps more effort should be made to promote trade liberalization, technological assistance, and tourism, and facilitate investment. When political will is absent, we must fall back on economics. Hopefully, mutual economic benefit will inject new dynamism into the process of monetary cooperation in East Asia.

NOTES

1 This paper is based on a presentation to the international conference on "International Economic Cooperation for a Balanced World Economy," held in Chongqing, 12–13 March 2005.

2 Grauwe, 2003, p. 60.

3 Trivisvavet, 2001.

4 Quoted in Kiss, 2000, p.

REFERENCES

Bayoumi, T. and B. Eichengreen. 1993. "Shocking Aspects of European Monetary Unification." F. Torres and F Giavazzi, eds. *Adjustment and Growth in the European Monetary Union*. Cambridge: Cambridge University Press. 193–240.

Chaipravat, O. 2004. "Developing an Asian Bond Market as a Means for Regional Financial Cooperation." Paper Presented at an International Conference on "East Asian Regionalism and Its Impact." Institute of Asia-Pacific Studies, CASS, Beijing, China. 21–22 October.

Calvo, Guillermo A. and C. M. Reinhart. 2002. "Fear of Floating." *Quarterly Journal of Economics* 107(2):379–408. May.

Dornbusch, R., and F. Leslie Helmers. 1988. *The Open Economy*. Oxford: Oxford University Press.

Eichengreen, B. 2003. "What to do with the Chiang Mai Initiative." *Asian Economic Papers* 2(1):1–49.

Frankel, J., and A. K. Rose. 1998. "The Endogeneity of the Optimum Currency Area Criteria." *Economic Journal* 108:1009–25.

Grauwe, P. 2003. *Economics of Monetary Union*. Oxford: Oxford University Press.

Kenen, P. 1969. "The Theory of Optimum Currency Area: An Eclectic View." R. Mundell and A. Swoboda, eds. *Monetary Problems of the International Economy*. Chicago: University of Chicago Press. 41–60.

Kiss, E. Fishman. 2000. "Optimum Currency Area: Euro as a Practical Paradigm?" First International Conference on Banking and Finance, Kuala Lumpur, Malaysia, Rutgers University and the State University of New Jersey.

Kuroda, H. 2004, "Transitional Steps in the Road to a Single Currency in East Asia." Seminar on "A Single Currency for East Asia—Lessons from Europe." Asian Development Bank. Jeju. 14 May 2004.

Kwan, C. H. 2000. *Yen Bloc*. Washington, D.C.: Brookings Institute Press.

McKinnon, R. I. 1963. "Optimum Currency Area." *American Economic Review* 53:717–25.

Mckinnon, R. I. 1998. "Exchange Rate Coordination for Surmounting the East Asian Currency Crisis." *Asian Economic Journal* 12(4):317–29. December.

———. 2000. After the Crisis, the East Asian Dollar Standard Resurrected: An Interpretation of High-Frequency Exchange Rate Pegging. Economics Department, Stanford University. Available at:

http://www-econ.standford.edu/faculty/workp/swp98010.pdf

Mundell, R. 1961. "The Theory of Optimum Currency Areas." *American Economic Review* 51:657–65.

———. 1997. "The International Monetary System in the 21st Century: Could Gold Make a Comeback?" Letrobe, PA: St. Vincent College. 12 March.

Obstfeld, M. and K. Rogoff. 2005. "Global Exchange Rate Adjustments and Global Current Account Balances." Brookings Institution. 67–123.

Sharma, S. 2003. *The Asian Financial Crisis*. Manchester University Press.

Shinohara, H. 1999. "On the Asian Monetary Fund." *IIMA Newsletter*. Institute of International Monetary Affairs, Japan. 31 March.

———. 1999. "On the Asian Monetary Fund." *Institute of International Monetary Affairs Newsletter*. Tokyo: Institute for International Monetary Affairs. 31 March.

Trivisvavet, T. 2001. "Do East Asian Countries Constitute An Optimum Currency Area?" Durham University. Unpublished manuscript.

UNCTAD.2001. *Trade and Development Report*. 2001. Geneva: UNCTAD.

Williamson, J. 2005. "A Currency Basket for East Asia." *Policy Briefs* 5–1. Institute for International Economics. July.

Yu, Y. 2000a. "China, Case for Capital Controls." Chapter 12 in W. Bello, N. Bullard, and K. Malhotra, eds. *Global Finance: New Thinking on Regulating Speculative Capital Markets.* London: Zed Books Ltd.

————. 2000b. "China's Deflation during the Asian Financial Crisis, and Reform of the International Financial System." *Asian Economic Bulletin* 17(2):163–174. August.

————. 2001. "China's Macroeconomic Outlook." *World Economy and China* 9(1).

————. 2003. "Overcoming the Fear of Floating and Achieving a Balanced Development." *Guo Ji Jing Ji Peng Lun* (*International Economic Review*) 9–10.

————. 2004. "Understanding the Current Macroeconomic Situation." *Guo Ji Jing Ji Peng Lun* (*International Economic Review*) 5–6.

Zhang, Z. 2000. "Exchange Rate Reform in China: An Experiment in the Real Targets Approach." *The World Economy* 23(8):1057–82.

PART 3

Global Imbalances and their Implications for the International Monetary System

---

CHAPTER 3.1

Understanding Global Imbalances[1]

RICHARD N. COOPER, Maurits C. Boas Professor of International Economics,
Harvard University

T he large and growing US current account deficit has elicited increasing
concern, even alarm, and claims that it is unsustainable (see Table 1).
This paper argues that the large US deficit is a natural consequence of
two significant worldwide developments, globalization of financial markets,
and demographic change, and that, far from being unsustainable, it is likely to
endure for some years, and indeed from a global point of view to enhance
world welfare.

Table 1: The US current account deficit[a]

	(US$ billion)	(% GDP)
1995	114	1.5
1996	125	1.6
1997	141	2.6
1998	214	2.4
1999	300	3.2
2000	416	4.2
2001	389	3.8
2002	475	4.5
2003	520	4.7
2004	668	5.7
2005	805	6.4
2006[b]	864	6.5
2007[b]	899	6.5

Notes:
  a. Balance of payments concept
  b. Projected by IMF staff

Source: IMF, 2006.

The foreign exchange market for the US dollar is not subject to systematic US intervention; the US dollar floats against other currencies that are allowed to float. The US current account deficit is large because foreign investment in the United States is large. Table 2 shows foreign capital inflows, private and public, and US capital outflows, for the period 2000–2005.

Table 2: Capital flows in the US balance of payments (US$ billion)

	2000	2001	2002	2003	2004	2005
Foreign Capital Inflow	1,047	783	794	889	1,440	1,293
Private	1,004	755	678	611	1,045	1,072
Official	43	28	116	278	395	1,74
US Capital Outflow	561	383	294	328	856	492
Private	559	377	291	330	860	513
Official	1	5	3	−2	−4	−22
Statistical Discrepancy	−69	−10	−24	−38	85	10

Source: www.bea.com.

Over US$1 trillion in foreign private funds entered the United States in 2004—much larger than the current account deficit in that year—and again in 2005. Indeed, foreign private capital inflows have exceeded the US current account deficits, usually by substantial amounts, in every year since significant deficits began in the early 1980s. In addition, nearly US$200 billion of foreign official funds, reflecting a build-up of foreign exchange reserves in foreign central banks, also entered the United States in 2005. It has been said that foreign central banks are financing the US current account deficit and, incidentally, the US budget deficit. This is an inappropriate attribution of selective inflows against selective outflows in the US balance of payments. It would be as true to say, as France's President DeGaulle did in 1963, that foreign central banks (partially) financed US capital outflows, which exceeded US$500 billion in 2005.

Why are so many foreign funds being invested in the United States? The answer lies partly in the attractiveness of US financial assets, which are claims on a robust, innovative economy, with good yield, liquidity, security, and relative stability. But the answer lies also in high savings relative to investment opportunities in other economies, particularly, but not exclusively, in other rich countries. Investment opportunities have been limited in Japan and continental Europe while savings remain relatively high. The excess private savings have been partially, but only partially, absorbed by large budget deficits in other major countries, such as Japan and Germany. The difference has been invested abroad. In addition, since the rise in world oil prices started in 2003, oil-exporting countries have seen their export revenues soar, and along with them their current account surpluses. Table 3 provides data on the world allocation of current account positions in 1997, 2000, and 2005.

Table 3: World current account balances

	1997	2000	2005
USA	−141	−16	−05
Japan	97	120	164
Germany, Netherlands, Switzerland	41	5	205
Other rich economies	68	23	−75
China	34	21	159
Other developing Asia	−27	26	−3
Central and Eastern Europe	−21	−32	−63
CIS	−9	48	90
Middle East	11	70	196
Latin America	−67	−48	30
Africa	−6	7	15
Discrepancy	14	176	87
NB: fuel exporters	16	149	347

Source: IMF, 2006, April.

An increase in the US deficit of about US$400 billion over 2000–2005 has been matched by significant increases in the surpluses of Japan, Germany—with its close economic associates Netherlands and Switzerland—China, Russia, and the Middle East, the last two mainly reflecting oil prices. Central Europe and other rich countries (mainly Spain, Britain, and Australia) experienced negative movements in their current accounts, while Latin

America—including oil-exporting Venezuela but also Brazil—experienced a significant positive movement. For all years, there is a significant statistical discrepancy, indicating higher recorded deficits than surpluses.

The surpluses of the members of OPEC—mainly Middle Eastern countries plus Venezuela and Nigeria—will undoubtedly decline after several years, as oil prices decline, and as the oil-exporting countries learn to spend their higher income, which accrues initially to governments in almost all significant oil-exporting countries. The IMF staff, however, projects these surpluses to rise somewhat in 2006, and to remain high through 2007.[2] Thus, these surpluses can be considered transitory, although enduring for several years.

Japan and augmented Germany have the largest surpluses after the oil-exporting countries. Table 4 provides data for recent years on national saving and domestic investment in Japan and Germany, along with newly rich Asian economies (Hong Kong SAR, Singapore, South Korea, and Taiwan, China) and developing Asia.

Table 4: National saving and domestic investment (% GDP)

		1992–1999	2000	2005
Japan	Saving	30.6	27.8	26.8
	Investment	28.1	25.2	23.2
Germany	Saving	21	20.1	21.3
	Investment	21.9	21.8	17.2
Newly rich Asian economies*	Saving	33.8	31.9	31.8
	Investment	31.1	28.4	25.7
Developing Asia	Saving	31.8	30.3	38.2
	Investment	32.3	28.2	34.3

* Hong Kong SAR, South Korea, Singapore, Taiwan (China)
Source: IMF, 2006 (April, Table 43).

Saving has declined in Japan, and private saving even more since 2000, as the large public sector deficit declined from 7.7 to 5.8 percent of GDP, 2000–2005. In Germany, saving rose slightly, and private saving even more since the government deficit rose by four percentage points in the years 2000–2005. Saving remained roughly unchanged in the four Asian tigers, and rose a remarkable 8 percentage points in developing Asia, dominated by China, but also including India, Indonesia, and a number of other significant developing countries. All these regions record significantly higher saving than the United States, as indeed do other regions of the world, including Latin America and Africa, but there is reason to believe that true saving in the United States is relatively greater than the recorded difference drawn from the national accounts (Cooper, 2006).

What is more noteworthy is the decline in investment in most other rich economies, including Japan, Germany, and newly rich Asia. Recorded physical investment remains higher in most places than in the United States. Germany (along with the United Kingdom) is the major exception; investment there has been in a slump for some years. In developing Asia, by contrast, investment has risen sharply, led by China where investment exceeds 40 percent of GDP and is considered, both by Chinese authorities and by some foreign analysts, to be too high—the only such case of a developing country with too much investment (as distinguished from investment in the wrong places) that I can recall. But the growth of investment has fallen short of the increase in saving. Rapid growth permits consumption to rise rapidly even when the rate of saving increases.

Recall that, apart from measurement errors, the current account position (= net foreign investment) is the difference between domestic investment and national savings. Thus saving in excess of domestic investment (or private saving in excess of investment plus government deficits) implies investment abroad, net of inward flows of foreign investment. Why are several of the world's major economies investing so much abroad?

A major part of the answer, I believe, lies in demographic trends. Birth rates have declined in all rich countries, although differentially, and in many developing countries as well, most notably China, which introduced its one-child policy in 1979. The result is the prospect, or the actuality in Japan and Germany, of declining population, despite an increase in longevity in most countries. More pertinent than total population for saving and investment is the change in the age composition of populations. The aging of societies, with its implications for pensions and health care, has been widely discussed. Less widely discussed has been the decline in the population of young adults— those who receive contemporary education, enter the labor force, form new households, and require housing and, for their children, schooling. Table 5 shows the age 15–29 population in 2005 and projections to 2025 for Japan, Germany, China, and the U.S., the four largest national economies.

Table 5: Population aged 15–29 for 2005, projected for 2025

	2005 (million)	2025 (million)	Change (%)
China	321	259	−9
Japan	22.6	17.8	−1
Germany	14.2	11.9	−6
USA	61.9	66	7

Source: US Census Bureau.

Apart from the United States, where birth rates have declined less than in other rich countries, and where immigration continues to be an important source of new young adults, the decline in this age group is remarkable. Yet this is the age group that provides the most educated, most flexible (occupationally and geographically) new members of the labor force. A decline in this age group implies not only a loss in economic flexibility, but also a decline in the need for investment to equip new members of the labor force, of investment in housing and its accoutrements, and of investment in new schools. Housing investment, in particular, is reduced to less than full replacement, plus some allowance for geographic mobility in rich countries. In poor, growing countries, such as China, demand for housing will remain robust, as the population upgrades housing quality, as well as moving from rural to urban areas.

With these demographic trends, the prospects for significant increases in domestic investment in rich countries are limited. Replacement of obsolete equipment, necessary in a world of continuous technological change, will continue to take place; and some capital deepening will continue to occur, although that implies lower returns to capital, making such investment unattractive, as compared with investment abroad. Investment in Japan and Germany is closely related to export prospects. If these weaken due to appreciating currencies, investment is likely to suffer.

The United States stands out among rich countries as having in prospect a continued rise in population, especially of young people, partly because the fertility rate has declined noticeably less in the United States than in other rich countries (to 2.1 children per woman of child-bearing age, compared with 1.4 in Japan and Germany and 1.0 in Hong Kong SAR and Singapore), partly because of continuing immigration on a significant scale.

The real needs of aging, low growth societies with limited domestic investment opportunities can be met by profitable external investment. (Excess private savings can be, and in Japan and Germany have been, absorbed in financing budget deficits, but most government expenditures are not oriented toward increasing future income.) That is what is happening. Most countries with prospective declines in new entrants to the labor force show significant current account surpluses, reflecting their foreign investment. Spain is a notable exception, as are several central European countries. These are below the rest of Europe in per capita income and are still in a catch-up phase, requiring additional productive investment; and Spain is building vacation and retirement homes for many northern Europeans, as well as upgrading Spanish housing.

This is what financial globalization is all about: a decline in home bias in the disposition of savings and investment, especially when indicated by structural changes such as the demographic developments discussed above. Where should such investment take place? Conventional economic theory suggests it should take place in relatively poor countries, with low ratios of capital to labor, because returns should be higher there. But conventional theory is a vast over-simplification of the complex conditions that both attract investment—investors want assurance that their investments are secure, subject only to business risk—and that make investment productive, which in addition requires an appropriate social and political infrastructure, such as social order, physical security, rule of law, secure property rights, impartial dispute settlement, etc. Many of these conditions are not present in the world's poorest countries, and some of them are not present even in middle-income countries. Argentina, Russia, and Bolivia have reminded investors in recent years how insecure private property rights can be from political action, particularly foreign private property rights. So investors approach very poor countries hardly at all, unless they have exploitable natural resources, and they approach many "emerging markets" warily. And after the financial crises of 1994–2001, many emerging markets also approach international borrowing warily. As those painful experiences recede in time, however, private foreign investment in emerging markets has begun to pick up, aided by low interest rates in capital-exporting countries and a desire by investors for higher returns. During 2004, for instance, an estimated US$300 billion in private funds flowed to developing countries, up from US$180 billion in 2000. This went mainly to East Asia (primarily equity) and to central Europe (primarily debt), but a significant amount of foreign direct investment also occurred in Latin America.[3]

However, it is not surprising that much of the surplus saving in other rich countries went to the United States. The US economy accounts for around 30 percent of world economic output. The social system is stable, private property is respected, and dispute settlement is reasonably quick and fair. Nearly half of the world's marketable securities (stocks and bonds) are in the United States. Returns are better on average than in other rich countries, and more secure and reliable than in emerging markets. The American economy is innovative and relatively flexible. Prospects for the future are bright. In these circumstances, it is not surprising that a growing fraction of world saving should be invested in the United States.

Indeed, in a fully globalized world economy, with no home bias, one would expect roughly 30 percent of world saving outside the United States to be invested in the United States—and 70 percent of US saving to be invested abroad. Saving outside the United States in 2004 was around US$7 trillion, 30 percent of which would be US$2.1 trillion. US private saving was about US$1.8 trillion, 70 percent of which would be US$1.2 trillion. The difference is US$900 billion, larger than the US current account deficit in 2004, or even that in 2005. Of course, home bias continues to be important, so investment abroad has not yet reached these large two-way amounts. But fifteen percent of world saving, which will rise in value from year to year, does not seem to be an unsustainably large number to invest in the United States; if anything it is on the low side. Yet that was enough to cover American investment abroad—less overseas loans by US banks, which are directly financed abroad—plus the current account deficit.

Some people are troubled that a significant amount—although a small fraction—of foreign investment in the United States is by monetary authorities, in the form of additions to their foreign exchange reserves that are held in US Treasury or other securities. Japan added US$480 billion to its reserves during the period 2000–2005, and together the newly-rich Asian economies added over US$300 billion. Emerging markets and developing countries taken together (including OPEC members) added an astounding US$1579 billion to their reserves, exceeding the net private capital inflow into these countries. Why?

The reasons are varied. Oil-exporters have experienced an unexpected increase in export receipts because of strong world demand and rising oil prices over the past five years. Their imports have not grown correspondingly, but this is likely to be largely a question of timing. Oil prices may be expected to decline in the future, and oil-exporting countries will gradually move the higher earnings, initially accruing to governments, into the income stream, and ultimately into higher imports.

It should be noted that total foreign exchange reserves have grown enormously since the introduction of floating exchange rates in the mid-1970s, contrary to expectations of the advocates of floating exchange rates. Clearly countries are not comfortable with freely floating rates, desire at least to have the possibility of managing them, and therefore feel they need higher reserves as economies and foreign trade grow in value. This sentiment was strongly reinforced by the financial crises of 1994–1999, in which reserves in several important countries proved to be totally inadequate to deal with the financial pressures on their currencies, initially more from residents than from non-residents. Even a country such as Switzerland built up its reserves substantially, from US$37 billion in 1999 to US$55 billion in 2004. The major exceptions are the United States, Canada, and the European Central Bank since 1999.

In some cases the growth in reserves is the incidental by-product of an active exchange rate policy, designed to slow appreciation of the currency or even to prevent appreciation altogether. The growth in reserves is not necessarily unwelcome in these circumstances, although it does create problems of monetary management, since it is the equivalent of open-market purchases in foreign rather than domestic securities.

But the currency policy may itself be motivated by fundamental factors. As noted above, it makes sense for aging Japan to invest heavily abroad in assets with positive yields, rather than investing at home for lower yields or, worse yet, investing in government securities which finance construction projects with negligible social return. Yet private Japanese savers are extraordinarily conservative; households keep much of their saving in the postal system, backed by the government, but with very low returns to savers and perhaps, given the use of these funds, none to the nation as a whole. By buying foreign exchange reserves, the Ministry of Finance is assuring future real returns—command over real resources in the international market—to the entire nation, which through their conservative behavior would not be obtained by relying on private savers alone. In short, the monetary authorities are acting as financial intermediaries, converting what private savers want now into what they will need in future years. Foreign exchange risk is real to the individual, but not to the nation: by investing abroad, even in US bonds, it secures a future claim on goods and services in the international market. (Given the magnitude of their reserves, Japanese authorities might be well advised to diversify them into some higher yield foreign investments, as a number of other countries have done, and as Korea has recently decided to do.)

The most dramatic growth in reserves, along with OPEC's, has been experienced by China: an increase of US$655 billion from the end of 2000 to the end of 2005, out-stripping even its very rapid growth in imports. This growth in reserves has been made possible by a current account surplus, modest and without trend until 2005, when it shot upward to US$159 billion, 19 percent of exports, and by continued net private capital inflow, particularly of foreign direct investment.

But China still maintains severe restrictions on resident capital outflow. Given the rapid growth in income in China in recent years, the high savings rate, and the limited domestic menu of financial investments in which Chinese households can invest, mainly in bank savings accounts, the latent demand for investment abroad is probably very high. Partly on residual communist doctrinal grounds, partly for the pragmatic reason of not wanting to undermine their fragile banking system, Chinese authorities are hesitant to move soon to full currency convertibility and free movement of capital. Nonetheless, China's central bank, the Peoples' Bank of China, can be thought of investing abroad on behalf of the public, and against the day in which the currency will be fully convertible—a stated Chinese objective—and net capital outflow may be large. It is undoubtedly true that China, unlike Japan, has many potentially profitable investments at home. But it is also true that the banking system as it is currently constituted does a poor job of allocating capital, and that, as noted above, in recent years Chinese authorities have considered aggregate investment to be excessive. A similar argument may be made with respect to the more modest, but still significant, buildup of reserves by India and a number of other developing countries which continue to maintain controls on resident capital outflow.

Presumably savings will decline in other rich countries as their populations age. That is implied by the life cycle hypothesis. But the decline may be a very gradual one. Simple versions of the life-cycle hypothesis assume individuals know when they will die, or purchase annuities. But longevity is increasing, remarkably but unpredictably, so people do not know when they die. Relatively few purchase annuities on top of their defined benefit pensions (whether state-sponsored or private). And non-financial assets such as houses or family businesses are not easily liquefied in most countries. So savings continue into post-retirement ages. This is especially noteworthy in Germany and Italy (McKinsey, 2004), but it is true even in the United States. Table 6 shows the median net worth, in constant dollars, in the United States by age bracket for 1992 and 2001.

Table 6: US Median family net worth (US$ thousand, 2001)

Age	1992	2001
<35	11.4	11.6
35–44	55.1	77.6
45–54	96.8	133.0
55–64	141.1	181.5
65–74	121.7	176.3
>75	107.5	151.4

Source: US Census Bureau, 2006, Table 702.

Looking at either column alone suggests a decline in net worth, i.e. dissaving, as people age past 65. But different groups are being compared. People aged 55–64 in 1992 were nearly a decade older in 2001, and their net worth increased, despite passing age 65. Those who were 65–74 in 1992 also increased their net worth further, i.e. saved, by 2001. This behavior can also be observed by comparing 2004 with 1995. Thus it cannot be taken for granted that aging societies will dissave, at least not that they will do so quickly and reliably.

While the rest of the world may continue to produce saving available for investment in the United States, can the United States accommodate an ever-increasing amount of such investment? Table 7 shows household financial assets and net worth in the United States 1990–2004 (the figures include non-profit institutions). It also shows gross foreign claims on the United States.

Table 7: Household assets, net worth and foreign claims on the United States (US$ billion)

		Household assets	
	Foreign claims on U.S.	Financial	Total (net)
1990	2,459	14,731	20,374
1995	4,291	21,529	27,560
1996	5,091	24,015	30,062
1997	6,202	27,489	33,806
1998	7,250	30,362	37,297
1999	8,437	34,769	42,275
2000	8,982	33,679	41,770
2001	9,270	32,211	40,893
2002	9,263	29,967	39,144
2003	10,669	34,092	44,583
2004	12,515	36,759	48,525

Source: BEA; US Census Bureau (*Statistical Yearbook of the United States*).

Several points stand out: first, both household net worth and financial assets have grown faster than GDP over this period (6.7 percent a year for financial assets compared with 5.2 percent growth for GDP). This reflects, in part, increasing financial innovation and layering of financial assets over the physical capital stock, but it also reflects the growth in intangible capital not counted in official statistics.

Second, foreign claims on the United States have grown even faster, by 12.3 percent a year over this period. The foreign share of total household financial plus foreign assets has thus risen from 14 percent in 1990 to 25 percent in 2004—22 percent if US banking liabilities to foreigners, nearly offset by bank claims on foreigners, are excluded. Obviously a rise in share cannot continue indefinitely, although 22 percent remains far below the foreign share of 70 percent in a fully globalized economy. But a rise in value can continue indefinitely, so long as the US economy and its financial asset super-structure continue to grow. And growing foreign investment in the United States can be serviced indefinitely so long as it adds, directly or indirectly, to productive assets.

Third, the risk profile of foreign private claims on the United States is very different from the risk profile of US private claims on the rest of the world; it is tilted much more toward debt instruments, both short-term and long-term. For example, 58 percent of private US claims on foreigners are equity (foreign direct investment plus corporate shares), while only 37 percent of foreign private claims on the United States are equity. In this respect their claims on the United States mirror their behavior at home, at least for the largest rich countries for which data are readily available: Japan, Germany, Britain, France, Italy, and Canada, in order of economic size. At end-2004, equities made up only 21 percent of German household financial assets (62 percent of disposable income), for instance, 16 percent in Britain (64 percent of disposable income), and 8 percent in Japan (39 percent of disposable income), compared with 28 percent (116 percent of disposable income) in the United States.[4] Foreign official investment in the United States includes virtually no equity, so the bias is even greater with respect to total foreign claims on the United States.

The difference in risk profile goes part way toward explaining the fact that, although the United States is a substantial net debtor to the rest of the world, US earnings on its overseas investments continue to exceed its payments to foreigners on investments in the United States, although the gap has narrowed in recent years and may reverse in 2006 or 2007, as a result not only of continued net foreign investment in the United States, but also of rising interest rates on foreign short-term interest-bearing claims on the United States.

There is another significant asymmetry, seen from the US perspective: foreign claims on the United States are denominated overwhelmingly in US dollars, while US claims on the rest of the world reflect a mixture of US dollar-denominated assets and foreign currency denominated assets. Thus the net international investment position (NIIP) of the United States is sensitive to movements in exchange rates between the dollar and other currencies. Concretely, depreciation of the dollar, ceteris paribus, reduces the net debtor position of the United States, measured in dollars. Valuation changes, other than those arising from currency movements, also affect the NIIP, in particular movements in share prices and in the valuation of foreign direct investment. Thus, while the cumulative US current account deficit from 1990 to 2004 was US$4.47 trillion, the increase in the net debtor position of the United States was "only" US$2.60 trillion. Largely because of depreciation of the dollar, the NIIP of the United States actually increased by US$83 billion in 2003, despite a current account deficit of US$520 billion in that year. A current account deficit of nearly US$800 billion in 2005 was accompanied by a deterioration in the NIIP of less than US$100 billion.

Many have argued that the large US current account deficit is unsustainable. If they mean that recent trends in the deficit cannot continue, that is surely correct; the deficit cannot continue to rise indefinitely as a share of US GDP, as it has done for the past decade —with a brief pause in 2001. If, however, they mean that a large deficit cannot continue, that is neither correct nor likely. Demographic trends in Japan, Europe, and East Asia are likely to call forth current account surpluses for a number of years, to build up external assets that can be drawn upon in later decades as populations continue to age. Central banks are sometimes endogenous in this process, intermediating between domestic savers whose behavior (in the case of Japan) is too conservative to serve well the national needs, or who (in the case of China) are not permitted to invest freely abroad.

The United States has a vibrant, innovative economy. Its demographics are markedly different from those of other rich countries, in that natality has not fallen nearly so much and immigration, heavily concentrated in young adults, can be expected to continue on a significant scale. In these respects the United States, although rich and politically mature, can be said to be a young and even a developing country. It has an especially innovative financial sector, which continually produces new products to cater to diverse portfolio tastes. The United States has a comparative advantage, in a globalized market, in producing marketable securities, and in exchanging low-risk claims for higher risk assets. It is not surprising that savers around the world will want to put a small but growing part of their savings in the United States. As a consequence, the US current account deficit is likely to remain large for some years to come.

NOTES

1 This paper is a shortened version of a paper prepared for a conference on saving and investment sponsored by the Federal Reserve Bank of Boston, in June 2006.

2 IMF, 2006, p. 217.

3 World Bank, 2005, Tables A21–A27.

4 OECD, 2005, Annex Table 58.

REFERENCES

Bureau of Economic Analysis. Available at: www.bea.com.

Cooper, R. 2006. *Understanding Global Imbalances*. Boston, MA: Federal Reserve Bank of Boston.

International Monetary Fund. 2006. *World Economic Outlook*. Washington, D.C.: IMF. April.

McKinsey Global Institute. 2004. *The Coming Demographic Deficit: How Aging Populations Will Reduce Global Savings*. San Francisco.

Organization for Economic Cooperation and Development OECD). 2005. *Economic Outlook*. Paris: OECD. June.

United States Census Bureau. 2006. *Statistical Yearbook of the United States*. Available at: www.census.gov.

World Bank. 2005. *Global Development Finance*. Washington, D.C.: World Bank.

CHAPTER 3.2

Remarks on Global Imbalances

DIETRICH DOMANSKI, Head of Macroeconomic Monitoring, Bank for International Settlements[1]

Introduction

G lobal current account imbalances have reached unprecedented levels. The combined current account position of countries with external payment deficits exceeded US$1 trillion in 2005, equivalent to almost 2.5 percent of world GDP. The debate on current account imbalances has elicited a wide range of hypotheses on the causes of global imbalances and different views about likely adjustment scenarios. This paper aims to provide a framework for the discussion of the prospects for global rebalancing, by reviewing broad trends in current account balances during the global economic upswing which began in 2002. It also discusses the role of various adjustment mechanisms at the current juncture.

How did we get to where we are now?

Since 2002, the combined annual current account position of deficit countries has doubled in dollar terms and, perhaps more importantly, risen sharply as a percentage of GDP (Figure 1).

The largest single contributor remains the United States, where the external payment deficit reached almost US$800 billion in 2005, or 6 percent of US GDP. The other advanced economies have, on aggregate, recorded a current account surplus which has fluctuated in a range of about 1 percent of their GDP since 2002. This positive balance mainly reflects continued large, or even growing, surpluses of Japan (about US$150 billion in 2005 and US$100 billion in 2002) and Germany (US$100 billion in 2005 and US$50 billion in 2002). However, the external deficits of several other advanced economies have grown rapidly. For instance, relative to GDP, the current account deficits of

Figure 1: Global current account deficits

US$ billion

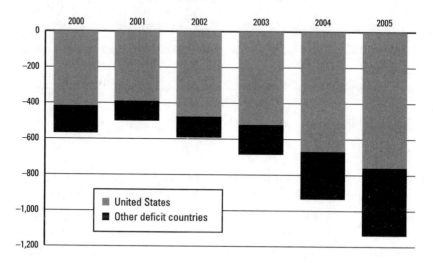

Percent GDP

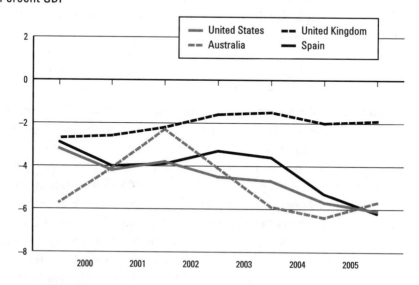

Source: World Economic Outlook (WEO) 2005.

Australia and Spain have widened broadly in tandem with the US deficit. Generally, sizeable current account deficits have become a more widespread phenomenon in industrial countries (Table 1).

To some extent, the widening current account balances among major advanced economies seem to reflect cyclical developments. Domestic demand growth in the G3 has been uneven during the current upswing. While aggregate spending in the United States recovered quickly from a relatively shallow recession, domestic demand growth in the euro area has consistently remained weak, and recovered only recently in Japan. Owing to the high income elasticity of US imports, the US trade deficit has grown even faster than US demand.[2]

Two related factors are of particular importance in explaining the unbalanced global economic expansion since 2002. The first is a different response of macroeconomic policies in the G3. In the United States, both fiscal and monetary policy was eased aggressively. The structural budget balance deteriorated by 4 percent of GDP from 2001 to 2004 and real interest rates turned negative. Macroeconomic policies were less stimulative in the euro area and Japan, where real interest rates fell, but did not become negative. Fiscal policy provided only a relatively small stimulus. Against the backdrop of already high headline fiscal deficits structural budget balances remained broadly unchanged.

Second, aggregate spending in the United States (and some other countries) responded more strongly to unusually low short- and long-term interest rates than in Japan and the euro area. One key mechanism has been lower mortgage interest rates which supported a boom in housing markets and a strong increase in housing prices (Figure 2).

In turn, rising housing prices boosted residential construction and private consumption through traditional wealth effects and, possibly even more importantly, housing equity withdrawal (HEW). HEW, measured as the difference between the increase in mortgage borrowing and residential investment, was equivalent to almost 4 percent of household disposable income and 3 percent of GDP in the United States in 2005, and slightly lower in the United Kingdom. At the same time, the level of corporate investment has remained low compared to earlier cycles, despite rapid profit growth, especially in surplus countries such as Japan and Germany, and very favorable financing conditions.

Table 1: Developments in current account balances, output growth and inflation

	Current account balance[1]			Real GDP[2]			Consumer prices[2,3]		
	2000–03	2004	2005	2000–03	2004	2005	2000–03	2004	2005
World	—[4]	—	—	3.1	4.4	3.9	3.3	3.2	3.2
Industrial economies	−297	−367	−601	2.0	2.7	2.3	1.9	2.0	2.3
United States	−450	−668	−790	2.2	4.2	3.5	2.5	2.7	3.4
Euro area	1	58	1	1.9	1.8	1.4	2.2	2.1	2.2
France	15	−8	−27	2.1	2.1	1.4	1.8	2.1	1.7
Germany	17	104	110	1.2	1.1	1.1	1.5	1.7	2.0
Italy	−9	−15	−28	1.4	1.0	0.2	2.6	2.2	2.0
Spain	−25	−55	−78	3.0	2.7	3.4	3.3	3.0	3.4
Japan	114	172	154	1.3	2.3	2.8	−0.6	−0.0	−0.3
United Kingdom	−30	−42	−44	2.7	3.2	1.8	1.2	1.3	2.1
Canada	16	22	21	3.0	2.9	2.9	2.6	1.8	2.2
Australia	−18	−40	−41	3.2	3.5	2.6	3.7	2.3	2.7
New Zealand	−2	−6	−9	3.7	4.3	2.5	2.4	2.3	3.0
Emerging economies	156	312	457	5.1	7.2	6.6	5.8	5.5	4.9
Net oil exporters[5]	70	156	271	4.3	6.3	5.2	11.2	8.8	9.1
Russia	36	60	93	6.8	7.1	6.3	17.9	10.9	12.7
Middle East	41	90	164	4.6	5.4	5.5	6.5	8.1	9.7
Saudi Arabia	16	52	77	3.1	5.2	6.1	−0.3	0.4	0.7
Mexico	−15	−7	−8	2.1	4.2	3.0	5.7	5.2	3.3
Venezuela	8	14	22	−2.6	17.9	9.7	20.7	19.2	14.4
Net oil importers[6]	88	135	155	6.3	8.0	7.7	3.8	4.4	3.1
Asia	99	161	188	6.7	8.2	8.2	1.8	4.3	2.9
China	30	69	124	8.1	9.5	9.9	0.4	3.9	1.8
Hong Kong SAR	11	16	20	3.9	8.6	7.3	−2.7	−0.4	1.1
India[7]	3	−5	−13	5.6	7.5	7.5	4.9	6.5	5.2
Other Asia[8]	55	81	57	4.5	5.6	4.2	1.8	2.8	2.9
Korea	9	28	17	5.6	4.6	4.0	3.1	3.6	2.8
Singapore	17	28	32	3.6	8.7	6.4	0.6	1.7	0.5
Thailand	8	7	−3	4.8	6.2	4.4	1.4	2.8	4.5
Central Europe[9]	−15	−18	−16	2.9	5.0	3.7	4.6	3.9	2.3
Poland	−6	−4	−4	2.5	5.3	3.2	4.5	3.5	2.1
Turkey	−4	−16	−23	3.1	8.4	5.1	44.4	10.6	8.2
South Africa	−0	−7	−7	3.4	4.5	4.9	6.5	1.4	3.4
Others[10]	−3	21	31	2.5	5.7	4.6	7.0	5.9	6.8
Argentina	1	3	4	−2.1	9.0	8.7	9.3	6.1	12.3
Brazil	−13	12	14	2.0	4.9	2.3	8.8	7.6	5.7
Chile	−1	1	0	3.4	6.1	5.9	2.8	2.4	3.7
Indonesia	8	3	4	4.5	4.9	5.6	8.4	6.1	10.5

1. In US$ billion; for the aggregates, sum of the countries and regions shown or cited; world figures do not sum to zero due to incomplete country coverage and statistical discrepancies.

2. Average annual changes, in percent; for consumer prices in Latin America, 12-month changes to December; for the aggregates, weighted average of the countries and regions shown or cited, based on 2000 GDP and PPP exchange rates.

3. For India, wholesale prices.

4. —, not applicable.

5. Economies with net oil exports > 0.5 million barrels/day.

6. Economies with net oil imports > 0.5 million barrels/day.

7. Fiscal years starting in April.

8. Korea, Singapore, Taiwan (China), and Thailand.

9. The Czech Republic, Hungary, and Poland.

10. Plus Colombia, the Czech Republic, Hungary, Malaysia, Peru, and the Philippines.

Sources: Consensus Economics, 2005 and 2006; IMF; BIS estimates.

Figure 2: Long-term interest rates and housing price/rent ratios

Ten-year government bond yields (%)

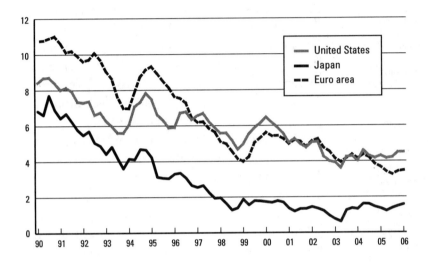

House price/rent ratios[1]

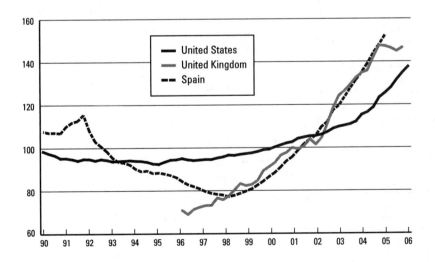

1. 1990 ± 2004 = 100; for the UK, 1996 ± 2005 = 100.
Source: National data.

Rising energy prices have led to both a further widening of current account deficits and a major shift in the composition of surplus countries during the past three years (Figure 3). Gross revenues from oil exports amounted to an estimated US$750 billion, about 1.75 percent of global GDP, in 2005, compared with about US$300 billion in 2002. The surplus of oil exporting countries has risen to about US$300 billion in 2005, compared to US$100 billion three years before. This amount is larger in dollar terms than the current account surplus of emerging Asia, and equivalent to about 4 percent of world gross savings. Relative to GDP of oil exporting countries, surpluses have reached 20 percent, raising questions about the absorption capacity of these countries. Correspondingly, the oil trade balance of advanced oil importing countries has deteriorated on the order of 1 percent of GDP. Hence, the higher oil bill accounts for about half of the deterioration of the US current account position since 2002.

High oil prices have had an even stronger impact on oil importing emerging economies, which typically have higher oil intensity of output. For instance, China's oil trade balance deteriorated by 4 percent of GDP between 2002 and 2005. Nonetheless, the current account surpluses of oil importing emerging economies have, overall, continued to rise. The combined surplus of Asian net oil importers (including China, Korea, Singapore) reached almost US$200 billion in 2005, compared to about US$100 billion in 2002. Net exports continued to provide an important contribution to GDP growth in emerging Asia (excluding China), and, especially in 2005, in China. Brazil also recorded rising surpluses, as it benefited from rising commodity prices and growing exports of manufactured goods. Central and eastern Europe stand out as the only emerging region that runs a current account deficit.

Growing current account surpluses contrast sharply with the orthodox view that emerging market economies with their higher growth potential should be net capital importers and hence run a current account deficit. Against this backdrop, the macroeconomic adjustment that has taken place in emerging Asian economies has been interpreted as a crisis response, with countries embarking on a strategy of self-insurance after the Asian crisis.[3] Two developments in particular support this view. First, accumulation of official reserves has been massive over the past few years in emerging Asia (excluding China), although it has slowed since 2005 (Figure 4).

Second, national investment rates dropped sharply in emerging Asia (excluding China) and have remained well below the levels seen in the run up

Figure 3: Global current account surpluses

In billions of US dollars

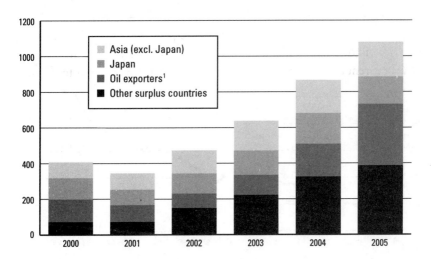

As a percentage of GDP

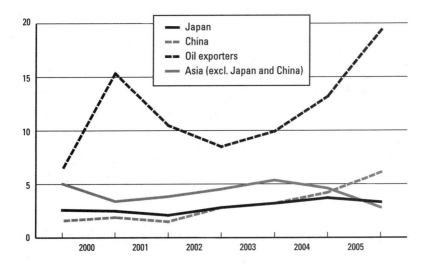

1. Middle East, Russia, and Norway.
Source: WEO, 2005.

Figure 4: Reserve accumulation and saving/investment balances in emerging Asia

Foreign exchange reserves (US$ billion)

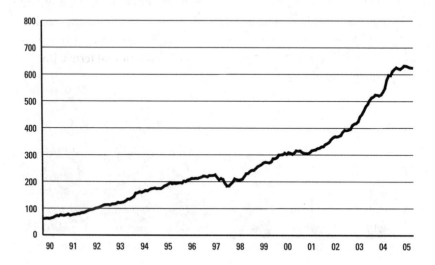

Investment and savings (% GDP)

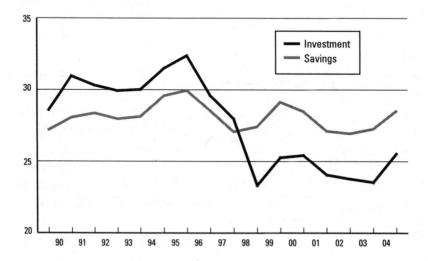

Note: Emerging Asia comprises India, Indonesia, Korea, Malaysia, the Philippines, Singapore, and Thailand.
Sources: IMF; WEO; International Institute of Finance (IIF); national data.

to the Asian crisis. From this angle, the growing current account surpluses in this part of Asia reflect an "investment drought" rather than a "savings glut."

For China, the picture is different. China's reserves, which have continued to grow apace, are now equivalent to about 40 percent of GDP. However, the massive growth in China's reserves before 2005 owes much more to capital inflows than to its global trade surplus. National investment rates have continued to rise, reaching about 40 percent of GDP in nominal terms. But national saving has risen even faster (Figure 5).

How to rebalance?

There is broad agreement among academics and policy-makers alike that current global external imbalances, and namely the US current account deficit, will require correction over the longer run. Yet views differ as to how such a process of global rebalancing might unfold. One camp argues that the rapid accumulation of external liabilities associated with the huge US trade deficit cannot be sustained in the longer run. In this view, a withdrawal of foreign investors from US assets could trigger an abrupt, and possibly disorderly, adjustment process.[4] Another camp sees the current configuration of current account balances as reflecting differences in the long-term growth potential of major economic regions. In this view, the US external deficit reflects strong capital inflows because of expectations of superior productivity gains in the United States. If these expectations materialize, the US deficit would gradually decline as a percentage of GDP.[5]

In both views globalization—"real" of the markets for goods and services, and "financial" in the form of globally integrated capital markets—is an important factor explaining the current pattern of global external imbalances. An obvious question is therefore whether globalization might have influenced the effectiveness of the mechanisms which might bring about external adjustment. Past current account reversals in advanced economies typically involved a combination of exchange rate and interest rate adjustments as well as rebalancing of global growth.[6] All of these adjustment mechanisms have been considerably muted in the past few years.

Exchange rate movements. The US dollar has depreciated in broad real effective terms by about 15 percent since its peak in March 2002 (Figure 6).

This is much less than in the mid-1980s, when it fell 35 percent between 1985 and 1988. It is also below estimates of the dollar depreciation required to

Figure 5: Reserve accumulation and saving/investment balances in China

Foreign exchange reserves (US$ billion)

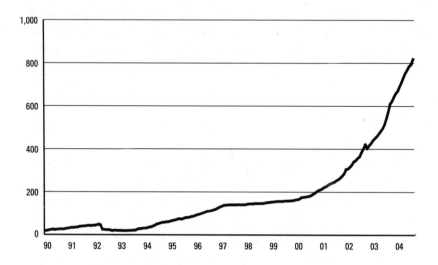

Investment and savings (% GDP)

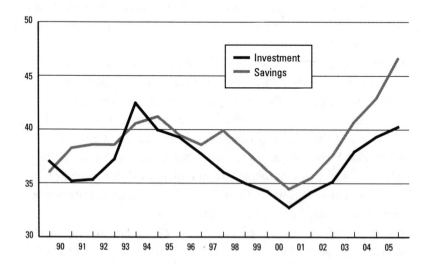

Sources: IMF; IIF; national data.

Figure 6: Real effective exchange rates

US dollar[1]

Major currencies and regional groups[1, 2]

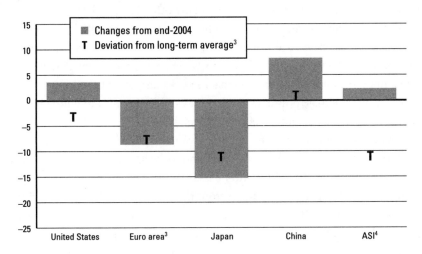

Notes:
1. In terms of relative consumer prices; 1975–2005 = 100.
2. February 2006, in percent.
3. January 1973 to February 2006; for China, January 1994 to February 2006.
4. Average for Hong Kong SAR, Singapore, and Taiwan (China).

Sources: National data; BIS.

reduce the current account deficit to a sustainable level (typically in a range of 25–40 percent real effective depreciation required to narrow the current account deficit to about 3 percent).[7] Since end-2004, the dollar has actually appreciated by almost 5 percent, supported by expectations of a widening interest rate differential in favor of the United States in much of 2005, and again since the beginning of 2006. At the same time, the euro and the yen have depreciated considerably, by 10 percent and 15 percent respectively. While supporting an export-led recovery in both economies, external imbalances widened further. The currencies of emerging Asian economies have appreciated since end-2004. While consistent with the expenditure switching which would be required to reduce their external surpluses, this process has been gradual, reflecting the hesitancy of a number of Asian countries to allow faster currency appreciation. As a consequence, real effective exchange rates in many countries in the region remain well below the long-term average.

Exchange rate pass-through. Lower exchange rate pass-through may have blunted the incentives to reallocate spending in the United States from imports to domestic goods, and to invest in the production of tradable goods. To maintain their market share in an environment of a declining dollar since 2002, foreign competitors have kept their US prices.[8] In some cases this has resulted in lower profit margins, but in many other cases, it has simply prompted foreign producers to find other ways to increase efficiency and cut input costs. For instance, unit labor costs (in dollars) have risen 8 percent in the United States while falling 1 percent (in euros) in Germany. Possibly reflecting this and related phenomena, the US share of global exports has fallen by 3 percentage points while the shares of Germany and China have risen by 4.5 and 3 percentage points respectively.

While well documented for major, advanced economies, the factors behind lower pass-through are not well understood.[9] More credible monetary policy and better anchored inflation expectations is one explanation. Another is heightened competition resulting from the integration of large emerging economies into a global marketplace. The large shift in the relative prices of commodities and manufactured goods supports this view. Against this backdrop, it remains an open question whether exchange-rate pass-through has declined in the long run. For instance, it is conceivable that a large movement in exchange rates, if perceived as permanent, might trigger a change in corporate price-setting and a sudden increase in pass-through.

Energy prices. A prolonged period of high oil prices would probably post-pone global rebalancing. This would be different from the last oil price shock, when a substantial part of the initial oil price increase was reversed relatively quickly. Long-term forecasts of oil prices are subject to large uncertainty. But both market expectations and demand and supply conditions support the assessment that oil prices might remain high. Oil futures have risen above the record levels of August 2005.

Recent IEA projections see oil demand growing by an annual rate of 2 percent until 2010, 50 percent faster than in the second half of the 1990s. This is consistent with the assessment that the recent oil price increase reflects primarily a permanent demand shock. At the same time, capacity remains tight. New capacity seems to take longer to come on line, as investment in oil exploration has been sluggish and qualified staff and equipment scarce.

Stronger demand growth in surplus countries. The scope for current account adjustment through stronger domestic demand in surplus countries appears limited, notwithstanding projections for continued robust global growth in 2006, and a significant narrowing of growth differentials among advanced economies.

First, euro area growth still depends on external demand as private consumption has remained weak. Second, both the euro area and Japan are forecast to grow at, or even above, potential in 2006, leaving little room for a sustained acceleration of growth without measures to lift potential growth. Third, while domestic demand in emerging Asia seems to be strengthening, the contribution of net exports to growth remained high in 2005 (Figure 7).

Fourth, oil-exporting countries seem to have spent a smaller proportion of additional oil revenues on imports in 2005 than in 2003–04, suggesting that their absorption capacity is limited in the near term.

Long-term interest rates. Unusually low interest rates during the current upswing have facilitated borrowing and lifted asset prices, increasing household wealth, especially in the United States. This has affected saving behavior, as by most measures, US households have stopped saving while steadily increasing their residential investment (to 5 percent of GDP in 2005, compared to 3.5 percent on average in the 1990s). At the same time, the corporate sector has hoarded cash (Figure 8). This combination does not raise US productive capacity in tradable goods and services. Hence, while saving rates of private households (and the public sector) appear unsustainably low, those of the corporate sector are probably higher than optimal.

Figure 7: GDP growth and net exports in China and emerging Asia

China

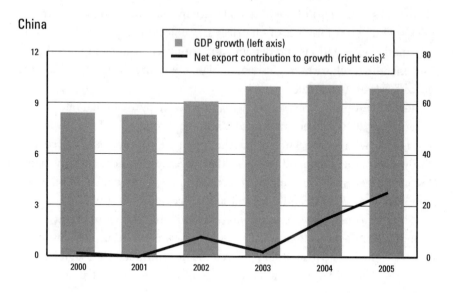

Emerging Asia[1]

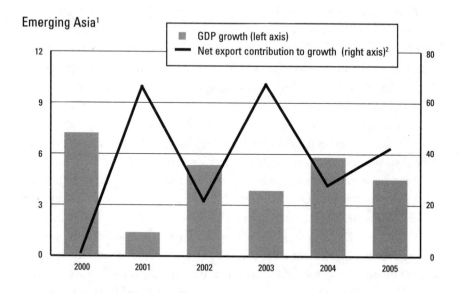

Notes:

1. Weighted average based on 2000 GDP and PPP exchange rates of the following economies: Hong Kong SAR, Korea, Thailand, Singapore, Taiwan (China); annual changes in percent.

2. As a share of output growth, in percent.

Sources: WEO; national data.

Figure 8: US net saving by sector

Private sector saving minus investment (% GDP)

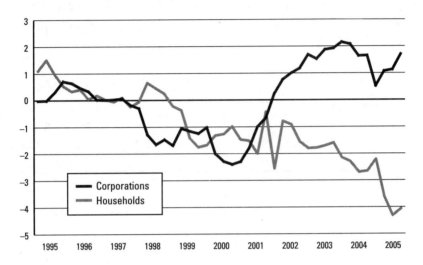

General government balance (% GDP)

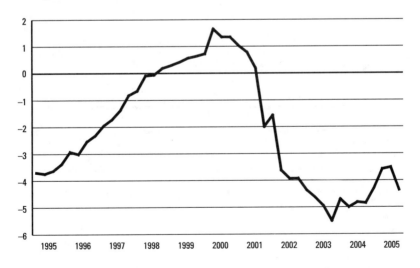

Source: National data.

The rebalancing of domestic demand would be required not just across countries, but also across sectors. In surplus countries, stronger corporate investment, especially in the non-tradeable sectors, appears key to raising productivity and stimulating domestic demand. The relatively low level of corporate investment relative to GDP in many countries is still puzzling in this regard (Table 2).

Table 2: Investment[1]

| | Total investment/GDP[2] | | Corporate investment | | | |
| | | | as share of GDP[2, 3] | | growth[4] | |
	2005[5]	Long-term average	2005[6]	Long-term average	2005[6]	Long-term average
United States	19.9	19.2	10.7	11.3	8.7	4.5
Euro area	20.4	21.3	—[7]	—	2.5	2.4
Germany	17.1	21.4	6.8	8.0	4.4	2.5
France	19.6	19.7	10.9	11.1	3.5	2.8
Italy	19.5	20.6	8.1	8.8	−4.3	2.2
Spain	29.4	23.4	5.8	6.8	5.8	4.1
Japan	23.3	27.9	14.9	15.8	8.6	3.5
United Kingdom	16.6	17.5	9.4	11.4	2.2	3.9
Canada	20.5	20.3	11.3	12.0	9.1	4.0
Australia	25.8	24.9	13.9	12.8	14.3	6.8
China	43.8	32.8	23.7	—	—	—
India[8]	25.9	22.0	—	—	—	—
Korea	29.3	32.0	8.8	12.3	5.1	7.9
Other emerging Asia[9]	21.8	25.6	—	—	—	—
Brazil	20.1	20.1	—	—	—	—
Mexico	19.7	19.8	—	—	11.6	7.2

Notes:
1. Gross fixed capital formation (GFCF); long-term averages are calculated on time series starting in 1980, except corporate investment for Mexico (1993).
2. In current prices, percentages.
3. Private non-residential GFCF/GDP; for Germany, Italy, Spain, China, and Korea, GFCF machinery and equipment.
4. Average annual changes in real private non-residential GFCF, in percent; for Germany, Italy, Spain, Korea, and Mexico, GFCF machinery, and equipment.
5. For China, and India, 2004.
6. For Spain, 2004.
7. —, not available.
8. Fiscal years starting in April.
9. Weighted average of Hong Kong SAR, Indonesia, Malaysia, the Philippines, Singapore, Taiwan (China), and Thailand, based on 2000 GDP and PPP exchange rates.

Sources: CEIC; Datastream; IMF; OECD; national data.

Conclusion

Broad current account trends observed over the past three years lend support to the view that responses to adverse shocks (including the bursting of the IT bubble in the United States and crises in Asia and Latin America) are the root cause of growing global current account imbalances. Other factors which have added to external imbalances (such as rising oil and commodity prices) or possibly delayed adjustment (such as declining exchange rate and commodity price pass-through) seem to have more to do with changes in the functioning of the global economy. These factors could re-structure the process of external adjustment. A better understanding of how external adjustment mechanisms work in today's world remains an important task for economic research.

Public policy might have to live with greater uncertainty about how global rebalancing might unfold. From this angle, policy measures aimed at reducing external imbalances should also be assessed from a risk-management perspective—does a specific measure reduce the risk of disorderly adjustment?—rather than just looking at the direct and immediate impact on the current account position, which may be hard to quantify anyway. This view provides a strong additional argument for removing government-induced distortions in external adjustment mechanisms, including high fiscal deficits, which are financed with foreign capital, massive reserve accumulation, or regulation, which prevents free trade in goods, services and factors of production. Policies aimed at reducing these forms of government intervention might well directly reduce external imbalances. More importantly, perhaps such policy measures would strengthen market mechanisms and facilitate private sector risk assessment and management.

NOTES

1 The author would like to thank Dubravko Mihaljek, Richhild Moessner, and Toshitaka Sekine for their helpful comments, and Michela Scatigna and Gert Schnabel for excellent technical assistance. The views expressed in this paper are those of the author and do not necessarily reflect those of the Bank for International Settlements (BIS).

2 Empirical estimates typically show an income elasticity of US imports of goods and services in the vicinity of 2 and the income elasticity of exports in a range of 1–1.5; see Brook et al. (2004) for an overview.

3 Rajan, 2006.

4 See, for instance, Roubini and Sester (2004).

5 See, for instance, Cooper (2005).

6 Freund, 2000.

7 See Jarrett (2005) for an overview.

8 See White (2005).

9 See Bank for International Settlements (2005) and Sekine (2006).

REFERENCES

Bank for International Settlements (BIS). 2005. 75th Annual Report. Basel.

Brook, A., F. Sédillot, and P. Ollivaud. 2004. "Channels for narrowing the US current account deficit and implications for other economies." OECD Economics Department Working Paper No. 390. Paris.

Consensus Economics. "Consensus Forecasts." 2005. December.

————. 2006. January and February.

Cooper, R. N. 2005. "Living with global imbalances: a contrarian view." IIE Policy Briefs in International Economics 05-3. Washington, D.C.

Freund, C. 2000. "Current account adjustments in industrialized countries." Federal Reserve Board International Finance Discussion Papers 2000-692. Washington, D.C.

International Monetary Fund (IMF). 2005. *World Economic Outlook*. Washington, D.C.: IMF.

Jarrett, P. 2005. "Coping with the inevitable adjustment in the US current account." OECD Economics Department Working Paper No 467. Paris.

Organisation for Co-operation and Development (OECD). *Economic Outlook* 78 database.

Rajan, G. R. 2006. "Perspectives on global imbalances." Remarks at the Global Financial Imbalances Conference. London. 23 January.

Roubini, N. and B. Setzer. 2004. "The US twin deficits and external debt accumulation: Are they sustainable?" Mimeo.

Sekine, T. 2006. "Time varying exchange rate pass-through: Experiences from several industrial countries." BIS Working Paper 202. March.

White, W. R. 2005. "Changes in productivity and competitiveness: Impact on the international allocation of capital and global imbalances." Presentation at the Banque de France International Symposium on Productivity, Competitiveness and Globalisation.

World Economic Outlook (WEO). 2005. Washington, D.C.: International Monetary Fund. September.

CHAPTER 3.3

Global Imbalances: The New Economy, the Dark Matter, the Savvy Investor, and the Standard Analysis[1]

BARRY EICHENGREEN, George C. Pardee and Helen N. Pardee Professor of
Economics and Political Science, University of California, Berkeley

Introduction

The longer the current global imbalances persist, the less agreement there is about how they will ultimately be resolved. The growth of the US current account deficit after the turn of the century was first met with warnings that such large deficits were unsustainable, that foreign finance would not be provided indefinitely, and that the situation would culminate in an abrupt interruption to capital inflows, sharp compression of the US current account, and a global slowdown, or worse.[2]

As equity inflows gave way to debt inflows, and as private purchases of US assets then gave way to foreign central bank purchases, these early warnings were echoed and amplified. But the longer the deficit persisted and the further it expanded without obvious adverse consequences, the larger swelled the ranks of the doubters. It was argued that foreigners would continue to direct substantial amounts of capital toward the U.S., thereby financing the country's deficit, because the flexibility of the American economy had delivered a permanent increase in the productivity and profitability of investment (Cooper, 2004). It was argued that the U.S. could run deficits and finance a large external debt at low cost—i.e., that the U.S. external position was sustainable—because US foreign investments earn a significantly higher return than foreign investments in the United States (Kitchen, 2006). The apotheosis of this view was the assertion that statistics are misleading and the US deficit is not, in fact, a deficit at all. That as late as 2005 America was officially receiving net interest income from abroad meant that the country still had more foreign assets than liabilities, implying the existence of significant un- or under-recorded US exports of goods and services (Hausmann and Sturzenegger, 2005).

In this paper, I sort through these interpretations with an eye to their consistency and compatibility. I raise questions about the internal consistency, conformity with the facts, and predictive content of each of the arguments challenging the mainstream analysis of US current account sustainability. Moreover, I show that several of these objections to the standard sustainability arithmetic are incompatible with one another. In other words, it is not always possible for the skeptics to take succor in one another's arguments.

The standard analysis

The standard analysis that the current pattern of global imbalances is unsustainable is based on arithmetically capitalizing the implied debt flows.[3] The indefinite maintenance of a current account deficit of 7.5 percent of GDP by a country whose rate of nominal GDP growth is 5 percent (3 percent real growth plus 2 percent inflation) implies an eventual ratio of net external debt to GDP of 150 percent. For an economy like that of the U.S., with a capital/output ratio of 3, this means that foreigners end up holding half of the country's capital stock. Quite apart from whether foreign investors would be willing to allocate such a large share of their portfolios to claims on the productive capacity of the United States, there is the question of whether Americans would feel comfortable allowing them to do so. As evidenced by the reaction surrounding China's recent offer to buy the US oil company Unocal and the political backlash against the efforts of a Dubai-based company to purchase the right to manage six US ports, there would likely be a strong negative reaction against extensive foreign ownership of productive assets in the United States, which are regarded, rightly or wrongly, as essential to the national security in the post-9/11 world.

Note that the share of US capital stock owned by foreigners would be even greater to the extent that foreign capital is needed not only to finance the current account gap, but also to offset the balance-of-payments consequences of US investment abroad. To be sure, the share of the capital stock owned by foreigners would be less, to the extent that foreign holdings are in the form of other financial assets. But here, the fear would be that the U.S. would have a strong incentive to inflate away or otherwise expropriate the value of these claims. By implication, finance for the indefinite maintenance of deficits at current levels will not be forthcoming.

The only uncertainty, according to the standard analysis, is whether the adjustment begins early and proceeds gradually, with minimal disruptive effects, or whether it is delayed until an abrupt correction becomes unavoidable. In the first scenario, capital inflows begin tailing off relatively early, allowing the current account balance to be compressed by, say, .5 percent of GDP each year, permitting the deficit to fall to 2.5 percent of GDP by 2016, and the debt/GDP ratio to stabilize in the neighborhood of 50 percent.

The mechanism behind this adjustment is no mystery. The gradually declining foreign demand for additional US assets leads to a decline in their prices, including that of the dollar. Falling asset prices and their mirror image, rising interest rates, compress absorption in the United States.[4] Slowing domestic demand makes more US exports available, while the weaker exchange rate switches foreign demand toward them. The econometric rule of thumb is that a .5 percent improvement in the current account will require a 5 percent decline in the real effective exchange rate of the dollar.[5]

In the second scenario, capital inflows continue to finance current account deficits at current levels, or, what is worse, they continue financing the dollar at current levels, in this case implying that the deficit as a share of GDP will widen further.[6] The debt/GDP ratio is then on a path to 150 percent or higher, threatening portfolio equilibrium abroad and political equilibrium in the United States. At some point foreign investors pull the plug. Capital inflows fall sharply, precipitating a sharp fall in the dollar.[7] This produces sharply lower asset prices, sharply higher import-price inflation, sharply higher interest rates, and a sharp fall in demand in the United States and globally.[8] Such is the conventional wisdom.

The new economy

Three quite different arguments are made for why this standard analysis is incorrect: the so-called "new economy," "dark matter," and "savvy investor" views. The new economy view is that the conventional wisdom underestimates the appetite of foreign investors for claims on the United States. Rapid productivity growth and high corporate profitability make the United States attractive as a place to invest, so much so that the rest of the world will be prepared to continue providing foreign investment in the amount of at least 7 percent of US GDP for an indefinite period. Financing even a US$1 trillion current account deficit, which is what a 7 percent deficit currently implies, requires less than 15 percent of the more than US$8 trillion of gross foreign savings outside the United States.[9] And placing that share of foreign savings in the United States is attractive.[10] Claims on the United States are secure. The economy is buoyant. With the U.S. growing rapidly, this foreign investment will produce an attractive rate of return and the country's debt/GDP ratio will not rise explosively.

The fact that US economic growth will accelerate relative to trend is essential for this story. But it still implies that foreigners will hold an uncomfortably large share of the US capital stock. Say that the growth of output doubles from 2.5–3 percent to 5.5 percent, while inflation continues running at 2 percent.[11] A current account deficit of 7.5 percent of GDP still implies a debt/GDP ratio of 100 percent, or that foreigners will hold a third of the US capital stock. And the premise that it is the growth of the productivity of the real economy that is attracting foreign investors implies that they will concentrate their holdings in claims on US productive capacity, not on US debt securities. Hence, there is still reason to fear a political backlash against foreigners "buying up the US economy." If so, even sharply increased productivity growth in the United States, as assumed here, will not sustain external deficits at current levels indefinitely.

A further problem for the view that a permanent acceleration in productivity growth makes foreign investment in the United States more attractive is that productivity is growing even faster in China, which constitutes the single largest national source of finance for the US deficit. Another problem is that there is little evidence of a significant increase in US investment as implied by the story. On the contrary, the growth of the current account deficit reflects a significant decline in national savings.[12] In addition, net finance for the US deficit is being provided by foreign central banks, not by private investors motivated by considerations of productivity and profitability.[13] These doubts are reinforced by the uncomfortable fact that, since 2000, foreign funds have been flowing into debt rather than equity markets, whereas the latter would be the obvious place to bet on the rapid growth of productivity and profitability.

Finally, this interpretation implies that the rate of return on foreign investment in the United States should be high, when this has, in fact, not been the case by comparison with US foreign investment in other countries. US net interest income from abroad remains positive (or it did through 2005), despite the fact that the U.S. is now a net debtor to the rest of the world to the tune of more than 20 percent of US GDP, according to official estimates.[14] On average, then, US investment abroad continues to pay more handsomely than does foreign investment in the United States. The implied rate of return differential is on the order of 2 percentage points.[15] It goes the wrong way for proponents of the "new economy" view.

It could be that foreign investors regard the US economy as a "growth stock." Perhaps they expect substantial capital gains on their US investments which have not yet shown up in recorded payments of interest and dividends because US firms are plowing their profits into additional capital formation. But here, the fact that US equity investment abroad is larger than foreign equity investment in the United States is problematic. The net flows that finance the current account are debt flows, as noted above. It is hard to believe that foreign investors anticipate capital gains on their US treasury and agency securities, as implied by the growth-stock interpretation—interest rates being low, relative to the norm for this stage of the business cycle and the dollar being unlikely to rise still further.

The dark matter

If foreign investors do in fact anticipate capital gains on their US investments—which would seem to be the only way of reconciling the "new economy" view with the fact of relatively low interest payments to date on those assets—then this is fundamentally corrosive of the other rationale for dismissing the possibility of a sharp correction in the US current account, the so-called "dark matter" view. Hausmann and Sturzenegger (2005) have cast doubt on the assumption that the U.S. has in fact been accumulating a large external debt. They cast doubt, in turn, on official statistics for the current account, by observing that the country's net interest income from abroad remains positive. They argue that since net interest income from abroad remained positive at some US$30 billion in 2005, US foreign investments, properly valued to reflect their income-generating capacity, must exceed foreign investors' claims on the United States, similarly measured to reflect their true economic value.[16] Since US net interest income did not decline significantly in the 25 years through 2005, neither did the value of the country's net foreign investments, again "properly valued." In turn this must mean that the country has not, in some sense, been running current account deficits. The current account statistics must be failing to capture US exports of reputation—the brand value of companies like Disney and Coca Cola, and the reputation of the US government for preserving the value of its debts—which are packaged together with US exports of observable goods and services. In this story, three categories of US exports were un- or under-recorded: US liquidity services (seignorage), US insurance services (secure investments), and US knowledge services (organizational knowledge and brand recognition), because they were bundled with three types of financial instruments, respectively: US currency held by foreigners, US treasury bonds held by foreigners, and US-originated FDI (Buiter, 2006).

Objections to this analysis include the observation that US net interest payments on the debt securities in which foreigners disproportionately invest have been artificially depressed by the Greenspan Conundrum (the unusually low level of interest rates).[17] They include the observation that there is no reason to take the official figures on net income from abroad as accurate, while dismissing official figures for the current account as meaningless.[18] In fact, there is ample room for misstating income by using transfer pricing—to shift profits between national subsidiaries—and considerable incentive for doing so to minimize tax liabilities.[19]

Perhaps the most fundamental objection is, again, that foreign investors regard their investments in the United States as a growth stock that will yield higher income and thus capital gains in the future. If this is the case, then perhaps the "new economy" view is right. But, if so, the "dark matter" view must be wrong. US net income from abroad remains positive only because the high future returns on foreign investment in the United States have not yet materialized. As soon as they do, the value of US net liabilities to foreigners will rise sharply. So will US net income payments, assuming that foreigners begin to repatriate some of the associated income gains, once their investments have paid off. Once the capital gains have occurred, the incentive for foreign investors to take more such positions will be less, since the likelihood of further gains will have diminished. The dollar will have to depreciate in order to stimulate additional US exports, not just sufficiently to offset the decline in capital inflows, but now also to service the more expensive net external debt.

"Dark matter" and "the new economy" are two widely cited reasons for questioning whether there needs to be a sharp correction of global imbalances. In fact, one cannot be consistently skeptical on both grounds.

The savvy investor

The third view is that the U.S. can service a large external debt without serious discomfort, since US external assets earn a significantly higher return than US foreign liabilities, simply because US investors are more savvy than their foreign counterparts. Kitchen (2006) lays out the scenario in which historical rate of return relationships continue to hold, and the U.S. also continues to enjoy the same tendency for its foreign investments to appreciate in value, while foreigners suffer capital losses on their more poorly chosen investments in the United States.[20] He shows that in this case it will cost the United States less than one percent of GDP to finance a net external debt of 50 percent of GDP. Indeed, even if the current account does not adjust, the fact that foreigners continue to incur capital losses on their investments in the United States— relative to valuation changes for US investments abroad—implies that the ratio of net foreign debt to GDP stabilizes in the neighborhood of 75 percent, not the 150 percent implied by the standard analysis. It will still cost the United States less than 2 percent of GDP to service this net external debt, since US investments abroad are so much more remunerative than are foreign investments in the United States.

Whether this scenario is politically plausible depends on whether the political process in the United States is driven by the income effects of the debt service—which are modest and therefore pose no problems for "sustainability"—and not by xenophobia and national security concerns over foreign ownership of the American capital stock, since under these assumptions the share owned by foreigners would still be substantial. Whether it is economically plausible depends on whether US investments abroad continue to outperform foreign investments in the United States by a significant margin. The fact that some foreign investment in the U.S. takes the form of US cash and Treasury securities is consistent with the view that the United States is well placed to continue providing liquidity and insurance services to the rest of the world, and with the idea that historical rate-of-return differentials will tend to persist. But, as shown by Gourinchas and Rey (2005) and Buiter (2006), these factors can explain only a fraction of the overall differential between the effective rates of return on US foreign assets and liabilities. The rest reflects the superior performance of US FDI relative to foreign FDI in the United States. Kitchen (2006) shows that, abstracting from recession and near-recession years, this differential averages more than 5 percent.[21] (In contrast, the differential for other private investments is quite small.) When one compares the recent performance of Japanese auto companies' investments in the United States with the performance of US auto companies' investments abroad, one is led to wonder whether recent differentials will persist.[22] The move of foreign investors out of US Treasury securities in favor of agency securities, and their current efforts to pursue new forms of FDI in the United States provide additional grounds for skepticism about the persistence of historical yield differentials. So, too, is the fact that overall US external debt will be significantly larger in the future and therefore, presumably carry an additional risk premium.[23]

In any case, this view that even large current account deficits will lead to only moderate debts and small net interest payments to foreigners is, if not exactly incompatible, then certainly hard to square with the "new economy" alternative. The new economy view is that foreign savings will continue flowing to the United States in large amounts because foreign investment in America will now pay better than US investment abroad. Unless US investors have some unique ability to find better performing investments abroad, this implies that the historical rate of return differentials helping to sustain the US balance of payments position will not continue to hold. One can argue that the American deficit is sustainable because the US economy is incredibly flexible, productive and remunerative to investors, and also that foreign direct investors in the U.S. will continue to earn only half the yield of US investors abroad, only if one is prepared to take the savvy US investor (and dull non-US investor) assumption to an extreme.

In lieu of a conclusion

This paper has reviewed four perspectives on global imbalances. The standard analysis suggests that the US current account deficit cannot be sustained at current levels. It suggests that there will have to be significant adjustments in asset prices to compress US spending and significant changes in relative prices to crowd in net exports. At the same time, nonstandard analyses, focusing on the profitability of investment in the United States, the profitability of US foreign investment, and the differential returns on US foreign assets and liabilities suggest that US current account deficits may be easier to sustain than implied by the standard analysis.

As for which view is correct, only time will tell. But uncertainty about whether a disorderly correction is imminent does not justify inaction. That a category 5 hurricane strikes only once a generation does not absolve the responsible homeowner, living in a flood plain, from putting his house on stilts or investing in flood insurance. For the United States, insuring against a disorderly correction would involve progressively tightening fiscal policy and thus gradually narrowing the gap between absorption and production. The best way for China and other East Asian countries that export to the United States to meet this deceleration in US absorption growth would be by loosening fiscal policy (increasing spending on social security, health care, education, rural infrastructure and the like) and thus stimulating demand at home. With demand growth slowing in the United States and accelerating in Asia, relative prices, in the form of the dollar exchange rate, will tend to adjust. The argument for gradual adjustment starting now to limit the risk of a sharp, disruptive adjustment later is still sound even if an eventual hard landing is less than certain.

NOTES

1 Reprinted from *The Journal of Policy Modeling* (2006).

2 Obstfeld and Rogoff, 2000, 2004; Roubini and Setser, 2004; Mann, 2004; Mussa, 2004.

3 Mussa, 2004; Roubini and Setser, 2004; Yoshitomi; 2006.

4 Presumably, through a combination of rising household saving and declining corporate investment.

5 Note that this implies a 50 percent decline in the dollar over the decade in which the 5 percent of GDP swing in the current account occurs.

6 Other things being equal; the idea that capital inflows are forthcoming in the amount needed to support the dollar at current levels is a corollary of the view that emerging markets, committed to a strategy of export-led growth, are reluctant to see their currencies rise against the greenback; the classic statement of this view is Dooley et al. (2003).

7 The dollar must fall further than in the other scenario (other things being equal), because debt stocks are higher, adjustment having been delayed, and it is necessary to crowd in additional exports in order to finance them; this point is developed by Blanchard et al. (2005).

8 Model-based simulations of the two scenarios are in Faruqee et al., (2005).

9 This is where the so-called global savings glut (see Bernanke, 2005) and slowdown in investment in East Asia ex Japan (see Rajan, 2006) enter the story; careful readers will note that I have now alluded to all four components of the global current account: US savings/absorption (where I discussed the standard analysis), US investment (where I introduced the new economy view), and now foreign saving and foreign investment; not coincidentally, this is how I structure my discussion of global imbalances in a previous paper (Eichengreen, 2006).

10 Of course, more than 15 percent of gross foreign savings would have to be poured into the United States insofar as Americans also invest abroad; for more on this see below.

11 I chose this unrealistically rosy scenario to drive home a point: productivity growth in the non-farm sector has risen by half since 1995, from 1.6 to 2.9 percent, relative to the preceding ten years; see, for example, Bacjys and Kanbert (2005), Cooper (2004), Clarida (2005), Levy (2005), Mandel (2006), and Plosser (2005).

12 In point of fact, national investment in the United States fell by 2 percent as a share of US GDP between the 1990s and 2004; US gross national saving has fallen to 13.6 percent of GDP on the IMF's measure, down by 3.3 percentage points from the 1983–2000 average and barely half the level prevailing in the rest of the world.

13 To be sure, there have also been substantial private capital inflows into the United States, but these have been fully offset by private capital outflows, leaving it for official foreign finance to fill the financing gap.

14 More on these official estimates below.

15 See Gourinchas and Rey (2005) and Kitchen (2006).

16 The 5 percent interest rate they use to capitalize income streams has been attacked as arbitrary, but their essential point would still follow for any constant positive interest rate.

17 It is revealing that the average return on foreign investment fell from 3.6 percent in 2000 to 2.4 percent in 2003, just when US interest rates were declining (Setser, 2006).

18 As do Hausmann and Sturzenegger.

19 Hung and Mascaro (2005) note that this view is supported by the fact that the rate of return on US owned FDI in Ireland was triple that on overall US FDI between 1999 and 2003, which that on US FDI in Bermuda was double the overall average.

20 In this scenario, the capital losses on US investments suffered by foreigners are accentuated by the assumption that the dollar depreciates at least modestly against foreign currencies, something that is not also assumed in the next scenario in the text; Gourinchas and Rey (2005) provide a more detailed analysis of the role of exchange rate fluctuations in accentuating historical valuations effects.

21 Gourinchas and Rey (2005) estimate the differential to be smaller because they do not selectively eliminate recession and near-recession years.

22 Hung and Mascaro (2004) show that the difference in returns appears to be associated with the longer presence of US investments abroad than foreign investments in the United States; thus, as recent foreign investments in the US mature, associated with the recent growth of the US current account deficit, the rate of return differential may show a tendency to close; as the authors write (p.3): "As foreign-controlled companies become older, the pattern of returns on direct investment that has so far favored US companies abroad could diminish." Note that this interpretation is easier to reconcile with the "new economy" than the "savvy investor" view (see below).

23 As assumed by, inter alia, Roubini and Setser (2004).

REFERENCES

Backus, David and Frederic Lambert. 2005. "Current Account Fact and Fiction." Unpublished manuscript. Stern School of Business, New York University.

Bernanke, Ben. 2005. "The Global Savings Glut and the US Current Account Deficit." Washington, D.C.: Board of Governors of the Federal Reserve System. 10 March.

Blanchard, Olivier, Francesco Givazzi, and Filipa Sa. 2005. "The US Current Account and the Dollar." Brookings Papers on Economic Activity 1:1–49.

Buiter, Willem. 2006. "Dark Matter or Cold Fusion?" Global Economics Paper No.136. London: Goldman Sachs. 16 January.

Clarida, Richard H. 2005. "Japan, China, and the US Current Account Deficit." CATO Journal 25:111–114.

Cooper, Richard. 2004. "US Deficit: It is Not Only Sustainable, It is Logical." Financial Times. 31 October. A15.

Dooley, Michael, David Folkerts-Landau, and Peter Garber. 2003. "An Essay on the Revived Bretton Woods System." NBER Working Paper No.9971. September.

Eichengreen, Barry. 2006. "The Blind Men and the Elephant." Brookings Policy Brief. Washington, D.C.: The Brookings Institution. January.

Faruqee, Hamid, Douglas Laxton, Dirk Muir, and Paolo Pesenti. 2005. "Smooth Landing or Crash? Model-Based Scenarios of Global Current Account Rebalancing." Paper presented to the NBER Conference on G7 Current Account Imbalances. Newport, R.I. June.

Hausmann, Ricardo and Federico Sturzenegger. 2005. "Dark Matter Makes the US Deficit Disappear." *Financial Times*. 8 December. A15.

Hung, Juann and Angelo Mascaro. 2004. "Return on Cross-Border Investment: Why Does US Investment Abroad Do Better?" Technical Paper No. 2004–17. Washington, D.C.: Congressional Budget Office. December.

Hung, Juann and Angelo Mascaro. 2005. "Why Does US Investment Abroad Earn Higher Returns than Foreign Investment in the United States?" *CBO Policy Issue Brief*. Washington, D.C.: Congressional Budget Office. November.

Jarrett, Peter. 2005. "Coping with the Inevitable Adjustment in the US Current Account." Economics Department Working Paper No. 467. Paris: OECD. December.

Kitchen, John. 2006. "Sharecroppers or Shrewd Capitalists? Projections of the US Current Account, International Income Flows, and Net International Debt." Unpublished manuscript. Office of Management and Budget. February.

Levy, Mickey D. 2005. "Worries About the Growing US Trade Deficit are Overstated." Bank of America Economics Brief. 13 April.

Mandel, Michael. 2006. "Productivity, the Trade Deficit and Dark Matter, Part I." *Business Week*. 21 February. Available at: www.businesweek.com.

Mann, Catherine. 2004. "Managing Exchange Rates: Achievement of Global Re-Balancing or Evidence of Global Co-Dependence?" Unpublished manuscript, Institute for International Economics. July.

Mussa, Michael. 2004. "Exchange Rate Adjustments Needed to Reduce Global Payments Imbalances." C. Fred Bergsten and John Williamson eds., *Dollar Adjustment: How Far? Against What?* Washington, D.C.: Institute for International Economics. 113–138.

Obstfeld, Maurice and Kenneth Rogoff. 2000. "Perspectives on OECD Capital Market Integration: Implications for US Current Account Adjustment." *Global Economic Integration: Opportunities and Challenges*. Kansas City: Federal Reserve Bank of Kansas City. 169–208.

———. 2004. "The Unsustainable US Current Account Position Revisited." NBER Working Paper No.10869. October.

Plosser, Charles I. 2005. "A Perspective on the Global Economy." Unpublished manuscript. Simon School of Business, University of Rochester. January.

Rajan, Raghuram. 2006. "Perspectives on Global Imbalances." 23 January. Available at: www.imf.org

Roubini, Nouriel and Brad Setser. 2004. "The U.S. as a Net Debtor: The Sustainability of the US External Imbalances." Unpublished manuscript. Stern School of Business, New York University.

Setser, Brad. 2006. "Mandel versus Setser. Round 2. More on Intangible Exports and Dark Matter." 21 February. Available at: www.rgemonitor.com

Yoshitomi, Masaru. 2006. "Global Imbalances and East Asian Monetary Cooperation." Duck-Koo Chung and Barry Eichengreen eds., *Toward an East Asian Exchange Rate Regime*. Forthcoming.

CHAPTER 3.4

Ongoing Risks from the US Current Account Deficit[1]

BRAD SETSER, Director of Global Research, Roubini Global Economics, and Research Associate, Global Economic Governance Center, University College, Oxford

The 2006 US current account deficit is on track to approach US$900 billion, slightly under 7 percent of US GDP. A current account deficit of 7 percent of GDP is comparable in size to the deficit of Mexico prior to its 1994–95 crisis, to the deficit of Thailand prior to its 1997 crisis, or for that matter, to Turkey's current account deficit as of this writing (2006).

The risks associated with the US deficit are not directly comparable to the risks run by emerging economies with comparable deficits, in no small part because the United States is still able to borrow in its own currency at low nominal and real interest rates. However, the US deficit is of an unprecedented size for a large advanced economy.

Recently, the U.S. has financed its external deficit entirely with debt. That is a change from the late 1990s, when optimism in the new economy attracted large equity flows into the U.S. Indeed, setting 2005 aside—a year dominated by the impact of the Homeland Investment Act—American investment in foreign equities have exceeded foreign equity investment in the U.S. Consequently, sustaining the status quo requires that the U.S. place US$1 trillion of debt a year abroad to finance both the US current account deficit and US equity investments abroad. Much of the debt will be bought by foreign central banks and government-controlled oil investment funds.

Going forward, the current account deficit will only stay at around 7 percent of US GDP if the trade deficit starts to shrink. The current account deficit is the sum of the trade deficit, the deficit in transfer payments, and the balance between the payments the U.S. makes on its external debt and the income the U.S. receives on its investment abroad. From 2000 to 2004, the interest rate the U.S. had to pay on its rising debt stock fell from over 6 percent to around 3 percent. The interest rate on US external debt is now above 4 percent, and is poised to increase further. That, combined with ongoing growth in the US external debt stock is liable to increase interest payments sharply.

Rising interest payments imply that the current account deficit will continue to grow, even if the trade deficit (now about 6 percent of US GDP) stabilizes. Indeed, even if the US trade deficit starts to shrink as a share of US GDP, as part of an orderly adjustment, the current account deficit will likely remain close to 7 percent of US GDP for the next five years or so. If the adjustment process is delayed, the ongoing deficits associated with a gradual adjustment process will be larger and, perhaps more importantly, the risk that the adjustment process will not be gradual will be far larger.

This large deficit generates two distinct risks: one risk is that the external financing needed to sustain this deficit will not be available. Any shortfall in financing would likely result in a falling dollar, higher US interest rates, and slower overall growth. In such a scenario, sectors which have benefited from low interest rates would be hurt; sectors that export or compete with imports would benefit. The more abrupt the adjustment, the greater the losses in the sectors that stand to be hurt and the smaller the offsetting gains. Export industries do not develop overnight.

The other risk is that the US trade and current account deficit will continue to expand. The larger the deficit now, the larger will be the US future external debt, and the larger the share of future US income that will have to be devoted to making payments on the US external debt. Future US workers will be obliged to support a larger retired population in the U.S., and also contribute to the retirement income of Chinese, Japanese, and others who are now financing the United States. Yet the U.S. is currently taking on external debt to finance a mix of government deficits, current consumption, and investment in sectors (such as housing) that seem unlikely to generate the future export revenues needed to make payments on the United States external debt.

The United States net international investment position, the broadest measure of total foreign claims on the US economy[2] has not deteriorated as rapidly as many expected in the face of large trade deficits. US debts are almost all denominated in dollars, while many US assets abroad, particularly US equity investments abroad, are denominated in another country's currency.

Consequently, the dollar value of US assets abroad rises when the dollar falls—particularly when the dollar falls against the euro and pound—while the dollar value of US debts do not change. Moreover, foreign equity markets have performed far better than the US equity market over the past few years, pushing up the value of US investment abroad, while the value of foreign investment in the US stagnated.

Yet US liabilities still exceed US external assets by about 20 percent of US GDP. That gap is as high as it has been since the 1880s. The large creditor position the U.S. built up after World War 2 has disappeared. Barring another run of extraordinary good performance of foreign markets (raising the value of US assets abroad), and comparative poor performance of US markets (limiting the increase in value of foreign investment in the US), the gap between US assets and US liabilities is poised to expand further—even taking into account likely currency gains from the favorable composition of the US external debt and external assets. The IMF now projects that the US net international investment position will reach around 85 percent of US GDP, if the US trade and transfers deficit comes down in an orderly way.

Policy changes in both the world's surplus and deficit countries could help increase the odds of an orderly adjustment. Before highlighting these policies, though, it is worth exploring four analytical points in greater detail:

- The US current account deficit has risen, largely because of a fall in national savings and a rise in residential investment, and not because of a surge in business investment.

- The surpluses that offset the US external deficit are found primarily in the world's emerging economies, not in other advanced economies.

- Foreign central banks, not private market participants, have played a key role financing the increase in the US current account deficit. US data likely understates US dependence on financing from central banks and oil investment funds.

- Significant reductions in the trade deficit—and much faster export growth relative to import growth—will be needed to keep the US current account deficit stable, as the amount of interest the U.S. has to pay on its net external debt begins to rise sharply.

The rise in the current account deficit reflects a fall in savings

The current account deficit can be thought of as the gap between what the U.S. earns abroad—whether from selling goods and services or from its existing investments—and what it pays abroad. It is also reflects the gap between what the US saves and what it invests. A country that invests more than it saves must borrow savings from abroad, and in the process, runs a current account deficit. This basic macroeconomic identity makes intuitive sense: a country that does not save consumes and imports and a country with a high level of investment will often import capital goods. Consumption is around 70 percent of US GDP—a low savings country—and 40 percent of the GDP of China—a very high savings country. It is consequently not a huge surprise that the US imports savings from China.

In the late 1990s, both savings and investment were increasing, though investment increased more than savings. As seen in Figure 1, however, the recent increase in the US current account deficit stems from a steep fall in national savings between 2000 and 2003. More recently, the economic recovery in 2004 and 2005 pushed investment up from its lows, while savings stayed low, resulting in an increase in the current account deficit.

The rise in the current account deficit since 2000 consequently reflects a fall in savings, not a rise in investment. This fall in savings stems from both the shift from fiscal surpluses to fiscal deficits and the fall in household savings. The swing from fiscal surpluses to deficits caused government savings to fall sharply from 2001 to 2003. The recovery—particularly strong corporate tax revenues—have helped bring the deficit down. However, the improvement in the government's fiscal balance has been offset by a fall in household savings.

Large current account deficits are generally considered less of a concern if they stem from a surge in investment, particularly investment in sectors likely to generate future export revenues. A country that borrows to import the capital goods needed to develop a newly discovered large oil field is borrowing to invest in a project that will increase both the country's future income and its capacity to generate the export revenues needed to make payments on country's external debt. Unfortunately, as seen in Figure 2, the recent rise in US (gross) investment primarily reflects a surge investment in residential housing. Business investment is up a bit, but remains well below its levels in the late 1990s—and only about 1 percent of GDP higher than its recession lows.

Figure 1: US savings vs. investment (% GDP)

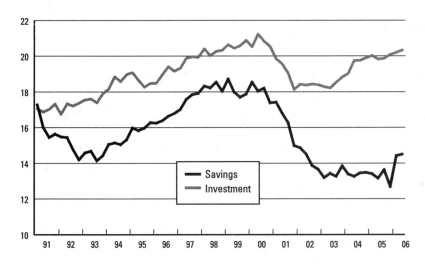

Source: US Bureau of Economic Analysis (BEA).

Figure 2: US real estate vs. business investment (% GDP)

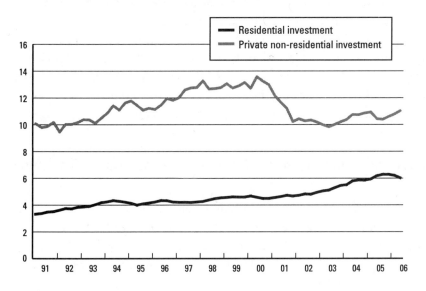

Source: BEA.

The US deficit is primarily financed by surpluses in the world's emerging economies

In the 1980s, the US current account deficit was balanced by surpluses in other major economies. Japan and Europe financed the United States (Figure 3).

The recent rise in the US external deficit, however, has not been associated with a rise in the surplus of either Europe or Japan. Japan continues to run a significant current account surplus, but its surplus has not risen along with the US deficit. Europe (excluding Norway) briefly ran a small surplus, but it now runs a substantial and growing deficit. The surpluses that are counter-balancing the US deficit are now generally found in the emerging world, specifically the rise in the surpluses of China and the major oil exporters.

In 2002 and 2003 most of rise in the emerging world's current account surplus came from the countries in emerging Asia. Beginning in late 2004 and continuing in 2005 and 2006, though, the surplus of the world's oil exporters surged along with the price of oil.

As seen in Figure 4, rising oil prices, however, did not reduce the aggregate current account surplus of emerging Asia, largely because of the rise in China's current account surplus. The surplus of other emerging Asian economies peaked in 2003. The recent surge in China's current account surplus is hard to understate. The US$150 billion increase in China's surplus from 2004 to 2006 is comparable in size to the swing in the current account balance of other Asian economies in the 1997 crisis (US$100 billion).

In the face of higher oil prices, the rise in the aggregate surplus of emerging Asia—along with the persistence of Japan's surplus— has had a profound impact on the global balance of payments. With the surplus of one oil-importing region (Asia) rising, balancing the global current account implied a rise in the deficits of the world's other two oil importing regions, the U.S. and Europe.

US data understates US dependence on financing from foreign central banks

In the late 1990s, the growing US current account deficit was financed in large part by a surge of foreign demand for US equities, along with a flight into safety after a series of crises reduced the attractiveness of investment in a range of emerging markets. By 2000, inflows of portfolio and foreign direct investment were at record levels.

Figure 3: Global current account (US$ billion)

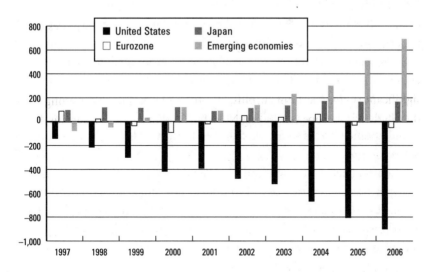

Source: IMF, 2006b.

Figure 4: Oil exporters and China vs. emerging Asia (US$ billion)

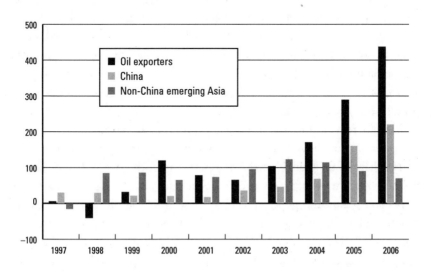

Source: IMF, 2006b.

Those equity flows have now disappeared. Recently, US investment in foreign equities—both foreign stocks and direct investment—has exceeded foreign investment in US equities.[3] As a result, the US current account deficit has been financed entirely with debt, and the bulk of the demand for US debt has come not from private investors, but rather from foreign central banks and oil investment funds. This is clearly visible in the US data for 2003 and 2004. In both these years, a surge in global reserve accumulation was matched by a surge in recorded central bank inflows to the U.S. In 2005, however, recorded official flows to the US fell, even though global reserve accumulation did not (Figure 5).

Central banks—judging from the data released by the IMF—did increase their purchases of euros, pounds, and other non-dollar reserves in 2005 (Figure 6). The available data suggests that central banks generally have tended to add more to their dollar balances in years when the dollar is under pressure, and added to their euro balances when the dollar is strong—helping to stabilize currency markets.

However, even taking growing purchases of euros and pounds into account, there is a US$200 billion gap between the estimated US$400 billion or so central banks added to dollar reserves in 2005[4] and the roughly US$200 billion in recorded central bank inflows to the U.S.

Central banks also built up dollar deposits in the international banking system, as shown in Table 1. These dollar deposits, as Lars Pedersen of the IMF has noted, indirectly helps to finance the U.S.,[5] even if such deposits are not formally recorded as inflows into the U.S. Combining the data on central bank offshore dollar deposits and the US inflow data, it is possible to track a large share of the increase in global reserves in 2003 and 2004, but not in 2005.[6]

The increase in the size of this gap is presumably explained by a change in the set of countries adding to their reserves in 2005. Japan accounted for a large share of the global increase in reserves in both 2003 and 2004. Japan not only keeps most of its reserves in dollars, but almost all purchases of US securities by the Bank of Japan seem to show up in the US data. In 2005, by contrast, all of the increase in the world's reserves came from emerging markets, and particularly from China and the world's oil exporters. A far smaller fraction of China's reserve increase than of Japan's typically shows up in the US capital inflows data.[7] The same point applies with even more force for the world's oil exporters. Recorded flows from the Gulf to the United States

Figure 5: Total debt flows track reserves (US$ billion)

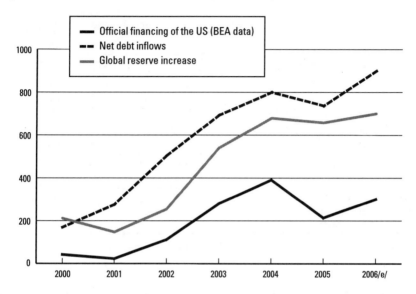

Sources: Official financing and debt flows data from BEA; 2006 based on data from the first half of the year, annualized; global reserve growth estimates from Roubini Global Economics, based on the IMF's Currency Composition of Official Foreign Exchange Reserves (COFER) data.

Figure 6: Estimated valuation-adjusted increase in reserves (US$ billion)

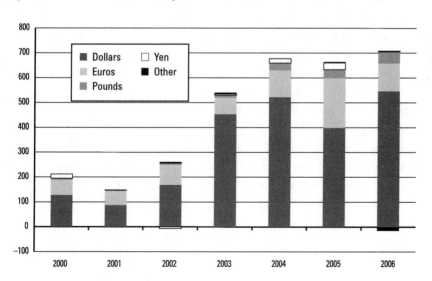

Sources: IMF (COFER) and Setser estimates.

Table 1: Comparing different estimates of US central bank financing

US$ billion	2000	2001	2002	2003	2004	2005
Official inflows (BEA data)	43	28	116	279	388	200
Japanese dollar/euro deposits in domestic Japanese banks (Japanese data, reported to IMF)	—	—	0	61	−2	−3
Dollar deposits in international banks (BIS table 5c)	32	−3	14	84	101	80
Total of these three	75	25	130	423	486	277
Setser estimate for increase in dollar reserves	127	87	168	453	537	405
Difference between US and BIS data and Setser estimate for dollar reserve increase	52	62	38	30	51	128

Sources: BEA, IMF (Japanese reserves data), BIS, IMF (COFER), and Setser estimates.

actually fell in 2005, despite the increase in oil prices and the rapid growth in Gulf foreign assets. Most observers believe that the Gulf States use London-based custodians for many of their purchases of US assets.

Counting the increase in the various oil investment funds of the Gulf States (estimated at nearly US$100 billion by the IMF) along with the growth in Saudi central bank assets, the total increase in official assets in 2005 likely approached US$800 billion. Far more than US$200 billion of that was invested in the U.S. Martin Feldstein of Harvard University has argued, correctly, that the BEA data now significantly understate true demand for US assets from foreign central banks and oil investment funds.[8]

Judging from the pace of their reserve growth, the central banks of China, Russia, and Saudi Arabia were the three most important sources of demand for US debt in 2005. The same is likely to be true in 2006. In the past—whether in the 1960s or the 1980s—most of the financing for US deficits came from close US allies—typically other large democracies. That is no longer the case.

The US trade deficit must fall in order to keep the current account deficit from rising

The US current account deficit will remain close to 7 percent of US GDP, even if the US trade deficit should fall. Over the past few years, a rise in the United States gross external debt has not led to a rise in interest payments. Interest payments actually fell from around US$275 billion in 2000 to US$185 billion in 2003, even though the United States gross external debt rose from US$4.35 trillion to US$6.2 trillion. Falling interest rates offset the rising stock—the interest rate on US debt fell from close to 6 percent in 2000 to around 3 percent in 2003. The interest rate has now started to rise, but it remained under 4 percent in 2005.

Unfortunately, with short-term rates above 5 percent, the average interest rate on US external debt is set to rise. The United States net debt is smaller than its gross debt, as some US external borrowing is offset by the loans US residents make to borrowers abroad. But US debt net of US lending is rising fast. In 2000, US lending exceeded US borrowing by US$1.5 trillion. In 2005, that total was more like US$4 trillion.[9] Barring a change in the composition of financial inflows into the United States, it will continue to increase by about US$1 trillion a year, even if the US trade deficit stabilizes.

US foreign direct investment (FDI) abroad has consistently had a higher reported return than foreign direct investment in the U.S., largely because reported returns on FDI in the U.S. are very low.[10] Combined with low US interest rates, the returns on US FDI kept the income balance[11] in surplus through 2005. That changed in the first part of 2006, and is set to change further.

Rising debt will soon combine with rising rates to generate a significant deficit in income payments. In some sense, the increase in interest rates will make the real cost of all the debt the U.S. has taken on to finance ongoing deficits more apparent—as falling rates will no longer hide the impact of a rising external debt stock (Figure 7).

The shift in the income balance has an important implication (Figure 8). Even if the pace of expansion of the US trade deficit slows, the overall current account deficit will continue to increase.

Even if the US trade deficit stabilizes at current levels—something that requires US exports to grow 60 percent faster than US imports on a sustained basis—the current account deficit will continue to expand on the back of rising net interest payments. Keeping the US current account deficit roughly constant

Figure 7: Falling rates will not offset rising stock

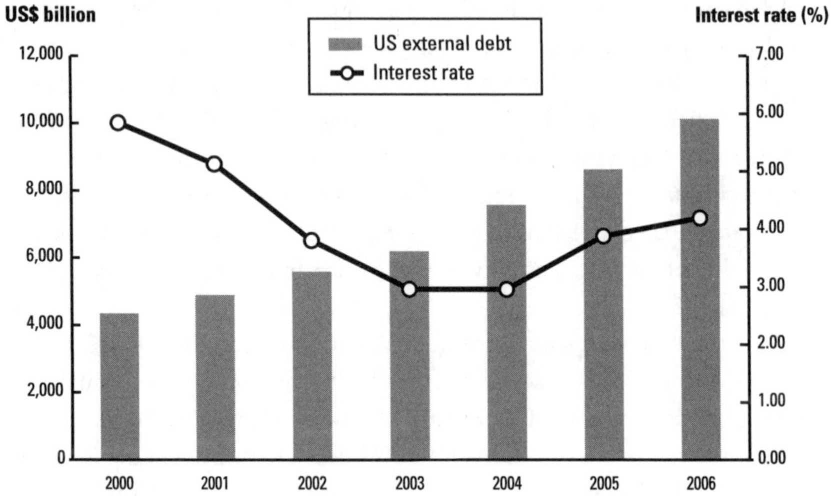

US$ billion   Interest rate (%)

Sources: BEA, 2006 interest rate based on data from the first half of the year, full year will be more.

over the next few years requires that the US exports grow about twice as fast as US imports—9 percent vs. 5 percent (Figure 9).

In both cases—a) where the US trade deficit continues to expand and b) the trade deficit begins to fall—total US external liabilities will increase much faster than US assets. The net international investment position of the United States—the broadest measure of the amount the United States owes the world[12]—will deteriorate substantially.

However, the United States is fortunate that it still has a favorable currency composition in its debt and external assets. Most US debts are denominated in dollars, while a significant fraction of US investment abroad is denominated in foreign currency. When the dollar falls, the dollar value of United States assets abroad rises, reducing the gap between US external liabilities and its external assets. This, along with the strong performance of foreign equity markets, is the key reason why the US net international investment position has not deteriorated substantially in recent years.

However, it would also be a mistake to assume that the rising (dollar) value of US investments abroad will continue to offset the rise in US external liabilities. The US has far more assets in Europe (and Canada) than in Asia, or

Figure 8: Unsustainable status quo (% GDP)

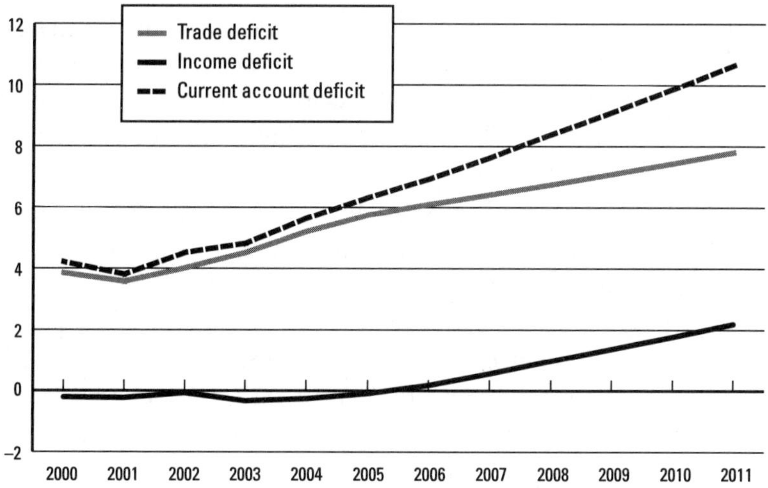

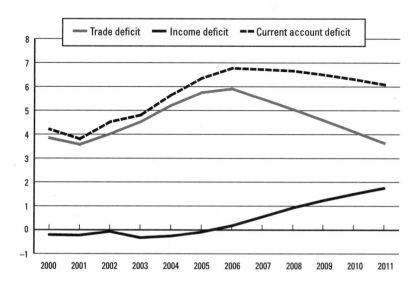

Source: BEA (historical data) and Setser projections.

Figure 9: Large US deficits (% GDP)

Source: BEA (historical data) and Setser projections.

in the world's emerging economies. If the dollar depreciates by more against Asian currencies than against European currencies—as one would expect, given the substantial adjustment that has already taken place in the dollar/euro—the U.S. will experience far smaller valuation gains. Moreover, if foreign equity markets continue to outperform US markets, it is hard to see how the United States will be able to attract the large net inflows needed to sustain deficits.

Indeed, the United States large valuation gains have come in part because foreign investors who have loaned to the U.S. *in* the U.S. have sustained large valuation losses—or, at a minimum, have not done as well as they would have, had they invested in other, competing assets—both the euro and European equities for example). Should the United States' foreign creditors start to demand interest rates on their lending to the U.S. large enough to | offset the risk of future currency losses, the deterioration in the United States external position could be far more dramatic.

Consequently, delaying adjustment carries two costs: first, it implies—barring a more rapid adjustment path—that the United States will end up with more net external debt. The United States is already in a position where the next generation of American workers will be obliged to help finance the retirement of Japan and China—not only the retirement of the United States' own baby boom. The amount future generations will have to pay, however, will be a function of the debts the U.S. accumulates now. Second, if the U.S. current account deficit continues to rise, the risk of a more abrupt adjustment rises. A more abrupt adjustment would limit the build-up of US external debt—but also generate more collateral damage to both the U.S. and the global economy.

Policy recommendations

Tim Geithner, President of the New York Federal Reserve Bank, has observed that private markets will eventually force the U.S. and the world to adjust, even if the policies of both the deficit and surplus countries remain unchanged. But he also noted that the risk of disruptive market moves that might significantly lower US growth during the adjustment process is far lower if that process is supported by appropriate policy changes.

The fall in US savings—and the offsetting rise in savings in many emerging economies—has not simply been the product of private market forces. US government policies that increased the US fiscal deficit have played a significant role in reducing the US savings rate. US tax policy encourages investment in residential real estate—and borrowing against rising real estate values. Government policies among key US trading partners have contributed to both a surge in savings, most notably by using the surge commodity prices to build up oil investment funds, and also blocked natural market pressures for their exchange rates to rise.

Private capital flows to emerging economies have returned to the levels seen before the 1997 Asian crisis. The current "uphill" flow of capital—that is the flow of capital from emerging economies with current account surpluses to wealthier economies in the United States and Europe—does not reflect private investment decisions.[13] Private investors have been willing to finance current account deficits in the emerging world. Instead, it reflects policy decisions to "bank" the recent surge in capital flows—and much of the commodity windfall—in the reserves of emerging economies central banks. The current pace of reserve growth in the world's emerging economies is truly unprecedented.

In the United States, reducing the budget deficit remains the most obvious way to increase overall national savings. Recent estimates by both the IMF and Menzie Chinn of the University of Wisconsin suggest that a one dollar reduction in the fiscal deficit could lead to a reduction of up to fifty cents in the US current account deficit. Bringing revenues in line with expenditures likely requires more than just spending restraint. Government revenues—excluding those revenues dedicated to Social Security—remain quite low. The recent improvement in the fiscal deficit reflects a surge in corporate tax revenues that may not be sustained.

Efforts to reduce US demand for oil could also help. Such measures would both reduce the volume of oil the US needs to import and, by taking pressure off global supply, help to reduce the price the US pays for its imports.

Policy changes are also needed in the world's major surplus countries. They include:

- Greater willingness by China, some other Asian economies, and many oil exporters to allow their currencies to appreciate against the dollar. Natural market pressures are pushing for appreciation: keeping the renminbi around 8 to the dollar requires that China's government intervene massively in the foreign exchange market. China's central bank alone likely spent US$250 billion[14]—over 10 percent of its GDP—in 2005 buying dollars. China likely will need to spend more in 2006, as its current account surplus has continued to grow. Many oil exporters' dollar peg has led to a fall in the real value of their currencies, even as their export revenues soared. The annual increase in global reserve accumulation was around US$150 billion in 2000 and 2001. It rose to nearly US$550 billion in 2003 and close to US$700 billion in 2004 and 2005.[15] Total reserve growth in 2006 looks likely to top 2005 levels.

- Greater distribution of the profits of Chinese firms, which are currently used to finance investment, and the development of a stronger system of social insurance in China. Both would help to lower China's exceptionally high savings rate—and turn China into an engine of global demand growth for a broad range of products, not only for commodities.

- Finding innovative ways to (prudently) inject more oil revenues into the economies of the oil-exporting countries. Right now the surge in oil revenues has led to a surge in the offshore dollar and euro deposits —and a surge in their purchases of euro and dollar-denominated securities—not to a surge in the purchasing power of the citizens of the world's oil states. Many oil exporters have budgeted for US$30/barrel of oil, even as oil prices surged. Oil fell off its peak in the fall of 2006, but given how much many oil states were salting away, there remains a substantial gap between many oil states export revenues and the amounts that have been distributed to the populations of these countries.

This list is heavy on policy changes in the world's emerging economies, since they now run the world's largest current account surpluses in the world. Europe now runs a small deficit, as deficits in Spain, France, the UK, and Eastern Europe offset surpluses elsewhere. While the euro zone combined deficit pales relative to the US deficit in absolute size, the pace of its recent deterioration has been comparable to the pace of deterioration in the US external balance. Since the end of 2004, the euro zone's combined current account has swung from a roughly 50 billion euro surplus to a 50 billion euro deficit. Looking forward, Europe's ability to sustain its recent domestic demand growth—particularly in the face of euro strength– will greatly facilitate rebalancing.

Japan also has a role to play, notably by not resisting pressure for yen appreciation, should such pressures emerge. Japan has resumed growth after a long slump, but its surplus has yet to fall, in part because the yen remains quite weak in real terms.

It is often argued that the necessary adjustment to close the US trade deficit poses little risk to the US economy, but a substantial risk to the economies of its trading partners. A weak dollar will help US exports and the US economy, while the United States trading partners no longer will be able to rely on a growing US trade deficit to spur their own economies. Moreover, dollar depreciation would increase the value of US assets abroad, while reducing the value of dollar-denominated loans to the U.S.

Both points are true, but they come with important caveats: first, if the global economy slows during the adjustment process—because other countries can no longer rely on the United States—it will be much harder for the U.S. to increase its exports. Adjustment would have to come mostly from a fall in imports, something that most likely would be accompanied by a slowdown in US growth. Second, the U.S. will still run large current account deficits in any gradual adjustment scenario. That means it will still need to import large sums of savings from the rest of the world even after the trade deficit begins to fall. If the United States' creditors increase the interest rates they charge to compensate for the risk of dollar depreciation, the negative impact of higher interest rates on the US economy would likely more than offset the positive impact of greater demand for US exports. The U.S. only "wins"—in a financial sense—from dollar depreciation, if its creditors do not demand adequate compensation for this risk.

The size and importance of the US market gives nearly everyone a stake in the orderly adjustment of the US deficit. But the U.S. should not base its own policies on the risky expectation that the U.S. is too big and too important a market for other countries to allow it to fail—or assume that any future shortfall in private demand for US assets will be offset by a surge in central bank financing. The world's central banks have shown a surprising willingness to extend an unconditional credit line to the United States over the past five years. But the United States must still recognize that there are likely to be limits to their generosity. Former Treasury Secretary Larry Summers reminded us recently that, just because large deficits have been financed relatively easily in the past does not necessarily mean that that they will continue to be financed so easily in the future. Experience teaches us that it is better to implement necessary policy changes when markets are calm, rather than waiting until markets demand change.

NOTES

1 This paper is based on material presented at the G-20 seminar in Adelaide Australia in March 2006. The author would like to thank Sangeetha Ramaswamy for assistance with the research of global reserve growth that underlies much of this paper. Nouriel Roubini and Menzie Chinn provided helpful comments on an earlier version of this paper. All remaining errors are the responsibility of the author.

2 The net international investment position is the difference between all US external assets—including US direct investment abroad—and all US external liabilities, including foreign direct investment in the U.S.

3 2005 is somewhat of an exception. However, the net equity inflow in 2005 stems entirely from the Homeland Investment Act. US firms with investment abroad stopped reinvesting ongoing earnings in their foreign operations and instead opted to bring their existing profits home. The result was a big fall in outflows. Net outflows resumed in the first half of 2006.

4 This estimate is derived from the IMF (COFER) data, adjusted to reflect reserves the People's Bank of China transferred to state banks and for the growth in the Saudi Monetary Agency's non-reserve foreign assets. It assumes that those countries that do not report data on the currency composition of their reserves—a set that includes China—have substantial dollar holdings. See Roubini Global Economics (RGE) Global Reserve Watch, Q2 2006 update.

5 Pedersen writes: "Over the same period (the year 2005 through September), deposits of all monetary authorities in BIS reporting banks denominated in dollars rose by US$110 billion. The largest offshore component of these dollar flows is not part of the US balance of payments although near-perfect arbitrage between offshore and onshore funding markets means these deposits effectively support the value of the dollar exactly as would an onshore deposit." (IMF, 2006a, box 1.6)

6 See McCauley, 2005. For more on different measures of US central bank financing, see Higgins and Klitgaard, 2004.

7 Interestingly, the annual survey data showed a much larger increase in Chinese holdings of US debt than was recorded in the monthly flow data (the Treasury international capital system data). Between the June 2004 and June 2005 surveys, Chinese holdings of US securities rose by US$186 billion. Net Chinese purchases of US securities in the monthly "flow" data over the same 12 month period totaled US$97 billion.

8 See Feldstein's December 2005 speech at the Central Bank of Mexico. Lars Pedersen of the IMF makes a similar point (IMF, 2006a, Chapter 1, box 1.6), noting that "[o]il exporter assets in mature markets are not fully reported, creating an understatement of official transactions. Chinese official asset-buying is more fully reported than the oil exporters, but together these official flows may be significantly understated in the US balance of payments." Pedersen observes that the "officially managed" assets of the large oil-exporting nations rose by between US$300 and US$450 billion in 2005. That total should be higher in 2006.

9 The US net international investment position can be divided into three parts: US borrowing net of US lending; US equity investment abroad net of foreign equity investment in the U.S., and US currency held abroad. The last is an interest free loan to the United States. At the end of 2005, the U.S. had borrowed US$4.45 trillion more from foreigners than it had lent to foreigners. However, US equity investments abroad (counting both FDI and portfolio equity investment) were worth about US$2.25 trillion more than foreign equity investments in the U.S. Foreigners held around 0.35 trillion in US currency. That implies a net international investment position of around negative US$2.55 trillion.

10 Daniel Gros of the Centre for European Policy Studies (CEPS) has noted that this difference largely stems from differences in reported reinvested earnings. US firms report large reinvested earnings; foreign firms operating in the U.S. report very low reinvested earnings. As a result, the reported return on foreign direct investment in the U.S. has consistently been below the interest rate foreigners could have earned if they had bought long-term US government bonds. Dr. Gros does not believe that this difference is real, but, rather, reflects data limitations. If Dr. Gros is right, the US income balance is already in a substantial deficit.

11 The income balance is the difference between what the U.S. has to pay on its external debt, the dividends the U.S. pays on foreign portfolio investment in the US stock market, and the returns foreign investors earn on their direct investment in the U.S., relative to what the U.S. earns on its investment abroad.

12 The net international investment position (NIIP) includes foreign direct investment and portfolio equity investments, as well as external debt.

13 Prasad et al., 2006.

14 China reported a somewhat smaller increase in its reserves in 2005. However, it reduced its reserve accumulation by transferring US$15 billion to one of its four large state commercial banks, and by another US$5 billion by engaging in various swap transactions. Moreover, the headline increase understates China's actual intervention, as the overall number was reduced by the falling dollar value of China's euro reserves. The US$250 billion estimated increase adjusts for such valuation effects, for the transfer to the state bank and for the currency swaps.

15 These totals are adjusted to reflect valuation changes and include the Saudi
    Monetary Agency's non-reserve foreign assets and reserves which China's central
    bank has transferred to three Chinese state banks. The valuation-adjustment
    assumes that some 65 percent of the world's reserves are invested in dollars,
    and around 35 percent in euros, yen, pounds, and other non-dollar assets. That is
    a slightly higher split than in the IMF data, but the IMF data include China or
    Saudi Arabia. Consequently, this split assumes that both China and Saudi Arabia
    hold a somewhat higher fraction of their reserves in dollars than the global
    average. This makes sense, given that both peg to the dollar.

REFERENCES

Feldstein, M. 2005. Speech at the Central Bank of Mexico. December.

Higgins, M. and T. Klitgaard. 2004. "Reserve accumulation: implications for global
    capital flows and financial markets. *Current Issues in Economics and Finance*
    10(10). Federal Reserve Bank of New York. September–October.

International Monetary Fund. 2006a. International Capital Market Report. April.

———. 2006b. *World Economic Outlook*. Statistical appendix. September. Available at:
    http://www.imf.org/external/pubs/ft/weo/2006/02/pdf/statappx.pdf

McCauley, R. 2005. "Distinguishing global dollar reserves from official holdings in the
    United States." *BIS Quarterly Review*. September.

Pedersen, L. 2006. *International Capital Markets Report*. Washington, D.C.: IMF. April.

Prasad, Eswar, Raghuram Rajan, and Arvind Subramanian. 2006. "Foreign Capital and
    Economic Growth." Washington, D.C.: IMF.

Roubini Global Economics (RGE). 2006. Global Reserve Watch. Available at:
    www.rgemonitor.com

Domestic Investment and External Imbalances in East Asia[1]

JONG-WHA LEE, Professor, Korea University, and Adjunct Professor,
the Australian National University
WARWICK J. MCKIBBIN, Professor, the Australian National University,
Lowy Institute for International Policy, and the Brookings Institution

Introduction

The financial crisis of 1997–98 was an adverse shock of unprecedented magnitude for East Asia, especially for the five countries directly affected by the crisis. The GDP growth rate plunged sharply in 1998. Real per capita GDP (the purchasing-power adjusted value) fell by 13 percent in Indonesia, 11 percent in Thailand, and 7 percent in South Korea and Malaysia (Figure 1).

The initial sharp contraction of GDP in 1998 was largely caused by the collapse in investment. Four of the Asian-crisis countries—Indonesia, South Korea (henceforth, referred to as Korea), Malaysia, and Thailand—suffered dramatic declines in 1998, by more than ten percentage points (Figure 2).

Although rates of economic growth in East Asia have partly rebounded since 1999, investment ratios in many crisis-hit East Asian economies have not recovered to pre-crisis levels. The failure of investment ratios to rebound significantly in these countries suggests that the crisis resulted in long-term adverse effects.[2] This is partly the result of excessive investment prior to the crisis. However, since 1997, investment rates as well as GDP growth rates have been depressed not only in the crisis-hit East Asian economies, but also in other East Asian economies, excluding China. Investors' perceptions of the risk inherent in East Asian economies have increased since the crisis. Growth prospects for the East Asian economies may also have changed permanently. As the East Asian economies continue to grow, rates of return on investment

Figure 1: Growth rate of GDP in ten East Asian countries, 1990–2005

A: Indonesia, Korea, Malayasia, Philippines, Thailand

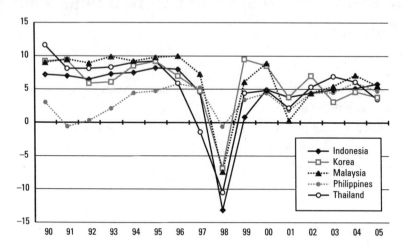

B: China, Hong Kong SAR, Japan, Singapore, Taiwan (China)

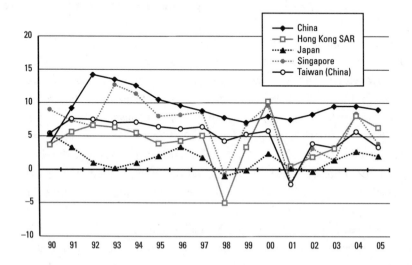

Sources: International Monetary Fund (IMF), 2005b.

Figure 2: Investment ratios in ten East Asian countries (as a percentage of GDP), 1990–2004

A: Indonesia, Korea, Malayasia, Philippines, Thailand

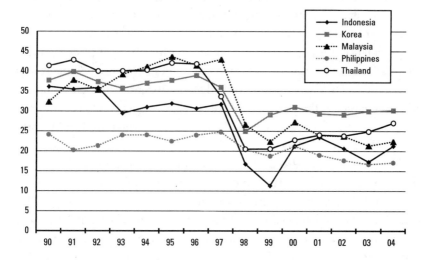

B: China, Hong Kong SAR, Japan, Singapore, Taiwan (China)

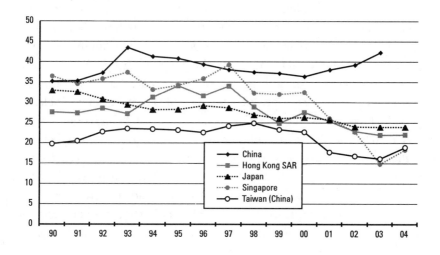

Source: IMF, 2005c; Asian Development Bank, 2005.

have declined. This will surely have an impact on future growth prospects in the region in the medium term.

The most important consequence of depressed investment is the widening of saving-investment imbalances in the region, reflected in rising current account imbalances. While saving rates remained relatively stable, the sharp declines in investment rates resulted in dramatic improvements in current account balances for East Asian economies after the financial crisis. Growing current account surpluses in East Asian economies have mirrored the continued current account deficit of the United States. External imbalances have never been larger in the post-war period. The growing current account imbalance between regions across the Pacific has provoked vigorous debates among policy-makers and scholars.

The purpose of this paper is to analyze the post-crisis evolution of the East Asian economies, focusing on domestic investment, and the consequences of this weak investment for global current account imbalances. The cause of the investment declines and subsequent current account surpluses in East Asia is assessed. In an earlier paper, we found that the changes in investment and current account balances in East Asia over the period from 1997 and 2004 are explained, to a large extent, by the adverse shock to private investment. Looking forward, we assess what events might reduce the global current account imbalances in coming years. The role of various policies, such as exchange rate revaluation, expansionary macroeconomic polices, and structural reform on domestic demand and external balances in the East Asian economies are summarized. Using a global general equilibrium model, we explore the impact of a fall in the equity risk premium in Asia and a surge in productivity growth on the imbalances. We also explore the impact of fiscal adjustment in the United States and a bursting of the US housing bubble.

We will first review the recent performance of East Asian economies in terms of GDP growth, investment, stock prices, and current account balances. The focus here is on assessing whether a permanent change has occurred to domestic investment in East Asia after the financial crisis. Next, we discuss the development of global current account imbalances, and evaluate diverse views on the causes and consequences of the imbalances. Finally, we examine various macroeconomic policies and shocks which might remedy the imbalances.

Economic performance in the East Asian economies after the financial crisis

Economic Growth

Figures 1A and 1B demonstrate the annual growth rate of real GDP for each of the East Asian economies from 1990 to 2005.[3] The sharp economic contractions in 1998 for the five Asian-crisis countries are evident: real GDP fell by 13 percent in Indonesia, 11 percent in Thailand, 7 percent in South Korea, and 7 percent in Malaysia, but only 1 percent in the Philippines. Other East Asian economies were also affected, but to a lesser degree: real GDP growth rate during 1998 was –5 percent in Hong Kong, –0.8 percent in Singapore, and –1 percent in Japan. The GDP growth rates were positive for China and Taiwan: 7.8 percent and 4.3 percent, respectively.

In 1999–2000, economies recovered, and the GDP growth rates were positive in all ten economies. Among the five crisis countries, the growth rate in 1999 was 9.5 percent in South Korea, 6.1 percent in Malaysia, 4.4 percent in Thailand, 3.4 percent in the Philippines, and 0.8 percent in Indonesia. For the other five economies, the rate was 7.1 percent in China, 6.8 percent in Singapore, 5.3 percent in Taiwan, 3.4 percent in Hong Kong, and –0.1 percent in Japan.

The rapid recoveries in the years following the crisis did not lead to the return to previous patterns of growth for the crisis-hit East Asian economies. In fact, the rebound of growth for 1999–2000 slowed down in subsequent periods. Thus, it looks likely that the financial crisis in 1997–98 had persistent negative effects on growth. However, the subsequent downturn over the period 2001–2002 may have come from the global recession. During the same period, the non-crisis East Asian economies also experienced a drastic fall in growth rates.

Since 2003, growth rates rebounded: the annualized per capita growth rates over the period of 2003–2005 were 6 percent in Malaysia, 5.9 percent in Hong Kong, 5.5 percent in Thailand, 5.3 percent in Indonesia, 5.1 percent in the Philippines, 4.1 percent in Taiwan, 3.8 percent in Korea, and 2 percent in Japan.

Looking ahead, East Asia's growth prospects are relatively bright. Japan is finally emerging from a decade-long recession. China continues its spectacular economic growth. Despite the favorable outlook, however, East Asian economies as a whole are expected to become inevitably adjusted to a lower growth path. In particular, despite the rebound of growth for 2003–2005, the average growth rates for the crisis-hit East Asian economies are lower than the high growth rates of between 7 and 8 percent achieved in the decades before the crises. These economies are unlikely to return to the high pre-crisis growth path. The East Asian economies have become so much richer than they were a few decades ago. However, they now face a much smaller gap in physical and human capital in the long-term potential levels attained in previous decades. Consequently, as the catch-up process through capital accumulation is expected to slow down over time, the economies will inevitably turn to slower economic growth.

Investment ratios

Figure 2A and B depict the investment ratios for the East Asian economies from 1990 to 2004. The ratios are for total capital formation (private plus public) relative to GDP.[4]

Four of the Asian-crisis countries: Indonesia, South Korea, Malaysia, and Thailand, showed dramatic declines in 1998, by well over ten percentage points. For the Philippines, which historically had a low investment ratio, the reduction in 1998 was comparatively small, amounting to approximately 4 percentage points. For the five countries in which investment declined sharply, no substantial recoveries occurred until 2004. The investment ratios in 2004 remained at 21.3 percent in Indonesia, 30.2 percent in South Korea, 22.5 percent in Malaysia, 17.1 percent in the Philippines, and 27.1 percent in Thailand.

With the exception of China, the other five non-crisis East Asian economies also exhibited decreases in investment ratios after the crisis. Investment ratios declined by 7 percentage points in Singapore and 5 percentage points in Hong Kong in 1998, and subsequently continued to decline. The investment ratios in Japan and Taiwan have also declined: in 2004, the investment ratios were 23.9 percent and 17.5 percent respectively, dropping by 5 and 7 percentage points from their peak ratios in 1997. However, investment ratios still remained high in China, increasing from 38 percent in 1997 to 45.8 percent in 2003. While both public and private investment declined in East Asia, the fall in private investment has been more dramatic.[5]

While the dramatic falls in the investment ratios in Indonesia, South Korea, Malaysia, and Thailand were specifically related to the Asian financial crisis, a situation occurred which permanently depressed private investment demand in East Asian economies, except China.

It is important to understand the factors resulting in these drops in investment in East Asia. First, they can be attributed in part to the increase in the prices of imported investment goods, due to considerable exchange rate depreciation. However, evidence shows limited 'pass-through' of exchange rate changes and therefore little effect of exchange rates on import investment goods. This means that there must be other more important factors contributing to the permanent depression in investment.

Second, the crisis-hit economies were forced to reduce excessive investment prior to the 1997–98 crisis. Many East Asian economies found themselves with large under-utilized capacity in manufacturing and vacant commercial and residential buildings constructed prior to the crisis. Despite the sharp decline in real interest rates, the existing excess capacity held back new investment in many East Asian countries. The adjustment in excessive investment contributed to some of the investment decline after the crisis, but cannot wholly explain the events. It would be inappropriate to argue that the adjustment has resulted in adverse effects on investment over a long period, such as eight years since the 1997 crisis in both the crisis-hit and the non crisis-hit East Asian economies.

Third, investors' perceptions of the risk for East Asian economies have increased. Investors have observed that structural problems in the corporate and financial sectors—such as the illiquidity of financial institutions, and the high leverage of the corporate sector—resulted in the overall economy being extremely vulnerable to financial panic and economic crisis in East Asia. This increase in perceived corporate and financial risk by investors caused the long-term decline in domestic investment after the crisis. Banks were required to reduce lending to the firms that were over-indebted and perceived as high risk. High-leverage corporate firms were more vulnerable to financial risk, and the associated investment demand declined substantially. Evidence in Korea reveals that *chaebol* (conglomerate)-affiliated firms with a higher debt-equity ratio prior to the crisis reduced investment more aggressively (Hong et al., 2006). While corporate and financial restructuring has been progressing, it has not completely resolved all the structural problems. Even if all problems were solved, Asian investors burned by the crisis have tended to be more conservative. Overall, less dependence on external borrowing and risky investment is preferred.

Fourth, it is also expected that productivity of investment will be declining in East Asian economies, as their economies continue to grow, and they approach the steady-state levels of capital stock. The "convergence" factor implies diminishing rates of return to new investment. From the perspective of the financial markets, the slow recovery in real stock market valuation since the 1997 financial crisis appears to reflect permanent negative effects of the shocks on the economic outlook of East Asian economies. A fall in an economy's stock market valuations likely reflects the belief that long-term market growth prospects have diminished.[6]

Fifth, in recent years, the capital intensity of East Asian products has declined, as industry structures have shifted to more skill- and knowledge-intensive structures, such as IT products and services. This shift has also contributed to weaker investment demand.

Lastly, there is the argument that China has attracted foreign investments which might otherwise have been directed to other Asian economies. However, evidence by Eichengreen and Tong (2006) and results from the McKibbin and Woo (2003) modeling framework used in this paper demonstrate that FDI into China encourages greater investment in other Asian countries, because they are interconnected in global production networks.

Investment demand in East Asia moderated in 2005, after a slight recovery in 2004. However, it is unlikely that East Asian economies will recover pre-crisis levels. As GDP growth decelerated, private investment revealed a declining trend in four East Asian NIEs. In China, policy tightening began to curb investment in a number of overheated sectors (IMF, 2005a).

Current account balances

In an open economy with capital mobility, a saving-investment imbalance leads to the current account imbalance, as the gap between domestic saving and investment is filled by net capital inflows. Recent current accounts in the East Asian economies have reflected changes in investment ratios, as saving ratios have been relatively stable. YESAs global capital markets integrate, low investment rates are likely to be converted to net capital outflows and current-account surpluses.

The Asian economies which experienced crisis reversed the current account position from one of deficit in the pre-crisis period to one of surplus after a crisis. In 1997, the current account deficits were 5.9 percent of GDP for Malaysia, 5.2 percent for the Philippines, 2.1 for Thailand, and 1.6 percent for

Indonesia and South Korea. All these countries have had substantial current account surpluses in the post-crisis period. In 1998, the surpluses were greater than 11 percent of GDP in Korea, Malaysia, and Thailand, where investment ratios declined significantly. However, despite a dramatic decline in investment ratio, Indonesia had a smaller current account surplus, amounting to 3.8 percent of GDP. This reflects a substantial decline in private saving rates in Indonesia. These economies continue to accumulate current account surpluses, but in 2005, Thailand is expected to exhibit current account deficits of approximately 2.5 percent of GDP.

In other Asian economies, current account balances have continuously revealed surpluses over time. Japan's current account surplus was 2.2 percent of GDP in 1997 and increased to 3.7 percent in 2004. China has persistently accumulated large amounts of current account surpluses, amounting to over 6 percent of GDP in 2005. Singapore and Taiwan have also revealed persistent surpluses before 1998 and afterwards. In 2004, the current account-to-GDP ratios amounted to 26 percent in Singapore and 6 percent in Taiwan.

The data demonstrates that for the five crisis economies in East Asia, the current accounts continued to improve until reaching a level permanently above that of the pre-crisis period. This can be attributed to the Asian financial crisis, which resulted in currency collapse and investment depression. For non-crisis countries, the continuing improvement in current accounts also reflects the decline in investment demand. In contrast, China's continuing current account surpluses are attributed to its higher saving rates, particularly in the corporate sector (see Figure 6A).

Global current account imbalances

The trans-Pacific imbalances

One of the major consequences of depressed investment and increased current account surpluses in East Asia is a growing global imbalance between regions across the Pacific. The current account surpluses in East Asian economies have mirrored the current account deficit of the United States (see Figure 3). The recent surge of the global current account imbalances are attributed to the regional saving-investment imbalances, particularly the fall in savings in the United States, and investment decline in emerging East Asian economies.[7]

Figure 3: Changes in global current account balances, 1990–2005

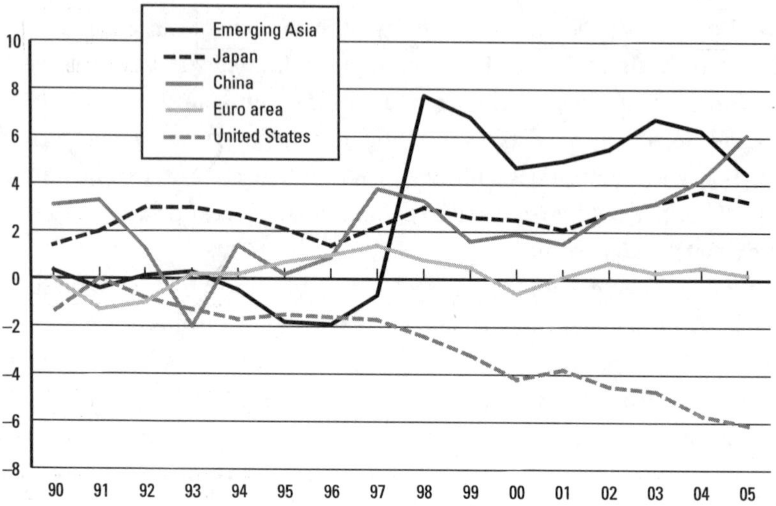

Note: Emerging Asia indicates Asian NIEs and ASEAN-4.
Source: IMF, 2005b.

The United States current account deficit has increased significantly in recent years. In 2004, the US deficit stood at US$666 billion, up from US$136 billion in 1997. This deficit amounts to 5.7 percent of GDP, increasing from 1.6 percent seven years earlier.

The principal cause of the US current account deficit is the low levels of saving rates relative to investment in the United States (Figure 4A).

The US gross private saving rates dropped continuously from over 19 percent in the 1980s to 15.1 percent in 2004. In recent years, corporate savings has risen substantially, offsetting lower household saving. In 2004 the US corporate savings rate is 11.5 percent of GDP, while the household savings rate is 3.1 percent (Figure 4B).

In particular, the recent deterioration in the US current account deficits reflects the deterioration of public savings.[8] During the 1990s, the US fiscal balance improved dramatically from negative savings to positive, peaking at 4.4 percent of GDP in 2000. However, in 2002, fiscal saving reverted once again to the negative, at –0.2 percent of GDP, when the US government loosened fiscal policy beginning in early 2001, as the US economy was heading

Figure 4A: Overall saving and investment in the United States (as a percentage of GDP), 1990–2005

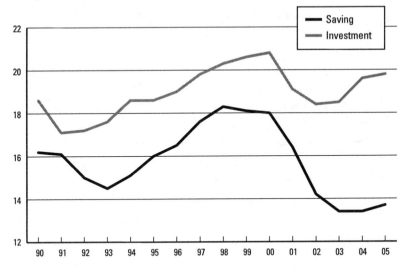

Source: IMF, 2005b.

Figure 4B: Saving in the United States by sector (as a percentage of GDP), 1990–2004

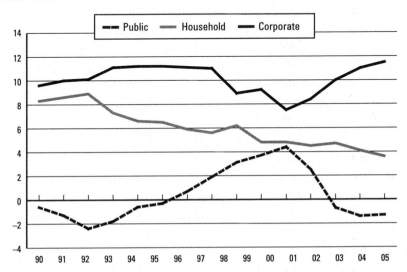

Source: IMF, 2005b.

toward a recession (Figure 4B). In 2004, the US public saving rate was –1.3 . percent of GDP.

On the other hand, the East Asian economies have continued to accumulate current account surpluses. The total surplus of 10 economies amounted to US$354 billion in 2004, up from US$120 billion in 1997. As the massive US current account deficit is attributed to low savings relative to investment, the East Asian current account surplus reflects their low investment relative to savings. In Japan, during the 1990s there was a secular downward trend in both saving and investment rates (Figure 5A).

However, investment declines have surpassed declines in savings. In 2004, the savings rate is 27.3 percent and the investment rate is 24.3 percent of GDP. While household and public saving rates have declined continuously, the corporate saving rate has risen significantly. In 2003, the Japanese corporate saving rate was 21.3 percent of GDP, while the household saving rate was 8.4 and the public saving rate –2.5 percent (Figure 5B).

As was indicated earlier, in East Asian economies other than China, investment rates fell dramatically after the financial crisis. In contrast, saving rates (both private and public) remain high, although they have declined steadily. In China, however, both the saving and investment rates revealed a declining trend during the latter half of 1990s, and since 2001, resumed their secular rising trend, reaching a record high of 46 percent in 2004 (Figure 6A).

There have been substantial increases in the corporate and public saving rates, offsetting the decline in household saving rate (Figure 6B).

The saving-investment imbalances have resulted in massive current account surpluses in East Asia (Figure 3). In recent years, East Asian economies have persistently accumulated large amounts of surplus on their current accounts, particularly after the 1997–98 financial crisis. In 2004, Japan had a current account surplus of US$172 billion, amounting to 3.7 percent of GDP, and the four East Asian NIEs, including Hong Kong SAR, Korea, Singapore, and Taiwan had a surplus of US$90 billion, or 7.2 percent of their GDP. The ASEAN-4 including Indonesia, Malaysia, Thailand, and the Philippines had a surplus of US$28 billion, amounting to 4.4 percent of GDP. China also had a surplus of approximately US$69 billion or 4.2 percent of GDP in 2004. For 10 East Asian economies, the total current account surpluses in 2004 amounted to US$386 billion. A significant portion of East Asia's current account surpluses originated from the region's trade with the U.S. In 2004, US trade deficit with 10 East Asian countries including Japan and

Figure 5A: Saving and investment in Japan (as a percentage of GDP), 1990–2005

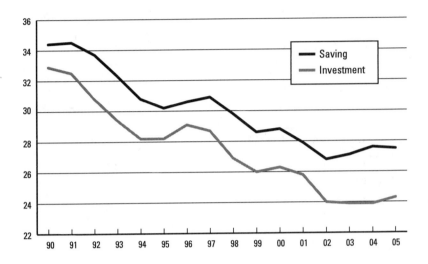

Source: IMF, 2005b.

Figure 5B: Saving in Japan by sector (as a percentage of GDP), 1990–2003

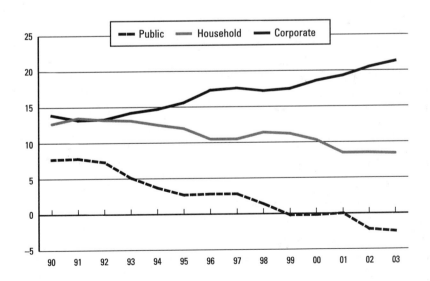

Source: IMF, 2005b.

Figure 6A: Saving and investment in China (as a percentage of GDP), 1990–2004

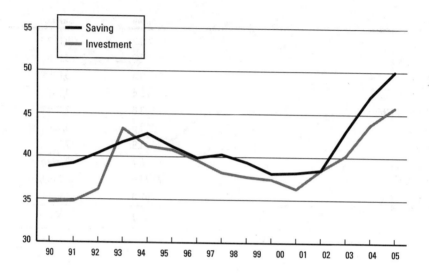

Source: IMF, 2005b.

Figure 6B: Saving in China by sector (as a percentage of GDP), 1990–2004

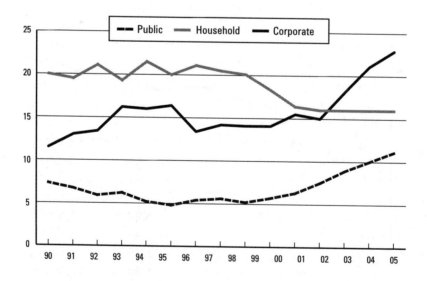

Source: IMF, 2005b.

Table 1. US bilateral trade with East Asian countries, 2004 (US$ million)

Economy	US Export to	US Import from	Balance
Japan	54,243.1	129,805.2	−75,562.1
Hong Kong SAR	15,827.4	9,313.9	6,513.5
Korea	8,955.2	14,650.6	−5,695.4
Singapore	19,608.5	15,370.4	4,238.1
Taiwan, China	21,744.4	34,623.6	−12,879.2
Indonesia	2,671.4	10,810.5	−8,139.1
Malaysia	10,921.2	28,178.9	−17,257.6
Philippines	7,087.0	9,136.7	−2,049.7
Thailand	6,368.4	17,578.9	−11,210.5
China	34,744.1	19,6682.0	−161,938.0
TOTAL	**182,170.7**	**466,150.7**	**−283,980.0**

Source: US Census Bureau.

China, amounted to US$ 284 billion (Table 1), which amounted to over 40 percent of the US current account deficit.

In 2005, current account surpluses in East Asia have generally declined, except in China. Interestingly, the current account surpluses of Indonesia and Thailand shifted into deficits. The current account surpluses of Korea and Taiwan also fell from 4 percent to 2 percent of GDP. The current account deterioration reflects rising oil prices and soaring import demand balances in most East Asian countries. However, in China, the current account balance continued to increase due to strong export growth.

Can the global imbalances be sustained?[9]

In recent years, there have been increasing concerns regarding the growing global current account imbalances. The most serious question is whether the US current account deficit can be sustained, as its accumulation has led to a substantial increase in US indebtedness to foreign countries. At the end of 2003, the net external debt of the United States was approximately 25 percent of GDP, amounting to over 250 percent of exports of goods and services, as exports are a small fraction of the US GDP—an indication that the United States cannot continue increasing its external debt at this pace (Roubini and Setser, 2004).

In theory, the persistent US deficit should ultimately result in real depreciation of the US dollar and an increase in US interest rates, thereby assisting in the reduction of the deficit. However, the US deficits has been sustained, despite continuous warnings of an imminent collapse, and currently, there has been almost no significant move toward reducing the global imbalances.

A number of research papers argue that an abrupt adjustment will take place sooner than later. For instance, Obstfeld and Rogoff (2004) argue that the reduction of US current account balance will be accompanied by a substantial change in real exchange rates, amounting to 40 percent depreciation. Substantial depreciation of the real exchange rate is required in order to switch spending on traded goods into non-traded goods, rendering the necessary reductions in trade deficits. This is because US spending on traded goods is a small share of total spending.

The US current account deficit has been sustained because foreign investors have continued to finance it. The majority of the capital inflows financing the US deficits have originated from surplus countries in East Asia, as well as the Middle East region.[10] Private investors as well as the official sector in these regions have maintained a strong appetite for US assets.

Foreign central banks have bought US treasury bills in order to accumulate international reserves as US assets. As a consequence of continuous interventions in foreign exchange markets, the international reserves of East Asian economies have increased significantly in recent years. East Asian reserves reached US$2.5 trillion in mid-2005, an excessive level compared to standard measures of reserve requirements. The hoarding of reserves entails cost. East Asian economies hold the majority of international reserves in low-yielding US treasury bills, while paying higher rates of return for securities held by foreign investors. The fiscal costs are involved with the sterilization. The continuing accumulation of foreign assets cannot always be successfully sterilized. A subsequent increase in the supply of money is bound to be translated into inflation of goods as well as real and financial assets. Foreign central banks may stop accumulating international reserves as US assets if the cost of intervention is considered too high. For instance, the People's Bank of China may stop purchasing US treasury securities, if the expanding reserve accumulations spill over into monetary creation that makes inflation soar above a certain policy objective.

The prospect of massive losses as a result of the fall in the dollar will force foreign central banks to reduce their large dollar-denominated asset holdings.

Recently, East Asian central banks appeared to begin to diversify their reserve holdings into other strong currency assets.

While foreign private investors continue to purchase US assets, they will also pull back from financing US deficits, once the dollar's decline is expected. Private equity and bond investors will most likely scale back their purchase of dollar assets and shift the composition of their portfolio.

Blanchard et al. (2005) attribute increasing global current account imbalances to an increase in the US demand for foreign goods, and an increase in the foreign demand for US assets. A large depreciation of the US dollar is anticipated when investors' preferences for dollar assets drop. The accumulation of the foreign debt makes the long-run value of the dollar continue to fall. Hence, the more prolonged US foreign borrowing, the sharper the adjustment of the dollar and the current account.

However, a number of other experts argue that the US current account deficit is sustainable, and that the adjustment, if it occurs, will take years, and will most likely do so in an orderly manner. Some argue that the widening current account deficit of the U.S. is not a problem. One view is that there is a global savings "glut." According to this view, the global current account imbalances occur largely as a result of a post-bubble global savings glut (Bernanke, 2005). Excess saving in East Asia, as well as Europe, has depressed global interest rates and required a large current account deficit in the global economy, particularly in the United States, because of the greater attractiveness of associated financial assets. Globalization of financial markets will continue to assist channeling of the supply of global savings to US markets. Thus, as long as excess saving persists and foreign investors continue to purchase American assets, the US current account deficit can be sustained.

While the savings glut story has intellectual appeal, the most accurate explanation for the global imbalance, particularly from the perspectives of East Asia, is insufficient investment, rather than excess saving by East Asian economies. While the high saving rates in East Asia, particularly in China, have contributed to the global imbalances, the recent surge of surpluses in East Asia is largely a result of the reduction in investment demand. As explained earlier, much of the increase in current account surpluses over the post-crisis period is explained by a sharp reduction in domestic investment demand in East Asia. In contrast, domestic saving as a proportion of GDP has remained largely unchanged in most East Asian economies. The flows of global savings into the US financial markets may not continue when foreign investors begin to worry about the sustainability of the US deficit, and the prospects of capital losses due to dollar depreciation. The adjustment will most likely occur when the US Federal Reserve Board does not continue to raise interest rates.

Another view, as argued by Dooley et al. (2003), is that East Asia's pursuit of an "export-led growth" strategy is most responsible for the continuous current account imbalances. In their view, the US current account deficit has persisted because East Asia is willing to finance these deficits by accumulating an unlimited amount of dollar reserve assets in order to keep exchange rates *undervalued*.

Dooley et al. called the current situation a "revived Bretton Woods system," where East Asian countries are pegged to the center's currency, the US dollar, as the European countries did under the Bretton Woods system. The periphery countries hoard their export earnings in low-yielding US treasuries bills and other dollar denominated assets, in order to maintain exchange rates stable vis-à-vis the US dollar.

The East Asian craving for dollar assets must have helped to maintain the US current account imbalance, or, more importantly, affected the price at which these imbalances are sustained. However, it is incorrect to argue that a conscious strategy of undervaluation by East Asian countries is the principle cause of growing global imbalances. Prior to the crisis, many East Asian countries ran large current account deficits in the course of promoting exports. The accumulation of reserves in East Asia after the crisis can be attributed to precautionary motives, rather than mercantilist ones (Aizenman and Lee, 2005).

Cooper (2005) claims that the US current account deficit is not only sustainable but also a natural feature of today's technology and globalization.[11] The United States attracts substantial investment in education and R&D, which has a high future payoff. The foreign capital inflows that finance the US deficits have been attracted by higher returns on investment due to higher productivity in the U.S. than in other regions, including Europe and Japan. Moreover, US financial assets are more secure and less volatile than those in many emerging markets. Hence, as long as foreigners continue to desire accumulation of US dollar assets, the US current account is sustainable.

An objection to this view is that the productivity differential between the U.S. and other regions, such as Europe, does not appear to be sufficiently large to result in a 6 percent-to-GDP swing in the US account balance

(Eichengreen, 2006). The results we present below support the view that productivity growth differentials do not have a significant impact on the current account because both savings and investment are affected. Critics also note that, in terms of financing the US deficits, the official sector plays a more important role than the private sector.[12] The motivation of differential in investment returns cannot explain the foreign official sector's accumulation of US financial assets in recent years.

How to adjust to the imbalances

The growing current account imbalances call for adjustment from East Asian economies, as well as adjustment in the United States. The accumulation of current account surplus per se should not be a primary policy objective. The continuing imbalances and massive reserve accumulation has created serious problems for East Asian economies. The appreciation of real exchange rates has discouraged investment in the non-tradable sector, such as the service industry, which in turn results in unbalanced economic growth. The continuing accumulation of foreign assets has not always been successfully sterilized. A subsequent increase in the supply of money has resulted in inflation of goods and services, as well as real and financial assets. While price increases have so far been modest in East Asia, it is inevitable that amassed current account surpluses and net capital inflows will increase the inflation rate. Recent data for China suggests a significant acceleration in inflation, jumping from 1.3 percent per annum in 2003 to 3.9 percent in 2004.

One policy that might be adopted to adjust the global imbalances is the appreciation of East Asian currencies. Various government officials, as well as a number of economists in the U.S. argue that East Asian economies should abandon the strategy of exchange rate undervaluation and increase exchange rate flexibility, in order to share the burden of global readjustments. An important issue is the extent to which an appreciation of East Asian currencies can assist in adjustment of the global current account imbalance. The impact depends considerably on the source of the currency appreciationæ whether it is effectively a currency adjustment, a change in monetary policy, or whether it is brought about through other policy changes. What matters for a sustained impact on the current account balance is a permanent change in real exchange rates. It is unclear whether a moderate adjustment of real exchange rates can assist in repairing global current account imbalances.

Some countries are increasingly resorting to public-private-partnerships (PPPs) to finance infrastructure demand in times of limited public resources. In infusing private capital and management, PPPs can deliver higher-quality and lower-cost public infrastructure than the government (Hemming, 2006). However, resorting to government guarantees to secure private sector involvement also entails an increase in potential fiscal costs and risks.

In order to revive the levels of investment as well as improve the efficiency of investment, macroeconomic adjustment must accompany structural reform polices. It is uncertain whether expansionary macroeconomic polices can raise investment rates to optimal levels. Furthermore, the stimulus of investment does not guarantee efficient allocation of investment funds. After the crisis, observed structural problems in the corporate and financial sectors in East Asian economies have increased investors' perceived risk sharply, resulting in a significant decline in domestic investment. During the crisis and subsequent recovery process, East Asian economies accomplished a great deal in improving the soundness and profitability of financial institutions and alleviating corporate distress. However, there still remain significant structural problems in these economies, impeding the recovery of investment, as well as the efficient allocation of investment. Unhealthy connections among large firms, financial institutions, and the government which undermined the allocation of capital and weakened financial systems have not been completely resolved. For many East Asian economies, financial institutions are still heavily influenced by government. Whether real practices in corporate governance and financial management and supervision have improved is still in question. Underdevelopment of equity and bond markets present substantial barriers to the efficient allocation of long-term investment funds in the region. More structural reforms will assist in diminishing corporate and financial risk and improve the rate of return on investment, thereby encouraging domestic investment.

In many East Asian countries, the lower productivity growth of non-tradable sectors, such as service industries relative to the manufacturing sector has also raised concerns (Lee, 2005). Reforms targeting stagnant service industries can assist in improving the productivity growth of the overall economy, and can also contribute to lowering trade surpluses.

Some advanced East Asian economies such as Hong Kong, Korea, and Singapore must focus on investment for technology development and human resource improvement, rather than on the accumulation of physical capital.

The importance of physical capital investment tends to decrease as the economy shifts from accumulation-driven growth to technology-driven growth.

According to the prediction of "convergence," it is likely that East Asian economies experienced slower factor accumulation than they had in previous decades.

Facing a diminished chance for rapid "catch up" through high rates of factor accumulation, the greatest challenge for the East Asian economies is to expedite its productivity growth.[15] Efforts to increase technology investment and to enhance the quality of human resources are crucial for productivity improvement. In this regard, fiscal expansion focusing on R&D and human capital investment will be more helpful in initiating sustained growth, in addition to reducing the current account imbalances. The available data reveals that many East Asian economies spend a substantial percentage of total GDP as R&D, education and health expenditure. However, in terms of the absolute amount or per capita expenditure, investments are far smaller than those of more advanced economies.[16]

We will now explore the sensitivity of current account balances and GDP growth to four possible scenarios based on simulations with a global general equilibrium model.[17]

1. A fall in equity risk premiums in Asia to levels consistent with investment rates prevailing before the Asian crisis.

2. A boost to productivity growth in Asia of 1 percent per year for a decade; this could be interpreted as a function of economic reforms in East Asia.

3. Fiscal consolidation in the United States sufficient to turn around the US fiscal position by 5.25 percent of GDP over three years.

4. A sharp fall in the housing market in the United States, due to the bursting of a housing bubble, modeled as a decline in the expected return to housing of 1 percent per year for a decade.

Results are presented in Tables 2 through 5 for the change in the current account and in investment (both as a percent of GDP), and the change in GDP. All variables are expressed relative to the baseline outcome, without the shock imposed. Each of the tables is preceded by a brief discussion of each of the above scenarios.

Fall in equity risk premium

The fall in the equity risk premium is calculated to approximate a rise in investment similar in magnitude to the average fall in investment as a share of GDP since 1996. The changes in the equity risk premia by country are: 2.5 percent for Indonesia, Malaysia, and Thailand; 1.5 percent for Korea and 1.2 percent for Singapore; and 1 percent for the Philippines and Taiwan. Results are presented in Table 2 for each country of interest.

The fall in the equity risk premium in Asian economies makes investment more attractive. This causes a rise in investment and the resulting flow of capital from non-Asian economies into Asia. This reallocation of global capital causes a worsening on the current accounts in Asia and an improvement in the current accounts outside Asia. In the United States, after 10 years, the current account has improved by 0.3 percent of GDP. Note however that the capital inflows into Asia are sourced globally, and although the current accounts of Asian economies deteriorate significantly, this is supplied by all countries and not only the United States. Thus, the impact on the US current account deficit is proportionately much lower than the impact on the Asian economies, even adjusting for relative country size. The reallocation of global capital is also reflected in the investment changes in non-Asian economies. Part of the capital is from investment in the rest of the world and part from increased saving in the rest of the world. This is also reflected in the outcomes for GDP outside Asia.

Rise in Asian productivity

The rise in Asian Productivity is modeled as a rise in the growth rate of labor augmenting technical change of 1 percent per year for 10 years in each of the Asian economies in the model. In many ways this rise in actual and expected productivity growth is similar to the fall in the equity risk premium. Capital flows into the Asian economies in anticipation of higher returns. Households within the Asia economies experience higher expected future incomes, which would tend to raise consumption at the expense of savings. But they also receive higher returns on savings, which would tend to raise saving. Households in the model also face inertia in adjusting consumption to expected higher incomes; so, initially private saving rises with higher economic growth, as is observed empirically. However the rise in investment dominates in the effect on the current account and much of the new investment comes from foreign economies. Part of this is from foreign savings and part from a

Table 2: Results for a reduction in Asian equity risk premia (change relative to baseline)

Economy	Change in current accounts (% of GDP)			Change in investment (% of GDP)			Change in GDP		
	Year 1	Year 5	Year 10	Year 1	Year 5	Year 10	Year 1	Year 5	Year 10
USA	0.12	0.25	0.30	-0.11	-0.36	-0.36	-0.05	-0.22	-0.31
Japan	0.21	0.55	0.73	-0.14	-0.68	-0.85	-0.07	-0.33	-0.63
United Kingdom	0.16	0.35	0.45	-0.11	-0.43	-0.54	-0.05	-0.24	-0.43
Europe	0.15	0.31	0.41	-0.12	-0.42	-0.52	-0.08	-0.28	-0.50
Canada	0.21	0.43	0.51	-0.15	-0.55	-0.55	-0.07	-0.33	-0.44
Australia	0.09	0.37	0.57	-0.07	-0.47	-0.67	-0.05	-0.26	-0.54
New Zealand	0.45	1.16	1.30	-0.39	-1.12	-0.92	-0.11	-0.70	-0.93
Indonesia	-2.50	-5.10	-5.69	4.96	12.16	14.38	1.76	9.31	16.22
Malaysia	-6.27	-15.84	-17.75	9.41	23.63	22.80	2.31	14.80	26.66
Philippines	-4.66	-10.61	-10.79	4.73	11.16	9.34	3.35	9.59	12.44
Singapore	-3.56	-9.51	-12.78	4.40	12.98	14.37	1.18	8.68	15.63
Thailand	-2.55	-5.64	-7.38	5.14	14.21	22.03	-0.18	10.61	26.66
China	0.13	0.32	0.36	-0.14	-0.54	-0.54	-0.09	-0.35	-0.42
India	0.18	0.33	0.37	-0.20	-0.51	-0.55	-0.14	-0.32	-0.49
Taiwan, China	-1.37	-3.40	-4.72	2.21	6.60	8.31	0.07	4.59	9.23
Korea	-2.64	-4.85	-5.33	4.92	11.64	14.85	2.24	8.50	15.89
Hong Kong SAR	-0.04	0.15	0.25	0.06	-0.03	0.02	0.05	0.06	0.19

Source: G-cubed (Asia Pacific) model - version 63A.

relocation of foreign investment into the Asian economies. After five years, the current accounts of non-Asian economies tend to improve, whereas the inflow of capital into the Asian economies worsens the current accounts of Asia (see Table 3). The global effect on GDP is positive. The fall in foreign GDP reflects the reallocation of global capital toward Asia where returns are higher. Note that the scale of this effect is smaller for the positive productivity shock than the risk shock in Asia, because the rest of the world gains income from the higher productivity. Thus, a positive productivity shock has a stronger positive impact on the global economy relative to a fall in equity risk.

US fiscal consolidation

The policy change is assumed to be a reduction in the fiscal deficit of the United States of approximately 5.25 of GDP, comprising a fall in government spending on goods and services of 2 percent of GDP, a fall in government spending on labor of 2 percent of GDP, and a rise in household taxes sufficient to generate the change in the fiscal deficit of 5.25 percent of GDP. The policy is assumed to be phased in over three years with the adjustment of one-third in year one, two-thirds in year two, and completed by year three.

Results are presented in Table 4. The reduction in fiscal spending and increase in taxes tend to reduce GDP through traditional Keynesian channels. US GDP is 0.74 percent below base in the first year, and 2.1 percent below base by year five. By year ten, US GDP is above baseline. The freeing up of resources by the federal government eventually is allocated by the private sectors, generating an increase in GDP relative to baseline forever. The growth rate of GDP eventually returns to baseline, because the long run growth rate is determined by productivity and population growth which is unchanged in the simulation. The fiscal adjustment in the United States reduces long term real interest rates and frees up capital to go into global capital stock accumulation. The transmission to the rest of the world is positive since the effects on financial markets through lower long-term real interest rates dominates the negative Keynesian spillover on demand for imports from the rest of the world. The fiscal contraction causes capital to flow out of the US which depreciates the US dollar and makes US exports more competitive, improving the US current account by 1.5 percent of GDP in the first year and 2.4 percent by year 5.[18] The current accounts of the rest of the world go into deficit as this capital is reallocated.

Table 3: Results for a rise in Asian productivity growth (change relative to baseline)

Economy	Change in current accounts (% of GDP)			Change in investment (% of GDP)			Change in GDP		
	Year 1	Year 5	Year 10	Year 1	Year 5	Year 10	Year 1	Year 5	Year 10
USA	0.01	0.10	0.24	0.01	-0.09	-0.31	-0.02	-0.05	-0.19
Japan	-0.04	0.17	0.56	0.08	-0.09	-0.69	-0.02	0.00	-0.35
United Kingdom	0.03	0.15	0.36	0.00	-0.13	-0.43	-0.03	-0.07	-0.27
Europe	0.02	0.13	0.34	0.00	-0.12	-0.43	-0.03	-0.08	-0.31
Canada	0.04	0.19	0.43	-0.01	-0.17	-0.49	-0.04	-0.10	-0.31
Australia	-0.11	0.00	0.35	0.13	0.13	-0.35	0.03	0.13	-0.08
New Zealand	0.03	0.33	0.86	0.00	-0.31	-0.75	-0.04	-0.13	-0.47
Indonesia	-0.21	-1.34	-2.68	0.57	4.69	8.65	0.49	3.71	8.20
Malaysia	-0.42	-3.06	-7.23	0.78	6.53	13.37	0.57	3.22	9.44
Philippines	-3.46	-10.35	-14.35	3.29	12.02	15.10	3.22	9.98	16.38
Singapore	-0.25	-3.26	-9.47	0.28	5.78	14.24	0.17	3.56	11.14
Thailand	0.62	-0.23	-2.60	-0.22	3.62	10.66	-0.06	1.27	6.60
China	0.07	-0.41	-1.17	0.02	3.84	8.58	0.26	3.30	7.78
India	0.06	0.17	0.31	-0.04	-0.21	-0.44	-0.06	-0.12	-0.31
Taiwan, China	-0.33	-2.15	-5.70	0.28	5.42	13.30	0.03	4.31	12.40
Korea	0.29	-0.47	-2.59	-0.31	4.76	13.74	0.22	3.66	11.60
Hong Kong SAR	-0.56	-0.38	0.10	0.82	1.13	0.75	0.72	1.42	1.91

Source: G-cubed (Asia Pacific) model - version 63A.

Bursting of the US housing bubble

Modeling the bursting of a housing bubble is difficult. In the model, part of household consumption is generated by a stock of household capital—in reality housing as well as white goods and automobiles—in which households invest each year in order to generate a flow of housing services over time. To capture the idea of a housing bubble bursting, we model the shock as a fall in the expected productivity of the investments that are made into the stock of household capital of 10 percent per year forever. Results are presented in Table 5.

The fall in the expected return to housing generates a reallocation of capital within the United States away from housing into other assets, such as government bonds and equities. However the fall in wealth from the sharp fall in the value of housing causes consumption to drop sharply and results in an economic slowdown, with GDP 4.1 percent below baseline. This recession causes much of the asset reallocation to go offshore, rather than staying in US assets, because returns to all asset classes within the United States are negatively affected. Thus, capital flows out of the United States into other economies. This capital outflow is reflected in an improvement in the US current account of 1.2 percent of GDP in the first year and 1.6 percent of GDP by the fifth year. The current accounts of the rest of the world worsen as a result. The reallocation of capital out of US housing into other countries raises the investment rate globally, but not in the United States, since the economic slowdown caused by the consumption contraction of 10 percent relative to baseline causes the return to capital in the US to be temporarily reduced. There are, thus, two effects on the rest of the world: a negative shock from the contraction of the US economy, and a positive effect from the reallocation of a significant amount of capital pulled out of the US housing market. To the extent that countries rely on the US market for demand, the shock tends to be negatively transmitted. Thus Singapore, the Philippines, and Hong Kong experience a slight decline in GDP relative to baseline in the initial year.

Conclusion

This paper demonstrates that since the 1997–98 financial crisis, there have been permanent depressions of domestic investment and output growth in many East Asian economies, mainly resulting from the increased financial risk and decreased rate of return on investment. The investment declines in East

Table 4: Results for a US fiscal adjustment (change relative to baseline)

Economy	Change in current accounts (% of GDP)			Change in investment (% of GDP)			Change in GDP		
	Year 1	Year 5	Year 10	Year 1	Year 5	Year 10	Year 1	Year 5	Year 10
USA	1.45	2.44	2.21	-1.19	0.27	2.67	-0.74	-2.11	0.43
Japan	-0.90	-1.06	-0.90	1.25	2.68	1.86	0.60	2.03	2.31
United Kingdom	-0.46	-0.84	-0.91	0.27	0.86	0.92	0.16	0.59	0.89
Europe	-0.46	-0.72	-0.73	0.66	1.70	1.63	0.55	1.46	2.15
Canada	-1.03	-2.77	-2.63	1.12	4.98	4.22	0.73	3.44	4.30
Australia	-1.01	-1.57	-1.53	0.58	1.56	1.46	0.38	1.23	1.69
New Zealand	-1.61	-3.15	-2.86	1.21	2.76	1.68	0.36	2.08	2.27
Indonesia	-0.69	-1.05	-0.79	1.52	1.60	1.12	3.01	1.18	1.31
Malaysia	-1.48	-3.29	-2.72	2.21	4.52	2.90	1.45	2.87	3.93
Philippines	-2.93	-4.13	-2.88	0.85	1.12	0.11	2.22	1.00	0.52
Singapore	0.14	-1.18	-1.84	1.41	4.74	4.31	0.49	2.94	4.90
Thailand	-1.26	-2.13	-1.78	0.75	1.28	0.92	0.79	0.81	1.29
China	-0.69	-1.04	-0.77	1.64	1.03	0.77	2.60	0.76	0.85
India	-0.55	-0.84	-0.74	1.08	1.02	0.96	2.14	0.68	1.01
Taiwan, China	-0.19	-1.00	-1.15	1.37	4.37	4.20	0.45	2.60	4.34
Korea	-0.97	-1.87	-1.48	2.26	2.77	1.93	2.56	2.30	2.69
Hong Kong SAR	-0.08	-0.17	0.05	1.31	1.31	0.88	2.04	1.10	1.5

Source: G-cubed (Asia Pacific) model - version 63A.

Table 5: Results for a bursting of US housing bubble (change relative to baseline)

Economy	Change in current accounts (% of GDP)			Change in investment (% of GDP)			Change in GDP		
	Year 1	Year 5	Year 10	Year 1	Year 5	Year 10	Year 1	Year 5	Year 10
USA	1.16	1.61	1.37	-1.55	-1.40	0.91	-4.11	-2.57	-0.33
Japan	-0.63	-0.73	-0.53	0.76	1.65	1.04	0.29	1.22	1.35
United Kingdom	-0.37	-0.54	-0.58	0.18	0.58	0.59	0.05	0.39	0.59
Europe	-0.41	-0.50	-0.46	0.42	1.06	0.94	0.25	0.88	1.29
Canada	-0.78	-1.82	-1.58	0.58	2.84	2.35	0.20	1.76	2.37
Australia	-0.63	-0.96	-0.91	0.35	0.99	0.90	0.20	0.75	1.05
New Zealand	-0.95	-1.87	-1.64	0.71	1.62	0.92	0.13	1.19	1.31
Indonesia	-0.52	-0.65	-0.47	0.48	0.92	0.65	0.36	0.64	0.74
Malaysia	-0.98	-2.11	-1.69	0.93	2.69	1.75	0.17	1.49	2.32
Philippines	-1.48	-2.55	-1.87	0.27	0.95	0.29	-0.14	0.64	0.56
Singapore	0.11	-1.18	-1.34	0.76	2.89	2.59	-0.03	1.60	2.97
Thailand	-1.00	-1.37	-1.13	0.40	0.94	0.65	0.05	0.54	0.94
China	-0.54	-0.67	-0.48	0.38	0.76	0.53	0.19	0.50	0.55
India	-0.41	-0.54	-0.46	0.31	0.63	0.59	0.17	0.39	0.60
Taiwan, China	-0.25	-0.88	-0.73	0.76	2.57	2.33	0.14	1.45	2.49
Korea	-0.76	-1.20	-0.93	0.64	1.68	1.23	0.35	1.17	1.58
Hong Kong SAR	-0.44	-0.30	-0.04	0.37	0.74	0.50	-0.53	0.42	0.87

Source: G-cubed (Asia Pacific) model - version 63A.

Asia outside of China, combined with the reduction in private and public saving in the United States, have led to a recent surge of global current account imbalances.

East Asia should adopt policies which raise investment rates and remain below what is likely to be the optimal levels. The revival of private investment will assist in diminishing the global imbalances, and, moreover, will contribute to robust economic growth for the coming decades. Continuous structural reforms in the corporate and financial sectors will help to reduce risk and improve rates of return on private investment. Expansion of public infrastructure investment is called for in most developing Asian economies. However, for maturing industrialized economies, an increase in R&D and human capital investment, rather than physical capital investment, will be crucial for sustained growth. In China, an increase in public spending on education, health care, social welfare, and housing would be helpful to reduce national saving, and thereby diminish current account surplus.

It is unclear whether, despite all the efforts of East Asia's expansionary adjustment, a reduction in East Asia's surpluses will necessarily lead to a significant reduction in the US current account deficit. The effects of the East Asian expansionary policies on the US current accounts are relatively minor in terms of the US GDP, because the expanding countries are small relative to the United States. Also, adjustment in Asia spills over to the entire world and not just into the bilateral relationship with the United States.

The saving and investment imbalances both in East Asia and the United States have resulted in global imbalances. Therefore, in correcting global imbalances, a concerted effort by both sides is required. The increase in saving rates is more effective for reducing the US current account deficit. A US fiscal contraction will have a much larger impact on the US current account deficit than the investment increase in East Asia or strong productivity-related growth in East Asia. Moreover, a fiscal adjustment in the United States is preferable to an adjustment in household saving which, for example, might be induced by a sharp correction in the US housing market.

NOTES

1 We are grateful to Max Corden, Yung Chul Park, Kwanho Shin, and participants at the Central Institute for Economic Management and the Australian National University Conference, the World Economic Forum Conference, and the Korean Institute for Economic Policy Conference for helpful comments and suggestions, and to Jong Suk Han and Joo Hyun Pyun for able research assistance. Financial support from the Korea Institute for International Economic Policy is gratefully appreciated.

2 Barro and Lee (2003) show evidence from a broad sample of 85 countries that currency and banking crises are associated with contemporaneously reduced values of economic growth and investment over the five-year period following a crisis. The magnitude of the typical effect is quantitatively similar to that observed in the recent period in the Asian crisis countries. The broad evidence indicates that while currency crises do not have a persistently adverse influence on economic growth, banking crises have had a long-term adverse effect on investment for over 10 years.

3 The underlying GDP data are from IMF (2005b).

4 The underlying data are from IMF (2005c) and the Asian Development Bank (2005).

5 According to the IMF World Economic Outlook Data, the average of public investment-to-GDP rate declined from 9.6 percent in 1997 to 6.2 percent of GDP in 2002 for East Asian newly industrialized economies (NIEs). Data on public investment in individual countries are limited.

6 See the details in the working paper version of this paper (Lee and McKibbin, 2006).

7 While saving-investment imbalance is focused on in both the US and East Asian regions, there are a number of different explanations of the global imbalance. Roubini (2005) summarizes five different views, and likens the existence of diverse interpretations of the global imbalances to the classic Kurosawa film *Rashomon*, in which a number of different witnesses give varying accounts of the same crime. Eichengreen (2005) considers that these different views are not incompatible, but that they explain only part of the facts, on the analogy of the parable of the blind men and the elephant.

8 It is generally controversial how strong budget deficits are associated with current account deficits. Critics point out that there is no strong positive co-movement of the budget and current account balance over the long run, and econometric studies show evidence of a relatively weak correlation between these variables, controlling for other important factors. See discussions in Eichengreen (2005).

9 See Corden (2006) for a clear analytical overview of the various arguments in this section.

10 Dooley et al. (2005) demonstrated that three-quarters of the increase in Asian and Middle Eastern savings over the period from 1999 to 2004 has been placed in international reserves as US assets.

11 This is also the view of Corden (2006), although with some qualifications.

12 In 2004, more than two-thirds of the external financing required for the US current account deficits came from the foreign official sector (Roubini and Setser, 2005). While purchases of US assets by private investors constitute the bulk—about 75 percent—of total foreign purchase of US assets, the private purchases of US assets by foreigners are largely offset by private purchases of foreign assets by Americans.

13 An alternative policy which East Asia, especially China, could adopt to reduce current account surpluses is lowering the saving rate. Chinese government may decrease public saving by raising spending on education, health care, social welfare, and housing. The resulting increased social security would, in turn, help to reduce private saving. Rapid population aging and financial market development will also help to lower private saving in China, as well as in other East Asian economies. However, this adjustment would likely take place over a long time. See the discussions in Eichengreen and Park (2006).

14 The effects of fiscal expansion may not be as large as expected if it crowds out private demand. The simulation in Lee et al. (2006) shows that the effects of fiscal expansion on domestic demand and external balances become smaller as crowding-out effects mitigate them. A permanent expansion of fiscal deficit by 2 percent of GDP in East Asia (except Japan) is estimated to have only a negligible effect on current account balances, ranging from no change to a decrease of one percent of GDP in five years following the shock.

15 See Lee (2005) for the detailed assessment of productivity growth performance and prospects for the South Korean economy.

16 See Tables 4 and 5 in the working paper version of this paper (Lee and McKibbin, 2006).

17 Our experiments are based on the Asia-Pacific G-cubed Model. See McKibbin and Wilcoxen (1998) and Lee et al. (2006).

18 This current account multiplier of roughly 0.4 percent of GDP change in the current account deficit for a 1 percent change in the US fiscal deficit has been a feature of the MSG3/G-Cubed models for decades.

REFERENCES

Aizenman, Joshua and Jaewoo Lee. 2005. "International Reserves: Precautionary versus Mercantilist Views, Theory and Evidence." National Bureau of Economic Research (NBER) Working Paper No.11366.

Asian Development Bank. 2005. *Key Indicators of Developing Asian and Pacific Countries*. Manila: The Philippines: ADB.

Barro, Robert and J-W. Lee. 2003. "Growth and Investment in East Asia Before and After the Financial Crisis." *Seoul Journal of Economics* 16(2):83–113.

Bernanke, Ben. 2005. "The Global Saving Glut and the US Current Account Deficit." Remarks at the Homer Jones Lecture. St. Louis, Missouri. 14 April.

Blanchard, Olivier, Francesco Giavazzi, and Filipa Sa. 2005. "The US Current Account and the Dollar." NBER Working Paper No.11137. February.

Cooper, Richard N. 2005. "Living with Global Imbalances: A Contrarian View." *Policy Briefs in International Economics* PB05-3. Washington, D.C.: Institute for International Economics.

Corden, W. Max. 2006. "Those Current Account Imbalances: A Skeptical View." Melbourne Institute Working Paper Series No. 13/06. Forthcoming in *World Economy*.

Dooley, M., Folkerts-Landau, D. and P. Garber. 2003. "An Essay on the Revived Bretton Woods System." NBER Working Paper No. 9971. September.

———. 2005. "Savings Gluts and Interest Rates: The Missing Link to Europe." NBER Working Paper No. 11520. July.

Eichengreen, B. 2005. "The Blind Men and the Elephant." A Paper prepared for the Tokyo Club Foundation's Macroeconomic Research Conference on the Future of International Capital Flows, Kyoto.

Eichengreen, B. and Y. C. Park. 2006. "Global Imbalances and the Asian Economies." Mimeo.

Eichengreen, B. and Hui Tong. 2006. "How China is Reorganizing the World Economy." *Asian Economic Policy Review* 1:73–97.

Hemming, Richard. 2006. "(Some) Fiscal Priorities for Development." Paper presented at CIEM and ANU Conference "Policies for Macroeconomic Adjustment, Growth and Development." Ha Noi, Vietnam. 23–24 February 2006.

Hong, K., J-W. Lee, and Y. S. Lee. 2006. "Investment by Korean Chaebols Before and After the Crisis." Mimeo. Forthcoming in *Japan and the World Economy*.

International Monetary Fund, Asia and Pacific Department. 2005a. *Regional Outlook*, September 2005.

———. 2005b. World Economic Outlook. Washington, D.C.: IMF. September.

————. 2005c. *International Financial Statistics Yearbook*. Washington, D.C.: IMF.

Lee, J-W. 2005. "Human Capital and Productivity for Korea's Sustained Economic Growth." *Journal of Asian Economics* 16:663–87.

Lee, J-W. and McKibbin W. 2006. "Domestic Investment and External Imbalances in East Asia." Brookings Discussion Papers in International Economics No. 172.

Lee, J-W., McKibbin W. and Y. C. Park. 2006. "Transpacific Trade Imbalances: Causes and Cures." *World Economy* 29:281–303.

McKibbin, W.J. and A. Stoeckel. 2004. "What if China Revalues Its Currency?" Available at: www.EconomicScenarios.com Issue 7. February.

McKibbin, W. and P. Wilcoxen. 1998. "The Theoretical and Empirical Structure of the G-Cubed Model." *Economic Modeling* 16(1):123–48.

McKibbin W.J. and W. Woo. 2003. "The Consequences of China's WTO Accession on Its Neighbors." *Asian Economic Papers* 2(2):1–38.

Obstfeld, M. and K. Rogoff. 2004. "The Unsustainable US Current Account Position Revisited." NBER Working Paper No.10869.

Roubini, N. 2005. "Global Imbalances: A Contemporary Rashomon Tale with Five Interpretations." Unpublished manuscript.

Roubini, N., and B. Setser. 2004. "The US as a Net Debtor: The Sustainability of the US External Imbalances." Unpublished manuscript.

PART 4

A New IMF in the Making?

CHAPTER 4.1

Sixty Years After Bretton Woods: Developing a Vision for the Future[1]

JACK BOORMAN, Former Counsellor and Director, Policy Development and Review Department, International Monetary Fund

T he International Monetary Fund (IMF or Fund) has changed enormously in the last ten years, continuing a process of evolution that has generally served it quite well in responding to a changing world. It has concentrated increasingly on crisis prevention and has refined its tools and analysis for that work. It has created new lending facilities for its members and closed down facilities that found little or no demand. It has transformed itself from something approaching a secret society to an exceptionally transparent institution. It has changed its staffing and structure to reflect changes in the world economy and in markets. It has vastly expanded its technical assistance and training—activities well respected and in heavy demand by the membership. And it has taken on a number of new responsibilities, some of which, however, in my view, represent a mixed blessing!

Notwithstanding the accelerated pace of change and adaptation in the Fund over the past ten years, issues remain. The important thing now is to build further on this record. I want to focus on three specific areas: governance, surveillance, and the Fund's activities with its emerging market members.[2] Under each I will raise some issues and make some suggestions.

Governance

Much has been written and said about various aspects of the governance of the Fund. Perhaps the broadest concern involves the voice and vote of members, determined to a large degree by each member's quota and by its representation in the Executive Board. Before dealing with that issue, however, let me raise two points. The first concerns the nature of organizations like the IMF. All such international institutions entail some yielding of sovereignty by the nation state to the broader international community. This may be more obvious for an organization such as the World Trade Organization (WTO) with its rule-making power and dispute resolution mechanism. But it is also true of the Fund. This is the essence of multilateralism. However, multilateralism has been under some threat in the last several years! It may well be that, as the world becomes more complex and more closely integrated, there may have to be a different balance found between ceding more sovereignty and applying the principles of subsidiarity. This is an issue, for example, in something as otherwise mundane as the formulation of internationally accepted standards and codes.

For multilateral institutions to work effectively, it is important that whatever sovereignty is ceded by the membership to the institution not be taken back over time in the context of individual decisions. Unfortunately, in the IMF, the G-7 and even a smaller number of the major shareholders, at times, try to do exactly that. Within the static context of quotas and voting power, there must be a fair playing-by-the-rules and an exercise of restraint by the major countries, in order to resist using political power *outside* the Fund to force decisions *within* it. The flip side is the need for the rest of the membership to resist the temptation to be passive when the major countries act this way. This has sometimes been the case in the past, even on issues of direct and immediate relevance to those countries.

The second point is that for the voice and vote of all members to be meaningful, there must be a renewed commitment on the part of all members to the search for consensus. That is an attitude and an approach which dominated in the past, but which has suffered a few blows in the recent past.

The broader, dynamic aspect of governance is the failure of voice and vote to keep up with changes in the world economy. We have all seen the examples of how distorted representation has become:

- Europe still has three full chairs (four including Russia), and leadership or representation in six others in an Executive Board of 24 chairs;

- Twelve EU countries have 28.3 percent of current calculated quotas, as compared to the 16.9 percent that they would have if trade between those countries was excluded from the quota calculations;

- Mexico, with more than three times the share of world GDP (in PPP terms) and nine times the population of Belgium, has about half its quota;

- The seven largest Asian countries (other than Japan) have somewhat lower aggregate quotas than seven European countries: Austria, Belgium, Denmark, Finland, Norway, Sweden and Switzerland, despite the fact that they constitute seven times the share in World GDP (in PPP terms), and vastly larger trade.

I am not making an argument for any particular quota formula, although I believe it would be best to base quotas primarily on members' participation in trade and financial flows. But, whatever the basis, surely something is askew and needs correcting. The legitimacy of the Fund's decision-making in the eyes of the membership and the general public can only be tarnished by such distortions.

Reforming the way the aggregate quota of the EU is calculated would provide some room for increasing the quotas of some of today's more egregiously under-represented member countries. Unfortunately, there appears to be little political will to take on this issue, although the draft EU constitution is said to provide the decision-making basis for such a change.

There should probably also be a reduction in the number of chairs on the Executive Board to improve the efficiency with which the institution works. Again, dealing with the over representation of the European countries would help. Putting the EU-25 countries into one or two chairs would significantly reduce the total number of chairs. It would probably be useful to take the size down even further. Combined with this, should be an upgrading of the seniority of Executive Directors within their own governments.

There is also the issue of the selection of the Managing Director. I expressed my view on this as the process unfolded. In the end, some greater transparency was injected into the process, but the unwillingness of the Europeans to part with the tradition of having a European as the Managing Director—presumably with the implicit agreement of the U.S.—was regrettable, doubly so, in light of the new principles and specific procedures for the selection process which were endorsed by Executive Directors in April 2001. Whatever one's views on the processes suggested at that time—and my own are not completely positive—it harms the institution to be seen as ignoring its own guidance when it comes time to take decisions.

Surveillance

I now turn to the most important of the IMF's responsibilities, surveillance. This remains a little understood responsibility of the Fund and of its members, visible in too many countries only to a narrow group of officials who deal with Fund matters. This is the disturbing conclusion of a survey conducted in the context of the current staff review of surveillance. Perhaps greater transparency will help, but so far its impact seems to be limited. The Fund is recognized as having staff that is fully capable of doing first rate work in this area, but there remain basic questions as to its purpose, its audience, and its effectiveness.

The purpose of surveillance is, of course, to determine if each member is respecting its responsibilities under Article IV of the Articles of Agreement, with regard to its exchange rate policies. We well know the breadth of policies this, in fact, encompasses. But the Fund is also responsible for advising and assisting its members through surveillance. This raises the question of what staff and the Executive Board bring to this exercise. Certainly, staff must bring a different perspective from that of most policy-makers, who are often predominantly focused on domestic issues. Prospects for the world economy and the region, and the impact of those developments on a country—and its own impact on the region and the world—should be a particular talent of Fund staff. This becomes absolutely key as the world is increasingly integrated and connected. One has only to look at the growing economic linkages between once distant countries, such as Brazil, Russia, India and China— the so-called BRICs—to see the point. This also raises important questions about the relative roles of bilateral and multilateral surveillance, and how they are integrated in the Fund's conduct of its business.

Beyond this, we hear repeatedly that, in addition to the macroeconomic assessment that is the stock-in-trade of surveillance, country officials want the Fund staff to bring the experience of other countries to the problems they are currently confronting. Policy-makers in any country seldom face problems which have not already been confronted—at least in their essence, if not in their specifics—in other countries.

But to be better able to share experiences and lessons across the membership, the Fund has to better distil the extraordinarily broad experience of its members and make sure that staff is conversant with those lessons. Some of this is done and done well![3] However, I believe that more could be done to assure that the Fund is the real center of knowledge and excellence on the economic and financial policies in its domain. It is not clear that staff assignments—or the incentives operating on staff—are well-tailored to this objective. Nor is it clear that the necessary information systems exist to help staff fully master the lessons of country experiences beyond their own assignments, and to bring those experiences to their own assigned countries, unless they were closely involved in those earlier experiences, or have easy access to those who were.

Some see other potential purposes for surveillance. There are proposals, for example, somehow to link the financial resources available to a country when it faces a crisis to the extent to which it took account of the Fund's earlier surveillance warnings about looming vulnerabilities. This reminds me of a parent's threat: "Do what I say this afternoon or no dessert tonight!" and it is likely to be equally ineffective. Hence, I do not believe this suggestion has much merit. Can the Fund, as a cooperative institution, say "no" to a member when it needs financial support, if it has misbehaved in the past? I would argue that it cannot, and should not, so long as the member is then ready to implement the needed corrective policies. The reality, of course, is that, frequently, by the time of the crisis, the Fund may be dealing with a new government that was not responsible for the earlier sin of ignoring Fund advice.

Beyond "purpose" is the question of the audience for surveillance. In its original construct, that was essentially the Executive Board and country officials, who were privileged to see Fund documents. That construct has gone by the boards with transparency, and that is all to the good. But I believe we may have drifted a bit here, without getting real agreement on some of the key issues raised by transparency. Surely, it is a better world with surveillance reports—as well as the documents related to the newer surveillance tasks of assessing countries' progress on various standards and codes such as ROSCs and FSAPs[4]—available to markets and to the public at large. These documents contain analysis and policy commitments which should be the stuff of public debate in democracies.

To date, much of the push toward transparency has been done voluntarily, but with a very strong element of peer pressure. However, the old challenge as to how this would affect the Fund's role of confidential advisor and spur to policy action, versus its new role as informer of markets, has not been fully resolved. There are, of course, questions about the extent to which the Fund really serves as a confidential advisor. But, at the same time, there is little doubt that officials in many countries open up to Fund staff in a way that they do not open up to others. That helps staff understand the operational realities and political feasibilities of domestic policies and helps avoid some naivety in policy assessments. But can this be preserved if the staff is also writing for markets? This is tricky business and some country officials themselves say no!

This leads to questions about the effectiveness of surveillance. The first requirements for effectiveness are obviously technical competence and some degree of political savvy. But another requirement is the ability to get country authorities to take the proper action when vulnerabilities threaten. This is the essence of crisis prevention. Is this done best by private persuasion or by public warnings? Look at the Fund's surveillance of Thailand in late 1996–early 1997. That exercise succeeded insofar as vulnerabilities were identified and assessed, and representations to deal with them were made to the Thai authorities at the most senior levels. But surveillance failed, insofar as the Fund did not get the authorities to address these vulnerabilities and to change policy. Would the Fund have been more effective if it had gone public? Or would it have been seen as precipitating the crisis? The Thai, and before that the Mexican, and later the Korean experience, were the catalysts for the unprecedented moves to make the Fund more transparent. But I remain unconvinced that the potential conflicts inherent in the roles the Fund is being asked to play have been resolved, and whether the transparency issue has yet been sufficiently clarified.

Here an aside, to indicate why I believe these issues surrounding governance and surveillance are so important. The Asian crisis, and the Fund's response to it, have left an unhappy residue in much of Asia. There is still, I believe, less agreement than would be desirable, even on something as basic as the diagnosis of the Asian crisis. But beyond this, the voice and vote and representation issues—and the refusal of the major countries to deal with them—are further aggravating relations. And the push toward transparency—without trying to better reconcile it with the traditions in some Asian cultures—may be further weakening relations. Is it any wonder that this atmosphere, together with the incredible build-up of reserves in the region, is giving renewed strength to those calling for an Asian Monetary Fund—the value of which I believe to be questionable for Asia as well as for the Fund, but which could also be a bell-wether for other regions if, they too, become disaffected from the Fund.

The Fund's role in emerging market countries

I now turn to the third issue, the Fund's role vis-à-vis its emerging market country members—hopefully an expanding group over the next decades. This is where the rubber hits the road on transparency issues, in particular, as the markets pay close attention to Fund views and to Fund moves in these countries!

But let me take up some of the other issues related to the impact of Fund policies in emerging market countries. Besides the fundamental matters of governance and the size of the Fund touched on earlier, four issues, in particular, are worth brief mention: signaling, access policy, debt workout mechanisms, and the Fund's policy on lending into arrears.

Signaling is, of course, a close relative of transparency, even though the Fund has been sending signals since long before transparency came into vogue. This was most obvious through its approval (or not) of financial arrangements with members. But transparency opens new, more subtle doors and the growing appetite of markets for information has created demand. In a transparent world, virtually anything the Fund does or says may be interpreted as a signal regarding its views on a particular country. The most obvious signals derive from approving, continuing, delaying, or halting lending arrangements with countries. But the nature of the arrangement also contains signals. Approval of a stand-by arrangement (SBA) or an arrangement under the extended Fund facility (EFF), where there is money involved, may signal something quite different from a Fund-monitored program, and surely something different from a staff-monitored program.

There are continuous calls for Fund signaling mechanisms, but some attempts at response have faltered. The Short-Term Financing Facility (STFF) which was discussed in 1994 and which would have provided something akin to a credit line linked to Fund surveillance, died with the Mexican blow-up before it could be tested. Contingent Credit Lines (CCL), created in 1999 and modified in 2000, were intended to protect countries from contagion. However, the CCL had many of the same characteristics as the STFF, failed from lack of use, and has been allowed to expire. The problems with such facilities are well known: creditors wanted more conditionality and slower disbursements, borrowers less conditionality and more money up front; the entry signal would likely be positive and welcome, but the exit could be a problem; some saw moral hazard, others saw policy discipline; more broadly, some saw the risk for the Fund to gravitate toward a rating agency. In the end, none of these issues was successfully resolved and I suspect they will continue to bedevil attempts to create new, more imaginative signaling mechanisms in the Fund. Perhaps the answer is to stay with the blunt instrument of approval of an SBA, make greater use of precautionary SBAs, and the more subtle— and public—assessment of a staff appraisal in the context of surveillance, and give up the search for something in between.

Let me turn to access policy, which determines a member country's window to Fund resources. I believe it also remains unsettled, even though there is some appearance of agreement. Those wanting more limited access to Fund resources have succeeded in imposing tighter procedures for the approval of access beyond the traditional limits, in terms of the member's quota, of 100 percent/annual and 300 percent/cumulative. But exceptional access clearly remains an option. Putting the burden of proof on those recommending exceptional access is probably appropriate, although I am one of those who believe that access would not look so exceptional in so many cases, if the Fund and Fund quotas were appropriately enlarged!

The calls to restrict access are motivated by: moral hazard considerations, the alleged benefits of greater predictability for markets, and a desire to clip the wings of Fund management, post-Mexico, -Asia, -Russia, etc.

But each of these motivations is subject to challenge. Few see moral hazard on the debtor side: most governments do not survive crises and are unlikely to invite them simply because the Fund may be there with large amounts of money. On the creditor side, there is an issue, but is it overriding, and is limiting access to Fund resources a necessary element of a sensible response to this phenomenon? Similarly, on predictability, I have never understood the appeal of having the Fund deal more predictably vis-à-vis markets. Is that not a recipe for one way bets and well-timed exits, instead of appropriate caution? In any case, the Fund will always be somewhat unpredictable in its responses, if only because of the judgmental element in deciding between liquidity and solvency problems. And as liquidity needs can at times be large—and it can be appropriate to fill them (as in Mexico in 1995, Thailand, and Korea in 1997, and other cases)—the Fund should be able to respond appropriately. In sum, I think the current access policy pretends too much, at least as regards its contribution to predictability. Hopefully, it will not tie the hands of the Fund when large resources are appropriate for a country in trouble. Given the discretion permitted, I would guess there will be cases of exceptional access in the future, as there have been in the past.

Related to access policy in crisis cases is, of course, the matter of debt workouts. On the positive side, I believe the debate and discussion on the Sovereign Debt Restructuring Mechanism (SDRM), Collective Action Clauses (CACs), and codes of conduct has been enormously productive. Not only has it pushed practice forward by moving emerging market countries to include CACs in their bond issues—perhaps because they perceived the threat of something worse, but it has vastly increased the understanding of the international community of the issues involved. This is important, because I believe we will be back to the discussion of some kind of statutory mechanism in the not too distant future. I do not believe that CACs have the power to do what is needed in more complex cases, although the international financial system is better than it was before with their more extensive use. So I think we should keep all the good, institutional, academic, and legal work done in the context of the recent debate on a nearby shelf.

An aside on this: we must be careful about how the Argentine experience is interpreted after a deal is struck between Argentina and its private creditors—whenever that may be. Whatever the deal, I hope that it will not be interpreted to mean that the markets, together with the debtor country, had the capacity to find a satisfactory solution to an obvious need for debt write-offs and restructuring, even in a case as complicated as this. Everyone has to keep in mind the enormous cost—on the part of both creditors and the Argentine society and people—that will have been endured by the time a settlement is reached. The cost is enormous, and continues to be paid, and will not be reversed by any restructuring. I believe a good case can be made, as well, that much of that cost could have been avoided.

Having raised the case of Argentina, I will conclude with the Fund's policy on lending into arrears. The policy is straight forward and based on experience: if a country falls into arrears to its private creditors, the international community cannot hand the discretion to help that country to those same creditors who may be demanding that agreement on a debt deal be struck before the Fund lends. At the same time, the official community must recognize the legitimate rights of creditors. The Fund's policy on lending into arrears attempts to strike a balance. The country must be judged to be acting in good faith with its creditors in finding a solution to its debt problem, in order for the Fund to initiate or continue lending to that country. That policy was given more flesh in September 2002, when the Fund Board agreed to certain principles and more specific criteria to be used to judge the dialogue taking place between debtors and their private external creditors. We could argue for a long time to come, I suppose, about whether those criteria have been met in the case of Argentina. But I wish to make a somewhat different point: I am concerned about the absence of a more specific medium-term analysis of Argentina's debt service capacity in the Argentine arrangement with the Fund.

We have been told by some that this is a new policy of the Fund, i.e., to leave the determination of the medium-term fiscal path—beyond that required to service debt to the international financial institutions (IFIs)—to the debtor and its private creditors. But I have not seen a policy paper on this issue, and I know of no formal discussion in the Executive Board of the Fund on this important matter. More importantly, I believe the stance is not tenable. Ultimately, the Fund will have to make a judgment on the sustainability of Argentina's position under any debt deal that is struck. Consider the possibilities: if a deal is not struck, the Fund will have to decide whether to resume and to continue lending to Argentina; that decision will have to rest in part on whether Argentina rejected an offer of the creditors which was, in fact, within its capacity to pay; And that judgment will require assessment by the Fund of Argentina's medium-term prospects, and of its capacity to adjust in a socially acceptable manner. Similarly, if a deal is struck, the Fund will have to judge the sustainability of Argentina's external position under that deal and its capacity to service its obligations to the Fund. If the deal lies outside what a sustainable medium term path would suggest and the position does not look viable, the Fund cannot continue to lend.

But even before this point is reached, I believe the passivity of the official sector may have made finding a solution more difficult. Effectively, the Argentine authorities have been told to negotiate not only a debt deal but also their macroeconomic program—most importantly the path for the primary surplus—with their private external creditors. This may well make giving any ground to the creditors more difficult for the Argentine authorities to sell domestically. I also wonder if the many creditors involved—who will have to find common ground on the elements of what is likely to be a very complex debt deal—will also be able to find agreement on the parameters of a medium term macroeconomic scenario. The passivity of the official sector may also make it more difficult to play a constructive role at a moment when a nudge in a particular direction could help the parties find agreement. As Nouriel Roubini has said: "The IMF's hands-on role in the restructuring process is part of what makes the sovereign debt restructuring process work in the absence of the supervision of a bankruptcy court; (it is) not an unwarranted official interference in a private commercial dispute."[5] I agree completely with this. This seems to be the view of many in the private sector as well, some of whom suggest that, if the Fund is to distance itself from the process as it has, perhaps its preferred creditor status should be rethought. I believe that would do irreparable harm to the Fund, and to its role in the future in helping countries deal with the debt crises which will, unfortunately, but inevitably, continue to occur.

Conclusion

Life in the Fund continues to be characterized by all the implications of the famous Chinese saying about "living in interesting times." The times are indeed interesting and the Fund will serve the purposes for which it was founded only if its members interpret those times correctly so that it may continue to evolve in the way in which it deals with them.

NOTES

1 Taken from speech presented to the meeting of the Reinventing Bretton Woods Committee, World Economic Forum, and the Ministry of the Economy and Finance, Italy, in Rome, 22–23 July 2004.

2 There a many important and challenging issues confronting the Fund in its work with its low income member countries. However, these issues are beyond the scope of this presentation.

3 See, for example, IMF (2003 and 2005).

4 Reports on the Observance of Standards and Codes (ROSC) and Financial Sector Assessment Program (FSAP).

5 Roubini, 2004.

REFERENCES

International Monetary Fund. 2005. "Stabilization and Reform in Latin America. A Macroeconomic Perspective on the Experience since the Early 1990s." Occasional Paper of the IMF No. 238.

———. 2003. "Lessons from the Crisis in Argentina." SM/03/345. 10 September.

Roubini, N. 2004. "The Reform of the Sovereign Debt Restructuring Process: Problems, Proposed Solutions, and the Argentine Episode." First Reading, *Journal of Restructuring Finance* 1(1):1–12.

CHAPTER 4.2

Assessing the Future of the IMF: Its Role, Relevance, and Prospective Reform

JOHN LIPSKY, JPMorgan[1]

T hat the International Monetary Fund (IMF) is ripe for fundamental reform is an idea whose time has come. The G-20 Finance Ministers and Central Bank Governors issued a "Statement on Reforming the Bretton Woods Institutions" at their October, 2005 meeting that asserted "more innovative approaches and renewed commitments are needed." While some critics claim that the Fund itself is an anachronism, the G-20 authorities anticipate that a reformed Fund will retain a critical role in international governance: "The IMF should primarily focus on national and international macroeconomic and financial stability, exercising enhanced surveillance of the global economy, international capital markets and strengthening crisis prevention and resolution." The Fund itself is actively engaged in the reform process: The Fund's Managing Director, Rodrigo de Rato, recently issued a "Report on the Fund's Medium-Term Strategy,"[2] while a blue-ribbon, IMF-sponsored panel is preparing a review of the Fund's work on financial markets.[3]

Despite the widespread consensus on the need for IMF reform, there is no parallel consensus regarding the specific content of that reform. Not surprisingly, this lack of consensus in large part reflects diverging views on the Fund.[4] Nonetheless, there is a critical, practical, and systemic role that the Fund can fulfill uniquely: To create the legal foundation for the international financial system, and to exercise surveillance of members' adherence to the obligations of Fund membership. At stake is the preservation of a multilateral, non-discriminatory rule-based financial system that seeks to support global growth and to preserve financial stability, while accommodating structural change. The challenge at present is to adapt the institution to a series of developments which in many ways have superseded the Fund's original organization and standard procedures.

Thus, innovations are needed in both the Fund's existing structure and processes to insure its future relevance and effectiveness, even taking into account the innovations introduced in the past few years. In the broadest terms, Fund reform should be focused on those issues and circumstances where it can make a unique and positive contribution, to create a forum for cooperation in those areas where its contribution is not unique, and to eliminate those activities which have lost their effectiveness.

To accomplish these goals, the Fund must adjust its governance to recognize powerful shifts in the global economy. At the same time, the Fund must sharpen its understanding of and interaction with international financial markets. New amendments to the Fund's Articles of Agreement may not be required to effect the needed changes, but its operations and focus inevitably will shift in many important ways.

What is the Fund for?

To put the current reform momentum into perspective, it is worth reviewing the essential aspects of the Fund's original role, and to summarize the forces that have created the conviction that change is necessary. While it is often claimed that the Fund's original responsibility was to operate the post–World War II dollar-based fixed exchange rate system, in fact, the Fund's central purpose was much broader.[5]

The IMF Articles of Agreement formed the legal basis for creating a multilateral and non-discriminatory international monetary system. No equivalent agreement existed previously. Accepting Fund membership also entailed making a commitment to eliminate, over time, all restrictions on current payments for balance of payments purposes.[6] When the Fund was created, such restrictions were the rule, even in the largest economies. The notion that foreign exchange would be available freely for all permitted international trade and debt service transactions—something taken for granted today almost everywhere—was at the time a distant memory from the late 19th century. Moreover, even the pre–World War I gold standard lacked a formal basis. It was merely a pragmatic arrangement.

Therefore, the Fund was intended to promote structural changes in the global economy. Its key role was to create a financial system based on international law, which would reliably support the liberalization of global trade, while preserving financial and economic balance. Critical to the Fund's systemic role was its unique and unprecedented responsibility for conducting surveillance. That is, the Fund's Articles created legal obligations for its members, and the Fund was charged to make sure that those obligations were being fulfilled, with the threat of sanctions for non-compliance.

The Fund's lending facilities—originally created somewhat as an afterthought, with no clear vision of exactly how or when they would be used—were intended to provide an incentive for member countries to avoid "beggarthy-neighbor" policies in correcting balance of payments deficits. At the time the Articles were drafted, the availability of such public international funding was novel. Both private and official cross-border capital flows were rare, while international capital markets as we know them today simply did not exist. Even short-term trade finance was often subject to severe restrictions. Direct foreign investment was minimal by modern standards, and controversial. Moreover, the percent of global output accounted for by international trade transactions in the Fund's early existence was the lowest since before World War I.

New challenges

Several key developments have fundamentally altered the challenges facing the Fund, including:

- The move to nearly universal Fund membership, expanding from the original 40 countries in 1945 to 184 today. In the process, the trading and monetary systems the Fund helped to create have also become universal. While this means that Fund membership is now virtually complete, the rapid growth in Fund membership led naturally to a sharp increase in Fund technical assistance, including to formerly centrally planned economies.

- The elimination of current payments restrictions in most economies —or at least substantial progress toward their elimination. In other words, one of the Fund's critical original missions is well on the way to having been achieved. This represents a monumental accomplishment, but one that is rarely remarked upon in the discussion of potential Fund reforms. In an important sense, one justification for the current re-examination of the Fund's role is that one of its principal systemic goals has largely been accomplished. One important caveat: relevant remaining payments restrictions are concentrated in large, formerly centrally-planned economies which are becoming systemically relevant, and in the poorest economies.

- Private sector cross-border capital flows have become massive. Today, such flows still take place in the more traditional form of direct investment and bank lending, but there has been explosive growth in cross-border trade in marketable securities and derivative instruments. Cross-border securities transactions often involve new institutions, including hedge funds and private equity funds. One result has been the increasingly tight linkage between international and domestic financial markets. Thus, both public and private entities in major economies can access international capital markets to a degree that was never contemplated by the framers of the Articles.

- Monetary and exchange rate policies in several cases have taken on a regional character not contemplated in the Articles, and not reflected clearly in the Fund's governance. Most important has been creation of the euro. In addition, the movement of key Asian economies away from pegged exchange rates has sparked proposals for new forms of regional cooperation. The dramatic growth in global trade, viewed by the Fund's founders as a key contribution to increased economic well-being, has tended to be more rapid within principal regions then between them. Put another way, globalization in large part has meant regionalization—at least so far.

- The dramatic global decline in inflation during the past decade or so, particularly in emerging market economies, has reflected an improvement in monetary and fiscal policy management, in addition to the forces of globalization. At the same time, the profound demographic shifts underway in the developed economies are creating powerful, longer-term challenges to their fiscal policies. In other words, the most striking policy challenges increasingly are medium- and long-term in nature, but they are potentially very serious. The emergence in the past few years of a record US current account deficit, along with the unprecedented form and ease of its financing, has produced strongly divergent views regarding the Fund's role. Many analysts claim that a US current deficit equivalent to nearly 7 percent of GDP provides *prima facie* evidence that the Fund has failed to forestall a serious threat to systemic stability. At the same time, other observers interpret the ease with which the US deficit has been financed as evidence that the Fund's systemic role should be re-examined and re-interpreted, to allow for a more up-to-date view of what constitutes systemically worrisome payments imbalances.

- The increase in transparency in many economies, in terms of both data availability and policy clarity, has made it easier to analyze and understand policy alternatives, and to gauge risks more accurately than in the past. The Fund itself has played a major role in improving the quality and availability of economic and financial data. Much more could be accomplished. Of course, it must be asked whether data reporting requirements should be created in the interest of transparency, even if none exist now.

Taken together, these changes have substantially altered the environment in which the Fund operates. Many issues that previously demanded significant amounts of staff effort, in terms of intellectual, manpower, and financial resources, have faded in importance, while others have become more prominent.

The momentum for reform

In its first decades, the Fund's efforts were focused on establishing a standard framework for analyzing member country's economies. This included creating conceptually consistent data and developing standards for member countries' policies that were in line with the demands of Fund membership. At the same time, the Fund developed the now-standard procedures for the use of Fund resources, including Stand-By Arrangements and subsequent innovations. Several large industrial countries were early users of Fund Arrangements, dominating the overall use of Fund resources in the institution's first decades.

The only previous period of fundamental Fund reform occurred in the early 1970s, following the collapse of the fixed-exchange rate system, and its replacement by a system of floating rates. This shift was accommodated by amending the Fund's Articles. However, it was not the debt crises of the 1980s, or the wide swings of key exchange rates and the associated record payments imbalances at that time that created a consensus that the Fund was in need of serious restructuring. Rather, it was the emergence during the 1990s of massive securitized private international capital flows—and the repeated, unnerving demonstrations that the Fund was simply not able to cope within its standard procedures with the implied systemic strains—that led to the current reform consensus.

In the wake of the 1994–95 Mexican crisis, the Fund's Interim Committee—itself created following the abandonment of fixed exchange rates in 1973—endorsed at its September 1997 meeting amending the Articles to make capital market liberalization a formal goal of Fund membership. Implicitly, the proposal would have given the Fund authority to guide the capital account liberalization process in a fashion analogous to its earlier responsibilities with regard to current account liberalization.

It was the rapid unfolding of the Asian crisis of 1997–98, the Russian debt default of 1998, the Brazilian devaluation of 1999—coupled with the market crisis generated by the failure of Long-Term Capital Management (LTCM) in the third quarter of 1998—left the proposed Amendment moot. In the wake of these repeated crises, it was accepted, virtually universally, that the crisis prevention and resolution mechanisms embodied in the Fund's Articles and the Fund's practices had become dysfunctional. In its place came a widely-supported, but vague, call for a "New International Financial Architecture." What ensued was commonly referred to as a "repair of the plumbing," but not a "new architecture."[7]

Assessing the "repairs"

The failure to agree on a new architecture was not for lack of trying. Numerous reforms were proposed, including the Fund's own plan for a Sovereign Debt Restructuring Mechanism (SDRM). Five important changes were adopted, although none of them required an amendment to the Fund's Articles of Agreement. Perhaps the most important of these was the de facto agreement among governments that, henceforth, all sovereign debt issues denominated in foreign currency—even those of G-8 members—would contain collective action clauses (CACs).[8]

Once a transition period is complete, future sovereign debt restructurings will no longer take place in the wake of a formal default, as the debt contract itself will spell out the procedures by which the terms can be renegotiated. In theory at least, the use of collective action clauses will virtually eliminate the situation where the Fund faces "lending into arrears." Moreover, a set of voluntary Principles[9] (often referred to as a "Code of Conduct") has been negotiated between private creditors and official borrowers, and endorsed by the Group of 20 authorities. The Fund's prospective role in a debt restructuring conducted under the CACs remains undefined in many important respects.

The second of the five changes involved the adoption in 2003 by the Fund's Executive Board of a policy of more formal limits on access to Fund resources. In essence, by establishing criteria for exceptional access and by requiring that the Fund issue an "exceptional access report," a more effective budget constraint has been created, making "the IMF, rather than official creditor governments... [now] responsible for large scale loan financing."[10] At the same time, it was agreed to seek greater clarity regarding the division of responsibilities between the Fund and the World Bank, and that the Fund would focus on its core responsibilities of supporting macroeconomic balance, through surveillance of monetary, fiscal, financial and exchange rate issues. Finally, it was agreed in April 2005 that the Fund would create "program monitoring arrangements," in which a member country could receive formal Fund endorsement of its economic program, but without drawing on the Fund's financial resources.[11]

Looking forward

As the support for some sort of Fund reform builds, it is worth pausing to take stock of the Fund's probable future, and whether the current challenges call for "New Architecture," or rather for another round of "repairs" to the "plumbing."[12]

The prospect for future demands on Fund resources remains murky. Even if the international economic environment becomes less favorable, the call on Fund resources is likely to recede sharply, unless the largest borrowers again experience serious difficulties. This implies that the relevance of the new policy on exceptional access is still to be tested. If the countries representing the largest current users of Fund resources have graduated from Fund support— as the G-7 countries have done over the past 30 years—the practical importance of the Fund's financing role will diminish.

Issues which have been raised repeatedly, such as whether the Fund should create a true "lender of last resort" facility, a "conditional lending facility" or even a "deadbeat's refinancing facility,"[13] will almost certainly remain

moot. However, the Fund's traditional role as the primary official international lender of last resort[14] will seem less controversial, if the amounts remain
modest, relative to recent experience. In this case, calls for a substantial
increase in Fund quotas are not likely to find a sympathetic audience, at least
not where it will make a difference. Moreover, the pending issue of a new
allocation of the Fund's Special Drawing Rights (SDRs) likely will remain
pending, as will the issue of whether the Fund will undertake new gold sales
in the interests of providing new support for its poorest members.

Two approaches to evaluating reform needs

Starting from the current situation, there are two basic approaches to the
issue of Fund reform. One is to begin with the structural and systemic issues
facing the Fund, and to assess the changes needed to confront them. The
other is to examine the Fund's probable operational needs, starting with a
typology of the Fund's member countries.

Beginning with the former approach, it seems clear that the prospect for
many proposed structural reforms will hinge on a set of interlocking issues to
which there are no clear answers at present. Much depends on whether a
redistribution of voting power within the Fund takes place.[15] Progress on this
question has proven to be very difficult, and it is uncertain whether forward
movement is imminent.[16] And related directly to the matter of voting redistribution is the possible expansion of the Fund's quotas, and a possible new
allocation of the Funds' Special Drawing Rights.

But regardless of whether there is progress on these structural issues,
there is little doubt that improving the Fund's effectiveness will require new
advances in the organization's work on international capital markets. Systemic
stability, debt sustainability, and capital market liberalization are all within the
Fund's responsibilities and expertise, and there is little doubt that the Fund is
uniquely equipped to take a leadership role in these critical areas.

Whether or not support will reemerge for the 1997 proposal—to amend
the Articles of Agreement and give the Fund a direct, formal role on capital
market liberalization—the Fund's knowledge and involvement of financial
market issues needs strengthening. The recent G-20 statement left no doubt of
the Fund's mandate in this area. To accomplish this, however, the Fund will
have to increase its formal cooperation with other international bodies, such

as the Basel Committee, the Financial Stability Forum and the various organizations which supervise and regulate specialized financial markets.

In fact, the scope and effectiveness of the Fund's multilateral surveillance activities, and even the authority with which it can address issues of appropriate exchange rate policy will depend to a large degree to its ability to speak with real authority on financial market developments—a distinct challenge. Far from having to master an entirely new body of knowledge, the Fund has to play a vanguard role in understanding better the forces that govern international financial markets, and in advancing analysis on the appropriate role for public intervention in what have become largely private markets. The intellectual and practical challenges are daunting, but they will have to be met if a reformed Fund is to be successful.

Viewed from a different perspective, four categories of Fund members can be discerned:

1. Countries which can access international capital markets in their own currency;

2. Countries which can access international markets in foreign currencies;

3. Countries which do not have market access at present, but which can aspire to attain access in the near term;

4. Countries not likely to enjoy market access for some time to come.

In each case, the Fund's role will be different. Obviously, the G-7 economies can access international markets in their own currency. The prospect that detailed Fund bilateral surveillance will be welcomed or heeded in these cases seems unlikely. Moreover, the prospect that these countries might fail to honor their own local currency debt is remote. The efforts of Fund staff with regard to these economies would be more fruitful if they could be focused on issues of systemic stability and financial market developments, rather than on conventional consultations.

For countries with access to markets in foreign currency, greater financial market expertise could be important in making the Fund's policy advice relevant. Issues of debt sustainability will be important, as many observers worry that the current large users of Fund resources could face significant new problems in the future. It is worth noting that the cutting edge in emerging markets is the growing interest of investors in the local currency securities of major and/or well-managed emerging economies. This new interest might not survive a less favorable international environment, but for now it surely reflects the better macro-economic outcomes registered in recent years by many key emerging economies, and improvements in their domestic financial markets. If sustained, this trend toward local currency financing would be striking, and could potentially boost systemic stability. It would also imply a reduced role for Fund financing. In any case, the use of CACs by these countries should also diminish their need to draw on the Fund's financial resources in the future.

For countries without current market access, but with plausible near-term prospects of gaining such access, the Fund must be able to support that process. Here again, the Fund will require reliable expertise regarding the necessary and sufficient conditions for market access. Of course, that will require the Fund to have a point of view regarding the country's macro-economic policies, but also regarding its financial system, regulations, and other considerations, such as those reviewed in the Fund's Financial Sector Assessment Programs.

For those countries whose market access is a distant prospect, international institutions are likely to play a large role on a sustained basis. Broad issues, such as whether assistance should be in the form of grants or loans, will, no doubt, be relevant. It is reasonable to ask whether the Fund's current targeted programs, such as the Poverty Reduction and Growth Facility, represent a useful innovation, or a confusing overlap with the World Bank and/or regional development banks. In any case, these countries require a cooperative approach by the relevant official institutions. A separate assessment of their needs is warranted, a function extending far beyond the Fund's prospective role.

Concluding postscript

Since this paper was written, there has been substantial progress on Fund reform. The Managing Director's Medium-Term Strategy (MTS) was published in April 2006 and endorsed by member countries at the Fund's 2006 Spring Meetings. The MTS includes a broad range of proposals that respond to virtually all of the Fund's major challenges:

- *Fund surveillance activities are being broadened and strengthened.* The Fund has initiated multilateral consultations, where important issues are discussed among a relevant group of countries. The first consultation is focused on global imbalances, and involves the United States, Japan, the Euro area, China, and Saudi Arabia. A review of the 1977 Executive Board Decision governing the Fund's surveillance of exchange rate policies has been authorized, with the goal of sharpening the Fund's analysis of its member countries' exchange rate policies. At the same time, a revamping of the Fund's financial sector analysis is underway, including regular reviews of member countries economies and policies;

- *A new Fund lending instrument for emerging market countries* is being considered, with the goal of improving the Fund's crisis-prevention capabilities;

- *The Fund's support of low-income member countries is being bolstered.* Already, the Fund has provided debt relief to low-income countries through the Multilateral Debt Relief Initiative, and introduced the non-lending Policy Support Instrument for low-income countries that seek Fund support for policy formulation, but which do not face a Fund financing need. A new Exogenous Shocks Facility has also been approved. Moreover, a blue-ribbon panel of experts is reviewing the collaboration between the World Bank and the Fund;

- *A reform program of the Fund's governance structure* was endorsed by member countries at the 2006 Annual Meetings in Singapore. This program is designed to better align member countries' representation in the Fund with their economic importance, while also safeguarding the voice of LICs in the institution's governance.

NOTE

1 The opinions expressed in this paper are those of the author, and do not necessarily represent the views of either JPMorgan or the International Monetary Fund. This paper was written in November 2005 and first published in February 2006; as of September 2006, the author has become the IMF's First Deputy Managing Director.

2 IMF, 2005.

3 Note that the *Report* was completed, and posted on Fund website.

4 For an excellent summary of the issues and of alternative views regarding IMF reform, see Truman, 2006.

5 After all, how big a staff is needed to "oversee" a system of fixed exchange rates operated by national central banks?

6 In other words, the Fund's Articles set current account convertibility as an obligatory goal of Fund membership.

7 For an excellent description of the New Architecture effort, see Eichengreen, 1999.

8 The case for collective action clauses was made first in this context by Eichengreen and Portes, "Crisis? What Crisis? Orderly Workouts for Sovereign Debtors" 1995, Centre for Economic Policy Research.

9 Principles for Stable Capital Flows and Fair Debt Restructuring in Emerging Markets.

10 Taylor, 2005.

11 This creation of so-called "non-borrowing" arrangements essentially harks back to the origins of the Fund's Stand-By Arrangements, in which the use of Fund resources was optional to the member country, as long as their policies remained in compliance with the Arrangement.

12 As of August 2006, the Fund has 45 active programs, involving the use of SDR18 billion in Fund resources, today worth about US$26 billion. However, 60 percent of Fund resources is absorbed by three cases (Turkey, Indonesia, and Uruguay), and only nine new programs have been approved during 2006.

13 The latter is a serious proposal (albeit with an ironic title) by former IMF Research Director Michael Mussa. See, Mussa, 2006.

14 Following Mussa's terminology, op. cit.

15 Detailed discussions of this issue can be found in Truman (2005 and 2006), Bini-Smiaghi (2006) and Kahler (2006).

16 At its September 2006 Annual Meetings, the IMF's Board of Governors approved a two-year program to review the Fund's quotas and adjust voting shares.

REFERENCES

Bini-Smiaghi, L. 2006. "IMF Governance and the Political Economy of a Consolidated European Seat." E. M. Truman, ed. *Reforming the IMF for the 21st Century*. Washington, D.C.: Institute for International Economics. April. 233–55.

Eichengreen, B. 1999. *Toward a New International Financial Architecture*. Washington, D.C.: Institute for International Economics.

Eichengreen, B. and R. Portes. 1995. "Crisis? What Crisis? Orderly Workouts for Sovereign Debtors." London: Centre for Economic Policy Research.

International Monetary Fund. 2005. "The Managing Director's Report on The Fund's Medium-Term Strategy." Washington, D.C. September.

Kahler, M. 2006. "Internal Governance and IMF Performance." *Reforming the IMF for the 21st Century*. Institute for International Economics. April.

Mussa, M. 2006. "Reflections on the Function and Facilities for IMF Lending." E. M. Truman, ed. *Reforming the IMF for the 21st Century*. Institute for International Finance. April.

Taylor, J. B. 2005. "Recent IMF Reforms: Are They Working in Practice?" Remarks at the Conference "The IMF in a Changing World." Frankfurt, Germany. 8 June.

Truman, E. M. 2005. "Rearranging IMF Chairs and Shares: The Sine Qua Non of IMF Reform." Paper presented at the IIE Conference on IMF Reform.

———. 2006. "International Monetary Fund Reform: An Overview of the Issues." E. M. Truman, ed. *Reforming the IMF for the 21st Century*. Washington, D.C.: Institute for International Economics. April.

CHAPTER 4.3

Reforms of the International Monetary System[1]

JOHN WILLIAMSON, Senior Fellow, Peterson Institute for International Economics

T
he issues currently engaging our attention were laid out with admirable clarity by Edwin Truman in a lengthy background paper for an Institute for International Economics (IIE) conference on The Future of the IMF in September 2005. He divided the topic into four areas: the IMF's systemic role, its governance, lending facilities, and financial resources. I propose in this paper to focus on the first of those four areas.

This should not be taken to imply that the other three areas are all unimportant. Perhaps one can for the moment dismiss the last of them, since the Fund is currently very liquid and is likely to remain so, unless and until lending picks up in a major way. The third issue, of lending facilities, has two aspects. One is whether the Fund should create a replacement for the never-used Conditional Credit Line (CCL)—now abolished—or whether it should otherwise change its methods of supporting emerging-market countries in crisis. I do not see a strong case for reviving something like the CCL. Nor am I among those who see advantage in cutting back on support for middle-income countries in crisis. It is true that lending as a percentage of quota has increased over time, but this was a natural reaction to the fall in IMF quotas, relative to all other relevant magnitudes, combined with the end of borrowing from the Fund by the industrial countries. The other issue is whether the Fund should shift its Poverty Reduction and Growth Facility, intended to support low-income members to the World Bank. Personally I am in favor of the latter rationalization, but it is a proposal that enjoys little support outside the United States, and is, therefore, unlikely to be implemented any time soon.

But even if one can ignore the latter two of Truman's four areas, one can certainly not similarly dismiss reforms to IMF governance. The inadequacies here are obvious and widely resented, being reflected not just in Truman's paper and the pronouncements of the G-24, but also in the Managing

Director's Strategic Review and in the speech to the IIE conference by Timothy Adams (the US Under Secretary for International Economic Affairs). There is little doubt about the nature that the reforms here will ultimately take: loss of the West European right to name the Fund's Managing Director in favor of a meritocratic process open to all, and a significant shift in voting power in the IMF from Europe to Asia. The critical question is whether these reforms occur with European leadership or not. If, for example, Europe were to propose a single Executive Director for either the EU or the euro area, with a vote equal to that of the United States, it might exercise increased, rather than diminished, influence. One fears, however, that it is more likely to occur in the teeth of European resistance, and therefore mark a *loss* of European influence over the Fund, which will be further diminished when the inevitable loss of the European monopoly in naming the Managing Director finally occurs.

Management of the world economy

It is the other big issue, the systemic issue of how the world economy is managed, which I propose to focus on in this paper. At the moment it is basically not managed at all. The philosophy is that one relies on each country to manage its own economy, in what it perceives to be its own best interest, without giving much attention to global consistency. It is hoped that this will somehow lead to a satisfactory outcome for the world, just as the actions of self-interested individuals lead to a socially efficient outcome in an ideal market. And so far the world has indeed muddled through in this way, without any disaster remotely comparable to the global depression of the 1930s.

The question is obviously whether this can be expected to continue. The fact is that global imbalances have been expanding in recent years, and have now reached a point that most commentators regard as unsustainable. Yet there is no sign that the imbalances are in the process of being corrected. The dollar has fallen from its clearly overvalued level against the floating currencies of Europe and the English-speaking world, but, at best, this has served to level off the US current account deficit. Mention the need for a reduction in the US cyclically-adjusted fiscal deficit (which means a big tax increase), and the US administration recoils with the same horror that China does when one talks of the need for a 25 percent revaluation of the renminbi. Or, for that matter, that many Europeans do when one mentions the need for structural reforms to liberalize sclerotic European labor markets. In other words, there is not the slightest sign that any of the major players are preparing themselves to take the measures that might correct the current imbalances, despite the fact that there is very wide agreement on what set of measures is required. Yet if such measures are not implemented, and if the judgment that the present situation is unsustainable proves correct, the result is bound to be a crisis.

What form might one expect such a crisis to take? The most likely is a world recession. If there is, at some stage, a sudden collapse of confidence in the dollar, the values of the floating currencies of Europe and the English-speaking countries will surge against the dollar. The same will happen to the Asian currencies, if and when their central banks finally tire of accumulating dollars, although one cannot rule out the possibility that they will decide to accumulate more dollars for a long time to come, so as to maintain their exports. The shock to confidence could be expected to have a negative effect on demand in both the U.S. and the other industrial countries. Offsetting that in the United States—though perhaps only partially, at least in the short run—would be the switch of demand toward US producers, caused by the dollar depreciation. But in other industrial countries, the recession would be fed by both the income decline, caused by the loss of confidence and the switch of demand away from their producers as a result of the appreciation of their currencies. Even if Asian countries avoid appreciations, their output will still suffer from the loss of demand from the industrial countries. Given that both the industrial countries and the Asians have relied on export-led growth because of their difficulty in expanding domestic demand in recent years when there was no crisis, it is difficult to believe that they could suddenly replace foreign by domestic demand in the presence of a crisis. It is all too easy to imagine that in these circumstances a major world recession might develop.

The main purpose of an international monetary system should be to head off this type of disaster. Ideally the international monetary system should embrace a set of rules and practices that induce countries to adopt macroeconomic and exchange rate policies which add up to a satisfactory global solution. And the International Monetary Fund, as the instrument that the international community created at the time of Bretton Woods, should then ensure countries' adherence to those policies. Could one conceive of a set of rules and practices that would have these virtues and which the Fund would then be expected to police?

A reference rate system for exchange rates

I believe that any such system must start from the recognition that exchange rates are a key part of the solution, and that they are inherently matters of international concern. No country has a sovereign right to decide *its* exchange rate, because an exchange rate is a relationship between the values of at least two currencies.[2] If one is to have any sort of governmental policy on exchange rates—rather than leaving them entirely to the market—then more than one government has a right to be involved in what is decided. In practice, it is much preferable to have each country deal with the IMF representing the international community of nations, than to have bilateral disputes between pairs of countries. Even if countries could reach bilateral deals, problems of potential inconsistency would arise. This makes it natural to ask whether one could devise an exchange rate system that would at the same time be compatible with such basic characteristics of current economic policy-making in most countries as floating exchange rates and inflation targeting, and would also encourage countries to adopt globally consistent macroeconomic policies.

In my view this is indeed conceivable. I see the key being IMF development of a system of reference rates for exchange rates. A reference rate is an estimate of the equilibrium effective exchange rate, whereby each country agrees *not* to follow policies (notably intervention policy) which would have the effect of pushing the exchange rate *away* from that rate. Since there is no corresponding obligation to hold the exchange rate close to the reference rate, this is indeed a system that is compatible with floating exchange rates and inflation targeting, the two major features of macroeconomic policy in most industrial countries and many emerging markets today. There is no question of forcing countries to adopt policies that might precipitate a crisis.

Why would such a system help to secure global policy consistency? First, because it would outlaw national policies like those of China (and some other Asian countries) today, which are focused on the preservation of disequilibrium exchange rates. Second, because it would require an internationally-agreed vision of a set of current account imbalances that would be mutually consistent, since one could not calculate a set of reference rates in the absence of such a vision. Third, it would permit IMF surveillance to become far more effective, not only because the Fund would be charged with ensuring that its members did not violate their obligations by inappropriate intervention, but also because it would close a loophole that permits countries to defend inappropriate demand-management policies.[3] Fourth, provided the reference rates were public knowledge—and it is difficult to believe that in this day and age they could be kept secret even if an attempt were made to preserve confidentiality—they might provide the market with information that would make speculation more stabilizing. Public reference rates might also make public discussion of exchange rate movements more rational; newspapers might be more inclined to comment on whether an exchange rate movement was toward equilibrium instead of equating strengthening with virtue.

Why should member countries take note of Fund advice structured along these lines, when it is well known that they largely ignore such advice as the Fund gives in its current surveillance operations? First, because the Fund would be drawing on a body of analysis that is not available to individual member countries. Without the reference rates and the background of an analysis that sets out a consistent global picture, the IMF offers nothing more than the countries can figure out for themselves. Since each of the major member countries have far more trained economists available to them than the IMF can deploy in any one country, it is rational to take little note of what the Fund says. This changes fundamentally if the Fund is drawing on a body of analysis of what is needed to produce a globally desirable outcome, an analysis which is not available to individual member countries. Second, because the outlines of the desirable outcomes will already have been agreed upon in setting the reference rates; thus, to refuse to comply with surveillance that is guided by those outcomes would be to refuse to will the means to effect an end that has already been mutually agreed to.

Would the Fund obtain sufficient additional leverage by agreement on these ends, such that members would start changing their policies to conform to Fund advice? Or would it also be desirable to change Fund surveillance procedures? My own view is that the main problem has been the lack of a vision of where we want the system to go. I am skeptical that any changes in procedures are likely to have much impact on the major countries, such as the United States and China. If countries have leaders who understand that national interests are advanced by undertaking actions that are consistent with satisfactory global outcomes, and the world has a Fund that can advance a convincing picture of what actions those are, there is some chance that, say, the US Congress can be persuaded to modify its actions. I cannot see it changing its actions because it is bullied by the Fund, no matter what procedural innovations are introduced.

Determining the reference rates

Operating a system of reference exchange rates is obviously dependent on the ability to reach international agreement on what the set of reference rates would be. What would be involved in reaching such an agreement? Is it even conceivable that countries could ever reach agreement?

The IMF now uses two different approaches to calculating estimates of equilibrium exchange rates. One involves an adjusted PPP approach, adjustment being made for factors that are known to influence the equilibrium exchange rate, such as net foreign assets, relative productivity growth, the relative output of manufacturing, and commodity prices. Naturally, this also involves the selection of a base period when the exchange rate appeared to be in rough equilibrium. The other involves a series of partial equilibrium models in which calculations are made of how much impact the restoration of ubiquitous internal balance would have on the balance of payments, after which an elasticities-calculation is performed to find how much exchange rate change is needed to secure external balance as well. An attempt is made to ensure multilateral consistency.[4]

Neither of these approaches, nor any of the other methods that can be found in the literature, claim to be able to identify an equilibrium exchange rate with any precision. In my early work, I suggested that this is one reason for preferring wide target zones, of the order of +/– 10 percent. Some subsequent writers have suggested that even this is over-ambitious, and that a range of +/– 15 percent (as used by the EMS in its final years) is more realistic. One implication is that it is unreasonable to expect that countries will accept obligations to hold exchange rates at levels that can only be calculated subject to such a wide margin of error, but of course a reference rate does not impose such an obligation. Presumably, many countries would not object to the much weaker restraint imposed by a reference rate: of not intervening to push the rate away from what is believed to be the equilibrium rate. This does not, of course, mean that one should not anticipate initial resistance from countries such as China and several other East Asian countries, which are currently maintaining their rates at levels that now fall outside reasonable estimates of equilibrium. But the question to ask is whether it would have appeared unreasonably onerous to them to join a system that contained such a rulebook, and whether, if they had joined, they would not have played by the rules. Some have argued that they have already violated the IMF's rules (by "manipulating" their currency), but in my view the current IMF guidelines on this subject are so ambiguous as to be unenforceable. A well-defined rule might have been expected to elicit the same respect that China has paid to its other international commitments.

The process of determining a set of reference exchange rates might resemble the following: the IMF staff would use their favored approach, or perhaps a variety of approaches, in order to generate a suggested set of reference rates for all IMF member countries. They would present these to the IMF Executive Board at regular intervals (quarterly or half-yearly). Some countries would doubtless object that their proposed reference rate was too strong, and occasionally there might also be a complaint that a proposed rate was too weak. Their Executive Director would make this case to the Board, using a mix of technical arguments—for example, challenging some aspect of the IMF's model, or claiming that the current account target that the IMF had assigned was inappropriate, or arguing that the Fund staff had overlooked certain special factors—and political pleading, as is customary in such contexts. The Board might find itself impressed or unimpressed by the case as made. Where it declared itself impressed, the staff would amend their recommendations appropriately, using a procedure that guaranteed that the set of reference rates remained globally consistent. It would then present its revised recommendations to the Board. If some countries remained dissatisfied, the process might be repeated, in principle, more than once. But it would be necessary for the Board to reach agreement by a defined date, and it would therefore be necessary to agree *ex ante* a process for resolving any differences of opinion that could not be argued out in this way. I do not see that there is an alternative to allowing the (weighted) majority of the Board the ultimate right to impose its views on a minority.

Once agreement had been reached, the set of reference rates would apply for the next three to six months. They would be expressed as effective exchange rates rather than bilateral dollar rates, so that movements of third currencies would not distort policy. Rapidly inflating countries—those with an inflation of more than, say, 10 percent a year—could also have their reference rates adjusted periodically, perhaps monthly, on publication of a pre-specified relevant price index, so as to keep their real reference rates more or less constant.

Is reform conceivable?

Most countries would not see their interests adversely threatened by a reference exchange rate system, since it does not impose any obligation to undertake acts of which they might disapprove, such as defending exchange rates. But that clearly does not apply to all countries. Specifically, since it would prevent the defense of a disequilibrium exchange rate; any country that presently manages its exchange rate and is not confident that its current rate would pass muster with the IMF, would have a clear incentive to oppose reform. In practice, this means that China and a number of other Asian countries that have managed exchange rate systems would have an incentive to oppose reform.

Nevertheless, I see three situations in which reform might occur. One involves the passage of time. Exchange rates do not remain disequilibrium rates forever. Sooner or later, the countries that are currently attempting to defend undervalued currencies will experience adjustment, if not by nominal revaluation, then by inflation—as first discussed by David Hume in the 18th century. When that occurs, they will lose their incentive to oppose adoption of a reference rate system. The disadvantage of this strategy is, of course, that a world crisis of the sort previously outlined may occur before the classic Hume adjustment mechanism has a chance to work.

The second situation in which reform is conceivable is in the midst of a crisis. It can be argued that every significant international monetary change in history has resulted from crisis, not from carefully laid plans. (That assumes that introduction of the Special Drawing Right was not a significant change, but at this point in history one has to acknowledge that this was probably true, even if one might have wished otherwise.) If the world does, indeed, experience the sort of crisis described above, then it is entirely possible that world leaders will search for an alternative system. It behooves us to think now about what they should adopt under such circumstances.

The snag is that, once again, reform would not head off the danger of crisis that is now looming. The third possibility is that world leaders will come to see the need to head off such a crisis *ex ante*, and will therefore adopt such a reform without the spur of a crisis. I would like to believe that such a scenario is likely, but I will believe this when I see it.

REFERENCES

Truman, Edwin M. 2005. "Postponing Global Adjustment: An Analysis of the Pending Adjustment of Global Imbalances." Working Paper 05-6. Washington, D.C.: PIIE. July. Available at: http://www.petersoninstitute.org/publications/wp/wp05-6.pdf

NOTES

1 © Peterson Institute for International Economics: all rights reserved. A background paper written for the World Economic Forum, Davos, 2006. The author is indebted to Edwin Truman for comments on a previous draft.

2 In technical terms there are n countries but only $n-1$ exchange rates, so that equal rights to decisionmaking implies a need to reach multilateral agreement.

3 At the moment there is no clear criterion as to whether a country is pursuing excessively contractionary or expansionary policies. As long as these do not result in recession or inflation in that particular country, the IMF has no basis to complain, even if the set of policies being pursued by all its member countries is collectively inconsistent with a satisfactory global outcome. Adoption of the reference rate proposal would replace this situation by a criterion that is in principle well defined and consistent with an acceptable global outcome. A country would be judged guilty of excessively expansionary policies, if its level of domestic demand exceeded the sum of potential output plus its equilibrium current account deficit, even if an appreciation of its exchange rate above the reference rate were masking the inflationary potential inherent in this situation. Conversely, a country would be judged to have deficient demand, if its domestic demand was less than its productive potential by more than its equilibrium current account surplus, even if this shortfall were being masked by a depreciation of its exchange rate below its reference rate and an enlarged current account surplus.

4 This is inspired by the same philosophy as that from which my own estimations of fundamental equilibrium exchange rates were made, though these involved the simulation of macroeconometric models.

CHAPTER 4.4

The Future of the International Monetary Fund

NOURIEL ROUBINI, Professor of Economics and International Business, Stern School of Business, New York University, and Chairman, Roubini Global Economics

BRAD SETSER, Director of Global Research, Roubini Global Economics, and Research Associate, Global Economic Governance Center, University College, Oxford

---

Warnings issued by the International Monetary Fund (IMF) are rarely heeded. Voting weights on the IMF board no longer reflect countries' current economic clout, calling into question its legitimacy as a referee of global problems. Calls for regional institutions to address regional financial problems are growing. A key source of the IMF influence in the 1990s and early years of this decade—its ability to lend out its reserves to countries in need—seems less relevant in a world where many emerging market economies have too many reserves, not too few, and spend too little, not too much. No surprise, the IMF is in something of a funk.

There is no doubt that the IMF has to evolve along with the global economy. There also should be little doubt that a global economy needs an effective IMF. The policy choices of every country, acting on its own, or the actions of individual market participants, looking out for their own immediate interests, can put international monetary and financial stability at risk. A global institution like the IMF is needed to:

- Identify potentially dangerous imbalances in the global economy early on, and encourage countries to take action to reduce those imbalances. If imbalances do reach unsustainable levels, the IMF can help to ensure a coordinated global response to these imbalances. An effective policy response usually requires adjustments in both debtor countries (right now, the US) and creditor countries.

- Serve as referee for disputes over exchange rates. The IMF must ensure that countries do not use their exchange rate policies to prevent necessary adjustments to the global current account; the likely alternative to a global referee is unilateral action, and growing protectionism.

• Coordinate the provision of crisis liquidity—conditioned on necessary policy adjustments—when the uncoordinated actions of market participants result in liquidity runs that could give rise to costly crises. Crises in major emerging economies can impact the entire world, not just the individual country and its creditors. Plus, by lending when others cannot and thus helping to shape the policies adopted by a debtor in default, the IMF can help to coordinate a sovereign debt restructuring.

So long as the IMF shareholders, management and staff do not shy away from taking on the core problems of the global economy, the IMF will remain at the center of cooperative attempts to address global financial problems.

In the fall of 2005, Barry Eichengreen first called the IMF a "rudderless ship adrift in sea of liquidity."[1] The sea of liquidity has only grown larger since then. Global reserve growth continues at an unprecedented pace, with China and the world's oil exporters in the lead. But the repayment of many of the large loans which the Fund extended earlier this decade—both Brazil and Argentina repaid the Fund in full around at the end of 2005—seems to have helped the IMF find a rudder. Rodrigo de Rato is pushing for essential updates in the Fund's governance structure and a new process for multilateral surveillance has made the Fund a firm advocate for a coordinated global response to global imbalances.

Most key players in the global economy are likely to conclude that a reformed global institution capable of delivering global solutions is preferable to regional solutions. Countries' financial defenses are not tested when global growth is strong, when global interest rates are unusually low, and private capital flowing to emerging economies, but, rather, when growth slows, interest rates rise, and private capital flows out. The IMF should be taking advantage of this period of relative calm to update its lending policies. Demand for global policy coordination was weak during a period when the world's surplus countries happily financed a growing US current account deficit. But that situation may change if the American consumer is not willing to borrow quite so much—as US home prices fall—or if the rest of the world is no longer willing to increase the amount of credit it extends to the U.S. Disputes over exchange rates will likely become more vociferous should the global economy slow. The orderly resolution of global imbalances likely requires more, not less, multilateral surveillance.

Each of these points is worth exploring in more depth.

Regionalism is an unattractive substitute for reformed global institutions

Asia has been threatening to create an Asian Monetary Fund. The United States seems to be disillusioned with multilateral institutions, often preferring unilateralism. Europe is focused on its territory. A world where Asian economies work together to take care of financial troubles in Asia, Western Europe protects the accession countries in Eastern Europe, and the U.S. unilaterally responds to trouble in Latin America and the strategically important Middle East is not impossible to imagine.

That is a world in which global institutions like the IMF would be marginalized. Its function, in practice if not in theory, would be limited to countries that fall outside the orbit of regional "financial" hegemony. The IMF would set the macroeconomic policy framework for African countries dependent on concessional aid flows from the G-7 and other rich countries, but would do little else. The activities of the IMF and World Bank would become harder and harder to distinguish from each other.

This vision has serious problems. Its architecture leaves truly global problems unaddressed, at a time when a truly global problem—the so called global imbalances—looms over the world economy. The surpluses that finance the unprecedented US external deficit are found all over the globe: in Asia, in places with lots of oil, and even in Latin America. Coordinated global efforts to stimulate demand in all surplus regions would make it easier to bring down the US deficit—provided, of course, that the US is also willing to take steps to reduce its need for external financing.

Moreover, relying on regional hegemons and institutions to solve regional financial problems is not without its difficulties. The first impulse of the United States when confronted with a crisis in its backyard (Mexico) was to take care of the problem on its own. But the Clinton administration plan to have the US government guarantee a large Mexican bond issue ran into political problems in Washington. The Clinton administration concluded that it was better to share the burden of crisis lending globally—and worked hard to build up the IMF's lending capacity, not US bilateral lending capacity.

Ironically, the Bush administration, generally no friend of multilateral institutions or standing alliances, has, through its actions if not its rhetoric, recognized the wisdom of the multilateral approach. Look at the large IMF loans extended to Argentina, Brazil, Uruguay, and Turkey. Europe's own institutions for regional cooperation are well developed, but its institutions for extending rescue loans are not. Neither the Commission nor the ECB is set up in ways that would make the financial "bailout" to current and future accession countries easy.

An Asian regional response to financial troubles in a major Asian economy poses even larger problems. Asia's potential financial hegemons (Japan and China) are themselves strategic rivals. Their capacity to act jointly remains untested. Asia likes to complain about IMF conditionality, but it is not clear that either Japan or China—both traditionally stingy lenders on a bilateral basis—would be prepared to lend US$20 billion to an Asian country in distress without strict conditions. Yet concerns about regional solidarity may make imposing tough conditions by one Asian country on another difficult. Continuing to outsource crisis conditionality to global institutions remains a better alternative to developing effective regional institutions, as the world needs institutions able to reach agreement on the hard questions.

IMF governance reform

All three key regions in the global economy have reason to prefer effective global financial firefighting to purely regional solutions. And fortunately, the reforms needed to give the IMF renewed global legitimacy are relatively easy—at least compared to the reforms needed in the other key post-war international institutions. The needed reforms do not require changing the fundamental principle of IMF governance, which is one dollar (i.e. one SDR) one vote, not one country one vote or one person one vote. They simply require shifting the distribution of IMF "chairs" and "shares," so that they reflect countries current economic clout, not their economic clout in 1950, 1970, or even 1990. Right now, Europe is clearly overrepresented, and Asia is clearly underrepresented.[2] The basic outlines of a solution are well known: Asia's voting weight should be increased, and both Europe's voting weight and the number of chairs occupied by European countries should be reduced. Even if the euro zone is not willing to consolidate its representation into a single chair, there is no reason, for example, why the Benelux countries should have two chairs on the board.

The U.S. is not overrepresented, but revitalizing the IMF would clearly be far easier if both the U.S. and Europe showed greater flexibility. Europe must recognize that it will not maximize its real power if it maintains an overweight position in an institution that plays a smaller and smaller global role. And the U.S. must recognize that changing the way the existing pie is divided is politically far harder than divvying up a growing pie in slightly different way. The recent agreement on an "ad hoc" increase in the quotas of China, Korea, Mexico, and Turkey was easy. The Fund's total size increased only modestly, by around US$5 billion, and no one had to give anything up. The next step in this two-step reform will be far harder. Letting the IMF's resources grow in line with a growing world economy—a generalized increase in quotas—would make the redistribution of relative quota share from Europe to Asia far easier.

The IMF should be prepared for a more unstable world

The case against an expanded IMF is simple: the IMF currently has as much money as it needs. That view, however, is short-sighted. Capital is not going to flow from relatively poor emerging markets to the United States forever. High-saving Asia may be able to finance its own development, though traditionally, rapidly growing Asian economies have not financed both high levels of investment in their own economies and the savings-short U.S. But low-saving regions like Latin America and Africa are unlikely to be able to sustain the investment needed for rapid growth, without drawing on the world's savings. Private flows to emerging markets are already back at their pre-crisis levels, though right now, that private flow is financing the extraordinary levels of reserve accumulation in emerging markets, not large current account deficits.

But even today, not all emerging markets are in great shape. Some emerging market economies, above all China, clearly have more reserves than they need. But others, such as Turkey, Philippines, and Indonesia, do not. At least not yet. All these countries still have relatively large stocks of domestic debt and comparatively small reserves, and one of the lessons of recent crises is that, if a country's own citizens lose confidence in their own government's ability to honor its financial commitments, a crisis soon follows.

We should not forget that IMF lending peaked in 2003, not in 1998, and that the IMF had a larger stock of outstanding loans in mid-2005 than it did in mid-2000. Forecasts that the IMF no longer has to be ready to lend to countries which are temporarily short of hard currency are rather premature. The IMF should be using the current lull to draw lessons from this experience, and to put in place policies that clarify when it should lend, and when it should *not*. Neither large bailouts loans to countries short of foreign currency —temporarily, one would hope—nor major sovereign debt restructurings are likely to disappear.

But without the impetus of an actual crisis, the pressure to develop a more realistic IMF lending policy has disappeared. The IMF's major shareholders (The G-7 countries) are, in theory, committed to trying to get the IMF to go back to its traditional lending limits, which have not been upheld in major crises since Mexico. The irony is clear: the G-7 wants to scale back the ability of emerging economies to borrow reserves from the IMF at a time when those same emerging economies have concluded that they need far *more* reserves to navigate through the turbulence created by volatile international capital flows. The stewards of the global financial order want to scale back the insurance provided by the IMF, just as emerging markets—by their decision to build up their reserves, a form of self-insurance—decided that they needed far more insurance.

The absence of a greater willingness to engage in an honest dialogue about the IMF's lending role is unfortunate. There are plenty of important issues to resolve. Not only is there a large gap between the amounts the IMF says it will lend—in theory—and the far larger amounts that it has actually lent in recent crises, but it is also clear that the IMF has been pushed, in times of crisis, to do far more than just lend out reserves to meet short-terms financing needs, the classic role of a lender of last resort. It some cases, the IMF has acted more like a long-term financier of last resort to strategically important countries. Turkey is a prime example: the IMF financed a long-term program of fiscal consolidation to let Turkey grow out of a debt problem. Turkey looks to be a success, but it is still not clear to us that the IMF should be in the business of long-term financing for middle-income countries.

The G-7 claim—without much credibility—that IMF should *never* loan large sums again. Emerging economies often say the IMF should *always* loan large sums, to help avoid either a debt restructuring or any change in their exchange rate regime. Neither approach is right. A sensible compromise would raise the IMF's lending limits to reflect the higher levels of reserves countries need to navigate sometimes turbulent global markets, but also set out the stronger expectation that IMF funds would be loaned only for short-term needs.

An IMF structured in such a way as to make large loans, but only for truly short-term needs, would not be in a position to give every emerging market sufficient credit to avoid any debt restructuring. A key lesson from Argentina is that if a country starts out with high levels of debt—particularly in conjunction with an overvalued exchange rate—IMF funds should be used to soften the blow from the restructuring, not to finance a futile attempt to avoid any restructuring—and in Argentina's case, maintain an overvalued exchange rate. After Argentina defaulted, the IMF, in part because it lacked support from the US Treasury, largely abdicated its role as crisis manager, and did not work to set out an economic framework that would guide Argentina's debt restructuring. The United States wanted to leave economic policy negotiations to Argentina and its private creditors. In practice, this "hands-off" policy meant that Argentina unilaterally decided how much it wanted to adjust, and how much it could pay. Even when the IMF does not provide enough credit to avoid a restructuring, it should help a debtor in default (or in need of restructuring) to plan an economic adjustment program which creates the basis for rapid agreement on the terms of its debt restructuring with its creditors and promotes quick economic and financial recovery.[3]

Managing the international monetary system

Right now, the most pressing issues facing the Fund do not center around Fund lending, but rather on the Fund's capacity to encourage countries to take the steps needed to prevent financial vulnerabilities from rising to levels that risk a major crisis. And even more unusually, the greatest risk of a crisis comes not from the emerging world, but rather from the Fund's biggest shareholder, the United States.

In recent years, innovations in IMF surveillance have largely been motivated by the need to do a better job of identifying potential vulnerabilities in emerging market economies. The Fund is paying more attention to the health of countries' banking systems, as it must if its lending is often used to allow a national central bank to act as a lender of last resort in dollars (or other foreign currency) to its local banking system. The Fund has refined its analysis of debt sustainability, as it must if it wants to differentiate between temporary liquidity problems—which can be financed with short-term money—and deeper solvency problems which should not be financed. And it is looking more at so-called balance-sheet vulnerabilities, such as the currency mismatches which are still pervasive in many emerging economies. Indeed, its analysis of the balance sheet vulnerabilities of some key emerging markets, like those of Lebanon and Turkey, far surpasses typical market analysis in its depth and quality.

Now is hardly the time to stop worrying about these vulnerabilities. One of the advantages of a global institution is that it can learn from the problems of a wide range of countries, and help countries in one part of the globe avoid the same mistakes already made by others. Many emerging market economies remain a long way from a truly clean financial bill of health. Large external deficits and growing external debt loads are clearly less of a concern than they have been in the past. But domestic debt levels remain high. And, as was said earlier, in a globalized world, if a country's citizens lose confidence in the country's government or the local banks, they will quickly shift their funds abroad. If a) the global housing bubble bursts (slowing global growth), b) the growth of credit derivatives concentrates risk in the hands of leveraged institutions rather than dispersing it, or c) US interest rates rise suddenly, then some of these latent vulnerabilities may emerge.

Increasingly, though, Fund surveillance will have to do more than simply identify financial vulnerabilities in emerging markets early enough so that they can be corrected without a crisis. The Fund must also identify national policies that impede the global adjustments needed to bring about an orderly rebalancing of the world economy. And it must do so in forums that count. The IMF's research department has not hesitated to highlight the risks posed by widening imbalances in the *World Economic Outlook*. But, too often, the Fund's actual dialogue with its member countries neglected the need for national policies to support global adjustment.

Important steps have been taken to try to address this weakness. Agreement to launch a new multilateral surveillance process that would bring surplus and deficit countries together, to discuss how both can take constructive steps to promote global adjustment was enough to turn Morgan Stanley's bearish chief economist Steve Roach bullish. We are not quite that optimistic. The Fund has identified the right people to gather around the table. The Gulf Cooperation Council countries and China are now as important sources of the global current account surplus as Japan. A fall in the US deficit clearly would be far easier if Europe's current import boom continues, helping to support global demand growth during the adjustment process.

But getting the right group around the table is the easy part. Getting those countries to agree to change established policies is likely to prove far more difficult. Consider the most prominent deficit and surplus countries. The United States continues to argue that fiscal deficits have little link to current account deficits, and refuses to countenance higher taxes to help close its structural fiscal deficit—and restrain demand growth. China continues to argue that its exchange rate peg is not the reason for its soaring current account surplus. And it has shown little willingness to allow the renminbi to appreciate meaningfully. The nominal appreciation in the renminbi in the first six months of 2006 was less than 1 percent, barely enough to make up for lower Chinese than American inflation, and not enough to offset the dollar's depreciation against the euro in the same time period. China's willingness to allow a faster rate of appreciation of its currency remains unclear.

The Fund has not hesitated to call on the United States to implement a more ambitious program of fiscal adjustment, one that aims to eliminate the fiscal deficit over the course of the economic cycle. It has been less willing to identify the policy changes needed in surplus countries. IMF surveillance has been somewhat asymmetric. The IMF has, correctly, argued that the US fiscal adjustment program is insufficiently ambitious. The IMF's executive board has not said anything similar in public about China's (insignificant) renminbi revaluation. And it remains largely silent—at least when it counts—on the Gulf countries' policy of pegging their currencies to the dollar. Yet the recent growth in China's surplus has been every bit as impressive as the recent increase in the US deficit, and it hardly makes sense for the Gulf's real exchange rate to depreciate, even as the real value of their oil exports has increased. The fact that many surplus countries, including China and Saudi Arabia, have tied their currency closely to the currency of the world's biggest deficit country is clearly an impediment to effective global adjustment.

The Fund traditionally has been uncomfortable acting as a referee calling out inappropriate exchange rate pegs, and—ironically given its mandate—is generally far less comfortable doling out advice on a country's exchange rate policies than on a country's fiscal policy.[4] That was true when a country like Argentina intervened heavily to maintain an overvalued exchange rate, and it remains true when countries like China, Malaysia, Russia, and Saudi Arabia intervene heavily to keep their currencies from appreciating. Argentina's steadfast defense of its own exchange rate put its own financial health at risk. China's steadfast support for the US dollar has not directly put its own financial health at risk, as China's external balance sheet is strong. But the surge in domestic money growth associated with China's rapid reserve growth is one reason why China has had trouble controlling domestic credit growth, and preventing its economy from over-heating. Yet even with strong domestic growth, China's current account surplus is surging; it will likely top US$225 billion, or 8 percent of China's GDP in 2006. Reigning in domestic demand to curb over-heating, without letting the exchange rate adjust would likely lead to an even larger surplus.

The IMF must be more willing to publicly highlight countries with undervalued exchange rates, as well as those with inappropriate fiscal policies, but it must act with care. The IMF should focus on *all* exchange rates that impede global adjustment—not only those most politically salient in the U.S. If oil prices stay as high as the futures markets now predict, the oil exporters' dollar pegs are probably as large an impediment to global adjustment as China's peg. And the IMF should continuously remind the U.S. that if surplus countries adjust, deficit countries like the U.S. will be forced to adjust too.

Finally, the IMF should be aware that calling China's exchange rate regime an impediment to global adjustment may have a larger impact than calling US fiscal deficits an impediment to global adjustment. In fact, the United States largest creditors—right now, China, Russia, and Saudi Arabia—have not cut back on their financing of the U.S. after the latter signaled that it plans to ignore the IMF's fiscal advice. But the U.S. might start a process that would lead to much higher tariffs on Chinese goods, if China ignores a clear IMF signal that it is pegging to the dollar at too low a level.

The Fund's reluctance to go beyond vague calls for greater flexibility, and to identify countries with undervalued currencies, reflects its desire to avoid being a club that beats up on Asia—particularly at a time when Asia is under-represented inside the Fund. But the alternative to having the IMF act as an umpire that identifies when countries' exchange rate policies are acting as an impediment to global adjustment is not a continuation of the status quo. Trade tensions are rising. They could well boil over, particularly if the US economy slows, as now seems likely. If the IMF does not act, the U.S. will eventually take the law into its own hands and charge China of currency manipulation, thus acting as plaintiff, judge, and jury in that trial. Such unilateralism would not be a good outcome for the international financial system.

A renewed focus of IMF surveillance on exchange rates, exchange rate regimes, and the global balance of payments is not simply a necessary response to current conjuncture. Looking ahead, it is reasonable to expect significant changes in the world's monetary and exchange rate arrangements over the next few years. Hong Kong is unlikely to combine a de facto monetary union with the U.S. and a political union with China for ever. Asia more generally is likely to find another way to maintain stability in intra-Asian exchange rates, other than by linking their currencies, either formally or informally, to the US dollar. Oil exporters would be better served pegging to the Canadian dollar or another "commodity" currency than to the American dollar. Africa probably has too many currencies. New monetary unions may form. Some existing monetary unions may come under pressure. Some smaller countries may dollarize or euroize. As exchange rate arrangements evolve, the IMF has to work to make sure national choices are consistent with global interest in financial stability, and that countries do not solve national problems by pushing their costs onto the rest of the world.

Conclusion

A globalized world may finance domestic imbalances for a longer period of time, but it does not eliminate the risks created by sustained exchange rate misalignments or poor macroeconomic policies. Global imbalances and national financial crises that can spill over into global markets are best addressed by a global institution like the IMF. But the IMF's ability to act in the global interest hinges on a governance structure that is up to date, and reflects current global realities. A global institution like the IMF can both learn from all countries' experience, and draw on that experience to help assess country's debt sustainability, and also look for weaknesses in national financial systems and balance sheets. But crises in emerging markets will not disappear. The IMF's ability to lend in a crisis makes it the central institution for crisis resolution. The IMF can work to try to ensure that financial and current account imbalances are addressed rather than ignored, and that they are addressed by policies that are not destructive of global prosperity. The core insight of Keynes and Dexter-White, that a global economy needs global institutions, will continue to stand the test of time.

NOTES

1 Eichengreen, 2006.

2 Europe (including Russia) accounts for 40 percent of IMF's voting weight, and holds up to 10 of the 24 seats on the IMF's Executive Board; Spain and Mexico rotate sitting on the Board; Japan, China, India and the rest of East Asia account for only 16 percent of the IMF's total vote, and hold only five chairs.

3 US Under Secretary Tim Adams seems to have backed away from the "hands-off" policy of his predecessor, though his commitment to a stronger IMF role in future debt restructurings remains largely untested. For a more systematic discussion of the role of the IMF in crisis resolution see Roubini and Setser, 2004.

4 The Fund's articles allow a country to pick its own exchange rate regime; thus, every country clearly has the right to peg its exchange rate, if it so wants. But that does not mean that a country can peg its rate at any level it chooses and not be subject to external criticism. The Fund's articles explicitly give the fund a role in identifying exchange rate policies that are an impediment to effective global adjustment.

REFERENCES

Eichengreen, B. 2006. "The IMF adrift in a sea of liquidity." E. Truman, ed. *Reforming the IMF for the 21st Century*. Washington, D.C.: IIE. April. Available at: http://www.iie.com/publications/chapters_preview/3870/25iie3870.pdf

Roubini, N. and B. Setser. 2004. "Bailouts or Bail-ins? Responding to Financial Crises in Emerging Economies." Washington, D.C.: Institute for International Economics.

International Monetary Fund. Various years. *World Economic Outlook*. Washington, D.C.: IMF.

Rethinking the IMF Business Model: Proposals for Assessment and Reform of the IMF's Medium-Term Strategy

ANGEL UBIDE, Director of Global Economics, Tudor Investment Corporation, and Centre for European Policy Studies

Introduction

Since the Asian crisis, the IMF has undergone a deep process of soul searching. External criticism has been abundant, and all three of the IMF's main areas of work: surveillance, crisis prevention and resolution, and poverty reduction, have been called into question. Ten years later, there is a feeling that not much has been achieved, and key questions remain unanswered. As the world business cycle matures, and thus the likelihood of further crises increases, it is critical for the stability of the world financial system to seriously rethink what the IMF's business model should look like.

We approached this issue at a conference in March 2005,[1] where I made the proposals outlined below. In April 2006, the IMF presented specific proposals for its Medium-Term Strategy,[2] incorporating some of my suggestions, and these were discussed at the September 2006 Annual Meetings. However, as indicated below, while the IMF proposals are tentative steps in the right direction, they are likely to prove insufficient to tackle the challenges that the IMF will be facing in the near future. More importantly, they reveal a lack of direction and conviction on the part of the G-7 as regards the type of institution the IMF should be. It is worrisome to see that, following some of the worst practices in structural reform, the focus seems to be on the process rather than on the substance. Focusing on the quota formula is a way of avoiding the key question: what type of IMF does the G-7 want? A redistribution of power can easily be accommodated within the current algebra of quotas—provided that a political agreement is achieved regarding the US veto power and other sticky points. But the focus on the quota formula distracts us from the more important question: what should the IMF look like in order to be an effective player in the 21st century?

We also argued that recent market events reinforce my conviction that the proposal I made for the creation of an insurance facility is critical for the resolution of the global imbalance. In the last two years, sudden spikes in risk aversion—unrelated to emerging market fundamentals, including the downgrading of General Motors' debt in 2005 and the inflation scare in April and May of 2006—led to a sell off in emerging market assets. The behavior of the markets clearly indicated that, unless emerging markets are provided with a valid alternative, the incentive structure that leads these countries to accumulate reserves as a self-insurance mechanism will not change, leaving the global imbalance unresolved. It was telling that markets quickly differentiated between countries with current account surpluses and countries with current account deficits. This happened, despite the fact that the April-May 2006 event was a liquidity run, sparked by a sudden increase in risk aversion, originating in an inflationary scare in the United States paralleling a US dollar decline, and was, thus, completely unrelated to emerging market fundamentals. The hardest hit countries (Turkey, South Africa, and Hungary) all presented large external imbalances. Turkey, especially, had to raise rates significantly, in order to stem the currency decline, and its fundamentals were affected by the liquidity run. The message is clear: a large current account surplus and thus a large reserve pool is an effective insurance mechanism against sudden market panics that lead to capital flight to quality, as the spring 2006 episode clearly demonstrated.

The second message of that episode is that disorderly adjustments of the global imbalance, triggered mostly by increases in risk aversion, lead to a stabilization and even appreciation of the US dollar against emerging market currencies, as flight to quality prevails. Thus, emerging markets are well-advised to accumulate foreign exchange reserves. This flies in the face of countless statements and policy recommendations based on the hypothesis that a dollar collapse is imminent, which suggest that further and deeper analysis of the issue is sorely needed,[3] and that increasing politicization of the issue is clouding the focus of policy-makers.

What is the IMF business model?

The IMF has traditionally had three core competencies, combining a consulting company, a central bank, and an NGO, and carrying out the following functions: pro-bono surveillance and technical assistance, conditional lending at penalty rates to resolve external financing shortfalls, and conditional lending at concessional rates to alleviate poverty. Against this backdrop, globalization and capital market integration have changed the world economy in fundamental ways, and, simultaneously, the needs of the prospective clients of the IMF. Thus, the organization must adapt to the new circumstances or risk becoming largely irrelevant and losing its clients.

Therefore, a comprehensive rethinking of the IMF business model is a priority, both for its own purposes, and as fundamental input for a comprehensive review of the governance and the financial viability of the IMF. With participation in loan programs at its lowest level since the 1970s, and at the risk of losing its customer base, the financing structure of the IMF must be reconsidered. In what follows, I review the outlook for the three core business areas of the IMF, discuss its implications for governance and financing, and then assess the IMF proposals with respect to my diagnosis.

Surveillance

What is the value of IMF surveillance? Traditionally, IMF reports were highly valued because of their sophisticated analysis, privileged access to generally unavailable data, and privileged discussions with authorities. Nowadays, the comparative advantage of the IMF in these three fields has declined. In no small measure, this has come to pass because of the IMF's own data dissemination policies, and because economic and market data for a large variety of developing countries are now readily available. In addition, as a result of the post-1997 drive for more transparency in economic policies around the world—again promoted by the IMF as part of the crisis-prevention framework —open discussions between market analysts and policy-makers are now both frank and frequent, a far cry from the secrecy that was widespread a decade ago. The IMF continues to produce sophisticated analyses, but the distance between the institution and the markets has diminished, especially as regards the framework used, as investment banks have loaded their teams with former IMF staff. Moreover, the widespread use of inflation targeting around the world, with its requirements of frequent disclosure of sophisticated economic analyses, has reduced the relative superiority of IMF analysis.[4]

However, the IMF still retains two key advantages: the first is the longer-term focus, which allows it to concentrate on structural issues which markets may ignore; the second is its cross-country and regional work. But even in this area, competition is still tough, especially from the OECD.

Over this diminished value hovers an important question, namely the independence of its analysis, especially for the large countries. And the more countries grow in economic size, the greater will be the doubts about independence, since voting power at the IMF Board is biased toward the larger shareholders.

The surveillance process itself is not independent. When the clients are the shareholders, incentive problems are sure to arise, and conflict is almost guaranteed between providing useful but friendly advice and signalling politically difficult problems. Topics and issues in Article IV consultations are typically negotiated ex-ante, with countries strongly resisting the IMF analysis of sensitive issues, and some government making ample use of their right-to-deletion authority on politically sensitive issues, often masked as "market-sensitive." This has frequently led times to a don't-upset-the-authorities mindset, which results in less effective work. Looking ahead, this mindset is a major drawback in a world where some of the large countries pose a critical risk to the world economy. The current debate on exchange rate manipulation is a case in point, where there is strong suspicion that the political interests of the key players is behind the IMF's views, thus making the IMF largely ineffective in this critical area. The IMF should certainly adopt a more decisive role in uncovering the weaknesses of the developed economies, and in providing sound and critical advice. When tough messages have to be hidden in the *World Economic Outlook*, instead of being frankly and openly expressed in Article IV discussions, when critical aspects of the economy are simply not up for discussion, and when the outcome of the Article IV Consultations is published late on Friday afternoon in mid-summer—for it is countries, not staff, which decide on the publication time and date—something is obviously amiss.

Independence would likely improve accuracy. Eggertsson and Le Borgne (2004) argue that delegating policy to an independent official implies awarding a long-term job contract, which, in turn, gives the official an incentive to put more effort into the policy-making process than an elected politician. This extra effort translates, in expectations, into better forecasts and fewer policy mistakes, which increases social welfare—and the usefulness of the official— thereby making delegation compatible with incentive. Applying this principle to the surveillance work of the IMF suggests that the staff, and not the Board, should have the ultimate responsibility for surveillance.

Thus, it is clear that the IMF must regain its edge in its surveillance work, in order to strengthen its credibility and independence. It may become necessary to separate surveillance from lending activities, with surveillance work not requiring the tacit approval of the Board, given that no lending—and thus no financial risk—is involved and eliminating the right to delete market sensitive issues from surveillance documents. Thus, the staff should be able to evaluate the market sensitivity of its analysis. This would certainly improve the credibility and appeal of the surveillance work.

Conditional lending to alleviate poverty

The IMF has been involved in concessional lending since the 1980s. However, the recommendations of the Meltzer Commission[5] and recent research suggest that grants, and not loans, should become the bulk of the financing of poverty alleviation programs. The recent moves toward debt forgiveness in the context of the Paris Club are manifestations of this trend, culminating in the total write-off of all official loans to the poorest countries of the G-8 summit in July 2005. The conclusion from economic analysis is not clear cut. There is a basic trade-off in which, for a given level of assistance, more concessionality means less repayment obligations, but also fewer resources available for donors to offer to recipient countries. For the poorest countries, however, the result is unambiguous: providing them with larger, but less concessional, aid packages could negatively affect both their current and future growth performance, through the accumulation of a stock of eventually unsustainable debt.

This view is gaining proponents, and has shaped some of the features of the Heavily Indebted Poor Countries (HIPC) program. The donor community is moving toward the view that any new HIPC borrowing—after debt relief is granted—should be on highly concessional terms, preferably in the form of grants. This would avoid repeating the mistakes of the past, when large loans left poor countries both poor and more heavily indebted. Countries that are (relatively) richer, but highly indebted and/or have bad policy frameworks should also receive grants rather than loans, in order to minimize excessive debt accumulation and avoid exacerbating the suffering of the population due to the bad policies. This way, lending would—at least in theory—only be confined to the smaller subset of richer, less-indebted and better-managed countries.

In any event, the political momentum suggests that, in the future, grants will likely represent the bulk of financing for poverty alleviation, and that loans extended today will have a low probability of repayment tomorrow. This will certainly put further strain on the financing framework of the IMF, and raises the question of whether the IMF should continue to be in the business of poverty alleviation.

Conditional lending at penalty rates to resolve external financing crises

Implementing sustainable macro policies, developing strong and sound financial systems, and crafting robust institutions are objectives shared, in principle, by all countries. But this takes time, in many cases generations, and thus a bumpy road has to be expected in many cases. There will always be crises, and very likely they will be unexpected. The key is to reduce their frequency, duration, and cost, and to minimize the scope for contagion. In such instances, robust frameworks for crisis prevention and resolution are needed.

Since the Mexican and Asian crises, there has been intensive work to improve the crisis management capabilities of the IMF. Efforts have been focused on two main areas: crisis prevention and crisis resolution. Progress in crisis prevention has been achieved mainly in the area of data dissemination, surveillance, and transparency of policies. However, progress in crisis resolution has been scant, to say the least. Conditionality has been streamlined and Collective Action Clauses have become more popular. But the failure of the sovereign debt restructuring mechanism (SDRM) and the elimination of the contingent credit lines (CCL) at the IMF means that we are basically where we were ten years ago. And, as the Argentinean saga shows, the current framework is ill-suited to dealing with large-scale debt restructurings.

The main problem with the current and proposed frameworks for crisis resolution is that they do not tackle the transition between liquidity and solvency problems. A standstill (bankruptcy) process tries to minimize the costs of the resolution of a solvency problem, but it does not prevent a liquidity problem from spiralling into a solvency problem.

In the continuum of possible products, there is, therefore, a critical gap in the business model/framework of the international financial institutions (IFIs). There is a framework to deal with poverty, a framework to deal with external solvency problems in developing countries, and a framework to deal with solvent developed countries. But there is no effective framework to deal with temporarily illiquid, but solvent, developing countries. In other words, there are frameworks for crisis prevention and for crisis resolution, but not for crisis management.

The big difference between current account and capital account crises is that the latter develop very rapidly and easily become self-fulfilling through exchange rate/debt spirals. The key factor in these crises is a collapse in confidence, which, if not addressed quickly, can rapidly transform otherwise sustainable debt levels into unsustainable ones. It is no secret that the size of the IMF's rescue packages has increased significantly in recent years: since the Mexican crisis of 1995, there have been nine cases of very large programs, with total packages representing several multiples of the theoretical access limits. Given the ongoing integration of global capital markets, this is a clear indication of the shape of future crises. The intensification of regional integration will probably reduce these confidence crises, but the heightened interconnection will probably lead to fewer, but potentially more intense, crises. So a strategy for reducing the scope for contagion becomes a vital necessity.

Emerging markets are clearly signalling with their actions their desire for a crisis management framework that can tackle modern capital account crises. The process of regional integration in South East Asia and the development of regional cross-country initiatives—including the Chiang Mai Initiative and the Asian Bond Fund—and the accumulation of reserves by the region's central banks are clear moves toward the development of an insurance framework that minimizes the risk of solvency problems stemming from liquidity crunches.[6] As Kawai (2004) describes it, the Chiang Mai initiative is a liquidity support facility designed to manage regional currency attacks, contagion, and crises. And reserves at the major emerging markets have increased by over 300 percent in the last decade (Truman, 2005).

One fundamental principle of good management is to listen to your customers. Prospective Asian IMF clients are sending a clear message: they are not really interested in its current services of crisis resolution, and they would rather have (and pay for) an insurance framework that enables them to prevent crises and not have to resort to an IMF program to resolve them. After all, by the time an IMF program is put in place, a significant output loss has already been incurred. Another set of prospective IMF clients, the emerging economies of Eastern Europe, are gravitating toward the EU and counting on an EU anchor to avoid future recourse to the IMF. Liquidity crunches during the convergence process cannot be ruled out, but as soon as they enter Exchange Rate Mechanism II (ERM II), the European Central Bank will play a larger role in ensuring currency stability. They have, de facto, secured an insurance framework with the EU.

There is therefore a strong drive toward securing regional insurance mechanisms that reduce the risks of a liquidity crisis. It seems clear that only countries deprived of a strong regional anchor are likely to continue to form the client base of the IMF in its current form. And even those would likely prefer to have some form of insurance that minimizes the need for a fully fledged IMF program. In fact, Brazil has already proposed the establishment of a facility that prevents crises, particularly those related to changing market sentiment unrelated to emerging markets.

In order to pre-empt the criticism that an insurance facility could lead to moral hazard, let me stress that there is very little empirical support for the existence of moral hazard. As Frankel (2004) points out, a political leader in a developing country is twice as likely to lose office in the six months following a currency crash than otherwise. A far as lenders' moral hazard is concerned, Jeanne and Zettelmeyer (2004) argue that it is difficult to find any evidence of moral hazard in the data. And after the recent defaults of Ecuador, Russia, Ukraine, Uruguay, and Argentina, it should be clear to investors that default does happen.

Moreover, there is a clear confusion in terms. There may be at times a problem of "too big to fail," or "too big to unwind in an orderly fashion," which prevents the correct pricing of risks in some instances. But this is not a problem of moral hazard. And this applies to all large countries, emerging or not. Why is the United States being lent money at very low interest rates, despite its large fiscal and current account deficits, if not because it is considered too big to fail?

There are additional advantages to the establishment of an insurance facility. Eliminating the need for country self-insurance would also eliminate the current distortions in exchange rate markets, and contribute to a smoother resolution of global imbalances. In addition, countries will be more likely to implement structural reforms if the expected pay-off from these reforms is higher.[7] An insurance device would extend the planning horizon of policy-makers and improve the incentive structure to undertake costly structural reforms.

What would an insurance facility look like? I would argue for an insurance mechanism which, by means of a liquidity window at pre-determined interest rates, provides eligible countries with a line of credit that caps the rollover cost in the event of a liquidity run. The technical details would be along the lines of Cordella and Levy-Yeyati (2005): countries could temporarily borrow from the facility, with a spread above pre-crisis levels, but capped at a level that does not threaten solvency. It would, in many respects, be similar to the liquidity assistance provided by a central bank to its banking sector. If a country, after using the facility for a short period, is still in need of assistance, an IMF program would then be negotiated, in the same way that the central bank starts the process of prompt corrective action.

In parallel to the central bank liquidity provision framework, where all banks are covered by it, this IMF insurance system should be inclusive: all emerging countries not currently under the umbrella of an IMF program would be eligible for this insurance facility. After all, if they do not need a program, their solvency seems not to be in question, and this facility may lead to deeper assessments of whether countries are indeed solvent. Inclusiveness would eliminate the problem of the CCL—countries did fear the negative impact of applying for it—and the threat of being declared non-compliant would provide enough incentive for countries to implement reforms, similar to the convergence process under ERM II. The Chiang Mai initiative is also inclusive, with a surveillance mechanism to ensure soundness of policies through peer pressure. Article IV consultations and ad-hoc staff visits would provide the necessary monitoring, similar to the regular supervisory visits to the banking sector. Under this proposed framework, all IMF member countries would be covered by an IMF facility: developed countries by surveillance, solvent emerging markets by the insurance, insolvent emerging markets by the standard IMF programs, and poorer countries by the poverty-alleviation programs.

How would this mechanism be financed? Ideally, it would be through a large increase in quotas, buttressed by open-ended lines of credit from the main shareholders which could be tapped automatically in moments of stress.

As with any line of credit, this would pay interest to the lender, and thus it would not represent any further use of taxpayers' money, a point which must be stressed to the American audience. The key to the credibility of any insurance device is that it has to be able to deploy more-than-needed resources— the Colin Powell military doctrine applied to financial markets. In its current form, the IMF would certainly not be able to perform this role.

In brief, an insurance framework is missing from the IMF business model capable of making crisis management viable and attractive to its customers. An inclusive and automatic insurance mechanism would bridge the existing gap in the international financial architecture and significantly reduce the potential extent and impact of financial crises. Without it, countries will continue to develop their own, probably imperfect, insurance schemes, which are exacerbating global imbalances, and recourse to IMF programs will likely diminish dramatically.

Implications for the governance and financial viability of the IMF

There are two main conclusions to be drawn from the above discussion: first, the IMF, especially in its surveillance activities, must be made more independent; second, the IMF must significantly enhance its capitalization, as it faces a greatly reduced revenue stream from its core activities, and the insurance facility proposed here would require a sizable increase in resources.

As argued above, eliminating the need for Board approval in its surveillance activities would greatly enhance the credibility of the surveillance work. In addition, overall independence would be greatly enhanced by fixing the current model of shared chairs on the Board, starting with the US veto and the EU representation on the Board. Under the current system, the combined EU countries exercise about 32 percent of the total voting power, and play a role in the election of 10 of the 24 Executive Directors (plus one ECB observer). This may sound excessive, compared to one US Executive Director and an 18 percent vote, and one would think that the EU exerts too much power on the Board. But the reality is precisely the opposite. Despite attempts at coordination, each country, in the end, pursues its own agenda, which in the case of shared chairs has to be negotiated with the other constituencies (Bini-Smaghi, 2005). As a hypothetical example, it is unclear that the joint chair Spain/ Mexico/Venezuela could have had a policy toward Argentina that is fully in line with the policy of the EU—assuming the EU had a unified policy—given the very diverse interests at play. This shared agreement clearly undermines the influence of each of the three countries. The result is that the United States has no effective counterbalancing power on the Board, and therefore the IMF jeopardizes its credibility by being perceived as the hand of the US administration.

Therefore, in a world economy with a clear trend toward regionalization, the current arrangement of shared chairs makes little sense, and a redistribution of chairs to better reflect current economic realities is long overdue. At a minimum, the EU chairs should be integrated, and the South East Asian economies should be re-arranged so as to better correspond to their increasing regional integration and economic power. A regional distribution of chairs would make much more sense.

Moreover, the dominance of the US at the IMF looks increasingly anachronistic. With growing doubts about the role of the dollar as a reserve currency, and the long-term solvency of the US economy, with the greater role of the euro as a reserve currency, and increased weight in the world economy of many emerging markets, it makes little sense that the U.S. continues to have veto rights on the IMF Board. The world is no longer in the post–WW II era, when the U.S. provided the bulk of financing for a battered world. In fact, the United States today represents one of the main *risks* to the global economy. Thus, a single EU chair would add another veto-wielding power to balance the current situation. Voting shares—and quotas—should be redistributed to better reflect the new realities of the world economy, allocating more votes and financing burden to the emerging economies. Increasing the voting power and financial burden of the major emerging economies will, in addition, have the positive side effect of better aligning their incentives with their risks, perhaps leading to better economic policies.

In terms of financial viability, it is critical to understand that as countries repay their loans, and as some loans are converted into grants, the main revenue stream of the IMF will disappear. And if my hypothesis is correct, and countries do try to avoid requesting IMF assistance through self-insurance mechanisms, then the IMF's financial outlook is grim. A large increase in quotas is therefore long overdue. The total size of quotas has declined from 1.4 percent of world GDP in 1978 to barely above 0.5 percent today, while the size of global capital markets has increased several times. This quota increase, supported by additional credit mechanisms to be tapped in times of stress, would adapt IMF capitalization to the realities of the global economy, and allow for the redistribution of power argued above. Given the strong opposition to a quota increase in the U.S., the EU should take the lead in this process, by offering the unification of its chairs on the Board in exchange for an overhaul and increase of the IMF's finances. Such a move could be the catalyst for this long-overdue reform of the IMF, and hopefully lead to the implementation of some of the proposals argued here.

In this vein, selling the IMF's gold for debt-relief purposes makes little sense. The IMF needs more, not less capital, and selling gold would permanently deplete the capital base of the institution. If there is agreement about debt relief, it should be accomplished with budgetary allocations from the member countries, many of which are still far from allocating the agreed 0.7 percent of GDP to official development assistance.

What is the IMF proposing? Assessing the IMF's Medium-Term Strategy

I have argued that the changes in the world economy, both in terms of size and policies, are rendering the IMF's business model increasingly obsolete. Substantial change is needed to adequately cope with the risks that future crises will pose. There is a fair amount of guesswork in forecasting the shape of future economic developments, but when the customers are demanding change and acting on it, it is always wise to listen. I am proposing that a more independent surveillance process, a change in the distribution of power and chairs at the Board, an insurance facility, and a substantial increase in the capital base of the IMF will enhance the stability of the world economy. It is vitally important to understand that this is a comprehensive proposal, in which all the elements are interlinked and mutually reinforcing, and that a piecemeal approach will surely fail.

The IMF has responded to these proposals by reviewing its Medium-Term Strategy, which does address some of these issues. It includes, inter alia, three actions: a new approach toward multilateral surveillance, an ad hoc quota increase, and a new high-access lending facility. Interestingly, the IMF adopted the proposed language concerning its future financial viability, stating that "a *new business model* (my emphasis) is needed to finance Fund activity in the future, with less reliance on margins from lending and more on steady, long-term sources of income." Unfortunately, as discussed below, the proposals are more a patchwork of amendments, rather than a comprehensive, long-term review of the business model.

Surveillance

In terms of surveillance, specific proposals include "(i) a new approach to multilateral consultation to facilitate discussions within groups of countries on issues of systemic importance; (ii) broadening the IMF's internal consultative group on exchange rates to include all major emerging market currencies; (iii) strengthening the analysis in the World Economic Outlook and Global Financial Stability Report of macroeconomic risks and their interactions; and (iv) formulating regional work plans, focusing on the main policy issues facing the region."[8]

The process of multilateral surveillance is welcome, and, if successful, could replace the currently inoperative G-7. Its main feature would be its variable geometry, as its composition and terms of reference can be redefined for each particular task. It now includes the G-3 plus the key financiers of the US current account deficit: China and the oil producing countries. The main risk in this process is the lack of enforcement mechanisms. Their absence basically reduces it to a peer pressure device. In this regard, the experience of the Stability and Growth Path in Europe is illuminating, for it shares the same organizing principles: peer pressure to achieve some shared objective: European fiscal sustainability in the case of the SGP, and global financial stability in the case of the multilateral surveillance process.

From the SGP experience, it became evident that domestic political agendas can lead the process astray quickly. It will thus be important to protect the process from political interference as much as possible, so that it is able to name and shame as needed, thus approaching my proposal of independent surveillance. If the outcome of the multilateral surveillance process has to pass the political filter, then it is doomed to fail—witness the move by the Japanese authorities to delete the assessment on the degree of undervaluation of the yen from their 2006 Art IV Consultation documents. Anchoring the future of IMF surveillance on quantitative assessments of equilibrium exchange rates is a strategy fraught with downside risks.

Crisis prevention

As regards crisis prevention, the IMF's proposals include: "(i) clarifying the framework for high-access Fund financing in situations other than capital account crises; (ii) allowing for high-access contingent financing through a new instrument available to countries with strong macroeconomic policies, sustainable debt, and transparent reporting, but still facing potential balance sheet weaknesses and vulnerabilities; and (iii) standing ready to support regional and other reserve pooling arrangements, including by signaling sound policies."[9]

The proposal for a high access facility is welcome and moves one step closer to an insurance facility, but falls critically short in two key conditions: capitalization and, more importantly, automaticity. The failure of the CCL lay precisely in that countries had to apply for it. Thus, there was a stigma associated with it—in addition to its being slow to deploy. This new facility looks like another version of the CCL, and is as likely to fail—if it ever sees the light of the day. In addition, the lack of progress with increasing the capitalization of the IMF (see below) will make this facility totally ineffective. As proposed, this high access facility will not change the incentives to accumulate foreign exchange reserves, and will not contribute to a better allocation of global savings, or to the resolution of global imbalances.

Governance

In terms of governance, the Fund states that "fair voice and distribution of quotas are central to the legitimacy and effectiveness of the Fund. Emerging market and other countries need to have a voice in the IMF commensurate with their weight in the world economy."[10] After a heated debate, the first stage—involving ad hoc quota increases for the most underrepresented members (China, Turkey, Mexico, and South Korea) was approved at the 2006 Annual Meetings. Agreement on an increase in basic voting procedure, key for strengthening the voice of the smallest members, was left for a second phase. This, once again, is a step in the right direction, but one which falls short of what is needed. The ad-hoc quota increase represents less than 2 percent, with no impact on the general lending capacity of the Fund or on the distribution of voting power. In fact, it was designed with the restriction that the veto power of the United States would be retained. The discussion on a revision of the quota formula is a tremendous waste of resources, given that the current formula gives plenty of room for an increase in capital and a redistribution of power. What is missing is the political will to seriously adapt the IMF to the new circumstances. In addition, there has been no discussion whatever about increasing the independence of the surveillance process, a key point in my judgment.

Conclusion

In this paper, I have argued that the IMF should undergo comprehensive reform in the following four areas: an independent surveillance process, a redistribution of power and chairs on the Board, establishment of an automatic insurance facility, and a substantial increase in its capital base. With this in mind, the proposals included in the Medium-Term Strategy, while seen as welcome steps, fall far short of addressing the medium-term needs of the IMF. In fact, the IMF seems to be behaving in the same manner for which it strongly criticizes its member countries, that is, taking half-hearted measures which are aimed more at calming their constituencies than addressing key structural problems.

The IMF requires deep, comprehensive, structural reform. It should start by deciding whether it wants to be a main player in the international financial architecture, or whether it wishes to remain only a trusted advisor. If it wants to be a key player, it must greatly increase its independence, boost its financial capacity and adopt an automatic insurance facility. Otherwise, its influence will be dependent on the political skills of its managing director. As regards its function as facilitator in the multilateral surveillance process, it will be critical to craft political agreements which will solve thorny issues. Moreover, unless emerging markets are provided with a viable insurance facility, it will be very difficult to induce the needed changes in the incentive structure that leads these countries to accumulate massive foreign reserves.

NOTES

1 "International Economic Cooperation for a Balanced World Economy," sponsored by the Reinventing Bretton Woods Committee and the World Economic Forum, in Chongqing, China.

2 IMF, 2006.

3 See Gros et al. (2006) "A World out of Balance" for a comprehensive discussion of the multiple aspects that have led to the current constellation of current accounts.

4 This is not the case for smaller countries, which are not covered by market analysts, and where the advice of IMF surveillance and technical assistance teams is still invaluable.

5 International Financial Institution Advisory Commission set up by the US Congress, under the chairmanship of Allan Meltzer, to study the role and effectiveness of the International Monetary Fund and the World Bank (see Meltzer Commission, 2001).

6 See Aizenman et al. (2004) for a theoretical discussion.

7 See Cordella and Levy-Yeyati (2005) regarding emerging markets and Gros et al. (2004) regarding monetary policy in the euro area.

8 IMF, 2006, p. 2.

9 Ibid., p. 3.

10 Ibid, p. 4.

REFERENCES

Aizenman, J., Y. Lee, and Y. Rhee. 2004. "International Reserves Management and Capital Mobility in a Volatile World: Policy Considerations and a Case Study of Korea." NBER Working Paper 10534.

Bini-Smaghi, L. 2005. "IMF Governance and the Political Economy of a Consolidated European Seat." European Central Bank. Manuscript.

Cordella T. and E. Levy-Yeyati. 2005. "A (New) Country Insurance Facility." IMF Working Paper 05/23.

Eggertsson, G. and E. Le Borgne. 2004. "A Political Agency Theory of Central bank Independence." IMF. Manuscript.

Frankel, J. 2004. "Contractionary Currency Crashes in Developing Countries." 5th Mundell-Fleming Lecture. IMF Annual Research Conference. Washington, D.C. 10 November.

Gros, D., T. Mayer, and A. Ubide. 2004. "Europe is ready for the carrot, not the stick." *Financial Times*. 31 August.

International Monetary Fund. 2006. "A Medium-Term Strategy for the IMF: Meeting the Challenge of Globalization." Washington, D.C.: IMF. April.

Jeanne, O., and J. Zettelmeyer. 2004. "The Mussa theorem and other results on IMF-Induced Moral Hazard." IMF Working Paper 04/192.

Kawai, M. 2004. "Regional Economic Integration and Cooperation in East Asia." Paper presented at the Experts' Seminar on the Impact and Coherence of OECD Country Policies on Asian Developing Economies. Policy Research Institute of the Japanese Ministry of Finance and the OECD Secretariat. Paris. 10–11 June.

Meltzer Commission. 2000. Report of the International Financial Institution Advisory Commission to the US Congress. March. Available at: http://www.house.gov/jec/imf/meltzer.htm

Truman, E. M. 2005. "International Monetary Fund Reform: An Overview of the Issues." E. M. Truman, ed. Reforming the IMF for the 21st Century. IIE Special Report 19. Washington, D.C.: IIE.

About the Authors

Patrick Artus

Patrick Artus is Chief Economist and Head of Market Research of IXIS Corporate and Investment Bank, a subsidiary of NATIXIS, the joint banking entity of the Caisse d'Épargne and Banque Populaire groups. In 1975, he began working in economic forecasting and modeling, first in the Economics Department of the OECD (1980), and later as Head of Research at the ENSAE. Thereafter, he taught a seminar on research at Paris Dauphine (1982). He taught at a number of universities, including Dauphine, ENSAE, Centre des Hautes Études de l'Armement, École Nationale des Ponts et Chaussées, and HEC Lausanne. He is now Professor of Economics at École Polytechnique and at University Paris I (Sorbonne), where he combines teaching responsibilities with his research work. He has published widely in the field of political economics and is presently a member of the council of economic advisors to the French Prime Minister. He is a graduate of École Polytechnique, of École Nationale de la Statistique et de l'Administration Économique, and of Institut d'Études Politiques de Paris.

Jack Boorman

Jack Boorman currently serves as Advisor to the Director of the International Monetary Fund Independent Evaluation Office and Chairman of the Investment Committee of the Board of Trustees of LeMoyne College. He was Director of the IMF Policy Development and Review Department for more than eleven years, and during the latter years Counselor and Special Advisor to the Managing Director. He held several other positions in the Fund, including in the European and Asian Departments, and as Resident Representative in Indonesia. Before joining the IMF, he taught at the University of Southern California, from which he received his PhD in Economics, and at the University of Maryland. He also served as a Financial Economist in the Research Department of The Federal Deposit Insurance Corporation. Dr. Boorman is the author of a number of books in the areas of development, structural adjustment, and developing country debt, emerging market country issues, international insolvency, governance, and IMF policies and country operations.

Michael Buchanan

Michael Buchanan is a Director of Global Macro and Markets Research at Goldman Sachs International, based in London. He is primarily responsible for the group's research on global thematic issues and the world economy. He is also responsible for the firm's coverage of emerging markets asset class issues, including bond restructurings, reforming the financial architecture, etc. For seven years, prior to joining Goldman Sachs in 2000, he was an economist at the International Monetary Fund based in Washington D.C., focusing on Russia, Pakistan, bond restructurings, Brady swaps, and other issues relating to the global financial architecture. He lectured at Jesus College Oxford from 1991 to 1993. He was a Rhodes Scholar from Australia, graduating from Oxford University with an M.Phil. in Economics after obtaining his Bachelors degree in Economics at the University of Tasmania (Australia).

Richard N. Cooper

Richard N. Cooper is Maurits C. Boas Professor of International Economics at Harvard University. He is Vice-Chairman of the Global Development network, and a member of the Trilateral Commission, the Council on Foreign Relations, the Executive Panel of the United States Chief of Naval Operations, the Aspen Strategy Group, and the Brookings Panel on Economic Activity. He has served in several capacities in the United States Government, as chairman of the National Intelligence Council (1995–97), Under Secretary of State for Economic Affairs (1977–81), Deputy Assistant Secretary of State for International Monetary Affairs (1965–66), and senior staff economist at the council of Economic Advisers (1961–63). He also served as chairman of the Federal Reserve Bank of Boston (1990–92). As a Marshall Scholar, he studied at the London School of Economics, and earned his PhD at Harvard University. He is widely published in the field of crisis management and future studies.

Gordon de Brouwer

Gordon de Brouwer is a senior official at the Australian Treasury, currently General Manager of the G-20 and APEC Secretariat set up to organize policy and logistics for Australia's hosting of these forums in 2006 and 2007. He was previously Professor of Economics at the Australian National University, and a senior official at the Reserve Bank of Australia working on economic modeling, research, and international financial markets. He has published widely on Australian and

Asian economic systems, international finance and integration, and international economic relations. He has a PhD in Economics from the Australian National University.

J. Bradford DeLong

J. Bradford DeLong is Professor of Economics at the University of California at Berkeley. He is also co-editor of the *Journal of Economic Perspectives*, a Research Associate of the National Bureau of Economic Research, and a Visiting Scholar at the Federal Reserve Bank of San Francisco. He served in the US government as Deputy Assistant Secretary of the Treasury for Economic Policy from 1993 to 1995. Before joining the Treasury Department he was Danziger Associate Professor in the Department of Economics at Harvard University, Assistant Professor of Economics at Boston University, and Lecturer in the Department of Economics at M.I.T. From 1988 to 1991, he was responsible for Harvard University's undergraduate programs in Economics, as Head Tutor of the Department of Economics. He received his PhD from Harvard University in 1987. He writes on such topics as the evolution and functioning of the U.S. and other nations' stock markets, the course and determinants of long-run economic growth, the making of economic policy, the changing nature of the American business cycle, and the history of economic thought.

Dietrich Domanski

Dietrich Domanski is Head of Macroeconomic Monitoring at the Bank for International Settlements in Basel (Switzerland). From 1992 to 2000, he worked as economist in, and since 1994 as head of, the capital market section in the economics department of the Deutsche Bundesbank. During that time, he lectured under the technical assistance programs of the Bundesbank and the IMF in several countries in Central and Eastern Europe. He was also a member of the Committee on Financial Markets at the OECD. From 1998 to 1999, he was IMF adviser on monetary operations in Indonesia, and from 2000 to 2005, he worked in the Secretariat of the Committee on the Global Financial System at the Bank for International Settlements. His main research interests include the interaction of monetary policy, financial markets and real economy, and financial intermediation and economic development.

Barry Eichengreen

Barry Eichengreen is the George C. Pardee and Helen N. Pardee Professor of Economics and Professor of Political Science at the University of California, Berkeley, where he has taught since 1987. He is also a Research Associate of the National Bureau of Economic Research, Research Fellow of the Centre for Economic Policy Research, and a fellow of the American Academy of Arts and Sciences. He is the convener of the Bellagio Group of academics and economic officials. He has held Guggenheim and Fulbright Fellowships and was a fellow of the Center for Advanced Study in the Behavioral Sciences. Professor Eichengreen has published widely on the history and current operation of the international financial system. His recent works include "Global Imbalances and the Lessons of Bretton Woods" (2006).

Lauren Johnston

Lauren Johnston is a Global Leadership Fellow with the World Economic Forum, responsible for relations with international organizations. In addition to promoting the multilateral aspects of the global agenda, she has provided assistance to the Forum's International Monetary Convention Project, in particular regarding low-income country issues. Previously, she served as Senior Economist for the Ministry of Planning and Economic Development, Sierra Leone, and Senior Economist in the Ministry of Finance, Guyana. Her role in both countries centered on the external assistance requirements of the country programs with the IMF and the World Bank. She began her career with KPMG in China, and is a graduate of the Universities of London (SOAS) and Melbourne.

Masahiro Kawai

Masahiro Kawai is Head of the Office of Regional Economic Integration of the Asian Development Bank (ADB), and Special Advisor to the President. Before joining the ADB in October 2005, he was Professor of Economics at the Institute of Social Science of the University of Tokyo. He worked as Chief Economist for the Division of East Asia and the Pacific Region of the World Bank from 1998 to 2001, and as Deputy Vice Minister of Finance for International Affairs of the Japanese Ministry of Finance from 2001 to 2003. Dr. Kawai taught in the economics department of Johns Hopkins University, and at the Institute of Social Science, University of Tokyo. He has published widely in the areas of economic globalization, regional financial integration and cooperation in East Asia, including lessons from the Asian crisis, and on the international currency system. He received his PhD in Economics from Stanford University.

Carina Larsfälten

Carina Larsfälten has headed the International Monetary Convention Project at the World Economic Forum since its inception in 2004. On leave from the European Commission, where she holds a permanent post in DG Industry and Competitiveness, she has been with the Forum since 2000, working on financial and competitiveness-related issues. From 2003 to the present, she has also been responsible for IGWEL, the Informal Gathering of World Economic Leaders in Davos. Previously, she was a Senior Manager in the Corporate Staff for Development at Skanska, and a Senior Officer at the Swedish Ministry of Finance. She started her career at the Swedish Trade Council in Paris and has an MSc from École Supérieure de Commerce de Paris.

Jong-Wha Lee

Jong-Wha Lee is Professor of Economics, Director of the International Center for Korean Studies at Korea University, and adjunct professor at the Research School of Pacific and Asian Studies of Australian National University. He received his BA in Economics from Korea University and his MA and PhD in Economics from Harvard University. He has worked as an economist at the International Monetary Fund and taught at Harvard University as Visiting Professor. He has been a consultant to the Asian Development Bank, the Harvard Institute for International Development, the Inter-American Development Bank, the International Monetary Fund, the United Nations Development Programme, and the World Bank, and has held research positions at the Center for International Development at Harvard University, the Central Bank of Chile, the Hoover Institution, Kobe University, the National Bureau of Economic Research and the Korea Institute of Finance. He has been a member of National Economic Advisory Council and the Financial Development Committee in Korea.

John Lipsky

John Lipsky assumed the position of First Deputy Managing Director of the International Monetary Fund on 1 September 2006. Before coming to the Fund, he was Vice Chairman of JPMorgan, advising principal market risk takers, and publishing independent research on the principal forces shaping global financial markets. Previously, he served as Chief economist and director of Research for Chase Manhattan Bank, and as Chief Economist of Salomon Brothers, Inc., directing its European Economic and Market Analysis Group. He worked for ten years at the IMF, helping to manage the Fund's exchange rate surveillance procedure and analyzing developments in the international capital market. In 2000, he chaired a Financial Sector Review Group, to provide the IMF with an independent perspective on the Fund's work on international financial markets. He is a member of the Board of Directors of the National Bureau of Economic Research. He received his PhD in Economics from Stanford University.

Augusto Lopez-Claros

Augusto López Claros is an international economic consultant based in Geneva, Switzerland. He served from 2003 until September 2006 as Chief Economist at the World Economic Forum and Director of its Global Competitiveness Programme, a research project whose aim is to determine the impediments to economic growth in more than 120 countries. Before joining the Forum, he was Executive Director and Senior International Economist with Lehman Brothers International in London. Earlier he was on the staff of the International Monetary Fund in Washington, serving from 1992 to 1995 as Resident Representative in the Russian Federation. He received a PhD in Economics from Duke University (USA), and a degree in Mathematical Statistics from Cambridge University, England. With an abiding interest in the growth and development of global interdependence and cooperation and the importance of international institutions in their principal role of promoting and safeguarding human prosperity, he has written extensively on a broad range of economic and financial issues, including those affecting transition economies, aspects of economic integration, and the development challenges confronting emerging markets.

Warwick McKibbin

Warwick McKibbin is Professor of International Economics in the Research School of Pacific and Asian Studies, Director of the Centre for Applied Macroeconomic Analysis at the Australian National University, and a Professorial Fellow at the Lowy Institute for International Policy in Sydney. He is also a non-resident Senior Fellow at the Brookings Institution in Washington D.C. and a member of the Board of the Reserve Bank of Australia and a member of the Australian Prime Minister's Science, Engineering and Innovation Council. Dr. McKibbin received his PhD (1986) from Harvard University. He is a Fellow of the Australian Academy of Social Sciences and was awarded the Centenary medal in 2003 "For Service to Australian Society through Economic Policy and Tertiary Education." He is internationally known for his contributions to global economic modeling.

Yung Chul Park

Yung Chul Park is Research Professor and Director of the Center for International Commerce and Finance at the Graduate School of International Studies, Seoul National University. He is a member of the National Economic Advisory Council. He was an ambassador for International Economy and Trade for the Ministry of Foreign Affairs and Trade from 2001 to 2002, and Chairman of the Board of the Korea Exchange Bank from 1999 to 2001. He previously served as Chief Economic Advisor to Korean President Doo Hwan Chun, as President of both the Korea Development Institute and the Korea Institute of Finance, and as a member of the Bank of Korea Monetary Board. He was Director of the Institute of Economic Research at Korea University, and a Visiting Professor at both Harvard and Boston Universities. He received his PhD from the University of Minnesota, and has published widely in the field of economic liberalization and integration and new financial structures in East Asia, and the financial development of Japan, Korea, and Taiwan.

Nouriel Roubini

Nouriel Roubini is Professor of Economics at the Stern School of Business, New York University and co-founder and Chairman of Roubini Global Economics LLC, a web-based economic and geo-strategic information service and economic consultancy. As a senior academic researcher in the field of international macro-economics, his views are regularly cited in the press and media. Professor Roubini received his PhD in Economics from Harvard University, and taught economics at Yale University (1988–95). He was Senior Economist for International Affairs on the White House Council of Economic Advisers, later Senior Advisor to the Under Secretary for International Affairs, and Director of the Office of Policy Development and Review at the United States Treasury Department, working on the resolution of the Asian and global financial crises of 1997–98 and the reform of the international financial architecture after these crises. He has published widely in the areas of theoretical, empirical and macroeconomics, on economic policy, on specific and global financial crises, emerging markets, the reform of the international financial system, and on global economic imbalances.

Li Ruogu

Li Ruogu is now Chairman and President of China Exim Bank, and a member of the Academic Committee of the Postdoctoral Research Station of the Financial Research Institute of the People's Bank of China, after serving as Director-General of the International Department and Deputy Governor. Earlier posts included Executive Director of the Asian Development Bank, Alternate Governor of the International Monetary Fund, Alternate Governor of the African Development Bank, Alternate Governor of Caribbean Development Bank, and Alternate Governor of Eastern and Southern African Trade and Development Bank, in each case dealing with affairs relating to China. He has published widely in the fields of economic globalization, China's financial reform, international economic integration, and financial control. He received his MA in Law from Peking University in 1981, and his MA in Public Management at Princeton University in 1983.

Richard Samans

Richard Samans is Managing Director of the World Economic Forum, responsible for the Forum's public-private partnership initiatives and its relations with governments, international organizations, NGOs and other non-business constituencies. Working at the Forum since early 2001, he directs the Forum's Centre for Public-Private Partnership and advises on the global issues program content of Forum meetings and other activities. Before joining the Forum, he served as Special Assistant to the President for International Economic Policy in the US White House. As a senior member of the National Economic Council staff and Senior Director of the National Security Council's International Economic Affairs directorate, he assisted President Clinton on a broad range of international trade and financial policy matters. He served previously as Economic Policy Advisor to former US Senate Democratic Leader Tom Daschle (D-SD), assisting him and the Senate Democratic Caucus on international trade and financial, fiscal and other economic policy issues. A former international banker, he has served in a number of additional capacities in government, the private sector and research institutions.

Brad Setser

Brad Setser is Senior Economist at Roubini Global Economics and Research Associate at the Global Economic Governance Programme at University College, Oxford. He is the author, with Nouriel Roubini, of *Bailouts or Bail-ins? Responding to Financial Crises in Emerging Economies*. He was an international affairs fellow at the Council on Foreign Relations, and a Visiting Scholar at the

International Monetary Fund. He served in the United States Treasury from 1997 to 2001, where he worked extensively on the reform of the international financial architecture, sovereign debt restructurings, and US policy toward the IMF. He ended his tenure at the Treasury as the acting director of the US Treasury's Office of International Monetary and Financial Policy. He received his undergraduate and graduate education at Oxford University, Sciences-Po (Paris), and Harvard University.

Robert Skidelsky

Professor Lord Skidelsky is Professor of Political Economy at the University of Warwick, author of *The World After Communism* (1995) and a biography of the economist John Maynard Keynes. He was elected a Fellow of the British Academy in 1994. He was elevated to the House of Lords in 1991 and served as Chief Opposition Spokesman on Treasury Affairs (1998–99). From 1991 to 2001 he was Chairman of the Social Market Foundation. Since 2002 he has been Chairman of the Centre for Global Studies (London). Lord Skidelsky is a non-executive director of Janus Capital Inc, Chairman of the Greater Europe Fund, and a Director of Transnational Insights Ltd. A Russian speaker, he is Director of the Moscow School of Political Studies and Founder and Executive Secretary of The UK/Russia Round Table. He is also a Trustee of the Manhattan Institute and Chairman of the Governors of the Brighton College.

Edwin M. Truman

Edwin M. Truman has been a Senior Fellow at the Peterson Institute for International Economics since 2001. He served as Assistant Secretary of the US Treasury for International Affairs from December 1998 to January 2001. He directed the Division of International Finance of the Board of Governors of the Federal Reserve System from 1977 to 1998, and was one of three economists on the staff of the Federal Open Market Committee. Truman was a member of the Financial Stability Forum's Working Group on Highly Leveraged Institutions (1999–2000), the G-22 Working Party on Transparency and Accountability (1998), and the G-10 Working Group on the Resolution of Sovereign Liquidity Crises (1995–96). He is the author, co-author, or editor of *Reforming the IMF for the 21st Century* (2006), *A Strategy for IMF Reform* (2006), *Chasing Dirty Money: The Fight Against Money Laundering* (2004), and *Inflation Targeting in the World Economy* (2003).

Philip Turner

Philip Turner has been with the Bank for International Settlements (BIS) since 1989. He is at present Head of Secretariat Group in the Monetary and Economic Department, responsible for economics papers produced for central bank meetings at the BIS. In an earlier position at the BIS, his main area of research interest was financial stability in emerging markets and he has written extensively on banking systems and on bank restructuring in the developing world. Between 1976 and 1989, he held various positions, including Head of Division in the Economics Department of the Organisation of Economic Co-operation and Development (OECD) in Paris. From 1985 to 1986 he was a Visiting Scholar at the Institute for Monetary and Economic Studies in the Bank of Japan. He received his PhD in Economics from Harvard University in 1976.

Angel Ubide

Angel Ubide is the Director of Global Economics at Tudor Investment Corporation, a leading global funds management company. He is an active member of several international economic policy organizations, including the Euro50 Group, the ECB's Shadow Governing Council, the Atlantic Council of the U.S., and the Center for European Policy Studies. He is a frequent contributor to the Spanish media, and writes a bi-weekly column on international economics for *El País*, the leading Spanish newspaper. Dr. Ubide has written numerous academic and policy papers on international macroeconomics, banking, and exchange rates, and his work has been published in major international journals and leading newspapers. Dr. Ubide was formerly an economist at the International Monetary Fund. He holds a PhD in Economics from the European University Institute in Florence (Italy).

Marc Uzan

Marc Uzan is the Executive Director of the Reinventing Bretton Woods Committee, an organization which he founded in 1994. The Committee is a think-tank focusing on issues related to international financial architecture through a regular dialogue between markets and governments. He also coordinates the activities of the Euro50Group. He is editor of a number of prominent publications, including *Financial System Under Stress—An Architecture for the New World Economy* (1996), *Private Capital Flows in the Age of Globalisation* (2000), *Capital Flows without Crisis?* (2001), *The Future of the International Monetary System* (2004), and a handbook on the international financial architecture with

Nouriel Roubini. He is the author of several academic papers on the new architecture for the international financial system. He has been a Visiting Scholar at the Department of Economics of the University of California, Berkeley.

John Williamson

John Williamson is Senior Fellow of the Peterson Institute for International Economics, with which he has been associated since 1981 as a specialist in international monetary issues. He was Project Director for the United Nations High-Level Panel on Financing for Development (the Zedillo Report) in 2001, and on leave as Chief Economist for South Asia at the World Bank from 1996 to 1999. He received his undergraduate education at the London School of Economics and PhD from Princeton. From 1962 to 1981, he taught economics at the Universities of York and Warwick in England, Massachussetts Institute of Technology, and the Pontifícia Universidade Católica of Rio de Janeiro, Brazil. He served as adviser to the International Monetary Fund on questions of international monetary reform related to the work of the Committee of Twenty, and as economic consultant to the UK Treasury. He is author, co-author, editor, or co-editor of numerous studies on international monetary and development issues.

Yu Yongding

Yu Yongding is an academician-member of the Chinese Academy of Social Sciences, Director-General of the Institute of World Economics and Politics, President of the China Society of World Economics, and Editor of *China and World Economy*. He was formerly the academic member of the Monetary Policy Committee of the People's Bank of China and a member of National Advisory Committee of the 11th Five-Year Plan of National Reform and Development Commission. He received his MA in Economics from the Graduate School of the Chinese Academy of Social Sciences and his Phil.D. in Economics from the University of Oxford. He has authored, co-authored, and edited more than ten books, and published widely on macroeconomics, international finance, and other subjects. His main research interests are in macroeconomics and world economics.